THE YEARBOOK OF LANGLAND STUDIES

YLS welcomes submissions dealing with *Piers Plowman* and related poetry and prose in the traditions of didactic and allegorical alliterative writing. Papers concerning the literary, historical, religious, intellectual, codicological, and critical contexts of these works are also invited. Submissions are double-blind peer reviewed. In preparing their manuscripts for review, authors should avoid revealing their identity within the essay itself and follow the MHRA Style Guide (available at http://www.mhra.org.uk/Publications/Books/StyleGuide /download.shtml). Please submit essays electronically in Microsoft Word to all of the editors: Andrew Cole (acole@princeton.edu); Fiona Somerset (somerset@duke.edu); and Lawrence Warner (lawrence.warner@sydney.edu.au).

Individual subscriptions are available at a discounted rate for members of the International *Piers Plowman* Society. To become a member, visit our website (www.piersplowman.org). Information on institutional subscriptions should be sought from Brepols Publishers (periodicals@brepols.net). Back issues of volumes 1–19 may be ordered from Medieval Institute Publications, Western Michigan University, 1903 W. Michigan Avenue, Kalamazoo, MI 49008–5432 (http://www.wmich.edu/medieval/mip/). Back issues starting with volume 20 can be acquired from Brepols. The complete run of *YLS*, from the first issue in 1987, is available online to those whose institutions subscribe to the e-journal through Brepols (see http://brepols.metapress.com).

THE YEARBOOK OF LANGLAND STUDIES

24
(2010)

Edited by

Andrew Cole, Fiona Somerset,
and Lawrence Warner

BREPOLS

D/2010/0095/214
ISBN 978-2-503-53274-5
ISSN 0890-2917

Printed in the E.U. on acid-free paper

CONTENTS

Reviews

ILLUSTRATIONS

Grindley

Figure 1, p. 65. 'Incipit Passus 3', London, British Library, MS Cotton Caligula A. xi, fol. 180^r. Early fifteenth century. Reproduced with the permission of The British Library.

Horobin

Figure 2, p. 93. Oxford, Bodleian Library, MS Digby 102, fol. 9^v. Reprinted by permission of the Bodleian Library.

Figure 3, p. 95. London Metropolitan Archives, CLC/L/BF/A/021/MS05440, fol. 50^r. Reprinted by permission of the Brewers' Company and the City of London Corporation.

FOREWORD

George Kane, editor of the Athlone edition of *Piers Plowman* A and a generous collaborator on the edition's B and C volumes, died on 27 December 2009, and so it is with this volume of the *Yearbook of Langland Studies* that we pay tribute to his career. Readers will find not a retrospective but a special cluster of essays presenting scholars' newest reflections on the manuscripts and versions of *Piers Plowman*, as well as work on Middle English editing more generally. Kane's influence is evident everywhere here, in an atmosphere of closely engaged and deeply considered debate that we think he would have relished.

Andrew Cole
Fiona Somerset
Lawrence Warner

George Kane and the Invention of Textual Thought: Retrospect and Prospect

Ralph Hanna

The proportions of Charlotte Brewer's excellent survey of the editorial history of *Piers Plowman* demonstrate that one cannot overestimate the magnitude of George Kane's editorial achievement, nor of its impact on our chosen area of study. As R. W. Chambers's latest, and surely most distinguished, student, Kane brought to a satisfactory conclusion his mentor's goal of subjecting *Piers Plowman* to suitable modern editorial treatment. Kane's painstaking scrutiny of every line of every manuscript of the poem, in all three versions, will long remain unequalled as an intellectual monument of passionate, and usually persuasive, engagement. And this will be the case, whatever local controversies the Athlone edition has stimulated (and this essay will remember Kane by examining a few instances).[1]

Quite simply put, George Kane remains, and will remain, the greatest editorial mind — and the greatest scholar of texts — who has ever engaged with Middle English. Moreover, his efforts with *Piers* have transformed the editing of Middle English generally. After Kane, no editor with any pretentions to explaining her

---

[1] See Charlotte Brewer, *Editing 'Piers Plowman': The Evolution of the Text*, Cambridge Studies in Medieval Literature, 28 (Cambridge: Cambridge University Press, 1996), pp. 219–433, fully half her study. To understand certain unevennesses in Brewer's account, one needs to consult as well Kane's compelling proof that the text exists in only three *authorial* versions, 'The "Z Version" of *Piers Plowman*', *Speculum*, 60 (1985), 910–30.

Ralph Hanna (*ralph.hanna@keble.ox.ac.uk*) is Professor of Palaeography, University of Oxford.

Abstract: The late George Kane revolutionized the editing of Middle English texts. He brought both a severely logical stance and an artist's eye to the discipline. On the one hand, Kane demonstrated the inability of stemmatics to deal with complex traditions; on the other, he was inventive in imagining the modes of transmission by which errors might have emerged in copying. Yet these two powerful contributions sit uneasily together, and Kane is a hard (and not always consistent) master to learn from. Two examples of recent scholarly misunderstanding, predicated upon Kane's prickly difficult explanations of his procedures, indicate some limitations of his contribution and imply the need for thoughtful reconsiderations not as yet undertaken.

Keywords: George Kane; editorial theory; Aberystwyth, National Library of Wales, MS 733B; Cambridge, Corpus Christi College, MS 201; Athlone editions of *Piers Plowman*; textual transmission; conjectural emendation; versions of *Piers Plowman*; Charlotte Brewer.

10.1484/J.YLS.1.102106

text critically can with impunity adopt a purely diplomatic or 'best-text' attitude toward the readings of her manuscripts.

This contribution is enshrined in Kane's great monument, his first effort with the text of *Piers Plowman*, the groundbreaking edition of the A version.[2] As an early footnote clearly indicates, Kane seeks here to bring the rather dilettantish world of Middle English editing into creative contact with the most sophisticated brands of textual thought.[3] These are essentially those developed over centuries, their great modern master (whom I would imagine Kane's model) A. E. Housman, for application, in a considerably more dire editorial situation, to the remnants of classical literature.

Kane's appropriation of these techniques is marked — as a great deal of his writing — by a considerable logical rigour. For in the foundational pages of his introduction to the A version, Kane not only appropriates, but he absorbs and recasts. Logic here serves a project that must (and should) be seen as fundamentally theoretical — in this case, the development, through induction, of a set of useful working postulates about scribal behaviour.

Kane's demonstration begins by analysing readings surely wrong because utterly isolated in attestation, the freak of a single scribe. Examining and explaining the mechanisms that created these certain errors allow Kane to develop principles that might identify the generators of error in readings more complicated and contentious. The argument, often left largely implicit, is that identifying a specific type of scribal behaviour as operative in such a contentious site allows the identification of a prior, sometimes a non-transmitted, reading, the demonstrable source of all the competing readings.

Kane's shorthand for this process manages to obscure more than it enlightens. Significantly, it is a Latin proverb, and one with a lengthy history in classical editorial thought, 'Durior lectio potior est'.[4] Enshrouded in the statement (and in a good deal of Kane's own practice) is precisely what Bentley calls 'ratio', that inductive thought that produced application/appropriation.

---

[2] Particularly *Piers Plowman: The A Version*, ed. by George Kane, rev. edn (London: Athlone; Berkeley and Los Angeles: University of California Press, 1988), pp. 53–64, 111–72.

[3] *The A Version*, ed. by Kane, pp. 53–54 n. 3.

[4] Its more rambunctious version is Richard Bentley's proud 'Nobis et ratio et res ipsa centum codicibus potiores sunt'. So far as I can see, Bentley only strives to state what was obvious to the thoughtful Kane, that no one should engage in editing without being able to distinguish more and less plausible readings on their face.

For Kane's editorial procedures do not simply reflect looking at a heap of variants, choosing the 'hardest' one, and inserting it in the text. Other careful logical processes are at work; these Kane either takes for granted that careful readers will intuit or decides do not really merit elucidation.[5] Yet increasingly clearly in the writings, Kane enunciates a view that the fundamental scribal process is 'the substitution of similars'. Generally at an implicit level, Kane sees these as of two types: substitution of a word similar in form, or substitution of a word similar in sense (homeographs or synonyms). His great innovation — and the artistic skill he brings to his project — consists in displaying copious examples of both types of (mis)readings and of indicating how they might be brought to bear on individual lections.

Single examples of the procedure are apparent everywhere in Kane's texts and ultimately underwrite his most flamboyant moments of brilliance. For example, at A.Prol.34, the editor faces alternatives: 'And gette gold wiþ here gle giltles [but the majority 'synneles'] I trowe.' The two readings here are basically identical in lexical terms, and one of them presumably represents a synonymous substitution for the other. But 'giltles' may obviously be identified as correct because Langland's metre requires that any word in this position should be a homeograph of the form 'g---les'. Similarly, in the unique B.Prol.159, 'Seide for a souereyn help to hem-selue/alle', 'help', although unanimously attested, clearly substitutes for some form homeographically 's----'. Kane and Donaldson's projected correction, the more precise but partially synonymous 'salue', supposes the form more narrowly 's-lu-', partly echoed in 'h-l', partly in the line-ending 'selue'. Indeed, the scribes may have provided 'help' precisely to dissimilate the midline reading from the form at the line's end.

Such logic in relatively unproblematic instances proves extensible by induction, and it supports a great many more complicated examples. At B.5.197, for instance, homeographic 'welthe' (probably simple confusion of the very similar *ch* and *th*) and synonymous 'web' 'bracket' the correct 'welche', attested in the B tradition only by LR. And the supreme brilliance of the unique and reconstructed B.12.130, 'Dyuyneris toforn vs viseden and markeden', explicitly rests on an extreme extension of the same principle visible in simple instances.

---

[5] This reticence creates that effect that leads Lee Patterson, in a fine analysis, to identify Kane's (here also E. Talbot Donaldson's) methods with 'the way of genius', an intuitive brilliance that resists logical explanation; see *Negotiating the Past: The Historical Understanding of Medieval Literature* (Madison: University of Wisconsin Press, 1987), pp. 77–113. Paradoxes, such as the scrupulously logical Kane as beyond logic, will proliferate as my argument proceeds.

The discussion of this line is unusually succinct in identifying the problems at issue.[6] Yet the note is perhaps a bit cavalier in its generalized attribution of the hash in the manuscripts as 'visual errors'. The disastrously transmitted line at least began to degenerate when the archetypal B scribe did not recognize its opening word and construed the *upper loop* of anglicana *D* as the similar form that consitutes the whole of anglicana *L*, thereby assimilating the form to a common word.[7] But as this scribe continued, having destroyed not only the alliteration, but also the meaning of the line, he remained acutely aware of his difficulties and produced careful homeographic facsimiles of the readings he saw, in hopes that they would communicate with someone. (In this case, they didn't, not even to the poet who wrote the lines, who at C.14.72–74 reverted to a paraphrase restatement of what he hoped he had written.)

But whatever the quality of explanation, the emendation is brilliant stuff, skilfully deployed, Patterson's 'genius'. And whatever the explanation, the guiding error types that Kane explicitly identifies in his *A Version* discussion form a universal scribal *Schriftsprache*. As such, in identifying and explicating them, Kane's work lays the foundations for their extension and use by other editors in a wide variety of textual situations, not limited just to Middle English. This is what one properly calls a seminal contribution to the discipline.

However, even within simple examples, complications lurk — and these fore-shadow difficulties in, as well as extensions of, Kane's logic that will shape the second half of this essay. Above I identified A.Prol.34 'giltles' as an unproblematic litmus of Kane's innovative editorial behaviour. But what is one to make of the parallel B.Prol.34, where the only reading attested in the B tradition is the rejected 'synnelees' of most A copies? I *hope* Kane is right in repeating his A procedures and reading 'giltlees' here; my hope rests on the easiness of the example and that the poet could or would have corrected the erroneous 'synnelees' automatically.

But Kane's explanation for his procedures — 'synnelees' is an 'easier reading', surely agreed — doesn't quite address what is at issue here.[8] Is the reading 'easier' because A offers evidence of another, and there is no reason to suppose the poet

---

[6] See *Piers Plowman: The B Version*, ed. by George Kane and E. Talbot Donaldson, rev. edn (London: Athlone; Berkeley and Los Angeles: University of California Press, 1988), p. 115.

[7] In so doing he may have made a further error of a sort Kane readily identifies elsewhere (and to which he thereby alerts his reader), haplography (or perhaps, homoteleuthon). Converting *diuineres* into *liueres* involves writing only one set of double minims, not two (and/or the scribe may have missed an abbreviation).

[8] *The B Version*, ed. by Kane and Donaldson, p. 85, and cf. p. 137.

should have revised to eliminate alliteration? Has Kane (here with Donaldson, of course) considered the possibility that Langland's revision copy for B was one of those majority A manuscripts that read 'synnelees'? Is it possible that the poet, as he was to do on a number of occasions in C, just nodded, and failed to correct an error in his 'standing copy'?

One's judgement here, which Kane's 'easier reading' simply overrides, can only be aesthetically, rather than textually, driven. One emends to 'giltlees' to spare the poet his blushes, and because of a faith that he would surely have corrected this reading, had he noticed it. Alternatively, one prints 'synnelees' from a conviction that B transmission should differ from A transmission (although hypothetically capable of repeating the same simple error-types, here the substitution *gilt-* > *synne-*) and that it should be respected on that basis. At the same time, one must be aware of the paradox that Kane's laudatory interest in 'textual result', a powerful edition, may at some moments obviate the very kind of thoughtfulness that had made the edition possible in the first place.

That I have felt compelled to write the preceding paragraphs indicates something about Kane and the nature of his contribution. Although certainly the greatest editorial mind to have engaged Middle English texts, there are certain kinds of limitations on his performance as an editor. Among these, and the logic for the preceding paragraphs of discussion, is his rather prickly refusal to offer ready explanations — and the resulting need to read his explanatory materials with a critical eye.[9]

Indeed, it is striking that Kane never performed one basic editorial act, to write explanatory annotation about his texts.[10] For that reason, he probably must share

---

[9] Underlying, for example, the (in)famous conclusion to the introduction to the B version, a challenge to the unconvinced to do it over again themselves from scratch; see *The B Version*, ed. by Kane and Donaldson, pp. 211–13, 220.

[10] This is not to say that Kane did not consider the poem critically. Indeed, he made a number of salient contributions, in *Middle English Literature: A Critical Study of the Romances, the Religious Lyrics, 'Piers Plowman'* (London: Methuen, 1951), as well as in the essays collected in *Chaucer and Langland: Historical and Textual Approaches* (London: Athlone, 1989). As his critical writings indicate, Kane generally viewed *Piers Plowman* as a religious document, one both inspiring and consoling. Indeed, he strenuously resisted, and was sharply critical of, a variety of recent views that decentre religious ideas. This reading strategy represents Kane's inheritance from his mentor R. W. Chambers; cf. what stood until late in the 1950s as the standard critical account of the poem, '*Piers Plowman*: A Comparative Study', in *Man's Unconquerable Mind: Studies of English Writers from Bede to A. E. Housman and W. P. Ker* (London: Cape, 1939), pp. 88–171. For Kane's distaste, see 'Langland: Labour and "Authorship"', *Notes & Queries*, 243 (1998), 420–25.

the title 'greatest editor of Middle English' with another fine eclecticist, Walter Skeat. For where Kane's contribution repeatedly demonstrates the limits of Skeat's editorial acumen (and perhaps interest), Skeat throws up a convivial and utterly capacious knowledge of medieval literary traditions and ideas, and he delights in making this available to the reader, in a form readily accessible and, in many cases, still unsurpassed.[11]

Although he was a man of great generosity and a civility almost chivalric in its courtesy, my strongest memories of interacting with Kane concern his prickliness — and his single-minded devotion to Langland's text. Most of my dealings with Kane might be described as interrupted efforts at a conversation, a state of things largely created by what he must have found an adversarial bumptiousness. Most typically, I would try offering him suggestions about — what probably no one else would want — places where I felt he might have been more sceptical about the text he printed. His usual response was in the form of self-citation: 'You should go read an essay I once wrote on conjectural emendation.'

On the one hand, Kane might be perceived as finding it too much of a bother to address an ignorance he had already dealt with. Yet equally, I came to see this conversational move as a feature of Kane's fearsomely logical grasp on textual issues, and his uncompromising faith in the explanations he had offered through such logical constructions. The published formulation would be more powerful than conversational correction of the neophyte; any local application of principle could (and should) not be disengaged from the considered formulations that had produced it. And although off-putting as a conversational (or sometimes epistolary) style, there was in Kane's general reference, an implicit faith in the power of the closely reasoned published account to convince even the obdurate.[12]

---

[11] Skeat's notes, in Volume II of his 1886 edition (*Piers the Plowman: Together with Richard the Redeless* (Oxford: Clarendon Press)), remain a *de rigueur* account, and will do so, along with others in his many editions of Middle English poetry, even after the completion of the five-volume 'Pennsylvania Commentary'. This new tool, of course, will absorb all Skeat's explanations, for he indeed knew everything. One might also adduce the example of *Piers Plowman: The Prologue and Passus I–VII of the B Text as Found in Bodleian MS. Laud Misc. 581*, ed. by J. A. W. Bennett, Clarendon Medieval and Tudor Series (Oxford: Clarendon Press, 1972), with brilliant annotation from a scholar who, unlike Skeat, eschewed editorial judgement completely.

[12] See George Kane, 'Conjectural Emendation', in *Medieval Manuscripts and Textual Criticism*, ed. by Christopher Kleinhenz (Chapel Hill: University of North Carolina Press, 1976), pp. 211–26, a reprint of the original 1969 publication, in a Festschrift honouring Kane's King's College colleague, G. N. Garmonsway. Among the more plausible examples I can now recall — I generally took on this expert advice and forgot most of them — are, at B.3.211, emending 'to alle men' to 'to Allemeyns' (i.e., Hanseatic merchants, who had their own special London entrepot,

On another occasion, Kane concluded a disccussion of John Bale's role in the reception of *Piers Plowman* with a question: 'So what does this change about the text?'[13] This response seems to me a rather typical revelation of Kane's deep aversion to historicizing the text, his general disinterest in the history either of its witnesses or of its reception. On the one hand, this dismissal spoke to one revolutionary strength of his logical method — his thorough demolition of stemmatic editing as, alternatively, either a massive example of *petitio principii* or a statistically flawed operation.[14] Attestation of readings, which is revealed by a stemma and is essentially the history of the text's transmission, could be of no interest, a precursor of difficulties to which I will turn in the second part of this essay.

It does, however, strike me that there is a downside to Kane's resoluteness here. His 'open analysis' of the variants cordons off the text from the history that has produced the evidence for it. It isolates the individual instance and flattens the variant-evidence into a single temporal plane. All readings, whatever their antiquity, are equally present and potentially equal in evidentiary value. This is a powerful antidote to the circularity Kane found to mar stemmatic thought, in all its manifestations. But it equally throws into relief the care that must accompany the art of analysing the variants.

At this, Kane will always remain without peer. His strictly logical underlying theory may generate some systemic failures to recognize certain classes of readings.[15]

'the Steelyard'); and at B.14.41, emending 'þe wilde worm' to 'þe wilde woond/wonte' (cf. the pulpit *versus* on which Langland here embroiders, *'On the Properties of Things': John Trevisa's Translation of Bartholomaeus Anglicus 'De proprietatibus rerum: A Critical Text*, ed. by M. C. Seymour and others, 3 vols (Oxford: Clarendon Press, 1975–88), II, 1161, ll. 2–8).

[13] See his discussion, George Kane, *'Piers Plowman': The Evidence for Authorship* (London: Athlone, 1965), pp. 37–45 and Plate 3.

[14] See, most notably, Kane's destruction of *Piers Plowman: A Critical Edition of the A-Version*, ed. by Thomas A. Knott and David C. Fowler (Baltimore: Johns Hopkins University Press, 1952), at *The A Version*, pp. 54–114. Kane quite properly points out that constructing a stemma for editorial purposes depends upon a capacity to recognize some errors (the resulting stemma then 'automatically' generates massively more examples); but, his argument would run, were one able actually to identify errors, one would not need a stemma at all, but could, as Kane did, construct the text variant by variant.

[15] Most notably what I think of as the undue A-radiation of the B version. This is among the trenchant points made by Robert Adams, 'Editing *Piers Plowman* B: The Imperative of an Intermittently Critical Edition', *Studies in Bibliography*, 45 (1992), 31–68. But the process had been noted almost immediately by the late David Fowler, in 'A New Edition of the B Text of *Piers Plowman*', *Yearbook of English Studies*, 7 (1977), 23–42.

But Kane's local editorial work shows a keen sense of where things have gone badly wrong, and an impressively tasteful capacity to suggest how to set them right. Indeed, the complaint lodged against Kane's technique, that it changes too much, that too much relies upon a faith in Kane's good judgement, often strikes me as the reverse of the case. This raises another paradox, for, in spite of his aversion to considering his witnesses, Kane is always intuitively aware of central lessons of medieval book history and offers a constant sage reminder of the difficulty of medieval books generally. As analysis after analysis reveals, Kane repeatedly indicates the manuscripts' intensely provisional status, that their makers are just as prone to visualize themselves engaged in 'representing' a text as they are to imagine 'faithful transmission' of it.

II

These thoughts suggest Kane's aversion to 'user friendliness', where his scholar-ship was concerned. As a result, one difficulty of remembering Kane, given his uncompromising stance, is in discovering what it is that one should remember, negotiating the simultaneous breadth and detail of his contribution.[16] A great deal of post-Kane discussion of the text of *Piers Plowman* might be described as 'uncomprehending', and much of this incomprehension could be attributed to Kane himself. The severity of argument does not make easy reading, utterly rebuffs dip-in consultation, and requires a particularly thoughtful absorption attentive to implication (sometimes the unsaid), and more than occasional 'read-ing against the grain'.

In the second part of this essay, I examine what I consider a couple of examples of forgetting Kane, failing to comprehend what I should think the writings reveal that he meant (and had sometimes obscured).[17] The first of these studies argues that a strikingly deviant manuscript of the A version with C continuation, Aberystwyth, National Library of Wales, MS 733B (C siglum N^2) offers evidence that the initial promulgation of the B and C versions was simultaneous. In the

---

[16] Hence the useful efforts of a sixteen-year-old California kid, Peter Barney, 'Line-Number Index to the Athlone Edition of *Piers Plowman*', *YLS*, 7 (1993), 97–114; and the less necessary Peter Barney, 'Line-Number Index to the Athlone Edition of *Piers Plowman: The C Version*', *YLS*, 12 (1998), 159–73.

[17] For these examples, see Lawrence Warner, 'The Ur-B *Piers Plowman* and the Earliest Production of C and B', *YLS*, 16 (2002), 3–39; and 'The Ending, and End of *Piers Plowman* B: The C-Version Origins of the Final Two Passus', *Medium Ævum*, 76 (2007), 225–50.

second case, the argument is extended further, largely on the basis of evidence provided by the B-version copy, Oxford, Corpus Christi College, MS 201 (B siglum F). In this account, the last two passūs of BC were originally the property of the C version alone and have later been conflated into B from that source.

To each of these views, Kane offered what I should consider much more plausible alternatives, but perhaps not in so collected and so germane a fashion as to be readily compelling to a frustrated reader. Indeed, they prove to be cases in which Kane himself did not follow the implications of his own logic. In what follows, I will apply Kane's methods, or what I take to be their spirit, to some points at which, it will emerge, he did not push his analysis far enough.

Kane and Russell take up the text of N^2 in an exceedingly dispersed discussion within their introduction to the Athlone C text.[18] Although the material has to be ferreted out, the fundamental point is signalled in statements that the text of this manuscript was 'formed, clearly, by both sophistication and authoritative correction', or, alternatively, 'We have here, so to speak, an editor.'[19] As I will suggest in a moment, the adjective *authoritative* in the first of these statements is probably predicated more upon theoretical hope than evidence.

The *C Version* introduction, carefully read, gathers quite categorical evidence that the readings of N^2 can have nothing to do with anything like Langlandian papers. N^2's C-version forms offer persistent, and fairly incontrovertible, evidence that the text has been formed from 'an editor['s]' consultation of multiple manuscripts. Moreover, these are manuscripts 'produced', that is, already filled with erroneous, rather than authorial, readings. The clearest exemplification involves nearly 150 readings, in which N^2 communicates one or another error peculiar to one of the 'two great families' which typify the general C transmission, *x* and *p*.

Troublingly, the readings are split about evenly. The text of N^2 shows affinities with both *x* and *p*, and in about an equal ratio. Further, as Russell and Kane point out, the readings persist to such a degree that identifying one set as accidental convergence in error with a foreign source proves an implausible scenario. The alternative is, of course, that the scribe of N^2 persistently consulted at least two manuscripts of his text (here a thoroughly unrelated pair), rather than a single copy.[20] But whatever the stripe of these two sets of readings, they cannot have

---

[18] *Piers Plowman: The C Version*, ed. by George Russell and George Kane (London: Athlone; Berkeley and Los Angeles: University of California Press, 1997), at least pp. 21, 32–35, 46–47, 55–58, 101–02, and 193 n. 7.

[19] *The C Version*, ed. by Russell and Kane, pp. 58, 59 n. 34.

[20] By the locution 'N^2' I understand, of course, 'either the surviving book, or one or more of its exemplars'. It is thoroughly possible both that multiple consultation happened more than once

involved consultation of even the archetypal papers of Langland's C version, because those readings that form x and p (and that N^2 transmits) developed only as the result of uniquely deviant copyings from the C archetype. They emerged in the first 'public' copying generation of the poem's manuscripts, not as part of Langland's, or his amanuenses', efforts.

Moreover, the editors' account offers ample evidence that N^2 can only have been produced much later in the transmission than even this belated split into 'great families'. Many of the distinctive erroneous agreements of N^2 imply that the scribe was copying very late in the tradition indeed, choosing readings from manuscripts at least three or four copying generations removed from Langland's archetypal materials. More prevalent than examples joining N^2 with either x or p are erroneous readings where this copy agrees with the books assigned sigla W (92x) and F (89x); further prominent examples would include 52 agreements with P^2, 46 with Ch, and 45 with N. None of these copies sits anywhere near the top of a transmissional diagramme of the C version, and they are scattered across the *stemma codicum* (ChP^2 representatives of x, WFN of p).[21]

The inference Russell and Kane should have drawn from their data would be that N^2 actually represents one of the most developed stages in the transmission, at best a representative of the fifth copying generation (since it can draw upon books produced in the fourth). Moreover, its scribe produced his text by comparing pre-existent, but already scribally well advanced, circulating copies of the text. It is exceedingly unlikely, then, that N^2 can offer any purchase on the nature of the C archetype. It is indeed a book formed by conflation, Russell and Kane's 'correction' by 'an editor'. In this process, readings, from whatever the scribe's primary source, were subjected to scrutiny and emendation in the light of at least one other scribally well-advanced, yet very different, manuscript version.

---

in the historical/transmissional procedures underlying the extant book, and equally possible that the scribe of N^2 may be responsible for none of it, merely passing on what he received. Neither option renders the readings I describe associable with authorial activity.

[21] To elucidate: x and p represent the first copying generation from something like authorial papers, the copy of Langland's autograph that formed the (in spots, already erroneous) archetype of all surviving copies. But to take, as an example, the production history underlying P^2: following the emergence of x, at least one further generation of copying was required to produce Russell and Kane's separate genetic groups TH^{2}Ch and XYJP^{2}UDD^2; at least one further generation, to generate the separate groups XYJP^{2}UD and D^2; and yet at least one further generation, to define the irreducible groups XYJP^2 and UD. For the evidence, see *The C Version*, ed. by Russell and Kane, pp. 41–46; my demonstration represents one example of reading the editors' account critically, since it is predicated on reversing their order of argument.

Given their construction of this history, one might wonder about the Russell-Kane claim for the manuscript's containing '*authoritative* correction' (my emphasis). This locution is designed to account for some forty-five readings,[22] in which N^2 preserves the correct readings of the B version, as against all other C manuscripts, here sharing erroneous readings. For Russell and Kane, this stands as a sign of the N^2 scribe's 'pre-archetypal' consultation; that is, in their account, he had access to Langlandian papers that pre-dated in the transmission the archetype variously misrepresented in x and p.

But one must, I think, view this claim as implausible, and a largely theoretical move, designed to preserve the integrity of the C tradition. In many, if not all, of these cases, brilliance persists: Russell and Kane are surely correct in suggesting that C should read as B. But their argumentative move is only designed to avoid outright importation of B-version forms into their C text as conjectures. Given the copious evidence of the N^2 scribe's persistent consultation of multiple copies, the logical inference (and the customary understanding of N^2 before 1997) would have been to see that among the scribe's various sources, one was a very good B manuscript. The correct B readings in the text simply reflect the scribe's usual eclectic procedures. Thus (another critical reading of Athlone materials), all these acceptable readings need to be seen as Russell and Kane's persuasive conjectural emendations of the C tradition on the basis of comparison with the readings of B. Nowhere in all this procedure can there be any evidence that B readings in N^2 indicate the simultaneous production of that version and the C text — the scribe only knew the latter in belated transmissional forms.

Yet like the example of B.Prol.43 'synnelees' that I discussed near the start, this turns out to be a case where the more interesting questions and implications have been left unposed. Essentially, Kane and Russell have been caught in a doublebind, not entirely of their own making. Half the dilemma is endemic in the very act of editing a text. To do this, one has first to ascertain that such an object exists; customarily, such a demonstration rests in a detrmination that such an object is, in gross, attested through a specific range of witnesses. In the case of *Piers Plowman*, such an 'in gross' demonstration is relatively straightforward, resting for example, on such a question as 'what follows A.Prol.95 in this manuscript?'[23]

---

[22] Listed in *The C Version*, ed. by Russell and Kane, p. 102 n. 23.

[23] A has nothing here comparable to the later versions, but passes to the equivalent of B.Prol.217, whilst B.Prol.97 only appears in C as Prol.125, delayed by the insertion of a biblical exemplum spoken by Conscience (who appears here in no other version).

But the difficulty emerging from this finding, the other half the bind, Russell and Kane have created for themselves. That is, having identified an 'in gross' textual version, they assume that all readings attested by books representative of one version properly belong to that version. The assumption then becomes supported by Kane's powerful piecemealism, the healthy postulate that every reading deserves, if not requires, independent scrutiny. As in the case of B.Prol.43 'synnelees', the intent and brilliant pursuit of an authorial reading never allows a pause to ask how such a reading might or could have been generated, or what it would mean that it was generated in this particular context. The powerfully helpful 'open analysis' of the variants has left out a step always considered a central act of textual criticism, 'examinatio', the construction of a plausible model of the text's transmission.

As I want to persist in suggesting, Kane's rejection of transmission history, basically an account of how his chosen witnesses were constructed, is an inherently healthy and constructive move. In *The A Version*, Kane powerfully demonstrates that a *stemma codicum*, the customary way in which the results of 'examinatio' are displayed, will not construct a text. What he fails to see, in reserving a stemma as a post-factum bow to scholarly convention,[24] is that a stemma, rather than identifying 'right readings', more or less automatically identifies aberrant forms of transmission. Such a diagrammatic record of the text's generation reveals that witness X customarily shares features consonant with witnesses A, B, and C — and thus, when X instead shows features of P, Q, and R, points up anomalies in X's construction.

Analysing such anomalies is traditionally the business of an editor, since they frequently indicate features of a witness that might qualify or enhance its value for constructing a text. But having rejected the procedure as an editorial tool altogether, Kane can only become aware of transmissional anomaly in his concluding fulfilment of scholarly convention. Again, I think Kane's arguments that this argumentative deferral should be the case absolutely compelling, but equally find the transmissional evidence worth a good deal more 'in-transit' attention than Kane is prepared to give it. N^2 demonstrates pretty conclusively, after all, that not all readings communicated in C-version copies indeed represent properties unique to the C version.

But the Kane-Russell explanation of N^2 exposes the paradoxical incongruities to which Kane's totalizing logic is sometimes subject. Preserving N^2's readings follows from the postulate that anything in an 'in gross' C-version manuscript

---

[24] See *The B Version*, ed. by Kane and Donaldson, p. 17.

represents the C version. Explaining their presence, however, requires a return of the repressed. Stemmatics plays no role in producing the text of the C version, but an essentially stemmatic argument ('recourse to a pre-transmission archetype') proves necessary to explain the unfortunate appearances — and that simply because of the logical structure within which Kane's editions have been conceived.

The second example of forgetting concerns the end of the poem. In this argument, the 'Dobest' portions of *Piers Plowman* were originally only the ending of the C version, and their appearance in all B manuscripts the result of infiltration from C. I would suppose that underlying such views is a considerable difficulty in aligning various of Kane's perceptions about the poem with the peculiarities of transmission here.

One has immediately to say that the thesis that B ends with passus 18 is inherently implausible. That view fails to grasp the poem in its broadest shape. While such an assertion does not address any textual data and does not constitute 'objective', or even 'external', evidence (like that presented by codicology), it remains worth heeding.

The primary question one would ask of this thesis is, 'How could a poem of such difficulty as *Piers Plowman B*, such a demonstration of a resolute effort to bring sense to the religious condition of England, arrive at a relatively simple (certainly widely available) pietistic conclusion, creeping to the cross on Good Friday (B.18.427–31)?' From this perspective, one that views the poem as personal religious odyssey, the concluding passus must be seen as an explanation of the difficulty the dreamer has encountered, actually remaining unresolved by the grandeur of Passion and Harrowing. Can the poem end in a moment of biblical historicism without measuring the (absence of) impact or transformation this has effected on a post-Incarnation world, the religious condition of England that is the poet's subject?

Moreover, one advocating the foreignness of B.19–20 to the B tradition must be immune to (and ignore) major thematic issues in the poem. One could point most particularly to two trinitarian patterns that the excision of at least passus 19 would leave incompletely accounted for. The poem contains a large-scale examination of the acts of the Trinity itself, and, as part of this pattern, acts specific to Grace/the Paraclete/the Holy Spirit and to the provision of pardon in this world emerge only in passus 19.[25] Moreover, the poem also associates the persons of the

---

[25] Everyone would probably agree that the poem's most powerful moment is Christ's magisterial speech at B.18.365–95 (C.20.403–38). But within that speech, the condition, 'Be it any þyng abou3t' (B.18.388), explicitly evokes the atonement theology associated with sacramental penance and signalled powerfully at the poem's end through 'Piers pardon þe Plowman, *redde quod debes*' (B.19.187).

Trinity with the three 'Do-states' repeatedly discussed (signalled at B.13.94, 102/C.15.102, 109). But again, that discussion is only completed in this portion. To these considerations, one might well add a bit of 'external' evidence, that the surviving authorial rubrics of B (they are the guides copied from Langland's fair copy into Oxford, Bodleian Library, MS Laud misc. 581) make it clear that the B version was always intended to include a 'Dobest'.[26]

Yet external evidence, although it is scarcely uncontroversial, exists that would imply the separate promulgation of the two versions. Steven Justice's discussion of *Piers Plowman* and the Peasants' Revolt implies the 1381 rebels' access to the poem in its B version (not A, as David Fowler always argued). In contrast, since all full C copies include the 'autobiographical passage' of passus 5, promulgation of this version, following Anne Middleton's detailed demonstration, must post-date 1388, if not 1390.[27]

The published argument for the C origins of the B 'Dobest' proceeds by two steps. On the one hand, a good deal relies upon the assumption of the textual identity of the two versions. This view, the argument that the C 'Dobest' is unrevised, is integral to Russell and Kane's strategy throughout their edition of C. While it is not strictly true to state that potential evidence for it is totally lacking, revision here is significantly lighter than elsewhere in the poem.[28]

---

[26] The guides, together with the scribe's refusal to transmit them formally (certainly support-ing Kane's usual refusal to countenance manuscript divisions) are accurately reproduced at C. David Benson and Lynne S. Blanchfield, *The Manuscripts of 'Piers Plowman': The B-Version* (Woodbridge: Boydell, 1997), p. 191. The logic for their authoriality depends upon M. L. Samuels's discovery of identical linguistic layers in Laud (L) and Oxford, Bodleian Library, MS Rawlinson poet. 38 (R); see 'Langland's Dialect', *Medium Ævum*, 54 (1985), 232–47 (p. 241). Following Samuels, these linguistic agreements can only have occurred through the two scribes copying and reproducing forms from the same exemplar, and the latest common source available to both scribes can only have been Langland's papers, from which exemplar, as is customary, the Laud scribe will have copied the rubrics as guides for filling in later. See the diagram of the transmission at *The Vision of Piers Plowman: A Critical Edition of the B-Text*, ed. by A. V. C. Schmidt, 2nd edn (London: Dent/Everyman, 1995), p. lvii.

[27] See Steven Justice, *Writing and Rebellion: England in 1381* (Berkeley and Los Angeles: University of California Press, 1994), pp. 104–11; cf. David C. Fowler, *'Piers the Plowman': Literary Relations of the A and B Texts* (Seattle: University of Washington Press, 1961). See also Anne Middleton, 'Acts of Vagrancy: The C Version "Autobiography" and the Statute of 1388', in *Written Work: Langland, Labor, and Authorship*, ed. by Steven Justice and Kathryn Kerby-Fulton (Philadelphia: University of Pennsylvania Press, 1997), pp. 208–317.

[28] Cf. for example, the deviant versions of B.20.381 and C.22.381, dragged into unity, to accord with theory, in the Athlone editions of B and C.

In the history of the poem's criticism, as well as of its editorial handling, the meaning of B-C congruity at the poem's end has proved contentious. Russell and Kane, for example, interpret this unusual identity as a sign of Langland's death, and the promulgation of the last version of his poem by an editor. But the assumption underlying this proposal, that Langland necessarily revised everything, and with equal thoroughness, is simply that, an assumption. Moreover, Middleton's recent demonstration that the poet was at work at least as late as 1390 leaves little room for anything other than the production of several generations of copying that lie between the poet and now-extant copies, some certainly of the 1390s.[29] The evidence of relative identity might imply, after all, that, at the end of his earlier version, the poet had actually achieved a presentation with which he was satisfied. The argument that the two versions achieve identity because the later has been intruded into the tailless earlier text must be seen in the context of competing explanations, and it strikes me as much the least plausible of the propositions.[30]

As a second step in presenting the argument for B.19–20 as an importation from C.21–22, much comes to rest on the peculiar state of the B manuscript assigned siglum F. This utterly fascinating book, parts of it certainly produced through a fairly attractive 'scribal poetics', has yet to have received anything like the full study it deserves.[31] But as Russell and Kane frequently notice, F's construction involves much the same difficulties as those already analysed in the case of N[2].

Indeed, Kane and Donaldson, as Adams has pointed out, frequently relied too heavily upon the book's unique readings as an argument for over-emending their B text to accord with the A version. It did not occur to the editors at the time that

---

[29] See *The C Version*, ed. by Russell and Kane, pp. 82–88, 90–91, but also Middleton, 'Acts of Vagrancy'. *The C Version* citation of John But (p. 83) is particularly ill-taken, since those materials likely post-date the promulgation of all three versions; see further Anne Middleton, 'Making a Good End: John But as a Reader of *Piers Plowman*', in *Medieval English Studies Presented to George Kane*, ed. by Edward D. Kennedy and others (Woodbridge: Boydell, 1988), pp. 243–66; and Wendy Scase, '"First to reckon Richard": John But's *Piers Plowman*', *YLS*, 11 (1997), 49–66.

[30] Russell and Kane consider, only to reject it, the possibility in reverse, that the C 'Dobest' has simply been imported from B (*The C Version*, pp. 82–83).

[31] Still among the most compelling accounts is the first, James Weldon, '*Ordinatio* and Genre in MS CCC 201', *Florilegium*, 12 (1993), 159–75. See further Andrew Galloway, 'Reading *Piers Plowman* in the Fifteenth and Twenty-First Centuries: Notes on Manuscripts F and W in the *Piers Plowman Electronic Archive*', *JEGP: Journal of English and Germanic Philology*, 103 (2004), 232–52 and passim.

the scribe provided such lections on the basis of multiple manuscript consultation. They reflected moments in his work when, as scribal editor, he preferred the locutions offered by his copy of A, rather than those present in the B manuscript he usually followed. Interestingly, in their prodigious logical effort to present F readings as part of the B tradition, Kane and Donaldson perform just as the scribe of F had already done, in choosing from the range of readings available to them the ones they like. Rather than examine F's behaviour critically, as one imagines textual critics are to do, they replicate it.[32]

So far as F is concerned, the argument for the intrusion of the C Dobest into the archetype of all B manuscripts rests upon this copy's behaviour between B.18.411 and B.20.26. At this point, F provides a steady stream of C readings, very frequently readings more persuasive than all other B copies and forming the text of this part of the poem in the Athlone editions of both B and C. In the argument for the C origins of B's 'Dobest', these readings loom large. As often in the poem, one might argue that the majority of the B copies (representing the archetype *b*) have erred, and that Langland's authoritative text, which read exactly as the C version, has been faithfully transmitted by the second B archetype *a*, here represented by F.[33]

All this would be fine, but for one fact: F's cognate manuscript R (mentioned in n. 26, above) has, at this point, lost a quire. This is a real difficulty, since editorial determination of the reading of the archetype *a* common to both manuscripts depends upon the agreement of the two books.[34] In the absence of one of them, we essentially have no assurance that we are looking at readings of the archetype *a* usually shared by both books. In this case, with R absent, we cannot

---

[32] See *The C Version*, ed. by Russell and Kane, pp. 102 n. 23, 131 n. 51, 193 n. 7, all suggestive of the editors' determination to persist in taking readings conflated into odd manuscripts from another version as evidence for readings of the archetype of the version currently under discussion (and cf. *The B Version*, ed. by Kane and Donaldson, pp. 165–73). See further Adams 'Editing *Piers Plowman* B'.

[33] The *locus classicus* for this view of the *a* copies' independence, often in rectitude, from the remainder of the B transmission, is their inclusion of about 175 B lines not elsewhere attested (as well as erroneous omission of about the same number); see *The B Version*, ed. by Kane and Donaldson, pp. 61–69 and passim.

[34] Or what comes to the same thing, the demonstration that the reading of one or the other copies is a plausible descendant of the other manuscript's reading and also foreign to the readings generated by the second archetype *b*. The A-radiation of the B version through F readings depends upon Kane and Donaldson's decision that, in certain places, R/F variation cannot reflect such descendant relations between the competing readings.

be sure that F may not be a representative of the C version, having divagated, for whatever reason, from its customary textual supply. Its readings, then, just as those of N², would have nothing to say about the state of the archetypal text of B, although they surely add to the piquancy of (and the imperative of closely examining) this striking bearer of Langland's text.[35]

Moreover, some external evidence might imply a very good reason for F's seeking an additional manuscript version here for its text. For at least one possibility is that R and F determine a separate B-version archetype *a* precisely because the second is a copy constructed mostly by consultation of the former, along with other copies. In the absence of a quire of his exemplar (which this scribe, who knew the text very well before he copied, will have noticed immediately), the scribe may have been forced to seek a textual source alien to that he customarily followed.[36] In the frequent medieval indifference to the poem's versions, the scribe could have taken up, as adequate for his task, a C version, without recognizing its deviations from the B version he customarily followed.

But the identity of R with the *a* archetype is scarcely the only plausible explanation that might be offered. R itself may be a page-by-page reproduction from *a*, in which case the archetype itself might either have been missing a quire, when F received it, or could have included a quire's worth of C materials. Such infusion of continuous sections from one version into a manuscript of another is much less frequent in *Piers* transmission than the relatively random momentary multiple consultation/conflation exhibited by N², F, and other manuscripts. But it does occur, and it is a factor (among several others) deserving attention, prior to such large-scale claims as those advanced for C origins of the B 'Dobest'.[37]

Again, Kane's practice here seems to me worthy of further interrogation. Kane accepts F, and often follows its readings, even when unique in the B tradition. But

[35] For this point, cf. *The B Version*, ed. by Kane and Donaldson, pp. 165–73, especially '[i]n XIX, where R is defective, F's character is obscure, since its relation to their exclusive common ancestor is not there determinable' (p. 172 n. 92, with my punctuation, more apt than the different statement in the text at p. 165).

[36] This view has been argued previously; see Sean Taylor, 'The F Scribe and the R Manuscript of *Piers Plowman* B', *English Studies*, 77 (1996), 530–48. One major reason for Taylor's finding is his belief that he had discovered in R writing in the hand of F, which may be, but is not provably, the case. Recently, in the course of his Oxford D.Phil. researches, James Wright has reaffirmed Taylor's view of the identity of notes in R with the hand of F.

[37] For example, the three copies BmBoCot (B sigla, LBO in C) reflect a single exemplar. Its scribe copied mainly from a headless manuscript of B, but, to achieve a full text, had to supplement it at the opening with quires from a C version.

if the scribe's archetype (and thus, functionally *a*) was the extant manuscript R, this decision raises considerable difficulty. In traditional terms, were F derived from R, the manuscript would constitute what is called a 'codex eliminandus', a book to be eliminated from any consideration in constructing the text.

This would be the case, were F's derivation from R accepted, because the manuscript, insofar as it follows its single archetype R, can provide no reading not already in that archetype, and thus already part of the evidentiary pool. Insofar as the scribe provides anything else, this material can only represent (a) individual innovations on what had been received (and thus already considered editorially); or (b) conflation of readings from a second source. The latter, if from other B manuscripts, would, again, be already editorially considered material; if from any other source, not germane to the B tradition at all.

This finding of editorial uselessness would affect the hypothesis that B.19–20 represent the C version every bit as much as it would any recourse to the manuscript by Kane and Donaldson. Just as using N^2 of the C tradition, using F, whether proper or improper, proves at various points advantageous to both parties; it enables inclusion in the B tradition of a variety of features which, otherwise, would need to be attributed to B only hypothetically or conjecturally. But editorial exclusion would not, by any means, compromise the very great interest of the book as an exceptionally vibrant and entertaining response to Langland's poem, and one deserving of intensive further study.[38]

On the whole, outright consultation of a C manuscript, prompted by a disruption of the scribe's usual exemplar, seems to me most likely to account for F's readings here. In particular, one should notice that such F dips into the C tradition do not end with the return of R (and some certainty about the readings of *a*). A bit sporadically, even after he has clearly returned to copying primarily from *a*, the scribe continues for a while to provide readings attested in C manuscripts but otherwise isolated in the B tradition, at B.20.42, 97, and 103. The first of these is clearly marked as not from the archetype underlying all C manuscripts, but from a circulating copy, a reading restricted to the *p* manuscripts. Several variants elsewhere may allow a more precise placement of F's second copy, since they represent specific readings of isolated C manuscripts, particularly N^2W (e.g., B.18.427/C.20.470, goddes] þe).

---

[38] Even down to the scribe's quite extraordinary thrift with his parchment (parts of the manuscript are written on preserved half-sheets, and in places here, the scribe has cut out additional leaves to reserve for later use).

I conclude this demonstration with a further point revealed in analysing the behaviour of F through B passus 19. As is his customary procedure, Kane (here with Donaldson) integrates the analysis of individual readings here into a global statement of manuscript relations, in this instance a demonstration of the efficaciouness of using C to correct B. The discussion relies extensively upon the evidence of B.19, and it reveals twenty-five occasions when F concurs with the B archetype in a reading revealed as erroneous, when compared with readings of C. In context, one might assume this to mean that the scribe of F had access to more than one textual version.

However, closer examination throws up yet another example of those paradoxes I have considered through this essay. Kane and Donaldson's comparison relies upon juxtaposing scribal B readings — and they are universally perspicacious in having rejected them — with readings of the edited (and scribally purged) C version. Yet examination of the mass of C variants Russell and Kane provide reveals that 60 per cent of the examples of universal B error (fifteen of them) are reflected somewhere in the C tradition, sometimes very widely so.

Thus, theory and brilliant application to the text lead Kane and Donaldson to produce a better version of B 19 than heretofore available. But the findings reaffirm theory in a second, less obvious way — as Kane always argues, errors (and identical errors) are 'convergent', infinitely repeatable, and they constitute the very nature of scribal copying. But if that is the case, their analysis may be particularly problematic here (although not in other, simple textual contexts), where so much material is repeated across all three versions, all of them susceptible to identical reduction to the same commonplace.[39]

This situation enables some concluding reflections about Kane's massive contribution. Even amidst moments taciturn, and perhaps even downright misleading, Kane unequivocally set down the fundamental principles of the craft, of use not simply to us, but across a wide range of disciplines. His rejection of stemmatics, *as conventionally practised*; his substitution of the bracketing synonymous/homeographic substitution as a tool; and the general good taste and sheer

---

[39] For Kane and Donaldson's demonstration, see *The B Version*, pp. 90–95 and passim. The presence of identical readings in the C tradition indicates that in the majority of the instances, F's conflation from C may accidentally converge with the remainder of the B tradition. The ten remaining readings, given the total number of variants quite a modest showing, appear in B.19.101, 148, 243, 251, 253, 280, 292, 301, 303, 308 — all whose appearance in F is capable of being explained either as convergence or spot-consultation of a B manuscript. For B errors widely dispersed in the C tradition, see e.g., B.19/C.21.429, 453, 477. I am extremely grateful to Lawrence Warner for drawing my attention to these.

brilliance with which he pursued an authorial text are absolutely seminal lessons to anyone interested in medieval texts and their transmission. Difficulties particularly emerge in the manner of his explanation and in the slippages perhaps inherent in attempting to transform an inimitable art, practised piecemeal, into a logically coherent and totalizing account of proceedings. This, I think, may actually falsify and misrepresent what had occurred in producing the editions. Particularly highlighted in these difficulties is the problem Kane rejected out of hand, the integration of local reading and general transmission history. Inextricably bound with Kane's substantial contribution is a massive structure, both theoretical and intensely detailed, that, on the evidence of some examples I have analysed, it will take at least another generation of textual scholarship to internalize thoroughly, to integrate carefully, and to advance beyond Kane's own applications.[40]

[40] I am grateful to Anne Middleton and Thorlac Turville-Petre, as well as *YLS*'s readers, for their readings of this article; their suggestions have only improved the piece, and they are not responsible for any of its crochets or failures.

EDITING THE C TEXT:
THE ATHLONE PRESS EDITION OF 1997

Derek Pearsall

Editing the C text is in some respects more straightforward than editing A or B; in some respects it is more difficult; and in other respects it is impossible. As to the first, there is no problem in the choice of copy-text, as there is in B, for of the two groups of manuscripts of C, one is clearly inferior. Skeat was tempted into choosing a manuscript from this latter group as his copy-text for C, since it offered an immaculately presented full text, with intelligent smoothing and 'improvement' to iron out textual difficulties. It was pleasantly accessible in the country house of Sir Thomas Phillipps in Cheltenham, where Skeat went to complete the collation.[1] As Charlotte Brewer points out, the attraction of the Phillipps manuscript was further enhanced by the fact that it had been the base text for Whitaker's edition of 1813 and Skeat could therefore establish his text by taking his own copy of Whitaker to Cheltenham, collating it with the Phillipps MS, entering corrections into it, and taking it home with him. The manuscript was later sold to the Huntington Library and is now MS Hm 137. R. W. Chambers

---

[1] Charlotte Brewer, *Editing 'Piers Plowman': The Evolution of the Text* (Cambridge: Cambridge University Press, 1996), pp. 161–62. For Skeat, see, *The Vision of William Concerning Piers the Plowman*, ed. by W. W. Skeat, pt III: *Text C*, Early English Text Society, o.s., 54 (London: Trübner, 1873) (this edition was reprinted with an abridged preface in 1959), and *The Vision of William Concerning Piers the Plowman, in Three Parallel Texts*, ed. by W. W. Skeat, 2 vols (Oxford: Oxford University Press, 1886).

Derek Pearsall (*derekapearsall@btinternet.com*) is Gurney Professor of English Emeritus, Harvard University.

Abstract: This essay assesses the problems George Russell and George Kane faced when preparing the Athlone edition of the C text, including the uncertain extent of Langland's revision of B in C and the fact that the poet based his C revision on a scribal copy of B with many errors. Their edition is acclaimed for its success in dealing with these problems and for its brilliance in the practice of conjectural emendation, though criticism is directed at their relatively limited textual commentary and the excessively dogmatic nature of their decisions about Langland's alliterative, grammatical, and syntactical practice.

Keywords: William Langland, *Piers Plowman*, the C text, editorial theory, editorial practice, editorial presentation, George Kane, George Russell, alliterative metre, alliterative style, conjectural emendation, debate of the Four Daughters of God, history of editing, authorial revision.

10.1484/J.YLS.1.102107

went to the Huntington Library in 1935 to inspect its *Piers Plowman* manuscripts and discovered in MS Hm 143, sold at Sotheby's in 1924, and unknown to Skeat, the manuscript with the strongest claim to be the base manuscript of the future edition of C. It was the leading member of the better of the two textual traditions of C, full and clear, with only some oddities of spelling and an irritating (but reassuring, in that 'improvement' was never a problem) general scribal carelessness to mar its claim to be the best representative of the C archetype. Chambers wrote an essay to advance his claim and in the next year published a facsimile edition of MS Hm 143.[2] The manuscript was first used as the basis for editing C by Pearsall and Salter in 1967, by Pearsall again in 1978, by Schmidt in 1995, by Russell and Kane in 1997, and by Pearsall again in his new edition of 2008.[3] There has been no question of its pre-eminence.

In the second place, that is, in respect of the difficulty of editing C, though there has been no question of the choice of manuscript to be used as base text, the base text, even when emended in the light of other manuscript evidence, can only be as good as the archetype. Here the problems are considerable. Langland's C revision was neither systematic nor complete. He did not revise his B text by beginning at the beginning and systematically working his way through to the end, but by focusing on passages that he was dissatisfied with and working his way outwards from these cores of dissatisfaction. Revisions ripple out from these passages as the reviser finds more to disagree with in what he earlier wrote: the version is, as Russell says, 'selective, sporadic, and local'.[4] Revision of this kind is

---

[2] R. W. Chambers, 'The Manuscripts of *Piers Plowman* in the Huntington Library and their Value for Fixing the Text of the Poem', *Huntington Library Bulletin*, 8 (1935), 1–25; *Piers Plowman: The Huntington Library Manuscript (Hm 143)*, reproduced in Photostat, with intro. by R. W. Chambers, and technical examination by R. B. Haselden and H. C. Schulz (San Marino, CA: The Huntington Library, 1936).

[3] *Piers Plowman: Selections from the C-Text*, ed. by Elizabeth Salter and Derek Pearsall, York Medieval Texts (London: Edward Arnold, 1967); *Piers Plowman, by William Langland: An Edition of the C-Text*, ed. by Derek Pearsall, York Medieval Texts, ser. 2 (London: Edward Arnold, 1978); *William Langland, Piers Plowman: A Parallel-Text Edition of the A, B, C and Z Versions*, ed. by A. V. C. Schmidt, I: *Text* (London: Longman, 1995); II: *Introduction, Textual Notes, Commentary, Bibliography and Indexical Glossary* (Kalamazoo: Medieval Institute Publications, 2008); *Piers Plowman: The C Version*, ed. by George Russell and George Kane (London: Athlone; Berkeley and Los Angeles: University of California Press, 1997); *Piers Plowman: A New Annotated Edition of the C-Text*, ed. by Derek Pearsall (Exeter: University of Exeter Press, 2008).

[4] George H. Russell, 'Some Aspects of the Process of Revision in *Piers Plowman*', in *'Piers Plowman': Critical Approaches*, ed. by S. S. Hussey (London: Methuen, 1969), pp. 27–49 (see

very likely to leave rough edges and unfinished seams at the transitions, which may create particular problems for the editor. The confession of Pride in C.6, like the other confessions of the Sins, includes large swathes of material cut out from the reported account of the sins of Hawkyn in B.13.273–456.[5] As a consequence, Langland has to adapt a reported account to a first-person confession. Pride, who started out as a woman but is now a man, speaks thus in C in the part of his confession adapted from the Hawkyn episode: 'And ȝut so synguler be mysulue, as to syhte of [þe] peple, | Was non such as [my]sulue ne non so pop-holy' (C.6.36–37). Instead of the second *mysulue*, which is the reading of most C manuscripts, the copy-text, MS Hm 143, known by the siglum X, along with three other C manuscripts, has *hymsulue*. This may be regarded as authentic, since *hymsulue* is not a plausible scribal error. Langland, in revising, has apparently allowed the third-person singular pronoun to slip through from the account of Hawkyn's sins that he is adapting from B.13.283. Other interpretations are possible, but it may be presumed that MS X, with its three companions, all reputable members of the superior textual tradition, preserve the authentic reading of their exemplar, which the scribes of other manuscripts have corrected in the light of the context. Emendation, which all editors are obliged to make, does not have to pretend that the mistake was the scribe's but assumes that the poet would have corrected it in a perfected revision.

The unsystematic and incomplete nature of the C revision is also evidenced in the partially digested state of some of its additional lines. The major example is in C.Prol.106–17, the Ophni and Finees episode, which, with their obviously imperfect alliteration and metre, have provoked considerable discussion.[6] Most

pp. 39–40); see also 'The Poet as Reviser: The Metamorphosis of the Confession of the Seven Deadly Sins in *Piers Plowman*', in *Acts of Interpretation: The Text in its Contexts, 700–1600; Essays on Medieval and Renaissance Literature in Honor of E. Talbot Donaldson*, ed. by Mary J. Carruthers and Elizabeth D. Kirk (Norman: University of Oklahoma Press, 1982), pp. 53–65.

[5] Many regret these changes, and especially the greatly reduced role of one of the 'human' characters of *Piers Plowman*, but Langland, I think, had two good reasons for the change. One was to avoid the déjà vu effect of yet another run-through of the seven deadly sins (there is still one to come, in the discourse of Patience, C.16.46–99); the other is that he did not want at this point a focus on personal confession — it jarred with the continuing role of the dreamer as a surrogate, and furthermore he had already provided such a confession in his own person in passus 5, at what might be thought the right point in the developing drama of the poem.

[6] See Derek Pearsall, 'The "Ilchester" Manuscript of *Piers Plowman*', *Neuphilologische Mitteilungen*, 82 (1981), 181–93; Wendy Scase, 'Two *Piers Plowman* C-Text Interpolations: Evidence for a Second Textual Tradition', *Notes & Queries*, 232 (1987), 456–63; *The C Version*, ed. by

would agree that they are an 'unworked' addition, material that Langland had roughed out ready to be shaped into proper alliterative form. The frustrated editor can neither dismiss them as inauthentic nor 'edit' them into conformity. There are other signs of incompleteness that the editor, likewise, has simply to accept: the haste or carelessness that has left some dreams twice begun or twice finished (the so-called 'inner dreams'),[7] and the exposed seams where new material has been patched to B without full attention to detailed congruence. Reference is preserved, for instance, to no longer extant antecedents, such as the mention of a companion for the fat friar of the feast of Patience who has long been excised from C,[8] or the description of the fruit of the Tree of Charity as 'Pers fruyt þe plouhman' (C.20.32), when Piers has already lost his job as keeper of the Tree (C.18.28). The process of revision, furthermore, seems not to have reached the last two passūs at all — or perhaps Langland was completely satisfied with them as they stood.[9] The editor's problem here is to decide whether to edit as if editing a direct descendant of the B archetype or to accept that Langland's admission of the two passūs without alteration has given them an unusual degree of authenticity. The problem is acute enough to prompt Russell and Kane to give special attention to it in their introduction, with many impressively detailed explanations of their editorial solutions.[10]

A third problem that faced Russell and Kane, to which Kane and Donaldson had devoted a whole chapter of the introduction to their B text, is so difficult as

Russell and Kane, pp. 186–94; Andrew Galloway, 'Uncharacterizable Entities: The Poetics of Middle English Scribal Culture and the Definitive *Piers Plowman*', *Studies in Bibliography*, 52 (1999), 59–87 (pp. 72–80).

[7] See notes to C.11.165, 13.214, 18.178 (as compared with B.16.20), in Pearsall, *Piers Plowman: A New Annotated Edition of the C-Text*. The B text is cited from *Piers Plowman: The B Version*, ed. by George Kane and E. Talbot Donaldson (London: Athlone, 1975).

[8] See C.15.47, corresponding to B.13.40–41 (emended out by Kane and Donaldson); C.15.101. For many further examples of uncompleted revision in C, see the introduction to *The C Version*, ed. by Russell and Kane, pp. 83–88.

[9] This last statement has to take account now of recent articles by Lawrence Warner who, as part of his theory of early BC contamination, suggests that C.21–22 were newly composed for C and not simply left unrevised from B. B never contained them, and ended on a note of high drama with the dreamer and his family creeping to the Cross on Easter morning. See Lawrence Warner, 'The Ur-B *Piers Plowman* and the Earliest Production of C and B', *YLS*, 16 (2002), 3–39; and, more particularly, 'The Ending, and End, of *Piers Plowman* B: The C-Version Origins of the Final Two Passus', *Medium Ævum*, 76 (2007), 225–50.

[10] *The C Version*, ed. by Russell and Kane, pp. 90–91, 118–36.

to be almost insoluble.[11] Langland's C revision was based on a scribal copy of his own B text in a quite advanced state of deterioration, though somewhat less so than the archetype of all surviving copies of B. It seems to us an inexplicable circumstance that Langland should not have had his own fair copy of his own poem, but so it appears to have been. He was thus forced to reconstruct his own poem, even as he revised it.

It must be acknowledged that the theory that C was based on a scribal copy of B and that therefore the C archetype is corrupt has not commanded un-questioning acceptance, and the fact that it was preceded, in the work of R. W. Chambers and Elsie Blackman, by a similar theory of the corruption of the B archetype might make one wary.[12] If the archetype of all manuscripts can be shown to be faulty, it is easier to disregard readings which have the attestation of all or a large majority of manuscripts, and to be dismissive of 'copytext matters', whilst freeing the editor to the joyful pursuit of conjectural and other kinds of emendation.[13] However, the theory has stood the test of time, and is true to the experience of following Langland minutely through his activity of revision. Watching the poet grope back through the jungle of scribal errors to recover what he had said in B or what he knew he had wanted to say is an unexpectedly intimate glimpse of Langland at work on his revision, as well as a witness to the tenacity of his poetic purpose. Here are some of the lines in which Hunger describes to Piers those who are to be the recipients of his charity. They appear thus in Skeat's B text and in all manuscripts of B except two that have 'no3t han' for 'nau3ty' (one manuscript by correction over an erasure): 'And alle manere of men that thow my3t asspye | That nedy ben and nau3ty helpe hem with thi godis' (B.6.225–26). Here are the same two lines, renumbered, as emended by Kane and Donaldson. The emended reading is drawn from the A text, where all manuscripts agree. No manuscript of B has the third line:

> And alle manere of men þat þow my3t aspie
> That nedy ben [or naked, and nou3t han to spende,
> Wiþ mete or wiþ mone lat make hem fare þe bettre]
> (B.6.222–24)

---

[11] *The B Version*, ed. by Kane and Donaldson, pp. 98–127, 'The C Reviser's B Manuscript'. See also *The C Version*, ed. by Russell and Kane, pp. 62–63, 70–75.

[12] For the early work of Chambers and Blackman, see Brewer, *Editing 'Piers Plowman'*, pp. 228, 260–61, 398.

[13] The reference to 'copytext matters' is in *The C Version*, ed. by Russell and Kane, p. 152.

Finally, here are the same two lines as they appear revised in C in the edition of
Russell and Kane. All manuscripts of C substantially agree:

> And alle manere [of] men þat thow myhte aspye
> In meschief or in malese, and thow mowe hem helpe,
> Loke by thy lyue lat hem nat forfare.
>
> (C.8.231–33)

It is the fact that Skeat's second line does not alliterate that alerted the editors of
B to the near-certainty of scribal corruption and prompted them to go back to
the reading of A. The C reviser recognizes both the semantic inadmissibility of
'nauȝty' in the context and the lack of alliteration and makes an evident effort to
reach back to the original meaning of B as it survived fragmented in 'helpe hem
with thi godis'. The effect of B's misreading, as preserved in Skeat, is profound. It
penetrates, for one thing, into dictionary-making. The *Oxford English Dictionary*,
faced with a contextually and historically implausible or even impossible meaning
('wicked') for 'naughty', produced a new signification for this reading alone, 'having nought, needy'. The *Middle English Dictionary* shows 'naughty' as early as
c. 1400 (in *Cleanness*) for the usual meaning 'wicked', but *Piers Plowman* remains
the only source for the signification 'in want', 'needy', that it provides, like the
OED, with another example cited from Oxford, Bodleian Library, MS Rawlinson
poet. 38, B.7.72, most likely the product of the influence of the reading earlier in
the text of the B archetype. In addition to the creation of a 'ghost-meaning' in the
OED, another consequence of the Skeat reading was the attempt of Coghill to
show that Langland was offering an unprecedentedly brave and outspoken new
solution to the problem of alleviating poverty (one must give even to the *wicked*),
and a sense of 'naughty' not otherwise recorded until 1526.[14] One could hardly
have a better example of the profound consequences of bad texts and the importance of good editing.

The final complication for the editors of C is that they have constantly to
decide whether inferior BC readings discarded in the Kane and Donaldson edition of B as scribal have been given authorial sanction by their admission into
manuscripts of C, or whether they have been readmitted by the scribes of the
extant manuscripts of C by convergent or coincidental variation, or whether they
have been inadvertently missed by the C reviser and should be corrected, or
whether indeed they were never inferior in the first place — a possibility which

---

[14] Nevill K. Coghill, 'Langland, the "Naket", the "Nauȝty", and the Dole', *Review of English
Studies*, 8 (1932), 303–09.

one can be sure is unlikely to be acknowledged by an editor in any acts of retro-spective emendation. These are not the only potential problems, and at times the situation of the editor, as I said at the beginning, is near to impossible.

There is all the more reason to salute the Russell and Kane edition of C as a monumental achievement, informed throughout by a deep knowledge of the poem and its way of working and an acute understanding of the processes of scribal transmission and corruption, and particularly the manner in which cor-ruptions may arise from hard readings. It is also a more 'reader-friendly' edition than the Athlone Press editions of A and B, and the Olympian tone of B, famously resounding in the final sentence of the editors' introduction ('Whether we have carried out our task efficiently must be assessed by re-enacting it'), is muted.[15] There are occasions when the editors venture emendations which they admit to not being entirely sure of, or where they acknowledge possibilities of doubt that would have been unthinkable in B. They explicitly concede the inevitability of 'subjectivity' in the editorial process and admit that on occasions the revising poet may not have 'got round' to revising inferior scribal readings, and that there may be 'nothing to choose between readings', and that at times it is 'possible only to speculate'.[16] This is probably less a change of heart than an acknowledgement of the peculiar difficulties of the C text, and of an edition that, given 'the unremitting contingency of uncompleted revision', must rest on 'arguments vastly more provisional than those underlying the texts of the A and B versions'.[17] There is the strong possibility too that George Russell exercised a moderating influence on Kane's enthusiasm for emendation. In his earlier writing on revision in C, Russell was notably cautious about the prospects for the radical editor of C:

> A reading originally scribal in origin is transformed by the fact of its admission by the C-reviser into a genuine reading of the C-version. It is, in my opinion, hazardous to edit these readings out of the C-version since we have no way of judging the motives which led to the retention. It may have been inadvertence: it may also have been a deliberate decision.[18]

Elsewhere, he expresses the same caution:

> It would seem also to be the case that the revising poet did not — for whatever reason — always concern himself with what we may venture to call the detail of the line. What may

---

[15] *The B Version*, ed. by Kane and Donaldson, p. 220.

[16] See *The C Version*, ed. by Russell and Kane, pp. 88, 90, 123, 132.

[17] *The C Version*, ed. by Russell and Kane, pp. 179–80.

[18] Russell, 'Some Aspects of the Process of Revision', p. 40 n. 21.

appear to a modern hypercritical eye as more explicit, more emphatic, easier, or accidental seems not always to have concerned the revising poet.[19]

Kane had a way of browbeating or persuading his fellow editors into acquiescence through the logically remorseless mode of argument that he favoured, but the occasional sweet reasonableness of the C edition may not be exclusively due to the special difficulties of editing C.

The editors of C have also responded, in their own way, to a criticism levelled at the editors of the B text by all readers and reviewers of that edition, namely, that in the absence of line-by-line textual notes it was very difficult and sometimes impossible to find the explanations of individual emendations.[20] All explanations were locked into blocks of examples, in the introduction, in small type, according to the standard classifications of scribal error made in the introduction to A. Anyone wishing to use the edition properly had first to annotate the text with marginal cross-references from text to introduction. In the edition of C, most of the routine emendations are recorded in the usual classification blocks in the introduction, and the effect, as usual, is to force the reader to an infinitely labourious turning of pages, and also, through the abbreviated form of reference to the causes of scribal substitution — 'minim trouble', 'uncompleted letter in exemplar', 'subconscious auditory variation' — to give the explanations a dismissively brisk force, as if to say 'further argument is obviously unnecessary'. However, there are also several series of substantial textual notes, in the intro-duction, still classified of course according to the taxonomy of error, dealing with the more interesting and contentious of the emendations. These textual notes, now that they have been admitted to be of value and have been admitted, are a demonstration of the practice of textual criticism at its best. It is rarely that they do not make a strong case. Yet at the same time, the systems of classification under which these textual notes are organized — emendation because of anormative alliteration, or lexical change, or misunderstanding of sense, or scribal tendency to greater explicitness or emphasis, and so on, which are useless to anyone looking for explanation of individual emendations, seem designed to disguise — even to

[19] Russell, 'The Imperative of Revision in the C Version of *Piers Plowman*', in *Medieval English Studies Presented to George Kane*, ed. by Edward Donald Kennedy, Ronald Waldron, and Joseph Wittig (Woodbridge: Brewer, 1988), pp. 233–42 (see p. 242).

[20] There is now, for both A and B, a valuable line-number index to the sources of textual decisions by Peter Barney, 'Line-Number Index to the Athlone Edition of *Piers Plowman*', *YLS*, 7 (1993), 97–114; and more recently a similar index to C also by Barney, 'Line-Number Index to the Athlone Edition of *Piers Plowman*: The C Version', *YLS*, 12 (1998), 159–73.

disguise from the editor — the patterns of manuscript affiliation which emendation is drawing upon, or eliciting, or reinforcing.

Given the quality of the textual notes, though, one can only regret that the editors did not similarly respond to equally widespread criticism of the B text for its practice of excluding indication, in the corpus of variants, of the source of certain of their emendations. The editors of C follow this regrettable practice, excluding any information about the source of emendations that are not drawn from the manuscripts of C.[21] It is obviously a sensible and helpful practice in critical editions to enter the source of an emendation and those witnesses that agree with it immediately after the square brackets following the lemma. The Athlone Press editors do not allow this, except, as I have said, where the emendation is drawn from the manuscripts of C, so that one has to work out for oneself where other kinds of emendation are drawn from: whether from the text of A or B as established earlier by the Athlone Press editors, or from conjecture. If all the manuscripts available are recorded as containing a reading or readings other than the one selected for inclusion in the text, then one has no way of knowing whether the chosen reading is a conjectural emendation or has been drafted in from another version. The complete absence of any mention of the B version in the corpus of variants as the source of an emendation (it is the source of many) is, above all, a perversity beyond imagining.

With that cry of pain from a dedicated and admiring user of the Athlone Press edition of C, it is a relief to turn to its many excellences.

In substantive emendation the editors are always persuasive, if not always compelling, and there are some brilliant major emendations with far-reaching implications for the interpretation of the text. One is the clarification of a passage in the passus 5 'Apologia' (C text only) which has always been puzzling in seeming to suggest that the scions of the aristocracy should be the ones who become clerics and administrative officials. A simple shift of three lines (C.5.62–64), the original mistake having been caused by eyeskip ('serue ... serue ...'), is enough to effect the remedy.[22] Another is an emendation which makes it clear that Piers Plowman is present in person at the feast of Patience:

---

[21] The practice of recording readings in the Athlone Press editions is explained in the introduction to *The A Version*, ed. by Kane, pp. 170–71, without any mention of this exclusion, and the same practice is consistent throughout A, B, and C.

[22] See the note in the introduction to *The C Version*, ed. by Russell and Kane, pp. 172–73.

[Pacience as a pore thyng cam] and preeyede mete *pur charite*;
Ilyk[e Peres] the [ploghman], as he a palmere were,
Crauede and cryede for Cristes loue of heuene,
A meles mete for a pore man or moneye yf they hadde.

(C.15.32–35)

Everything hangs upon the emendation here of 'Ilyk' (the reading in MS X and the majority of other C manuscripts) to 'Ilyke', which turns an adjective, 'like, resembling', into an adverb, 'alike, similarly, likewise'.[23] Peres, who is again referred to, a little later (15.130), as a palmer, 'þe palmare 3ent' (yonder, over there), just before he begins to speak, is now present throughout the following scene, not a 'spectral visitant'[24] but a living embodiment of *pacience*, as his opening words make clear when he is eventually prevailed upon to speak (15.137).

There are many further examples of happy emendations in Russell and Kane, some prompted by the needs of alliteration, some by the needs of good sense, and some by both.[25] They are derived from various sources. Some are plucked from a single manuscript of C: 'And bygge 3ow benefices, [here bonchef] to haue' (C.3.33).[26] 'Here bonchef' is taken up from MS F (Cambridge University Library, MS Ff.5.35), with better alliteration and better sense in the context than 'pluralites', the reading of all other C manuscripts. Another such emendation, also picked up from MS F, is beautifully apt as an example of *lectio difficilior*: 'The tarre is vntydy þat to þe [tripe] bylongeth' (C.9.263, RK, 164). For 'tripe' (a small flock of sheep), all other C manuscripts have 'shep', with complete loss of alliteration. Intelligent ad hoc emendation for metre on the part of the scribe of MS F might be suspected in these two instances, but the balance of probability is against it.

---

[23] Only three manuscripts have 'Ilyke'; six others have 'ylike to' or 'like to', which indicates that the final *-e* had ceased to be a widely recognized adverbial marker. See the note on the line in *The C Version*, ed. by Russell and Kane, p. 156. It should be noted that the editorial square brackets around 'Peres' and 'ploghman' record the erasure of these two words, as throughout the text of MS X, the work of a sixteenth-century user who associated them with the pope.

[24] *An Edition of the C-Text*, ed. by Pearsall, p. 252.

[25] Most of these emendations are discussed and all rejected by Schmidt, who shows a keen attachment to the copy-text and to his own edition of C, published two years before Russell and Kane's. See his 'Textual Notes' to C.3.33, 9.263, 21.76, 90, 11.143, 21.241, 10.249 in his *Parallel-Text Edition*, vol. II.

[26] For commentary, see *The C Version*, ed. by Russell and Kane, p. 162. In the examples that follow, the commentary of Russell and Kane is introduced under the abbreviation 'RK', followed by the page number.

Other emendations are taken from B, often from a single aberrant manuscript: 'Mirre and moche gold withouten merc[ede] askynge' (C.21.76, RK, 133). All manuscripts of C have 'mercy' for 'mercede' (reward), and all manuscripts of B likewise, except for one which has 'mercede' by correction and two which have 'mede', one of them by correction. The reading 'mercy' makes less good sense. Another example is a little more complex: '[For it shal turne tresoun] to riht and to treuthe' (C.21.90, RK, 134). For the first half-line, all C manuscripts and all B manuscripts except one (MS F, Oxford, Corpus Christi College, MS 201) have 'And resoun to riche gold', which is superficially plausible but inappropriate in the context. The relationship of MS F of B to the C text is of course a matter of some debate.[27]

Finally, there are the large number of successful conjectural emendations. Faulty alliteration is often the clue to where the text is ailing, and the cue for conjectural emendation, Kane's own partiality and gift for which have always been remarkable. One example provides Russell and Kane with occasion for quiet self-congratulation: 'And byleeflely how Goddes [l]o[u]e alyhte | On þe maide Marie for mankynde sake' (C.11.141–42, RK, 170). All C manuscripts, including MS X, have 'sone' for 'loue'. 'A very elegant justification of conjecture', Russell and Kane call it, not only restoring the alliteration but also providing better, and slightly harder, sense. The following emendation is taken over from B, where it is likewise conjectural: 'And somme to deuyne and deuyde, [figu]res to kenne' (C.21.240, RK, 131). The slightly more appropriate word (all C manuscripts, like all B manuscripts, read 'noumbres') restores f/v alliteration on the root syllables of 'deuyne' and 'deuyde'. Alliteration is not in question in this last example: 'Ac why þe world was adreynt, holy writ telleth, | Was for marriages [maugre kynde] þat men made þat tyme' (C.10.245–46, RK, 160). For 'maugre kynde' all C manuscripts have either 'of mankynde' or 'makynge', both equally lame.

Not all the many minor emendations in Russell and Kane may seem equally well advised, and particularly those emendations that aim to systematize and regularize alliteration, grammar, and syntax in unnecessary or fussy ways and that are not well supported by the witnesses (and where the possibility is very real that Langland himself may have accepted and thus authorized the rejected reading). Examples of such emendations include the imposition of $aa|ax$ alliteration, even though the evidence is quite plentiful that Langland was prepared to tolerate some variant forms of the alliterative line, not only $aaa|xy$, which the Athlone Press

---

[27] See *A Parallel-Text Edition*, ed. by Schmidt, II, 142–44; *The B Version*, ed. by Kane and Donaldson, pp. 63–64, and the articles by Warner cited in n. 9, above.

editors accept, but also *ax|ay* and *xa|ay*. In the following line, from a passage not present in B, the word 'ȝut' is introduced, without manuscript attestation, to restore *aa|ax* alliteration, even though the natural stress-pattern of the line seems thereby to be twisted out of shape: 'When y ȝut ȝong was, many ȝer hennes. (C.5.35, RK, 169). MS X and two manuscripts of the same genetic group read 'ȝong ȝong', which Russell and Kane somewhat implausibly maintain supports the emendation by suggesting that the first word was illegible (but why would the scribe insert such an odd substitute?). Similar editorial motives account for the insertion of 'clereliche' in this line: 'And sende vs contricion [clereliche] to clanse with oure soules' (C.16.25, RK, 170). The natural rhythm of the line is violated by the emendation: it cannot be read or spoken with any kind of ease.[28] Russell and Kane cite in support a use of 'clerliche' in B.18.391, but the structure of that line is quite different. Whilst suggestive of a certain rigidity in the application of normative alliteration, these emendations, and the many others of a similar kind, generally refrain from the far-fetched hypotheses of alliteration on unstressed syllables and minor function-words that occasioned such bewilderment or even hilarity to users of the Athlone Press edition of B.[29] Russell and Kane make little acknowledgement of the work of Hoyt Duggan, in a series of articles beginning in 1987, on the metre of *Piers Plowman*, but it is possible that his careful analyses have acted as a curb on such speculation.[30]

In addition to the emendations that aim to regularize alliteration, there are many types of minor emendation aimed at syntactical regularization where Russell and Kane prefer the reading of a manuscript or manuscripts other than their copy-text and its group affiliates. Some involve the omission of the second preposition in parallel prepositional phrases, e.g.,

> When me carpeth of Crist or clannesse of soule. (C.7.76, MS X, etc., 'of clannesse')
>
> Fro wastoures and wikked men þat þis world struyen. (C.8.27, MS X, etc., 'fro wikked men')
>
> For thogh me souhte alle þe sektes of susturne and brethurne. (C.16.295, MS X, etc., 'of brethurne')

---

[28] Other examples of similar emendations *metri causa* include C.16.174, 197, 20.310.

[29] Examples are the presumption of alliteration on 'ouer', 'his', and 'hem' in B.1.108, on 'Ne', 'none', and 'nas' in B.12.146, and on 'tho', 'thise', and 'for' in B.10.134. The editors have the grace to admit that the 'unobvious alliteration' of the last example would be likely to be missed. See *The B Version*, ed. by Kane and Donaldson, p. 196.

[30] See especially Hoyt N. Duggan, 'Notes Toward a Theory of Langland's Meter', *YLS*, 1 (1987), 41–70. The only acknowledgement of Duggan's work I have come across in Russell and Kane is in *The C Version*, p. 138 n. 2.

Others involve the omission (or insertion) of the second possessive adjective in parallel possessive phrases, e.g.,

> Bote oure spensis and spendynge sprynge of a trewe welle. (C.16.39, MS X, etc. 'oure spendyng')
>
> For his pouerte and pacience perpetual ioye. (C.16.56, MS X, etc. 'his pacience')
>
> Here moneye and [here] marchandise marchen togyderes. (C.Prol.61, MS X, etc. do not have 'here')

Others involve the omission of the second infinitive marker in parallel infinitive phrases, e.g.,

> To bynde and vnbynde as þe boke telleth. (C.Prol.129, MS X, etc., 'to vnbynde')
>
> And there to iangele and iape and iuge here Emcristene. (C.2.102, MS X, etc., 'to iape')
>
> To repenten and arise and rowe out of synne. (C.10.52, MS X, etc., 'to arise')

Although a hyper-delicate ear might conceivably distinguish one or the other as aesthetically preferable, the only reason for the changes seems to be the over-mastering desire for regularity and the attractive possibility of being able to locate the source of scribal corruption in 'adducement to parallelism with preceding', repeated over and over again in the editorial commentary.[31]

The other two groups of fussy and needless emendation appeal to grammatical rather than syntactical nicety, and involve the imposition, again, of a stricter regularity than was usual for a fourteenth-century vernacular writer. Many of the readings chosen and rejected, as with those of the previous group, are matters of indifference, where the copy-text may properly be allowed, in the absence of pressing evidence for change, to stand. First, there are examples of the elimination by emendation of superfluous negative particles as they appear in MS X and its affiliates, e.g.,

> Noþer goos ne gries but two grene cheses. (C.8.304, MS X, etc. 'Ne noþer')
>
> For noþer he beggeth ne biddeth ne borweth to ȝelde. (C.16.372, MS X, etc. 'ne beggeth')

Such superfluity of negatives is a characteristic feature of informal Middle English, as are the several kinds of ungrammatically colloquial forms of expression and of colloquial semi-appositional phrasing which are similarly pruned and tidied up by Russell and Kane, e.g.,

---

[31] For example, *The C Version*, ed. by Russell and Kane, p. 108.

Loke now where this lollares and lewede Ermites

Breke þis obedience þat beth so fer fram chirche. (C.9.241–42, all C MSS,
'Yf they breke')

Russell and Kane call the rejected reading 'grammatically out of true', and criticize
the repetition of the conditional already present in 'where' (whether), accusing
the scribe of mistaking its meaning.[32] There other examples of a kind of loose
appositional structure that seems to me both 'grammatically out of true' and
characteristically Langlandian: "'Parfay!" quod pacience, "propreliche to telle
[this] | In engelysch is ful hard Ac sumdel y shal telle the"' (C.16.118–19). Most
C-manuscripts, including MS X, have 'it' for 'this' (none have 'this'), and C
manuscripts of the X group have 'it is' for 'is'. Likewise,

> For hymsulue said, þat sire is of heuene,
> That Adam and Eue and all his issue
> [Sh]olde deye with doel
>   (C.20.302–04)

MS X and its group have 'said hit' for 'said'.

Generally, the editors tend to suppress the increased informality and collo-
quialism of C, which is made markedly evident in the frequent substitution of
unstressed *a* for masculine pronoun *he* (a feature of MS X only, but preserved in
Russell and Kane). The effect is often to impose the equivalent of a 'house style'
upon Langland, which usually involves the rejection of the reading of MS X and
the selection of a reading from the family of manuscripts that includes MS Hm
137 and are well known to be given to 'improvement' of the kind that Russell and
Kane in this instance seem to prefer. Finally, questions as to choice of reading
customarily decided by the application of the rule of *lectio difficilior* are complicated by the very real possibility that Langland himself, some years on, may have
given the nod to easier readings, where there was no significant difference of
meaning, in order to assist in ready understanding. This is not an argument for
best-text editing, which demonstrably has many defects, but for a more base-text-
friendly interventionism, something more akin to the moderate editorial course
pursued by Schmidt.[33]

---

[32] *The C Version*, ed. by Russell and Kane, p. 174.

[33] This simple characterization of Schmidt's editorial method must be set beside his own ex-
haustive discussion of the problems of editing C in his *Parallel-Text Edition*, II, 60–75, 165–207.

I will conclude with two examples, one tiny and not very important, the other of vast significance, of what I have called the 'impossibility' of editing the C text of *Piers Plowman*. The first is in the Confession of the Sins, where Envy appears, shaking his fist at Wrath, the next sin to appear, as if he envies him his place in the limelight: 'A wroth his f[u]ste vppon Wrath; hadde [he] wesches at wille | Sholde no lyf lyue that on his lond pissede' (C.6.65–66). The X group alone has 'pissede' (MS Y, 'pessede') and is followed by Russell and Kane; all other C manuscripts have 'passede'. It looks like a classic case of the scribal substitution of *lectio facilior*, with the added incentive for change of mild bowdlerization.[34] The problem is that 'pissing' on one's land would be annoying for anyone, not just a madly resentful man. On the other hand, 'passede' seems perfectly appropriate as an example of a harmless action that causes violent offence to a man full of jealousy and malice, and in its evocation of the familiar cartoon image of the landowner, with loaded shotgun and red face apoplectic, enraged with jealous possessiveness at finding trespassers on his land.[35] My image is anachronistic, but probably not untruthful to the nature of landowners. On the other hand, 'pissing' would be a calculated and gratuitous insult, and a cause of great annoyance even to an ordinary land-holder. Why couldn't the man wait? One would not need to be a personification to get very annoyed. Decision between the two readings here is as arbitrary as flipping a coin, and an editor might easily change his mind later. A story is told of Talbot Donaldson in his later years ruminating on the B-text edition of *Piers Plowman* and wishing that he had chosen a different reading. But then, he said, 'maybe I did'.

The other example comes from the speech of Peace in the debate of the Four Daughters of God that precedes the Harrowing of Hell. She is about to put forward the argument that the purpose of the Incarnation was so that man could appreciate by experience the difference between sorrow and joy — he had to undergo suffering so that he might truly understand the joy of Redemption — and so that God could experience for himself and so fully understand human suffering and the sorrow of death. It is a daring and unusual argument, and theologically

---

[34] A curious parallel, probably not relevant, may be observed in the crux at C.22.219, where a variant *pissing* in one copy is 'identified by a corrector as a subconscious overlay with *passing*, "extremely", and emended accordingly' (*The C Version*, ed. by Russell and Kane, p. 135).

[35] Comparison with the passage in C.3.33–64 about merchants and messengers and their contrasting fortunes when trespassing over men's corn is not helpful. The messenger gets away with it because he is known to be moneyless and cannot be 'fined', whereas the merchant can be relieved of his hat or his hood or his gloves or 'moneye of his porse' (13.49).

unorthodox on a number of counts. Our understanding of the whole speech is implicated in the choice of a particular reading in the first line of Peace's speech: "'And y shal pre[u]e," quod pees, "here payne moet haue ende | And wo into wele moet wende at þe laste'" (C.20.208–09). All C manuscripts except one have 'preye' for 'preue'. The reading 'preue' is taken by Russell and Kane from a single aberrant manuscript of C, Aberystwyth, National Library of Wales MS 733B.[36] It is also the reading of most manuscripts of B (likewise accepted into their edition by the Athlone Press editors), where 'preie' is found only in the RF family, which has a long and contentious history in *Piers Plowman* editing and has often been thought to have an association with archetypal C.[37] The reading 'preue', it will be seen, is at some kind of fault-line in the history of the textual tradition.

In every way, 'preue' is the more appropriate word in the context, since what Peace is offering in her speech is a demonstration or 'proof' that the Incarnation served God's desire to have experience of contraries — not good theology, perhaps, but clearly what Peace wishes to demonstrate. Furthermore, it has manuscript support and is accepted by the Athlone Press editors for both B and C: 'preye' is a feeble substitute and a classic *lectio facilior*.[38] The choice of 'preue' as a reading is so compelling that it is all the more surprising that Schmidt rejects it for both B and C. Indeed, he maintains a running battle with the reading 'preue' in both the banks of notes in his apparatus, bringing to bear a variety of arguments that have little relevance to the matter in hand.[39] He says, for instance, 'The religious truth of man's coming salvation through Grace is a matter not of evidence but of faith and is therefore an object not of proof but of prayer.'[40] This is of course true, but it does not change what Peace, in her speech, says. Later, Schmidt, having called Peace's arguments 'surprising', reprimands her sharply: 'Peace's argument risks blurring the distinction between God's choosing to experience what he is free to and man's choosing to know what he was forbidden

---

[36] This manuscript has played a large part in the speculations of Lawrence Warner (see n. 9, above). It is an A+C manuscript, the A part bearing the siglum N, the C part the siglum N².

[37] The debate about the status of the two manuscripts is briefly rehearsed by Kane and Donaldson and by Schmidt, as cited in n. 27, above.

[38] For discussion of the variant in C, including a characteristically ingenious explanation of the origin of 'preye' as 'induced' by 'preyer', line 205, see *The C Version*, ed. by Russell and Kane, p. 115.

[39] See *A Parallel-Text Edition*, ed. by Schmidt, II, 449, 691.

[40] *A Parallel-Text Edition*, ed. by Schmidt, II, 449.

to.'[41] Does Schmidt's argument necessarily imply that Peace is an unreliable witness? That would be difficult to accept, and of a different order of difficulty from acknowledging that, as party to a debate, she does not have access to the whole truth (yet she is the one who brings letters from 'loue'). Schmidt's motives for accepting 'preye' may have something to do with his generally strict adherence to his copy-text as best representative of the archetype (his guiding principle, invoked more than once, is 'When it is not necessary to emend, it is necessary not to emend'),[42] but it may also be that, since he finds Peace's arguments theologically unacceptable, he wishes to deny her the freedom to say that she *proves* them. There is a possibility — and this is the significant point — that C records the same hesitation on the part of the scribe of the C archetype or even on the part of Langland, who may in his revision have been hesitant about what he now per-ceived as unnecessary or gratuitous challenges to the reader. Such a possibility must leave the editor in a quandary.

A small example from this same speech by Peace may give further substance to this possibility: 'For til [*modicum*] mete with vs, y may hit wel avowe, | Ne woet no wyht, as y wene, what is ynow to mene' (C.20.225–26). The unusual Latin word is taken over into C by Russell and Kane from B, where it is the archetypal reading. All but one of the C-manuscripts, on the other hand (the exception being MS N[2], which has 'defaute'), have 'moreyne', a tame substitute, but one that Langland himself might have let pass, as an easier reading which would not halt readers in their tracks, when he found it in his copy.

Such possibilities of acquiescence on the part of the author in an 'inferior' reading leave the editor in an impossible situation. All he can do is to adhere to the only basic editorial rule left — *Show your working*. In one respect, Russell and Kane, like the Athlone editors always do, observe this injunction to the letter. Their record of information about variants is utterly comprehensive and astonish-ingly free from error. All the information one needs to criticize their edition is available somewhere. On the other hand, most of the information they provide, even in the excellent textual notes, where they appear, is restricted to individual variants, so that the larger patterns of manuscript affiliation which may be drawn upon or suggested or supported by their processes of emendation are hidden away, even, as I have suggested, from the editors themselves.

---

[41] *Parallel-Text Edition*, ed. by Schmidt, II, 691.

[42] For example, *Parallel-Text Edition*, ed. by Schmidt, II, 240.

MAKERES OF THE MIND:
AUTHORIAL INTENTION, EDITORIAL
PRACTICE, AND *THE SIEGE OF JERUSALEM*

Timothy L. Stinson

S cholarly editing usually entails many acts, or at least claims, of supersession; a new edition is meant to supersede its predecessors, a reading from one source text supersedes that found in another, and an eclectic text supersedes the exemplars upon which it draws. Indeed it may be said that supersession is inherent in every act of editing, for no one sets out to edit a document or text having decided that there is nothing that needs to be replaced or improved upon. This situation naturally lends itself to debate, ranging in scope from an argument over a single word to agonistic struggles between advocates of competing schools of textual criticism. During recent decades, these debates have been shaped by the much larger discussion concerning the impact of digital media on every activity that is central to humanistic enquiry, including reading, writing, researching, publishing, and archiving, as well as the implications of what many assume will be the eventual supersession of the codex as both the primary tool and the default final product of most humanities scholarship. Much of this conversation concerns broad effects of this upheaval, from hyperbolic claims of the potential of digital media to liberate us from the chains of print to alarmed predictions of a decline in literacy and the enervation of attention spans required to read the complex arguments that print media have facilitated.

It is my goal here to conduct a much more focused examination of the impact of digital media on the editing of Middle English texts by examining a specific example, the fourteenth-century alliterative poem *The Siege of Jerusalem*. A case-based analysis will be helpful, for while there are overarching rationales for

Timothy L. Stinson (*timothy_stinson@ncsu.edu*) is Assistant Professor of English, North Carolina State University.

Abstract: Drawing examples from the alliterative poem *The Siege of Jerusalem* and the forthcoming *Siege of Jerusalem Electronic Archive* (SJEA), this article examines the impact of digital media on the editing of Middle English texts, particularly those that survive in competing manuscript witnesses, and argues that digital media promise an advantageous supersession of print that will bring us far closer to the material conditions and transmission of medieval texts than print ever has.

Keywords: *Siege of Jerusalem*, Mary of Jerusalem, authorial intention, manuscript studies, electronic editions, textual criticism.

10.1484/J.YLS.1.102108

and consequences of the transition to digital media in editorial work, these also change from text to text: just as editors might approach a text in a variety of ways using print technologies, so too are we faced with a number of possibilities when employing digital tools. I will consider these questions: How has the medium of print shaped the editing, criticism, and reception of *The Siege* and, conversely, how can these activities be reshaped by digital media? What significant new opportunities greet us when editing the poem in a digital setting, and how can these best be realized? Throughout this essay, I will draw upon my work on *The Siege of Jerusalem Electronic Archive* (SJEA), which John Ivor Carlson and I are editing for publication through the Society for Early English and Norse Electronic Texts. The SJEA will be a peer-reviewed online resource that provides colour digital images of all of the 231 extant manuscript pages containing the poem, linked to XML-encoded transcriptions of all of the texts. Each manuscript will be accompanied by a critical introduction comprising a physical and linguistic description, analysis of scribal habits, and bibliography. The outcome will be a set of interconnected best-text editions of each manuscript copy of the poem: the user of the archive will be able to work with any manuscript individually or to conduct comparative searches across the entire corpus of texts, critical materials, and encoded annotations of scribal features such as additions, deletions, and modifications of texts. A series of critical texts of what Ralph Hanna and David Lawton have identified as the *alpha* and *beta* versions of the poem, as well as a new critical text of the archetype, will be linked to these documentary materials.[1] Thus the scholar consulting the archive in its final form will have access to an eclectic critical text reflecting the intentions of the *Siege*-poet as well as to alternative textual traditions of the poem; these texts will be linked to full facsimile editions of the manuscript witnesses rather than apparatus that present documentary materials in partial and abbreviated forms. The initial version of the archive will also include digital images, a transcription, and a translation of John of Tynemouth's *Historia aurea*, a major source for the *Siege*-poet recently discovered by Andrew Galloway.[2] We plan for future expansions of the archive to include additional source materials.

---

[1] *The Siege of Jerusalem*, ed. by Ralph Hanna and David Lawton, Early English Text Society, o.s., 320 (Oxford: Oxford University Press, 2003). Unless otherwise noted, quotations from the poem are taken from this edition. Hanna and Lawton provide a discussion of the relationships of the manuscripts at pp. lv–lxix, and provide a stemma at p. lxvii.

[2] Andrew Galloway, 'Alliterative Poetry in Old Jerusalem: *The Siege of Jerusalem* and its Sources', in *Medieval Alliterative Poetry: Essays in Honour of Thorlac Turville-Petre*, ed. by J. A. Burrow and Hoyt N. Duggan (Dublin: Four Courts, 2010), pp. 85–106.

Editing 'The Siege of Jerusalem'

The Siege of Jerusalem survives in nine manuscript copies:[3]

1. Oxford, Bodleian Library, MS Laud misc. 656 (L)
2. London, British Library, MS Additional 31042 (A)
3. London, British Library, MS Cotton Caligula A. ii (C)
4. London, British Library, MS Cotton Vespasian E. xvi (V)
5. Cambridge University Library, MS Mm. v. 14 (U)
6. Devon Record Office, Deposit 2507 (Ex)
7. San Marino, Huntington Library, MS Hm 128 (E)
8. London, Lambeth Palace Library, MS 491 (D)
9. Princeton University Library, MS Taylor Medieval 11 (P)

To date there have been three published editions of the poem. The first, by E. Kölbing and Mabel Day, was published by the Early English Text Society in 1932[4] and remained the only widely available text of the poem until the appearance of Hanna and Lawton's edition in 2003. The Kölbing-Day text is limited in two important ways. First, the editors did not have the advantage of knowing of all of the extant manuscript witnesses. The Princeton manuscript was unknown at the time, not appearing on the market and coming to the attention of scholars until its sale by Sotheby's in 1952; the Exeter fragment, meanwhile, was unknown until its discovery late in the twentieth century in the course of repair work on a sixteenth-century memorandum book.[5] Second, the editors were not able to account for the source of the six hundred or so lines in the poem that were derived from the *Bible en françois*, a puzzle that was not solved until several decades later when Phyllis Moe, working on Cleveland Public Library, MS W q091.92-C468, which contains an English translation of the work, realized the connection.[6] Hanna and Lawton's excellent edition, also an EETS publication,

---

[3] Of these nine, six are complete or nearly complete, two are substantial fragments (P and V), and one (Ex) is a binding fragment containing a portion of one column of text on either side. The manuscripts are described in the introduction to *The Siege of Jerusalem*, ed. by Hanna and Lawton.

[4] *The Siege of Jerusalem*, ed. by E. Kölbing and Mabel Day, Early English Text Society, o.s., 188 (Oxford: Oxford University Press, 1932; repr. 2001).

[5] Michael Swanton, 'A Further Manuscript of *The Siege of Jerusalem*', *Scriptorium*, 44 (1990), 103–04.

[6] Phyllis Moe, 'The French Source of the Alliterative *Siege of Jerusalem*', *Medium Ævum*, 39 (1970), 147–54. See also *The ME Prose Translation of Roger d'Argenteuil's Bible en françois: Edited*

was in every way an improvement upon its predecessor. In addition to making the changes mandated by the newly discovered manuscripts and source text, the editors also added a more substantial introduction, expanded textual notes, a more thorough and convincing explanation of the genetic relationship of the manuscripts, a new and more accurate analysis of scribal and authorial dialects, and an appendix of extensive data documenting manuscript affiliations. Both editions rely upon L as the copy-text, but Hanna and Lawton truly establish a critical text, whereas Kölbing and Day remain much closer to the copy-text, making far fewer emendations. As part of their effort to re-create the archetype, Hanna and Lawton establish seven major textual divisions as authorial, as opposed to Kölbing and Day's presentation of the text in four parts, the divisions presented by the scribe of L. In addition, Hanna and Lawton divide the poem into quatrains, a division present in E and C but not in L or any of the other witnesses (although U features eight-line divisions). Michael Livingston's edition is the most recent, appearing the year after Hanna and Lawton's text as part of the TEAMS series published by the Medieval Institute. Livingston's text of the poem differs very little from, and is much indebted to, Hanna-Lawton's;[7] it is an edition meant for classroom use that is inexpensive, features ample explanatory notes, and contains a concise, clearly written introduction.[8]

Both of the most recent editions of *The Siege of Jerusalem*, then, have articulated a goal — in one instance to produce an eclectic critical text with accompanying scholarly apparatus, and in the other to produce a volume designed for students and teachers — and accomplished it using the print format. Moreover, both have done an excellent job of meeting their goals using that medium. As utterly indispensable as the print codex has been to the dissemination of texts and knowledge to date, however, there are tasks that printed critical editions cannot do nearly as well as digital ones. This has, of course, been pointed out many times in the relatively brief history of electronic editing. Perhaps the best formulation to date of the problems presented by printed critical editions is Jerome McGann's:

---

from Cleveland Public Library, MS W q091.92-C468, ed. by Phyllis Moe, Middle English Texts, 6 (Heidelberg: Carl Winter, 1977).

[7] As Livingston openly and gratefully acknowledges: *The Siege of Jerusalem*, ed. by Michael Livingston, TEAMS Middle English Texts (Kalamazoo: Medieval Institute Publications, 2004), p. vii.

[8] In addition to the three editions discussed here, Thorlac Turville-Petre presented an edited text of lines 521–724, again using L as his copy-text, in *Alliterative Poetry of the Later Middle Ages: An Anthology* (Washington, DC: Catholic University of America Press, 1989).

Brilliantly conceived, these works are nonetheless infamously difficult to read and use. Their problems arise because they deploy a book form to study another book form. This symmetry between the tool and its subject forces the scholar to invent analytic mechanisms that must be displayed and engaged at the primary reading level — e.g., apparatus structures, descriptive bibliographies, calculi of variants, shorthand reference forms, and so forth. The critical edition's apparatus, for example, exists only because no single book or manageable set of books can incorporate for analysis all of the relevant documents. In standard critical editions, the primary materials come before the reader in abbreviated and coded forms.[9]

The goal of the SJEA is to provide tools that take full advantage of the opportunities of electronic editing while avoiding those difficulties that derive from 'deploy[ing] a book form to study another book form'. It is certainly true that 'no single book or manageable set of books' could accomplish the same tasks as a digital archive like the SJEA. Even if one were to find a publisher cooperative enough to publish full transcriptions and notes for each manuscript in *The Siege of Jerusalem* corpus accompanied by the requisite 231 photographic plates of facsimile images, this would not result in a 'manageable set of books'. What scholar or publisher could afford such a set of volumes? And, more to the point, how would someone wishing to use this set as a tool manage to get around in it? It would be most unwieldy, and the indexing necessary to make the texts usable would add such bulk as to make it considerably more so. But of course, even if such a set of volumes were to be produced, digital critical editions offer many advantages that are not available in printed critical editions regardless of the available budget or the size of the volumes. Many of these, such as the relatively inexpensive availability of numerous images, improved search capabilities, the interconnectivity of hypertext, and the replacement of apparatus, concordances, and other scholarly tools with more user-friendly digital versions, have already been noted repeatedly and found wide acceptance. I wish to focus my discussion more closely on advantages that digital critical editions offer to editors of medieval texts surviving in multiple competing manuscript witnesses, as well as to users of such editions. Such a situation, common in the editing of Middle English texts,[10]

---

[9] Jerome J. McGann, 'The Rationale of Hypertext', in *Electronic Text: Investigations in Method and Theory*, ed. by Kathryn Sutherland (Oxford: Clarendon Press, 1997), pp. 19–46 (p. 21).

[10] The other common situation is editing a work that survives in a lone manuscript. For a discussion of how digital media can facilitate this work, see John Ivor Carlson, 'Translating the Alliterative *Morte Arthure* into a Digital Medium: The Influence of Physical Context on Editorial Theory', *Arthuriana* 20. 2 (2010), 28–44. See also A. S. G. Edwards, 'Middle English Romance: The Limits of Editing, the Limits of Criticism', in *Medieval Literature: Texts and Interpretation*, ed. by Tim William Machan, Medieval & Renaissance Texts & Studies (Binghamton, NY: Center for Medieval and Renaissance Studies, 1991), pp. 91–104.

poses specific problems and offers specific opportunities, and demands a tailored response from editors.

The Siege of Jerusalem is an attractive candidate both for publication in a digital format and for discussing the merits of digital editions more broadly. The manuscripts are richly varied and feature complex relationships both to one another and to the lost archetype from which they descended; but there are few enough of them to make such variation manageable in one edition. The poem is long enough to warrant publication as a stand-alone edition, but brief enough to make undertaking a project such as the SJEA feasible from a perspective of both economy and time. Among long-line alliterative poems, *The Siege* is second only to *Piers Plowman* in the number of manuscript copies, but it fits more clearly into 'the central tradition of Middle English alliterative verse',[11] making it particularly valuable to a study of that verse form. I will discuss three significant advantages offered by digital media for the editing of *The Siege* and conclude with a case study that provides examples of how the SJEA might facilitate study of the poem.

The first advantage offered by a digital archive like the SJEA is its capacity to maintain competing textual authorities rather than forcing an editor to 'resolve' them into an eclectic text or to choose a 'best' text, the primary options of the print era (although, of course, printed facsimiles are also possible). Medieval texts, and particularly vernacular literary texts, were created in a context in which the existence of simultaneous competing authorities, that is versions of a text that have been, to various degrees, recomposed through scribal intervention, was the norm. Even if we envision the simplest possible level of complexity concerning medieval textual transmission — the solitary scribe copying from a single exemplar — we find competing authority, for we have both the exemplar and the (invariably altered) scribal copy. But of course, things frequently were not that simple. In the relatively small group of nine manuscripts in the SJEA alone, for example, we have evidence that the scribe of C worked from at least two exemplars that contained substantially different versions of *The Siege of Jerusalem*, and he seems to have switched between them 'on an essentially free-choice basis' for more than half of the poem.[12] Furthermore, we know that not only was the narrative of the destruction of Jerusalem widely known and attested in other texts, but that the source texts of *The Siege*, which themselves survive in multiple copies today, had wide circulation in the era. This wide availability of

---

[11] *The Siege of Jerusalem*, p. xxxvii.

[12] *The Siege of Jerusalem*, p. lxvii. The scribe apparently had access to an exemplar from both the *gamma* and *delta* subarchetypes, which represent two textual traditions within the larger *beta* subarchetype.

source texts creates a secondary layer of authority; the scribes likely knew the narrative, as well as at least some of the source texts, and understood that the poem was a reworking of those sources.

With *The Siege of Jerusalem*, then, we have a complex situation with respect to textual authority, and one that is inherent in the transmission of Middle English texts more broadly. An unfortunate consequence of printed critical editions is the tendency of, and indeed often the necessity of, elevating one extant version at the expense of all others. Vital traditions of recomposition and critical evidence of processes of transmission are thereby lost, or at best rendered 'infamously difficult to read and use', either through their displacement into apparatus or their (frequently tacit) expulsion from the final critical edition. *The Siege of Jerusalem* is a case where the need for preserving these traditions is especially pressing, for L, the version of the poem invariably chosen by editors as the base text, survives alone on one side of a bifurcated stemma. Thus editions have not only obscured the evidence of eight out of nine of the surviving manuscripts, but have done so when those eight form a separate tradition of the text. Hanna has argued that L, the only representative of the *alpha* tradition, 'is relatively isolated from all other copies', whereas *beta* 'was a "local text" circulating in areas reasonably proximate to the author'.[13] Moreover, there are separate textual traditions within *beta*, such as the 'southerly dispersal of *Siege*' represented by the *delta* group.[14] The SJEA attempts to preserve the simultaneity of competing authority and the resultant diversity of textual traditions by including each manuscript on equal footing. This is not to suggest, of course, that the manuscripts are equal for all tasks. L is indeed, as previous editors have demonstrated, the best text if our interest is authorial intention. But others have compelling traits to recommend them as well. For example, A, which we know was copied by Robert Thornton, provides important information about the habits of a scribe whose taste in texts is responsible for the survival of a significant portion of the extant corpus of medieval English alliterative verse.[15] Meanwhile the Huntington copy, one of the least desirable

[13] Ralph Hanna III, 'On Stemmatics', in Hanna, *Pursuing History: Middle English Manuscripts and their Texts* (Stanford: Stanford University Press, 1996), pp. 83–93 (p. 92).

[14] Hanna, 'On Stemmatics', p. 92.

[15] For a detailed discussion of the manuscript, see John J. Thompson, *Robert Thornton and the London Thornton Manuscript* (Cambridge: Brewer, 1987), and Ralph Hanna III, 'The Growth of Robert Thornton's Books', *Studies in Bibliography*, 40 (1987), 51–61. Michael Johnston offers a discussion of Thornton's habits and intentions as a compiler in 'Robert Thornton and *The Siege of Jerusalem*', *YLS*, 23 (2009), 125–62.

manuscripts if one's goal is the establishment of the authorial text, is probably the most fruitful if one's interest lies in studying extensive scribal recomposition and intervention.[16]

In making modern editions, however, the complexities of competing authority are not limited to those created by multiple medieval scribes and their texts. The meaning of the terms *author* and *authority* (and hence *auctor* and *auctoritas*, their etymological roots) have many nuances. The terminology of textual critics and medieval writers, along with everyday usage of the words, offer overlapping and sometimes competing interpretations. In order to sort out these meanings and how they influence editorial practice, it is perhaps best to begin with Mary Hamel's insights into how authorship was understood in the medieval era:

> Few if any Middle English texts, then, were 'original' in the sense 'not derived from something else'; the expectation was that any Middle English work would be derivative to a greater or lesser degree. The Middle English writer was most often, in fact, the direct translator of a single text in French or Latin or the compiler of several related texts in one or both of those languages.[17]

Multiple authors and authorities, then, were routinely present in single Middle English texts. This is certainly the case with *The Siege of Jerusalem*, where the poet is engaged in compilation and in translating from French and Latin, precisely the activities mentioned by Hamel. His authority is shared with that of the authors whom he translates and rewrites. The *auctoritas* of his sources is, of course, reflected in the usage of these texts by editors to emend scribal texts; those texts employed by the poet still possess not only relevance, but *authority* regarding what the final reading of a critical edition should be.[18]

---

[16] For a discussion of the extensive revision in this manuscript (much of which focuses on scribes other than the one who copied *The Siege*), see Thorlac Turville-Petre, 'Putting it Right: The Corrections of Huntington Library MS Hm 128 and BL Additional MS 35287', *YLS*, 16 (2003), 41–65, and the introduction to *The Piers Plowman Electronic Archive*, XI: *San Marino, Huntington Library Hm 128 (Hm and Hm2)*, ed. by Michael Calabrese, Hoyt N. Duggan, and Thorlac Turville-Petre (Cambridge: Published for the Medieval Academy of America and SEENET by Boydell & Brewer, 2008).

[17] Mary Hamel, 'The Use of Sources in Editing Middle English Texts', in *A Guide to Editing Middle English*, ed. by Vincent P. McCarren and Douglas Moffat (Ann Arbor: University of Michigan Press, 1998), pp. 203–16 (pp. 203–04); Hamel is here quoting the *American Heritage Dictionary*.

[18] In the introduction to their edition, Hanna and Lawton note that 'we have been both inspired and constrained by the poet's sources, which very often identify for us that variant extant

In addition to this, we have in the corpus of *Siege of Jerusalem* manuscripts, as in many corpora of surviving medieval manuscripts, the work of scribe-authors who produced new sites of authority, and new narratives and narrative traditions, as they altered and recomposed the texts they copied. This is evident in the poem's *beta* tradition, where we have evidence not only of scribal recomposition, but of at least two traditions of transmitting distinct versions of the text, designated by Hanna and Lawton the *gamma* and *delta* subarchetypes. This already complicated notion of authority is made even more complex by the terminology of textual criticism and by the roles of editors. Fredson Bowers has famously written about 'multiple authorities', by which he means any documents with the potential to point towards an authorial reading, a related but clearly distinct usage of the term.[19] In this sense, of course, all of the manuscript copies of the poem possess authority; the meaning in this context differs from, but is still related to, the medieval usage. Finally, it must be considered that the editor also assumes a significant role of authority in choosing which readings or manuscripts best represent the goals of the edition at hand, even if the goal of that editor is to reveal authorial intention. Try as an editor might to arrive at such intentions, her own judgement is everywhere visible, even in actions as purportedly routine as transcribing manuscript materials (a task which, as anyone who has attempted it can tell you, is rife with moments of editorial uncertainty and occasionally demands fiat).

Digital media are much more flexible in handling the simultaneity of, as well as the nuanced distinctions of, the many overlapping intersections of authority in both medieval manuscript contexts and critical editions. Whereas printed critical editions tend to force documentary materials into a marginal position, usually in an apparatus or appendix, digital media make no such restrictions: an eclectic critical text can be comfortably accommodated within an archive alongside documentary and best-text editions, and advantageously cross-linked to the documentary texts. The SJEA not only maintains multiple authority by presenting all extant manuscripts, but accounts for multiple forms of authority within each documentary text through the use of style sheets. This builds upon an

---

in the corpus most likely to represent the author's response to the Latin or French he was reading' (p. xci). See, for example, the textual commentary to lines 25 and 27–28 (p. 92), where decisions regarding authorial readings and quatrain divisions, respectively, are influenced by consultation of *Vindicta Salvatoris*.

[19] Fredson Bowers, 'Multiple Authority: New Problems and Concepts of Copy-Text', *Library*, 5. 27 (1972), 81–115.

innovation developed in *Piers Plowman Electronic Archive* publications, where style sheets allow users to choose a number of ways of viewing the text, including 'Diplomatic', which minimizes the judgement of the editor by displaying all scribal marks without editorial remark, 'Scribal', which presents the same text as 'Diplomatic' but calls attention to difficulties in the text through colour-coding conventions, and 'Critical', which increases the level of editorial intervention by showing the editor's judgement of scribal intention. Furthermore, the images of manuscript folios provide another level of access to authority for the user of the archive to explore, and the one freest from editorial manipulation and closest to the scribe's intentions and practices (although one that, of course, requires palaeographical skills). Digital media, then, are quite flexible in their ability to facilitate a representation of the many forms of authority present in critical editions of medieval manuscript materials in a way that would be impossible in printed volumes.

Closely tied to the ability of digital media to maintain competing textual authorities is their capacity for much greater flexibility in handling authorial intention, a feature that holds as much potential to enrich literary criticism as it does editorial practice. Recovering the intentions of the poet has been the explicit goal of previous editors of the poem: Kölbing and Day did so through light emendation of the manuscript deemed closest to the author's intended text, while Hanna and Lawton created a more eclectic text in pursuit of the same goal. The author's intentions have also been a dominant preoccupation of critics and the predominant theme of their criticism. The poem's early critics tended to dismiss the work on the grounds of the *Siege*-poet's alleged zeal for suffering and rank anti-Judaism; Dorothy Everett claimed that the poet's 'ghoulish relish for the horrible is so marked that one feels it may account for his having chosen the siege as his subject',[20] while Derek Pearsall saw in the poem 'an accomplished brutality of the visualizing imagination' and 'a crude and narrow vindictiveness'.[21] Recent critical opinion has been mixed concerning the poet's stance towards the violent subject matter of his source texts and how and why he deploys these in his own work, resulting in a rough division between those who see sympathy or antipathy on the part of the author. Christine Chism, for example, argues that the poet feels 'delight' at the sea of broken Jewish bodies upon which the horses trod after the

---

[20] Dorothy Everett, 'The Alliterative Revival', in *Essays on Middle English Literature*, ed. by Patricia Kean (Oxford: Clarendon Press, 1955), pp. 58–59.

[21] Derek Pearsall, *Old English and Middle English Poetry* (London: Routledge and Kegan Paul, 1977), p. 169.

first Roman victory detailed in the poem,[22] and Roger Nicholson notes that the poem seems 'pollutized by anti-Semitism, in the intensity with which it imagines and realizes its vindictive design'.[23] Elisa Narin van Court counters that 'the poem exhibits a tenuous, but fully articulated sympathy towards the Jews',[24] and Alex Mueller agrees, finding in the poet's handling of his source materials a sympathy for 'the pitiable fate of the Jews' and 'disgust for the cruelty of the Roman conquerors'.[25]

Of course, the goals of editors and critics with respect to authorial intention are not identical; editors consider textual variants, source texts, and metrical constraints in order to determine the text the poet intended to write, whereas critical concern over the poet's views towards violence and Judaism is a very different matter. But it seems fair to assume that the decision of editors to create editions designed specifically to present the poet's intended text has had a significant effect on literary criticism, for the way in which most critics encounter the poem is mirrored in the way that they write about it — as a single text in a modern printed edition with the complexities of its transmission and physical textual states marginalized, and with the intentions of the poet depicted as the most prominent and important aspect of the textual tradition. The print medium does not inevitably and invariably shape the work of critics in this way, as is evident, for example, in Bonnie Millar's mindfulness of the manuscript tradition in her efforts to contextualize the poem[26] and (as I discuss further below) Michael Johnston's thoughtful approach to understanding how scribal compilers shaped reception. Throughout the poem's reception history, however, we have also seen persistent and widespread speculation about the poet's personal bias, and it is difficult to believe that these critics' prioritizing of the intentions of an anonymous poet is unrelated to the same priority in the printed editions of the poem that they cite in their arguments.

---

[22] Christine Chism, *Alliterative Revivals* (Philadelphia: University of Pennsylvania Press, 2002), p. 167.

[23] Roger Nicholson, 'Haunted Itineraries: Reading *The Siege of Jerusalem*', *Exemplaria*, 14 (2002), 447–84 (p. 457).

[24] Elisa Narin van Court, '*The Siege of Jerusalem* and Augustinian Historians: Writing about Jews in Fourteenth-Century England', *Chaucer Review*, 29 (1995), 227–48 (p. 233).

[25] Alex Mueller, 'Corporal Terror: Critiques of Imperialism in *The Siege of Jerusalem*', *Philological Quarterly*, 84 (2005), 287–310 (p. 288).

[26] '*The Siege of Jerusalem* in its Physical, Literary and Historical Contexts' (Dublin: Four Courts, 2000). Millar devotes the first chapter of her book to 'The Manuscript Contexts of *The Siege of Jerusalem*'.

This criticism has in effect invented a figure — the 'makere of the mind' from my title — and energetically imagined his proclivities while ignoring much of the material evidence we have of his poetry. The title of this article is meant to recall D. F. McKenzie's famous study 'Printers of the Mind: Some Notes on Bibliographical Theories and Printing-House Practices', in which the author demonstrates how bibliographers working with only one type of evidence (physical evidence from books themselves) arrived at a set of assumptions about printers that were limited in their helpfulness and accuracy.[27] I suggest a parallel between McKenzie's presentation of evidence of an 'incredible', but mostly un-examined, variety of practices in seventeenth- and eighteenth-century printing houses[28] and the rich but underutilized physical evidence of textual production and transmission found in the manuscript witnesses and source texts of *The Siege of Jerusalem*. McKenzie argues that a lack of knowledge about conditions in printing houses 'left us disastrously free to devise them according to need',[29] and demonstrates the survival of a wide variety of evidence, including press accounts, vouchers, and ledgers, that challenges previous assumptions regarding the daily operations of printing houses. Similarly, many critics of *The Siege* have worked with only one type of evidence (the printed critical edition) and have devised assertions about the poet that rest on assumptions while ignoring the surviving primary evidence. While the evidence provided by manuscript copies of the poem cannot definitively resolve debates about the author of *The Siege of Jerusalem*, it does promise to lead to new debates and discussions founded on historical docu-ments and texts rather than assumptions about an unknown poet.

In the case of the extant body of criticism of *The Siege*, the almost exclusive focus on the poet's intentions amounts to a failure to consider the poem in a fully contextualized and historicized way; this is particularly the case with the lack of critical interest in manuscript contexts and textual variants, but has also been reflected in some studies through a lack of careful consideration of the rela-tionship of the alliterative *Siege* to its source texts, as well as to the much larger Vengeance of Our Lord tradition to which the poem and its sources belong.[30] In

---

[27] D. F. McKenzie, 'Printers of the Mind: Some Notes on Bibliographical Theories and Printing-House Practices', *Studies in Bibliography*, 22 (1969), 1–75.

[28] McKenzie, 'Printers of the Mind', p. 5.

[29] McKenzie, 'Printers of the Mind', p. 2.

[30] For summaries of the extent and popularity of the Vengeance of Our Lord tradition, see Bonnie Millar, *'The Siege of Jerusalem'*; Chapter 5 of Michael Hebron's *The Medieval Siege*

the case of critical editions, however, such a focus seems not a failure of any kind, but rather a well-reasoned choice and a consequence of physical limitations of format and medium. If, indeed, your medium only permits one primary goal, and usually a single way of presenting the text, reconstruction of authorial intention is an attractive one, and the one that is most likely to be desired by the majority of the edition's potential purchasers and users. And, of course, the impact of editing on criticism has been reciprocated; demand for eclectic texts over diplomatic texts and documentary archives has shaped the kinds of editions that publishers are willing to produce and promote. The medium of the printed book itself, meanwhile, has limited access to primary materials; it is not that they are missing entirely from printed critical editions, but that they 'come before the reader in abbreviated and coded forms', thus making them difficult to use and positioning them as far less important than the author's intentions. Usually, this has not been a shortcoming of editors. Indeed the very editors who create the 'abbreviated and coded forms' that serve to suppress the physical contexts of manuscripts to footnotes and appendices and to collapse their competing voices often have the greatest appreciation for the riches contained in primary materials. This certainly seems to be the case with *The Siege of Jerusalem*, where tendencies to ignore the poem's manuscript contexts and source texts have been countered by a recent and productive trend toward considering their importance. Following the footnotes of these discussions back to the source, one discovers that this awareness often stems in part, if not directly, from Hanna's thoughtful articles, as well as from the admirable job that he and Lawton do of contextualizing the poem in the introduction to their edition. In many ways, the Hanna-Lawton edition stands as a testament to just how sophisticated and complex critical editions can be in the print format, and their work in establishing the intended text of the poet is an important achievement of editorial and literary detective work that will remain invaluable to scholars and future editors for many years to come.

It is thus a testament to the power of digital media to transform how we edit and transmit the poem that there remains much work to be done on this corpus of manuscripts, for we now have the possibility of making authorial intention a central goal of an archive or edition without reducing documentary materials and

(Oxford: Oxford University Press, 1997); the introduction to *Siege of Jerusalem*, ed. by Livingston; and the introduction to Stephen K. Wright, *The Vengeance of Our Lord: Medieval Dramatizations of the Destruction of Jerusalem*, Studies and Texts, 89 (Toronto: Pontifical Institute of Mediaeval Studies, 1989).

scribal intention to abbreviated forms. In a digital medium, the meaning of 'encoded' forms has shifted, for the term now signifies more information, in the form of metadata, rather than less information in the form of abbreviation. Texts may be presented in multiple states, just as they circulated, and primary materials can be presented in a full and interactive manner. Thus the options available to us in creating printed editions remain, but we face far fewer limitations.

Finally, the use of digital media in editing Middle English texts reveals the long-standing and strongly contested debate between advocates of eclectic and best-text editions to be largely a result of the limitations of the print medium. This debate, which has at times been heated, collapses in the face of media that allow us to combine in one archive facsimile images, diplomatic editions, best-text editions of every manuscript in a corpus, and multiple eclectic critical texts, together with an interface that permits users of the edition to move from diplomatic to scribal to critical states of a text. A debate that once seemed counterproductive, since in fact best-text, diplomatic, and eclectic editions all had their places and merits in the print era, now seems futile since all of these may be combined in a mutually edifying manner in the context of one archive. In 1975, Fredson Bowers remarked that '[l]iterary critics, historians, general scholars, students of all kinds — these need as authoritative a reconstruction of a full text as the documents allow, not editions of the separate documents, except when the distance is so great as to make eclectic reconstruction impossible'.[31] Although Bowers acknowledges that facsimile editions are useful in some instances, one might have objected at the time that his argument does not recognize that, for example, historians interested in manuscript contexts or habits of scribal self-correction would probably be much better off with editions of separate documents, as would students studying medieval textual transmission or those brushing up their palaeography skills. Today, the SJEA could be of benefit to a great variety of 'critics, historians, general scholars, and students', whether their interest is manuscript transmission, Robert Thornton's habits, palaeography, or the disparity between the prestigious presentation of the poem in the Cambridge University Library copy and the unattractive and scrunched rendering of it in Vespasian E. xvi. At the same time, this does not preclude the simultaneous presence of eclectic texts in the archive, and indeed an eclectic text and its users will benefit greatly from the presence of the documentary materials.

---

[31] 'Remarks on Eclectic Texts', in *Essays in Bibliography, Text, and Editing* (Charlottesville: Bibliographical Society of the University of Virginia), p. 528.

Using the SJEA: A Case Study

Having articulated overarching benefits that digital media bring to the editing of Middle English texts generally and *The Siege of Jerusalem* in particular, I will turn now to an analysis of specific payoffs that the SJEA will offer in the study and criticism of one passage of the poem. The infamous scene in which a starving Jewish mother, Mary, kills and eats her own son serves as a good example for a number of reasons: it is one of the passages most frequently discussed by critics, it has a complex and much-studied relationship to its source texts, and it features interesting variants at both the archetype and manuscript level. The story of Mary, or Maria, was well known during the medieval era; Merrall Llewelyn Price has traced intermittent appearances in the late classical and early medieval periods followed by 'a continuous upsurge in the popularity of the motif' from the eleventh through the sixteenth centuries in works as diverse as chronicle histories, Dante's *Purgatorio*, *La Vengeance de Nostre-Seigneur*, the verse romance *Titus and Vespasian*, and religious dramas performed across the Continent.[32] In the alliterative *Siege of Jerusalem*, the episode precedes — and helps to precipitate — the Roman assault on and breach of Jerusalem's walls after a protracted standoff. It is one of several passages that vividly describe the suffering of the Jewish inhabitants immured within the city as famine sets in:

> On Marie, a myld wyf,　for meschef of foode,
> Hire owen barn þat 3o bare　brad on þe gledis,
> Rostyþ rigge and rib　with rewful wordes,
> Sayþ, 'sone, vpon eche side　our sorow is alofte:
> Batail aboute þe borwe　our bodies to quelle;
> Withyn hunger so hote　þat ne3 our herte brestyþ.
> Þerfor 3eld þat I þe 3af　and a3en tourne,
> Entre þer þou out cam',　and etyþ a schouldere.
> Þe rich roos of þe rost　ri3t into þe strete
> Þat fele fastyng folke　felden þe sauere.
> Doun þei daschen þe dore,　dey scholde þe berde
> Þat mete yn þis meschef　hadde from men layned.
> Þan saiþ þat worþi wif　in a wode hunger,
> 'Myn owen barn haue I brad　and þe bones gnawen,
> 3it haue I saued 3ou som',　and a side feccheþ

[32] Merrall Llewelyn Price, 'Imperial Violence and the Monstrous Mother: Cannibalism at the Siege of Jerusalem', in *Domestic Violence in Medieval Texts*, ed. by Eve Salisbury, Georgiana Donavin, and Merrall Llewelyn Price (Gainesville: University Press of Florida, 2002), p. 272.

Of þe barn þat 30 bare,   and alle hire blode chaungeþ.
Forþ þey went for wo   wepande sore
And sayn, 'alas in þis lif   how longe schul we dwelle?
3it beter were at o brayde   in batail to deye
Þan þus in langur to lyue   and lengþen our fyne'.[33]

Some critics have found evidence of sympathy here, others of antipathy. In the process they have often devoted a significant amount of attention to the poet's reworking of his source texts.[34] Chism cites the passage as an example of how 'the poem targets Jewish mothers in bizarrely flamboyant ways', and notes that the siege 'targets the generative capacities of the Jews because those capacities reflect the most intimate and intractable sites of Jewish vitality'. She sees this as part of an agenda that is reflective of a 'gathering darkness of specifically late medieval anti-Judaisms'.[35] Nicholson strikes much the same tone, noting that '[w]ithin the frame of the episode there seems to be real sympathy, but to stay with that would be to miss the point — that the Jew is confined to the carnal and therefore trapped within the pattern of abhorrence that the poem traces'.[36] Narin van Court reads the passage very differently, noting that '[t]he *Jerusalem* poet reworks the rhetoric of his sources and renders the act a result of desperation in a sympathetic account that invites not disgust but sorrow from the reader'.[37] Mueller agrees, arguing that 'the *Siege*-poet does not use Maria's cannibalism to condemn the Jews', but rather 'alters his sources and provides sympathetic commentary through eyewitness testimony'.[38] It is notable that underlying all of these accounts is an interest in the poet's intentions and an attempt to employ his source texts in order to discern those intentions.

---

[33] This citation from Hanna and Lawton's edition of *The Siege of Jerusalem*, lines 1081–1100. It should be noted that, depending upon date of publication, some critics cited below used the Kölbing-Day edition, wherein the corresponding lines are numbered 1077–96. The passage in the two editions is substantially the same, although Hanna and Lawton make a number of emendations both to improve metre (e.g., replacing *smel* with the alliterating *rich* at l. 1089) and sense (e.g., choosing *layned* over *loyned* at l. 1092).

[34] The most thorough consideration is provided by Bonnie Millar, who devotes an entire chapter to the motif in '*The Siege of Jerusalem*' (chap. 3, pp. 76–104).

[35] Chism, *Alliterative Revivals*, p. 166.

[36] Nicholson, 'Haunted Itineraries', p. 481.

[37] Elisa Narin van Court, '*The Siege of Jerusalem* and Recuperative Readings', in *Pulp Fictions of Medieval England: Essays in Popular Romance*, ed. by Nicola McDonald (Manchester: Manchester University Press, 2004), pp. 151–70 (p. 158).

[38] Mueller, 'Corporal Terror', p. 301.

Before turning to how the SJEA might contribute to these conversations, it is necessary both to offer a brief summary of the source texts in question and to consider a recently discovered source that will impact future considerations of how the *Siege*-poet composed this section of his poem. Josephus's *Jewish War* is the ultimate source of much of the narrative in the poem, including the account of Mary's cannibalism, but in order to understand his role in the creation of *The Siege of Jerusalem*, we must also consider the complex roles of Hegesippus and Higden in transmitting Josephan texts. Josephus was widely known throughout medieval Europe, especially in the Latin translation created at the behest of Cassiodorus in the fifth or sixth century. Hegesippus's translation was also in circulation; completed around AD 370, it abbreviates Josephus, combining his text with materials from other early authors, including Sallust and Tacitus. The fourteenth-century English chronicler Ranulph Higden used both Hegesippus and a Latin translation of Josephus in his *Polychronicon*, making the transmission of this material in late medieval England quite complex. Before all of this came Josephus's Greek text, the one from which the Latin translators worked. The prologue to the *Jewish War*, in turn, informs us that the Greek text is Josephus's own translation from his composition in Aramaic.[39] In addition to this already intricate textual history, Andrew Galloway has recently demonstrated that the *Siege*-poet relied on the *Historia aurea* of John of Tynemouth, a compilation that included both Higden and Hegesippus. Tynemouth's text replaces what Hanna and Lawton believed to be 'not only the poet's use of Ranulph Higden's widely known historical compilation, which quotes from Jacob of Voragine, Josephus, and "Hegesippus," but also further contact with a direct Latin translation of Josephus himself, deftly woven in'.[40] In some ways, Galloway's discovery makes for a simpler and more direct explanation of passages such as the Marian episode quoted above, as he demonstrates that it is possible for the poet to have accomplished with one source what it would have taken at least three sources to explain. It also serves to streamline arguments regarding the poet's reworking of those sources, as it is clear that the *Historia aurea* has been closely followed in this part of the poem. At the same time, this new information further complicates our account of the textual transmission of this episode in that it adds yet another intermediary between Josephus and *The Siege of Jerusalem*.

---

[39] For this summary of Josephus's textual transmission, I am indebted to Millar, 'The Siege of Jerusalem', pp. 60–63, and Hanna-Lawton's edition of *The Siege of Jerusalem*, pp. xxxvii–lv.

[40] Galloway, 'Alliterative Poetry in Old Jerusalem', p. 90.

One obvious way in which the SJEA can contribute to scholarly discussions of this passage is by providing access to the newly discovered materials by including images of those folios of Lambeth Palace, MS 10 that contain the relevant portions of Tynemouth's *Historia aurea* linked to a transcription and translation of the text. But I would like to suggest a more fundamental contribution that the archive can make over time by altering how source texts of the poem are handled and depicted, and consequently what uses scholars are able to make of these materials. A striking feature of most criticism of the passage cited above, as well as much other criticism of this poem, is how closely conceptions of why source texts matter and how they should be used mirror the rationales, methods, and format of printed critical editions. These usually at best contain brief excerpts of a few relevant passages of source materials in appendices. Not only is revealing the intentions of the poet the foremost goal of most critics, but, as in critical editions, the sources are consulted and valued only insofar as they can provide evidence and justification for assertions about these intentions. Just as this is a useful strategy for editors producing eclectic texts, it has also been a useful and productive strategy for critics, who have used it to contextualize and enrich our collective understanding of the poem; Chism and Narin van Court in particular have been instrumental in encouraging other scholars to see the possibilities of nuanced, historicized readings of the poem that attend to how the poet might have used his sources.

But consulting source texts in order to discern authorial intention can be *one* use among many that we make of them, and making sources available alongside documentary and critical materials has the potential to catalyse new paths of enquiry regarding the complex relationships of texts within the Vengeance of Our Lord tradition to one another. A useful model for understanding how sources have traditionally been represented in critical editions is the palimpsest. In the case of *The Siege of Jerusalem*, the surface of this palimpsest is an editorial reconstruction of the *Siege*-poet's intentions that modifies and partially obscures *The Siege* manuscript witnesses, the texts just below the surface. In the Marian passage, the next layer would be Tynemouth, discernable, but further fragmented and obscured by the activities of poet, scribe, and editor. Beneath this, texts recede further back into time — Higden, Jacobus de Voragine, Hegesippus, Josephus — and, as is always the case with a palimpsest, become increasingly difficult to discern. Early iterations of the SJEA will, admittedly, reflect the rationale of critical editions in that the direct evidence of one poem will be foregrounded, while source texts will be there by virtue of the fact that they are related to this poem. But just as we use digital media to maintain and represent the polyvocality of manuscript witnesses, so too can each layer of the polyvocal 'palimpsest' of source texts be shown with equal clarity, and we intend to expand the archive over time to facilitate research of a number of these interrelated texts.

Reading the Marian scene in John of Tynemouth is instructive because it simultaneously offers evidence of how the *Siege*-poet reworked his sources and how Tynemouth reworked Higden, the *Legenda aurea*, and other sources. While the *Siege*-poet borrowed rather directly from this passage, as Galloway has shown, he also borrowed selectively (perhaps a necessity given the length of Tynemouth's account), and the passage varies significantly in tone between the two works. Whereas in the alliterative *Siege* Mary is introduced simply as 'On Marie, a myld wyf', without further description to contextualize who she is, in Tynemouth Mary is depicted as famous, and her deed notorious: 'Tunc contigit illud factum tam horrendum quam famosum Marie alienigene' (Then occurred that deed, as horrific as notorious, of the famous Maria, not a native of the city).[41] In addition to being notorious, the Mary found in John of Tynemouth's chronicle is an outsider (*alienigene*), and is much more actively opposed to the men who break in her door. In the chronicle, she consumes her child not only due to hunger, but also as an act of revenge against these predators: 'veni igitur, esto matri cibus — predonibus furor, et sceleris fabula — Redde vel semel matri quod ab ea sumpsisti' (come, therefore, be food for your mother — a source of wrath for the predators, and a fable of crime: return once more to the mother what you have taken). While the *Siege*-poet has elected to elide Mary's notoriety and her active resistance of the 'predators' through her act of cannibalism, John of Tynemouth has borrowed his text verbatim from his sources; the first passage quoted above is taken unaltered from Higden, while the second is identical to the *Legenda aurea*. The inclusion of such sources in the SJEA offers the opportunity not only to understand how the story of Mary's cannibalism was altered by the *Siege*-poet, but also how the narrative had its own life and transmission history across many centuries, and how reception and intervention occurred at many moments in its textual life, with the *Siege*-poet's reworking of it being just one such moment.

While there has been some focus on the *Siege*-poet's use of his sources, only scant attention has been paid to manuscript contexts of the poem, including script, *ordinatio*, how the texts alongside which the poem was placed affected reception, and the textual variants found both within individual manuscripts and in the subarchetypes. As discussed above, this is likely due in large part to the format of printed critical editions. Such editions lack the ability to convey an

---

[41] Quotations and translations of John of Tynemouth are from Galloway, 'Alliterative Poetry in Old Jerusalem', pp. 90–91.

adequate sense of the appearance of manuscripts, prioritize authorial intention above other goals, and offer only partial and encoded accounts of manuscript readings. But there are questions that we may (and should) pose of a poem like *The Siege of Jerusalem* that do not rely on a recovery of its author's intended text: How was the text received and perceived by its audiences? How was reception shaped by the material presentation of the manuscript, including such features as script and layout? How did textual variants and the texts surrounding the poem reflect how the poem was understood by scribes and shape how it was interpreted by readers? Because the SJEA features complete cross-searchable transcriptions of all manuscript witnesses accompanied by colour images, it encourages and facilitates researchers wishing to pursue such questions. For example, an analysis of variants found in the Marian scene reveals the considerable impact that scribal texts might have on the interpretation of the passage, as the following excerpt from A makes clear:

> O saynt Marie a Milde wyfe for meschefe of fude
> hir awen barne that scho bare Made brede one the gledis
> Scho ruschede owte ribbe and rygere with rewefull wordis
> Sayse Enter thare þou owte come and Etis the rybbis
> and sone appone Ilke a syde oure sorowe es newe
> alle withowttyn þe burghe oure bodyes to quelle
> and withIn es hungre so hate that nere oure hertis brystis
> and therefore ȝelde þat þou ȝafe and aȝayne torne
> Enter þare þou owte come and Etis the childe
> the smelle rase of the roste righte in the strete
> that fele Fastande folke felide the sauoure
> and downe thay daschen the dore and hastely thay askede
> why that þat mete in þat Meschefe was fro men laynede
> than sayde that worthiliche wyfe in ane wode hungre
> Myn awen barne es my brede and I the bones gnawe
> ȝitte hafe I sauede ȝow some and a syde fechide
> Of the barne þat scho bare bot than thaire ble chaungede
> and furthe wente þay with woo wepande full sore
> and sayde allas in this lyfe how lange schall we lenge
> ȝitt were it better at a brayde in batelle to dye
> than thus in langoure to ly and lenghthyn oure pyn.[42]

---

[42] BL, MS Add. 31042, fol. 63ʳ. This transcription reflects Thornton's capitalization practices; further details of the script such as expansions and barred letter forms (*h* and *l*) are indicated in

Several variants found here are unique to this manuscript and have a significant impact on how a reader might interpret this passage. First, the passage begins 'O saynt Marie', which is apparently an invocation to the Virgin (this does not seem to be the cardinal *o*, as Thornton elsewhere uses *one* throughout).[43] As such the mother remains nameless, and thus a reader might be less inclined to infer that in this passage 'Mary the nurturer becomes Mary the devourer', thereby reversing 'Christian transubstantiation into cannibalism with vicious precision'.[44] Second, the line beginning 'Enter thare þou owte come' (l. 1088) is doubled in this manuscript alone, and the reading 'and Etis the childe' is also found only in this manuscript; in all other witnesses, the mother eats a shoulder of the child. In the line reading 'and downe thay daschen the dore and hastely thay askede', the b-verse is likewise unique, as other witnesses have some version of 'dey scholde þe berde' (l. 1091). Again, it is easy to imagine how these changes might guide a reader towards an interpretation that differs significantly in tone from the edited passage above. Emphasizing that the mother is eating her 'childe' rather than 'a schouldere' reminds us of both her motherhood and the humanity of the child who is being consumed. Meanwhile the men who break down the door are cast more favourably here, for they simply ask 'hastely' why meat had been hidden from them before fleeing — 'with woo wepande full sore' — when they comprehend the scene before them. In the other manuscripts, conversely, these men threaten Mary with death, as they do in Tynemouth (via Higden): 'Sed nidor incense carnis sediciosos allexit, qui in domum irruentes, nisi carnem prodat, mortem minantur' (But the odor of the burned flesh drew the rebels, who, rushing into the house, threatened her with death, unless she produce the meat).[45]

Variants in other manuscripts suggest additional readings. The scribe of E, for example, produces a text full of interesting, and often perplexing, alternate readings. Thus in this passage 'marion' is a 'mydwyf'[46] rather than a 'milde' (i.e.,

---

the transcription found in the SJEA. Thornton does not indicate a caesura in his copy of the poem.

[43] I wish to thank Michael Johnston for first calling my attention to this invocation, which he noticed in the course of his research on 'Robert Thornton and *The Siege of Jerusalem*'.

[44] Chism, *Alliterative Revivals*, p. 161.

[45] Galloway, 'Alliterative Poetry in Old Jerusalem', pp. 90–91.

[46] Hm 128, fol. 214[r]. This strange variant is also found in MS E at the line corresponding to *The Siege of Jerusalem*, l. 901, where it is part of a catalogue of atrocities committed by Nero. The manuscript informs us that he murdered 'his modire & his mydwyf'. In the Marian passage, E alone has this reading, however, whereas at l. 901 the reading is found in LUE.

gentle or well-born) wife and — in contrast to the overtones of A — the dehumanization suffered by her son when he becomes foodstuff is emphasized, rather than mitigated, when the remains that she producers for the intruders are described as 'a gobat red yroosted'. Manuscript variants also frequently occur in agreement in such a way that a subarchetype offers a different tone or emphasis. For example, in the final line of the passage we have been analysing, *alpha* alone (i.e., L) reads 'þan þus in langur to lyue [:] & lengþen our fyne', with all *beta* manuscripts reading 'pyne' or 'peyne' in place of 'fyne', a reading that Hanna and Lawton note 'is certainly the *durior*, in fact almost too good a, reading'.[47] Just before this passage, meanwhile, only D and E, two manuscripts from the *delta* subarchetype, preserve what is likely the reading of the *Siege*-poet's source when they record that the citizens in Jerusalem had no food for forty days; Mary's decision to eat her own son after only four days of hunger, as the other manuscripts read, might of course give a very different impression to readers.[48]

The corpus of manuscripts promises other productive avenues of study as well. As Michael Johnston has demonstrated with his careful study of Robert Thornton's collocation of texts in MS Add. 31042, scribal compilers could significantly influence textual reception through the variants they recorded or suppressed (either intentionally or unknowingly), the order in which they placed texts in miscellanies, and the incipits with which they introduced those texts. Johnston considers all of these features, and his argument that Thornton positions *The Siege of Jerusalem* in a manner that intentionally 'sells the poem as a piece of unqualified anti-Jewish propaganda'[49] provides a good example of how scholars might use the surviving manuscript evidence to understand medieval reception history, including how scribes were active agents in shaping and altering texts. Although the SJEA will initially include only images of those portions of manuscript witnesses containing *The Siege of Jerusalem*, digitization of these manuscripts in their entirety is a future goal of the editors. Furthermore, it is our hope that texts and images from the SJEA will be used in conjunction with other digital editions either already published or under development, such as the *Piers*

---

[47] *The Siege of Jerusalem*, note to l. 1100, p. 146.

[48] Hanna and Lawton note that most manuscripts of the French source, the *Bible en françois*, read 'par xl. iorz', and that the emendation to 'fourty' is 'simply commonsensical' (p. 145). While this reading is not unanimously attested by *delta* manuscripts, many variant readings throughout the poem are; see *The Siege of Jerusalem*, Appendix C, p. 170, for examples.

[49] Johnston, 'Robert Thornton and *The Siege of Jerusalem*', p. 128.

Plowman Electronic Archive edition of Hm 128,[50] a manuscript in which the text of *Piers Plowman* ends on the same folio where *The Siege of Jerusalem* begins, or John Carlson's forthcoming electronic edition of the Alliterative *Morte Arthure*, which is found in Lincoln, Cathedral Library, MS 91, the only other known manuscript copied by Robert Thornton.[51] Because all of these editions contain full transcriptions encoded in TEI-compliant XML,[52] with textual features such as expansions, abbreviations, erasures, and corrections encoded and searchable, they are together beginning to form a sizable body of texts that can be mined in order to study such topics as alliterative metre, patterns of scribal correction, and distributions of dialect, both within and across manuscripts.

Conclusion

In the essay 'Producing Manuscripts and Editions', Hanna diagnoses problems in contemporary practices of editing Middle English texts and discusses potential alternative forms that editions may take. Among the topics he covers is the inherent tension between the expectation that modern readers have that an editor will render a singular, canonical text and the plurality of the manuscript materials with which editors grapple, a tension that is clearly evident in editing *The Siege of Jerusalem*. First published in 1992, on the eve of the explosive growth of the World Wide Web during the mid-1990s, Hanna's essay does not mention digital media or their potential fundamentally to alter editorial theory and practice. It clearly outlines limitations in editorial practices that may be redressed through such media, however, and envisions alternatives that they may help us to realize:

> '[T]he editorial issue' should become, what varieties of mediation can modern textual consumption allow so as to address its public constituency, with its desire to canonize medieval works in forms consonant with those customary for presenting 'modern scripture' while still remaining in palpable contact with the extraordinary evidential plurality of manuscript culture? Most modern readers require the singularity of A Text

---

[50] *The Piers Plowman Electronic Archive*, XI: *San Marino, Huntington Library Hm 128 (Hm and Hm2)*.

[51] This edition is also slated to be published through SEENET, although no release date is available at this time.

[52] 'TEI' refers to the Text Encoding Initiative, 'a consortium which collectively develops and maintains a standard for the representation of texts in digital form'. Guidelines and further information about the consortium, its activities, and its aims are available at <http://www.tei-c.org> [accessed October 2010].

and, indeed, [...] canonicity in some sense demands one. But the manuscript situation in an equally absolute way requires some greater access to 'the evidence' than standard formats based on collation forms derived from print books allows: the text is only a series of human products, every bit as mediated in their own differing ways as the standard modern edition, each historically situated and incapable of being understood outside that situation.[53]

While digital media cannot provide 'palpable contact' with manuscripts, at least not in a literal sense, they can relieve us of the dilemma of choosing between 'A Text' and 'contact with the extraordinary evidential plurality of manuscript culture', for they facilitate experiencing both in an interconnected and mutually supporting way, as we plan to demonstrate with the SJEA. As such, they promise makers and users of scholarly editions an advantageous supersession of print, and one that will bring us far closer to the material conditions and transmission of medieval texts than print ever has.[54]

[53] Ralph Hanna III, 'Producing Manuscripts and Editions', in Hanna, *Pursuing History*, pp. 63–82 (pp. 74–75) (first publ. in *Crux and Controversy in Middle English Textual Criticism*, ed. by Charlotte Brewer and Alastair Minnis (Cambridge: Brewer, 1992), pp. 109–30).

[54] I am grateful to the Bibliographical Society of America and to the National Endowment for the Humanities for fellowships. Hoyt N. Duggan has been a nonpareil mentor and friend, while John Ivor Carlson has been an able and helpful colleague and co-editor. Andrew Galloway generously shared early drafts of his work on John of Tynemouth with me. Thanks too to Michael Johnston and the readers for *YLS* for thorough and helpful comments.

THE A-VERSION ANCESTOR OF BMBOCOT

Carl James Grindley

London, British Library, MS Additional 10574 (Bm), Oxford, Bodleian Library, MS 814 (Bo), and London, British Library, MS Cotton Caligula A. xi (Cot) present passus Prol.1–2.131 in the C version, 2.86–3.30 of the A version, and the balance of the text in the B version.[1] A study of the BmBoCot's composition is worthwhile because it both highlights a number of well-known problems in the Athlone critical editions and adds to our knowledge of late medieval scribal practice. The A materials, in particular, call for scrutiny. For one, although George Kane says that his critical apparatus 'shows all the evidence available for determining originality', his ignorance of BmBoCot's A-version texts in 1960 means that they are, in essence, as yet unpublished (an oversight he recognized in 'The A Text in 1988').[2] Second, the only substantial treatment of these manuscripts'

---

[1] All references to the text are cited according to *Piers Plowman: The A Version*, ed. by George Kane, rev. edn (London: Athlone; Berkeley and Los Angeles: University of California Press, 1988); *Piers Plowman: The B Version*, ed. by George Kane and E. Talbot Donaldson, rev. edn (London: Athlone; Berkeley and Los Angeles: University of California Press, 1988); and *Piers Plowman: The C Version*, ed. by George Russell and George Kane (London: Athlone; Berkeley and Los Angeles: University of California Press, 1997). Russell and Kane inadvertently confuse MSS Add. 10574 and Cotton Caligula A. xi, reversing not only their physical descriptions but also their sigla in the collation and apparatus criticus; see my review in *Envoi*, 10 (2004), 185–93.

[2] *The A Version*, ed. by Kane, p. 172.

Carl James Grindley (*carl.grindley@snet.net*) is Associate Professor of English at Eugenio María de Hostos Community College and Consortial Associate Professor of Communications and Culture at the School of Professional Studies, both of The City University of New York.

Abstract: Prompted by Bryan P. Davis's article in *YLS*, 11, this essay considers the A-version text in London, British Library, MS Additional 10574 (Bm), Oxford, Bodleian Library, MS 814 (Bo), and London, British Library, MS Cotton Caligula A. xi (Cot). The textual relationships of these three MSS and their close relatives, Cambridge, Trinity College, MS R. 3. 14 (T) and London, British Library, MS Harley 6041 (H²), are examined and BmBoCot's common A-version ancestor is reconstructed. Davis's theory on the extent of the A-version text in BmBoCot is confirmed, and as collations from these MSS were absent from Kane, an edition comprising 2.86–3.30 of the A-version text is included.

Keywords: English literature, 1100–1499, Middle English period, William Langland, *Piers Plowman*, London, British Library, MS Cotton Caligula A. xi, manuscript study, textual variants, role of scribe.

10.1484/J.YLS.1.102109

composition, by Bryan Davis, can be further bolstered and refined, especially with regard to his claim that the A materials extend to 3.30 rather than ending at the conclusion of passus 2 as Kane and Donaldson have it.[3] Third, a rigorous analysis of BmBoCot's A matter will help to resolve the conflicts between Kane and Donaldson's B edition and Russell and Kane's C edition regarding the production of these manuscripts. Finally, the benefits to be gained from a clearer under-standing of BmBoCot's textual relationships far surpass the editorial value of the texts themselves. This material has much to tell us about how Langland's early editors, scribes, and readers understood his poem. It is time, therefore, to revisit these manuscripts, determine the status of 3.1–30, and attempt to reconstruct BmBoCot's common ancestor.

The Extent of the A Text in BmBoCot

To begin, it is important to clarify the nature of BmBoCot's A-version text and obtain an understanding of how it fits into the A-version tradition. In his study of Bm, Davis explains that the process of redaction present in the BmBoCot shared ancestor was based on its B-version exemplar wanting some nine, forty-line leaves containing the Prologue, passūs 1 and 2, and the first few lines of passus 3. He had access to both other traditions, but 'A-text materials would not have filled the gap and would have lacked some widely recognized episodes; C-text materials would have been too lengthy and would have contained some unnecessary episodes'.[4] Kane and Donaldson's proposal that BmBoCot begins its B portion at 3.1 is hard to accept, Davis points out, because it forces us to posit that the preparer of Bm exemplar lost eight full leaves plus fifty-one lines of material from his copy while retaining twenty-nine lines from passus 3. It is much easier to grant that 'he used A- and C-text materials to construct nine full leaves of material including the first 29 lines of passus 3 (see Figure 1). The absence of Kane and Donaldson 3.18 from exemplar Bm, a line that is absent from all A manuscripts, supports this suggestion'.[5]

---

[3] Bryan P. Davis, 'The Rationale for a Copy of a Text: Constructing the Exemplar for British Library Additional MS. 10574', *YLS*, 11 (1997), 141–55.

[4] Davis, 'The Rationale for a Copy of a Text', p. 147.

[5] Davis, 'The Rationale for a Copy of a Text', p. 149.

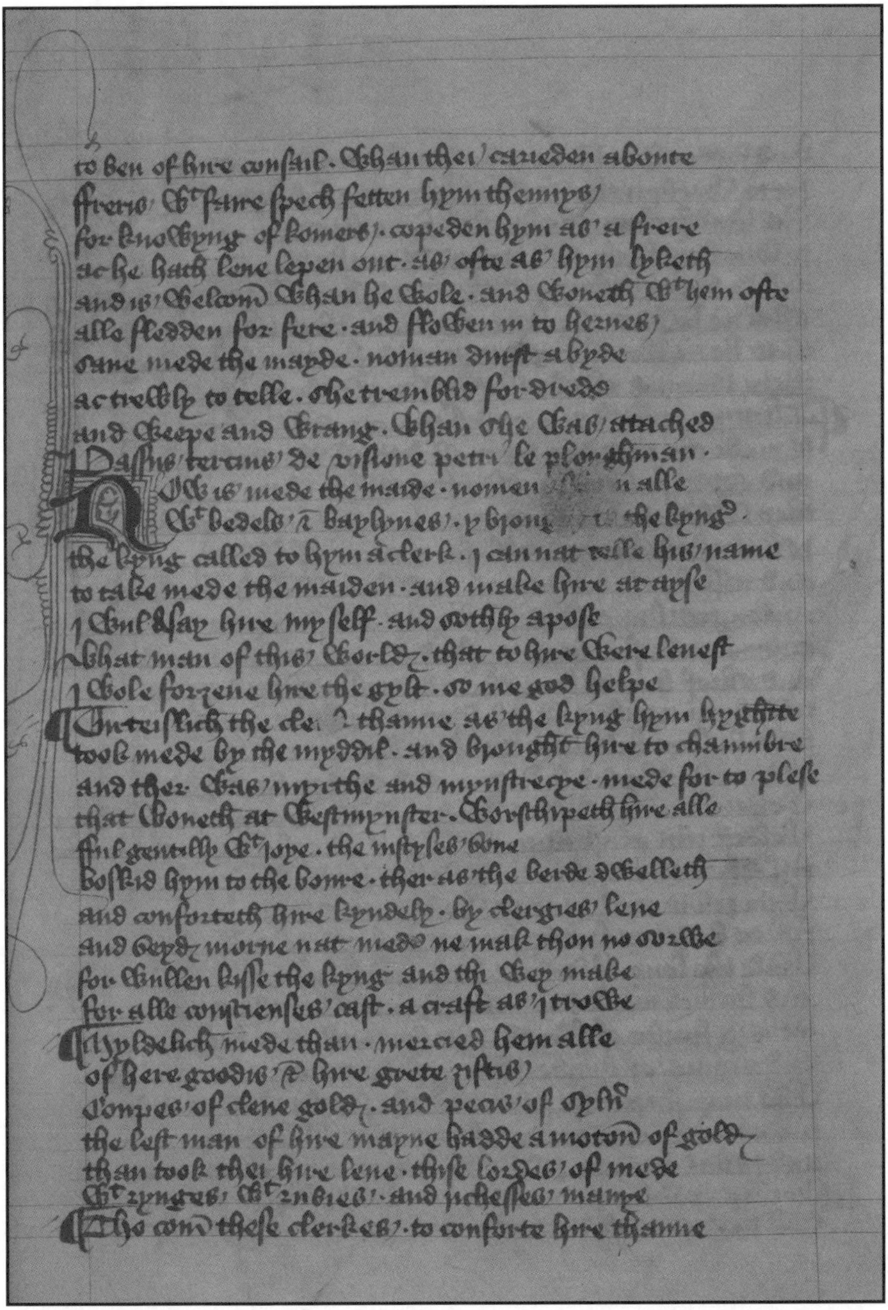

to ben of hire counseil. Whan thei carieden aboute
freris with faire speche fetten hym thennys
for knowyng of comers, copeden hym as a frere
ac he hath leve lepen out as ofte as hym lyketh
and is welcome whan he wole and woneth with hem ofte
alle fledden for fere and flowen in to hernes
save mede the mayde no man durst abyde
ac treuly to telle she trembled for drede
and weepe and wrang whan she was attached
Passus tercius de visione petri le plowghman.
Now is mede the mayde [illegible] n alle
With bedels & bayllyves y brought [illegible] the kyng.
the kyng called to hym a clerk I can nat telle his name
to take mede the maiden and make hire at ayse
I wil assay hire myself and sothly apose
What man of this world that to hire were levest
I wole forzeve hire the gylt so me god helpe
Curteisliche the cle[illegible] thanne as the kyng hym hyghte
took mede by the myddel and brought hire to chambre
and ther was myrthe and mynstrecye mede for to plese
that woneth at Westmynster worshipeth hire alle
ful gentilly with joye the justises some
bosked hym to the bowre ther as the berde dwelleth
and conforteth hire kyndely by clergies leve
and seyde morne nat mede ne mak thou no sorwe
for we wollen wisse the kyng and thi wey make
for alle consciences cast a craft as I trowe
Myldelich mede than merciede hem alle
of here goodnis & hire grete ziftis
Coupes of clene gold and pecis of sylver
the lest man of hire mayne hadde a moton of gold
than took thei hire leve these lordes of mede
With ryngis with rubies and richesses manye
Tho come these clerkes to conforte hire thanne

Fig. 1. 'Incipit Passus 3', London, British Library, MS Cotton Caligula A. xi, fol. 180r.
Early fifteenth century. Reproduced with the permission of The British Library.

Although 3.18 is also absent from Bo and Cot, similarities between passus 3 in the A and B versions and the noise created by convergent error make Davis's straightforward claim surprisingly difficult to prove. A collation of BmBoCot against the extant manuscripts of the A and B versions reveals ten readings unique to BmBoCot and absent from both A and B, five readings that would be unique variants in A but have B-version support, and six that would be unique in B but have A-version support.[6] Since these figures are so close, the attempt to determine the source of these thirty lines must factor in the status of the cross-versional support for each scenario: of the five A variants, three are from MS F alone, whereas one B variant, the omission of line B.18, is shared by all A manuscripts, and the other five appear in at least four copies each, with the TH²Ch group featuring in two and possibly three of these. Given that, as Kane and Donaldson point out, the eighty variants shared by BmBoCotF in their B texts must be attributable to convergent variation, since they conflict with the 250 errors shared by CBmBoCot,[7] there is no substantive B support for BmBoCot's variants from A, but extensive A (especially TH²Ch) support for variants from B. I therefore believe that Davis's conclusion that BmBoCot's A-version text runs from 2.86–3.30 is confirmed.

Variational Analysis of BmBoCot

Although it is well known that manuscripts Bm, Bo, and Cot are very closely related in their C- and B-version texts, there is still some debate regarding the exact nature of their stemma. Russell and Kane's summary points to the problem:

---

[6] The variants from both A and B would be: 6/6 hire] to hire. 7/7 *line om*. 14/14 þere] ther as. 20/21 goodness & gaf hem ichone] goodis and grete ʒiftis. 22/23 *line placed after 24/25*. 22/23 Rynges] With rynges. 24/25 at] of. 25/26 With þat come clerkis] Tho com*m* these clerkes. 26/27 be blyþe] blithe to be. 28/29 Hendely þanne heo] Ful hendly than she. Those readings that would be unique in the B tradition would be (A MS support in parentheses): 3.1 and] *om*. (RUH²VHJEWN). 5 I shall] I will (VEAM). 13 somme] sone (TChH²HEKW). 17 shape] make (TRUDChH²E). 18 *line om* (all A MSS). 28 þi] oure RUVHJLKWNM. Those readings that would be unique in the A tradition would be (B support in parentheses): 3.3 not] not tell BmCot (H). 9 hiʒte] hym hyghtte (F). 11 to] forto (G). 13 Ientily] Ful gentilly (F). 23 a] hadde a (F).

[7] *The B Version*, ed. by Kane and Donaldson, p. 47, although contra Kane and Donaldson, F is contaminated from A. Variants at 3.9, 3.13, and 3.24 are included by Kane and Donaldson in their collation of BmBoCotF.

'The relation of [BmBoCot] in their B portion, while unmistakably genetic, was also immensely complex. Here in C it is simple; they evidently have an immediate exclusive common ancestor. From the number of agreements in error, equivalent to 600 over the whole poem, it was not a good text.'[8] To explain the 'immensely complex' B version ancestry, Kane and Donaldson had proposed three different scenarios:

> I. There were three exemplars: the exclusive common ancestor B and two of its three known descendants. Where the variational group BmBo occurs *Cot* is a copy of B, and BmBo are copies of *Cot*; where the variational group BoCot occurs Bm is a copy of B and Bo*Cot* are copies of Bm.

> II. Again there were three exemplars: B and two of its three known descendants. Where the variational group BmBo occurs Bm and *Cot* are copies of B and Bo is a copy of Bm, *or* Bo and *Cot* are copies of B and Bm is a copy of Bo; where the variational group BoCot occurs Bm and Bo are copies of B and *Cot* is a copy of Bo, *or* Bm and *Cot* are copies of B and Bo is a copy of *Cot*.

> III. There were two exemplars: the necessarily posited exclusive common ancestor B and a hypothetical lost copy of this, B^1. Where the variational group BmBo occurs *Cot* is a copy of B and BmBo are copies of B^1; where the variational group BoCot occurs Bm is a copy of B and Bo*Cot* are copies of B^1.[9]

As difficult as it is to follow, and as unlikely as it seems, the Russell and Kane argument for the genetic affiliations of BmBoCot's C-version text is at odds with all three of Kane and Donaldson's proposed arguments for its B-version text. Although it is possible that BmBoCot could have been assembled from different component manuscripts simultaneously at the time of their mutual productions (Ralph Hanna gives Bm *s. xiv/xv²*, Bo *s. xiv/xv*, and Cot *s. xv¹*),[10] it is exceptionally unlikely. The Athlone editors seem to want to minimize the contributions of 'improving' scribes, and fail to consider that the scribes of copies such as T or even Bm might have been competent editors in their own rights. I believe that both Russell-Kane and Kane-Donaldson are wrong: the simplest situation is that Bm and Bo were copied from a lost exemplar which formed a genetic pair with Cot, and that deficiencies and disagreements between the texts are otherwise minor scribal errors, evidence of the dialects of their scribes, and the like.

---

[8] *The C Version*, ed. by Russell and Kane, p. 40.

[9] *The B Version*, ed. by Kane and Donaldson, pp. 40–41.

[10] Ralph Hanna III, *William Langland* (Aldershot: Variorum, 1993), p. 40.

The key to reconciling Russell and Kane's 'simple' with Kane and Donaldson's 'immensely complex' arrives through the careful understanding of BmBoCot's unstudied A-version materials. We need to begin by listing variational pairs of substantive, non-dialectal shared error where two manuscripts side against the remaining one (at this stage, it is unimportant whether the dominant readings are allied with the rest of the A tradition). Such an analysis reveals manuscripts CotBm in three agreements; CotBo in some fifteen agreements; and BmBo in some fifteen agreements.[11] On those occasions when Bo disagrees with Cot and Bm, it seems that sloppy scribal practice is to blame.[12] Similarly, on those fifteen occasions where Bm disagrees with Cot and Bo, thirteen seem to be due to different types of mechanical error. Only at 2.167 ('and if ʒe kacche lyʒere lete hym nat a-scape' for 'And if ʒe lacche liʒere, let hym not askape') and 3.1 ('Now is mede þe maide no mo of hem alle' for 'Now is mede the maide, nomen of hem alle') does it seem that the Bm scribe has presented a substantially different text.[13] Cot's disagreements with Bm and Bo, by contrast, seem to be rooted in Cot's exemplar rather than the practice of its scribe.[14]

It will clarify the situation to note that Kane's edition favours all three readings shared by Cot and Bm, and of the fourteen agreements between Cot and Bo, only the variants at 2.168, 3.1, 3.11, and 3.18 disagree with Kane.[15] Based on these

---

[11] CotBm: 2.86*a*, 87 and 98; CotBo: 2.116, 117, 144, 156, 162, 167, 168, 185, 188; 3.1, 3, 11, 16, 18 and 29; BmBo: 2.92, 95, 100, 103, 113, 114, 120, 125, 126, 130, 139, 149, 162; 3.17 and 30.

[12] For example, miscounted minims or a momentary lapse in Latin in 2.86*a*, same line eyeskip in 2.87, and a misread thorn in 2.98.

[13] Of these two, it can be argued that the change from <nomen> NO MAN to <no mo> NO MORE could have come about through Bm's scribe successfully restoring a line he realized was deficient in his exemplar. Similarly, <lacche> LACK to <kacche> CATCH could have come about through a myriad of different types of convergent variation: (a) scribal improvement on the part of the Bm scribe; (b) scribal simplification on the part of the CotBo scribes; (c) legitimate confusion over letterforms; (d) some combination of the above. Kane discusses sources of error at length on pp. 119–21, but does not suggest *i*/*k* confusion in his list of potential problems caused by unclear or incomplete letterforms.

[14] Of the fifteen disagreements between Cot and BmBo, the four variations in lines 2.95, 2.113, 2.114, and 2.120 show Cot siding with what Kane saw as potentially appearing in T's genetic lineage. Conversely, the five disagreements between Cot and BmBo in lines 2.126, 2.130, 2.149, and 2.162, and 3.17 show BmBo siding with T's genetic ancestor. The balance of Cot's error, are either mechanical matters or dialectal in nature (eg., 2.139 and 3.30).

[15] Although Kane's reading at 3.18 is supplied from A texts RVKWNM, and Kane's collation shows that TDH²HA read the same as CotBo, which argues strongly for the error to be genetic and originate in an early ancestor of that family of texts.

patterns of shared error and on Cot's systematic departures from BmBo and from Bm and Bo individually, and towards whatever common ancestor they shared with manuscript T, the most plausible relationship would be [Cot(BmBo)]. It seems likely that Bm and Bo were copied from the same lost exemplar, and Cot was copied from either the exemplar of the BmBo exemplar or from a manuscript forming a genetic pair with the BmBo exemplar. I have therefore decided to use Cot, corrected from Bm and Bo, as the basis of my reconstruction of the shared [Cot(BmBo)] ancestor (hereafter b1).

The important but previously unnoticed work of a second scribe in MS Cot enables us to minimize the influence that the manuscript's main scribe will have on an analysis of BmBoCot's genetic relationship, and test the theory that logically [Cot(BmBo)] must hold true across all three versions. In Cot, folios 173^{r-v} represent the work of a second scribe, whom I will call 'scribe B', responsible for C.Prol.205–1.42. This observation runs contrary to that of A. I. Doyle, who is cited by Kane and Donaldson in Cot's manuscript description as claiming that the manuscript is 'all by one hand'.[16] In my opinion, although Doyle was correct to posit an early fifteenth-century production, he was mistaken about the hand, perhaps overlooking the one folio on which this second scribe's work appears.[17] A collation of scribe B's work against Bm and Bo reveals that the latter two manuscripts have twenty substantive, non-dialectal variations from Cot (more or less demonstrating scribe B's lack of concern for what should be an alliterating text) against a single disagreement between Bm and BoCot (due to an obvious instance of intralinear dittography).[18] Any assertion that BmBoCot have a different

---

[16] *The B Version*, ed. by Kane and Donaldson, p. 5.

[17] Scribe B uses a distinctive, hurried-looking bastard hand with a less upright ductus than scribe A. Features of scribe B's hand include the occasional use of a terminal looped <s>, regular use of a looped <e>, a long tailed, left-leaning <y>, single compartment <a>, more frequent use of long <s> and long <r>, no clubbing on the minim of the anglicana formata <r>, a decorative hairline flourish leading to the left on the 2-shaped <r>, crossed ascenders, predictable initial line capitalization, a considerably lighter colour of ink, slightly different use of abbreviations, and a different pattern of punctuation (scribe A typically uses a hairline solidus after a word ending with a two compartment <s>, a dot for <i>, a hairline solidus following a terminal <i> — particularly in <thei> THEY — and almost always places a prominent punctus at the medial break and another punctus at the end of the line; whereas scribe B merely uses a punctus at the medial break approximately half of the time).

[18] These are: Prol.214 hit] þe BmBo. Prol.220 merie be] beþ merie BmBo. Prol.222 y] me BmBo. Prol.229 dryueth forth] dryueþ Bm. 1.2 yow telle] faire shewe BmBo. 1.4 faire] bi name BmBo. 1.7 on] vp-on Bm; out of Bo. 1.8 of] in BmBo. 1.12 este] tofte BmBo. 1.20 curteise] cur

genetic relationship for each text is therefore wholly insupportable. BmBo share one exemplar, and Cot another.

The Classification of MS b1

Although the text preserved by a reconstructed b1 represents a very small portion of the A version of *Piers Plowman*, it is more than enough to establish b1's genetic affiliations, and to provide some additional information on the relationships identified by Knott and Fowler, and verified by Kane.[19] In due course we will assess b1's unique readings, with an eye towards determining whether any of them might witness Langland's own text. First, though, it is necessary to understand the greater context of b1, including its relationship to other A-version manuscripts, and to understand how its scribes worked on their text.

Generally, b1 shares a number of readings with TH[2], some of which are presumably authorial, and were used by Kane. Yet b1 also offers a number of variant readings that link it more specifically with London, British Library, MS Harley 6041 (H[2]). The genetic ties of b1 and H[2] are already strong enough on their own to stand as evidence of their close relationship, but it should still be noted that H[2] also features emendations by a 'mid-sixteenth century hand' Kane calls 'the late corrector',[20] whose work pushes the two manuscripts even closer together.[21] If the rate of agreement between b1H[2] were extrapolated for the entire

---

curtesie Bm. 1.31 *line om.* Cot. 1.32 and thou shalt do the bettere] boþe day and ny3ttis BmBo. 1.33 om.] þou3 BmBo. 1.35 as to the soule] þat lief is þe soule BmBo. 1.36 hit] *om.* Cot. 1.37 betraye] bigile BmBo. 1.39 be war of her wyles] and seiþ in þin herte BmBo. 1.40 be war I wyse the beste] y-war what wolde þe disceyue BmBo. 1.41 quod I] *om.* BmBo. 1.42 worlde] molde BmBo; herre deth] kepen BmBo.

[19] *Piers the Plowman: A Critical Edition of the A-Version*, ed. by Thomas A. Knott and David C. Fowler (Baltimore: Johns Hopkins University Press, 1952), p. 26; *The A Version*, ed. by Kane, pp. 85–86.

[20] *The A Version*, ed. by Kane, p. 7.

[21] H[2] is a conjoint A/C manuscript, which is dated by watermark and hand to the first quarter of the fifteenth century. Of the twenty-three corrections apparently made to passus 2.86–198, fifteen bring H[2] into agreement with b1, four bring H[2] into disagreement with b1, and four do not have any impact on the relationship between H[2] and b1. The four emendations that do not affect agreement with b1 are: 2.98 Ihauntith] Ihaunditd. 113 To] when. 175 sewen] sellen. 3 1 nomme] nomor. The four that bring H[2] into disagreement with b1 are: 2.86 telliþ not] telliþ the not. 184 panis] penis. 3 6 molde] world. 18 a] or. The fifteen that bring H[2] into agreement with

poem, the two manuscripts would share approximately 100 or so substantive, non-dialectal readings. Taking into consideration Knott and Fowler's assertion that TH^2 represents a genetic pair, and given Kane's demonstration of the readings shared by those manuscripts, Table 1 represents the simplest possible stemma.

Table 1

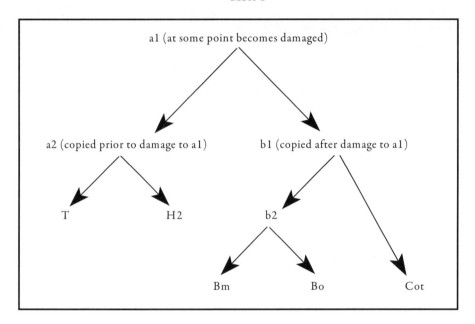

b1 are: 2.87 worth] worthi. 92 boþe] it boþe. 97 he] she. 100 laute] lawe. 127 fourty] fourthe. 142 vicailes] vitailes. 148 man] men. 163 heued] hedde. 172 *om.*] þe. 197 he] she. 198 he] she. 3.2 *om.*] þe. 24 hij] they; wordes] lordis. 25 clerc] clerces. 28 heo] sheo. Of these, the corrections to 2.97, 2.197, 2.198, and 3.28 probably argue for <heo> SHE being present in whatever manuscript served as the ultimate exemplar for both H^2 and the A version material in b1 (in the stemma below, this hypothetical manuscript is labeled a1). Owing to the lack of confusion of forms in BmBoCot, it is unlikely that b1 used <heo> SHE. Of those emendations that bring H^2 closer to b1, the correction to 2.100 creates a unique agreement in error, and the correction to 2.127 creates an agreement in error of b1H^2U. The tentative conclusion is that 'the late corrector' used either b1's exemplar or a manuscript closely related to b1 in order to supply the deficient readings. This may or may not have a bearing on the rest of H^2's text, which includes the balance of the A version, and a copy of the C version comprising 11.295a–14.200 and 16.24–22.386.

The first thing to note is that the proposed stemma in Table 1 can be reconciled with Davis's thoughtful reconstruction of what he calls the 'Bm exemplar' — b1. The only modification I suggest is to add b2 to explain the genetic differences between Cot and BmBo where Cot cannot be a copy of Bm. Similarly, if Davis is correct and b1 was a response to a deficient B version exemplar, then the most likely situation is that a1 became damaged after a2 was copied, and b1 was created in response. Since b1's scribe had access to an *i*-family C version-text, and since Cot shows signs typical of a turn of the century London copying, it is likely that a1 and b1 were created in the capital.

Although it is not a particularly cautious argument, it might be suggested that when b1 is in disagreement with T and in agreement with H[2] or with H[2] as emended by 'the late corrector', this agreement represents a feature of a2 and hence a1, and, therefore, T's reading is *likely* to be scribal. This theory, however, is for others to prove or disprove. Several readings demonstrate this effect, for example, passus 2.119:

> H[2] Þat he grauntiþ with vs to go wiþ a good wille
>
> b1 And that she graunted with vs to goo w*ith* a goode wille
>
> T Þat he grauntiþ to gon wiþ a good wille.

In this situation, there are four possible options: (a) similar to what Kane and Donaldson suggested for the BmBoCot B-version text, there are three exemplars and the manuscripts were cross-copied in the manner that is seen in the Synoptic Gospels; (b) the H[2] and b1 scribes, encountering a moderately difficult line, chose to 'produce what seemed to them a more correct, or a more emphatic, or a more elegant text'; (c) the T scribe has made a simple mechanical error and has omitted 'with vs'; or (d) the T scribe has 'perceived that his original was corrupt', and engaged in 'smoothing [...] conjectural emendation'.[22] I believe that a multiplication of exemplars is not necessary for this scenario to be quickly resolved. Although there are some periodic instances where the T scribe has allowed some mechanical errors to sneak into his text (for example passūs 2.190 and 2.190*a*), I do not believe that option (c) is necessarily true. The fourth of these options is probably the correct one, as other instances confirm.[23] The T scribe knew the

---

[22] *The A Version*, ed. by Kane, pp. 128–29.

[23] Another example of this may be seen at passus 2.185: H[2] 'Therof herden lechis & lettris him sente', b1 'Ther of hirde a leche and lettris hym sente', T 'Þanne louride lechis & lettris be sente'. Again, it seems unlikely that H[2] and b1 would emend independently from the T line to their own, but likely that T would 'improve' a line deficient in a2. Another case arises at passus 2.131: H[2]

general shape and lexicon of Langland's work well enough to consciously and expertly emended his text. As far as b1's classification is concerned, it takes this form $\{<[((TH^2)b1)Ch]D>RU\}$.[24]

Preliminary Analysis of the Dialects of BmBoCot and b1

Before unique A-version readings in b1 can be considered, we must come to some understanding of the role that the respective scribal dialects seen in BmBoCot play in either revealing or concealing what was originally present in their shared ancestor. A preliminary dialect analysis of BmBoCot has two goals: (a) to test the genetic conclusions reached following the study of the manuscripts' various types of shared errors; and (b) to attempt to reconstruct the dialect of their common ancestor.[25] Although the sample was only slightly more than 140 lines of text, each manuscript presented more than sixty items for analysis, and so, the dialects were at least partially recoverable, and as was expected, an analysis of the layering of dialects in BmBoCot mirrored the findings made regarding their textual affiliations obtained through the study of shared error. That is, the dialects of BmBo are nearly identical, and stand slightly apart from Cot, even while all three manuscripts contain relics of Langland's South-West Worcester dialect (see the

---

'Þere hadde notories non hors anoyed þei were', b1 'There hadden notaries noon hors; anoied thei were', T 'Þere had notories none anoyed þei were'. Again, it seems likely that the T exemplar contained the word 'hors,' and that the T scribe improved on his exemplar, and in the process, has inadvertently brought it towards what was surely Langland's intention. If a future editor wishes to reconstruct Ax, then T's reading, although it is probably what Langland intended, could not be used to argue as such.

[24] This relationship is supported by the following sets of shared error: *The manuscripts* b1H[2] *in some six agreements*: 2.129 softeliche] fetusly. 130 fe[int]liche] quentely. 131 none] non hors. 168a *om*.] not a-scape. 190 ʒer & elleuene dayes] terme of hire lyues. 190a *om*.] To ben of hire consail; whan thei carieden aboute. *The manuscripts* b1T *in some two agreements*: 2.126 for] forþ. 189 Mynstralis] And mynstralis. *The manuscripts* b1Ch *in two agreements*: 2.144 iotten] trotten. 3.24 lauʒte hy leue] took thei hire leue. *The manuscripts* b1TH[2] *in one agreement*: 2.86 textis] tixtis b; textis TH[2]. *The manuscripts* b1TChH[2] *in some three agreements*: 2.123 in shires abouten] aboute in shiris. 131 Þo] There. 142 of] fro. *The manuscripts* b1TDH[2] *in some two agreements*: 2.97 he] he. 186 wateres] and watres.

[25] Unless otherwise noted, all technical terms are taken from, and all dialect work is based on, *A Linguistic Atlas of Late Mediaeval English*, ed. by Angus McIntosh, M. L. Samuels, and Michael Benskin, 4 vols (Aberdeen: Aberdeen University Press, 1986); hereafter *LALME*. See also Michael Benskin, 'The 'Fit'-Technique Explained', in *Regionalism in Late Medieval Manuscripts and Texts*, ed. by Felicity Riddy (Cambridge: Brewer, 1991), pp. 9–26.

Appendix below).[26] For this exercise, A-version texts from BmBoCot were analysed according to the 'fit' procedure established by the authors of *The Linguistic
Atlas of Late Mediaeval English*.

In his essay 'Langland's Dialect', M. L. Samuels claims that the BmBoCot
manuscripts' B copies 'derive certain of their dialectal features from a north
Gloucestershire exemplar, itself presumably an intermediate copy in the chain of
descent from the B-archetype',[27] providing a list of spellings that includes '<huyre
(hiren)> HEAR, <hure> HER, <wul> (vb.) WILL, <wather> WHETHER, <ʒut (ʒit)>
YET, <silf, silue> SELF, <wurch> (vb.) WORK, <thorgh> THROUGH, <nat/naught>
NOT, <mony> MANY'.[28] Yet these findings are not consistently reproducible for
the individual manuscripts Bm, Bo, and Cot, and do not apply at all to their C-
version and A-version texts — but perhaps not for any reason rooted in their
shared ancestral exemplars. As Simon Horobin has demonstrated, Samuels failed
to factor in 'the phenomenon of "working in"',[29] whereby 'a scribe may begin
by translating unfamiliar forms into his own dialect, and subsequently switch
to literatim copying as familiarity with his exemplar grows'.[30] The situation
presented by BmBoCot's A-version spellings is complex but seems to support
Horobin. First, there are very few diagnostically important SW Worcs. features.[31]

---

[26] M. L. Samuels, 'Langland's Dialect', in *The English of Chaucer and his Contemporaries:
Essays by M. L. Samuels and J. J. Smith*, ed. by J. J. Smith (Aberdeen: Aberdeen University Press,
1988), pp. 70–85 (p. 85).

[27] Samuels, 'Langland's Dialect', pp. 77–78.

[28] Samuels, 'Langland's Dialect', p. 84.

[29] Simon Horobin, '"In London and Opelond": The Dialect and Circulation of the C Version
of *Piers Plowman*', *Medium Ævum*, 74 (2005), 248–69 (p. 253).

[30] Horobin, '"In London and Opelond"', pp. 253–54.

[31] None of Samuels's hallmarks of Langland's dialect (<oe> ME ō, <heo> SHE, <a> HE or
SHE, <noyther> NEITHER, <no> NOR, <ar> ERE or BEFORE, <ʒut> YET, <u> and <uy> for OE
y) is present. With regard to his list of SW Worcs. features observed in BmBoCot's B version texts,
the spellings <huyre (hiren)> HEAR, <hure> HER, <wather> WHETHER, <naught> NOT,
<mony> MANY, <wurch> (vb.) WORK do not appear in any of the manuscripts' A-version texts.
The form <ʒit> YET appears once across all three manuscripts, and both <wul> (vb.) WILL and
<thorgh> THROUGH appear twice each but only in Cot. As far as <silf, silue> SELF is concerned,
the manuscripts are mixed with BmBo favouring <silf, (silue)>, and Cot favouring <self, (selue)>.
Finally, Cot uniformly reads <nat> NOT whereas BmBo uniformly read <not> NOT. Even if a
minority position is taken where necessary to exaggerate b1's features, with <nat> NOT, <silf,
(silue)> SELF, <wul> (vb.) WILL, <ʒit> YET, and <thorgh> THROUGH, the distribution of these
forms is widely attested across a number of Middle English dialects.

The BmBoCot C-version texts, though, do show a clear layer of relict usage, with Cot standing out in both instances as a repository of specific forms associated with Langland.[32]

Horobin's ideas about the trademarks of a professional London copying by the circle of scribes responsible for disseminating Langland's C version suggests support for the hypothesis that Cot, like the very best manuscripts of the C version of *Piers Plowman*, was the product of a well-established London copyist who may have had experience with the copying other versions of Langland's poem. First, in keeping with some of Horobin's observations made regarding the *i*-group, Cot features a high quality and current hand, extensive contemporary corrections, a consistent thirty-two-line framework (which in itself would have involved detailed calculations as most of the manuscripts are consistently forty lines per leaf), careful and consistent punctuation, the remnants of a sophisticated *ordinatio* including alternating *paraph* signs, rubricated Latin quotations, and an elaborate twin sets of double bounding lines. Second, the main scribe demonstrates a sophisticated programme of 'working in'. The scribe significantly decoloured most of his exemplar's lexicon, but preserved what he must have considered to have been defining Langlandisms, but gradually allowing more and more SW Worcs. spellings to emerge as the poem develops (e.g. <ar> ERE, <arn> BE, <fram> FROM, <louye> LOVE, <siegge> SAY, <moch> MUCH, <naught> NOT, and so on), with the late passus of the B-version text showing considerably more such forms than the earlier passus.

BmBo's dialect initially appears at once to be more localizable than Cot's not because Cot is further removed from b1, but because Cot is closer to it. Instead, BmBo were copied by scribes working outside of the traditions represented by the Cot scribe, and worked from an already partially 'translated' copy of b1, hence the pattern of usage seen by Samuels. Conversely, Cot's C version text's dialect is at more distinctive than its A-version dialect *because* of 'working in'. That is, b1's A-version exemplar was considerably further removed from Langland's original (even though it was arguably better than any extant A-version manuscript), than

---

[32] For example, <oe> ō, <heo> SHE, <a> HE/SHE, <wurch> WORK, <wather> WHETHER, <naught> NOT, <u> and <uy> for OE y do not appear at all; and the balance of Samuels's suggested items appears to be. <ʒit, ʒut> YET, <er, (((ar)))> ERE, <self, (silf), (silue), ((selue))> SELF; and only in Cot, <nother, neither, neythur> NEITHER, <many, (((mony))), (((mayny)))> MANY, <wul, ((wullen)), ((wull))>, <hire, (((hure))), (((her)))> HER, <thorgh> THROUGH, <nat, (((not)))> NOT. In this case, if minority readings were adopted as being in the archetype, it would immediately localize to SW Worcs.

b1's C-version exemplar (which could not have been much removed from the original *i*-group ancestor).

To speculate further, the more removed from Langland a manuscript becomes, the more progressively decoloured its text becomes in the initial quires, whereas the more prevalent generalized features of SW Worcs. become in the latter quires, and the more ossified specific facets of Langland's linguistic habits become in the earlier quires. As a caveat, I acknowledge that this theory assumes that manuscript quires were copied in the order of the text. Finally, although the study of the dialects used in these manuscripts will require a great deal more work, the preliminary results support the decision to base an edition of b1's A-version text (and a later edition of b1's C-version text) on Cot.

It is relatively easy to verify the conclusions made regarding dialect by studying Cot's individualistic orthographic practices. Michael Benskin has described three different 'regionally conditioned' categories of usage of <þ> and <y>: the first 'as a single symbol, which may be <þ>-like or <y>-like in appearance'; the second as distinct symbols but confused usage; and the third as 'discretely distinct' symbols and usage.[33] For the first twenty-three or so folia, Cot's scribe A adheres to a clear orthographic distinction between <y> and <þ>, and follows the following basic practice: use of <th> versus <þ> in initial and final positions corresponding to <th> in Modern English (phonetic correlate θ); <th> versus <þ> in medial positions corresponding to <th> in Modern English (phonetic correlate ð); <ȝ> versus <y> in initial positions corresponding to Modern English <y>; <gh> versus <ȝ> in final positions corresponding to Modern English <gh>; and <ghtte> corresponding to <ht> in Old English and <ght> in Modern English. Indeed, in the early quires of Cot, <þ> is an exceptionally rare form, and only appears eight times prior to passus 5 (that is, 8 uses of <þ> versus 1082 uses of <th> in initial positions across some 1200 lines comprising some 12,000 words of text),[34] with two of those instances arguably by another hand, and three made under special conditions. Of those three special uses, it appears as if scribe A, rather than making a midline adjustment in the size of his hand, spontaneously employs <þ> in the second hemistych of a line when he realizes that the text is not going to fit easily inside the page's bounding lines.

---

[33] Michael Benskin, 'The Letters <þ> and <y> in Later Middle English, and Some Related Matters', *Journal of the Society of Archivists*, 7 (1982), 13–30 (p. 14).

[34] The other forms for passūs 1–5 are: 124 <ȝ> versus 4 <y> in [j]-segments; and 117 <gh> versus 20 <ȝ> in [x]-segments.

Following the start of passus 5, scribe A's pattern of usage changes. It appears as if <þ> for <y> confusion begins soon after the twentieth folio of scribe A's stint.[35] In general, although an orthographic distinction continues to be made between <y> and <þ>, <y> versus <þ> becomes predominant, and the appearance of <þ> versus <th> in initial positions increases. Again, those stray times when a careful distinction is maintained seem tied to those to occasions where scribe A runs out of space in a given line, as at folio 190^v.

In the situations where scribe A has preserved the distinction between <þ> and <y>, I would argue that the usage of <þ> is his own, owing to mistakes he makes calculating the necessary relative difference in character size from a 40-line to a 32-line format. At other times, for example, it seems that the confusion between <þ> and <y> does not indicate a consistent type of behaviour on the part of scribe A, but his periodic difficulty negotiating <þ/y> confusion in his exemplar, thus writing <sþnne> SIN on folio 193^r and <sauþour> SAVIOUR on folio 195^v. In the example of <sþnne>, some attempt has been made in the second example to draw a dot above the bowl of the <þ>, a feature that is reminiscent of five instances of dotted <y> earlier in the manuscript, on folios 170^r, 170^v, 175^r, 186^r, and 186^v. For the most part, scribe A settles into using <y> for both þ and y as he does on folio 193^v when he uses <y> for <yat> THAT and <tyme> TIME.

The effect of scribe A's 'working in' is profound. In Cot's text for the B version's passus 5, there are some 642 opportunities when he has to choose between <þ> or <th> in the initial position of a given word. If scribe A had followed the pattern he established in the first five passūs of *Piers*, one would expect to see approximately four uses of <þ>. Instead, and although there are some 586 uses of <th>, there are only some 56 uses of <þ>. An informal survey of the relative usage of <þ> versus <y> in initial positions in passūs 19 and 20 shows that this pattern continues and slightly increases towards the end of Cot's B-version text.

We can conclude, then, that the use of <y> for <þ> was part of the Cot scribe's passive repertoire, and he is willing to transmit it, but not to introduce it into his text. Conversely, <þ> is part of the Cot scribe's active repertoire, and he will substitute it for his exemplar's confused or indistinct use of <y/þ> or for his exemplar's use of <th>. The use of an indistinct form for <þ/y> is apparently not a feature of scribe A's usage, and, therefore, may have originated with the scribe/scribes of Cot's exemplar.

---

[35] Although he was using a thirty-two-line layout, he had just completed copying the sixteenth folio of his forty-line exemplar, which, if his exemplar was in eights, would have meant that he just finished the second gathering. See Davis, 'The Rationale for a Copy of a Text'.

Analysis of *b1*'s Unique Readings

Kane's collation reveals that across lines 2.86–198 and 3.1–30, b1 contains fifty-six or so unique readings not preserved by any extant manuscript of the A version. Our basic understanding of the text's overall affiliations and dialect enables a determination of whether any of these might be authorial. Many of these variants clearly appear scribal in nature.[36] About four appear to be genetic to a1, as is clear from their attestation as well with T and/or H[2].[37] Three line-length variants appear to violate Langland's poetic practice.[38] Of the remaining three variants, two seem scribal.[39] Having excluded all obvious scribal and genetic error, we are

---

[36] *Mechanical error*: 2.88 hire] *om*. 94 feyntles] feynt. 101 ʒif] om. 146 þe] *om*. 151 But] And. 125 þis] that. 158 Shal] Shal ther. 162 Feteriþ] Y hote ʒou to fetere. 3.6 hire] to hire. 7 *line om*. 22 *line placed after 24. Scribal amplification*: 2.109 go] fast goo. 121 ioyntly] to-gedre ioyntly. 122 fayn [...] als bliþe] ful faynn [...] ful blythe. 142 fetten] fette forth. 145 togidere] bothe to-gyder. 3.13 Ientily] Ful gentilly. 28 Hendely þanne heo] Ful hendly than she. *Scribal clarifications and simplifications (22):* 2.97 cosyn] cosyns. 99 lawe] as lawe. 107 signes] for his seignes. 116 certis [...] cesse shuln] for certeyn [...] ceese ne sholde. 119 Þat] And that. 124 alle be boun]also bonde men. 136 shal sitte on] sat vpon. 156 werchen] worcheth hem. 157 do hem hange] hange hem. 166 euere] eueremore. 177–178 Liʒtliche liʒere lep a-way þennes/Lurkyng þoruʒ lanes, toluggid of manye] Lythlich lyʒere lepe a-way, lurkyng thorgh lanes. 180 yhuntid] he was hunschid. 181 hadde pite] had of hym pite. 187 Spiceris [...] here ware] A spicer [...] hem here ware. 3.3 not his] not tell his Cot; not tell is Bm. 9 hiʒte] hym hyghtte. 11 to] forto. 14 þere þe] ther as the. 23 a] hadde a. 24 at] of. 25 Wiþ þat come] Tho com*m* these. 26 be blyþe] blithe to be. *Rejection of specific lexical items*: 2.148 on þis molde] in this world. *Homæographs*: 2.100 ʒif any Leaute] Yf that eny lawe. 123 segges] sissours. *Emendations made to correct same scribe error*: 2.105 ʒoure] to ʒour. 3.20 goodness & gaf hem ichone] goodis and grete ʒiftis. 22 Rynges] With rynges.

[37] Passus 2.115 to] and. 91 notories noye] notaries that sore anoyen. 168–168*a* I bidde/wayte hym wel late hym not ascape H[2]], 168a I bydde þee awayte hem wele let non of hem ascape. 185 Þanne louride lechis] Ther of hirde a leche.

[38] Passus 2.89, For al be lesinges þou lyuest, & leccherous werkis] For all is falsnesse and lesyngus, and lecherye that thou werkys. 161 for any tresour I hote] þat for no catel ʒe ne lette. 169 Dreed at þe dore stood & þat doom herde] That herde drede at the dore ther*r*e he stode al that hard*e* dome. For information on Langland's metrical practices, see most recently Hoyt N. Duggan, 'Notes on the Metre of *Piers Plowman*: Twenty Years On', in *Approaches to the Metres of Alliterative Verse*, ed. by Judith Jefferson and Ad Putter, Leeds Texts and Monographs, n.s. 17 (Leeds: Leeds Studies in English, 2009), pp. 159–86. He would argue that these variants do not necessarily represent tremendous departures from Langland's usual practice.

[39] The variant at passus 2.112, 'thei [...] and maken hire at here wille' for received 'he [...] and maken at my wille', presents an extreme of b1's agenda of clarification. Encountering a passage moderately difficult to follow, the b1 scribe decided to reject his exemplar's pronouns. The b1

left with a single plausibly authorial variant, at A.2.95: b1, 'He is a bastard ybore, of belsebubbes kynde' for received 'And as a bastard yborn of belsabubbis kynde.' MS T reads 'a bastard yborn of belsaboukis kynde'; D, 'a bastard born of belsabubbes kyn'; H², 'a bastard yborn of belsabouris kynde'; and Ch, 'And as a bastard born of belsabuckes kynde'. Given the overall soundness of {<[(((TH²) b1)Ch]D>RU}, and acknowledging the widespread support for <and> among the other traditions of the A version, it is likely that the problem is rooted in either Langland's periodic use of <a> HE or <a> AND. If the common ancestor of {<[(((TH²) b1)Ch]D>RU}, that is Ax, had read 'A is a bastard yborn of belsebubbes kynde' or something similar, the entire group of variants could be due to a handful of scribes having different reactions to the same intolerance for <a> HE/AND.

I believe that this was the reading of a1 and b1. The scribe of TH²'s exemplar, that is, the scribe of theoretical manuscript a2, seeing what he believed was a combination of intralinear dittography and mechanical error, removed the offending reading, as did a scribe independently in D's tradition. The scribe of Ch, seeing the same reading, changed <a> HE/AND to <and> and the <is> to <as>. The b1 scribe, on the other hand, merely substituted his own dialect's spelling for <a> HE/AND, and therefore, b1 through BmBoCot probably represents the closest reading to Langland's original.

Conclusions

The b1 scribe, this analysis has revealed, introduced the majority of errors found in BmBoCot, mostly through his desire to make the poem as transparent as possible. We can also infer that his exemplar, theoretical manuscript a1, seems to have used <a> HE and <heo, he> SHE. Theoretical manuscript a1 apparently already had some error, and so was not Langland's holograph, nor, in all likelihood was it Ax. As for Cot, it was probably the product of an elite London scribe, a professional who worked according to the standards that had been established for the C version. His dialect practices accord with Horobin's observations on

scribe's problems with this brief passage also leads to the manuscript's second to last unique variant: 2.111 floreynes ynowe] fele faire nobles. Apparently, the b1 scribe, fearing eyeskip in his exemplar with 2.108, invented a perfectly plausible Langlandian hemistich. If his understanding of this passage had been better, and if there had been any hint of confusion in the greater {<[(((TH²) b1)Ch]D>RU}, then the half-line might have been authorial, but as he showed some confusion, and as the error apparently did not exist in theoretical manuscript a1, the variant in b1's 2.111 is certainly scribal.

progressive de-translation, and comparison of Cot's C-version and A-version texts reveals the cumulative effects of different types of constraint on Langland's dialect.

Finally, it must be acknowledged that the effects of Kane's omission of 3.1–31 from his A edition were minimal. Although BmBoCot provide support for some of TH²ChD's text, BmBoCot would provide only one potentially authorial variant.[40]

A Note on the Transcription and Apparatus Criticus

It is not my intention in this study to describe any codicological findings regarding BmBoCot or to propose any codicological features of b1. These issues will have to wait for the publication of an electronic edition of the BmBoCot C/A version splice through the *Piers Plowman Electronic Archive*. Nor will I describe the scribal hands involved in the production of Cot further than to confirm that the A version material was written by a single scribe who employed a late Anglicana book hand with some stray secretary features.

The palaeographical practices employed in the transcription of Cot were adapted from the various writings of Malcolm Parkes, and the apparatus criticus has been adapted from Kane. In brief, the text is cited according to its line number in the Kane edition of the A version. The reading found on the left-hand side of the bracket is that which was selected for b1, which for the most part will be the reading given in Cot. The reading found on the right of the bracket will be the disagreeing text, followed by the manuscript's sigil. If only one manuscript is given, then it is assumed that the third shares the same reading as the reading selected for the edition. Finally, the punctuation used in this edition was adapted from Kane.

[40] I would like to thank the National Endowment for the Humanities for their generous support through the Summer Stipend Program. Thanks also go to the Research Foundation of The City University of New York for their funding through the PSC CUNY Grants Program. I would also like to recognize the National Endowment for the Humanities Editions Grants Program for their continuing support of the *Piers Plowman Electronic Archive*. My research would have been impossible without the transcriptions made by the PPEA's editors and adjunct editors. Thanks also go to Bryan P. Davis and Gail Duggan for graciously allowing me to cite their collations of manuscripts Bo and Bm respectively. Finally, this article would not have been possible without the encouragement of Hoyt Duggan and Lawrence Warner.

Piers Plowman, A.2.86–3.29, the b1 Text

86   'The tixtes telleth nat so, treuthe wot the soth.

86*a*   *Dignus est operarius mercede sua.*

87   Worthi is the workman his mede to haue,

88   And thu hast fastnede *with* fals, fy on thy lawes!

89   For all is falsnesse and lesyngus, and lecherye that thou werkys;

90   Symonye and thyselue shenden holi cherch;

91   ʒe and the notaries that sore anoyen the peple;

92   [ʒee] shullen biegge [it] bothe, by god that me made.

93   Wel ʒe wyten, wirnardes, but yf ʒour*r*e wittes faile,

94   That fals is a faytour and feynt of his werkes.

95   He is a bastard ybore, of belsebubbes kynde;

96   And mede is mulere, a mayden of goode;

97   She myghtte kysse the kyng*e* for cosyns if he wolde.

98   Worcheth by wysdom, and by wyt after;

99   Ledeth here to londou*n* ther as lawe is handlid

100   Yf that eny lawe looke [wole] that thei lieggen to-gedre.

101   And the iustyse iuge hire to be ioyned *with* fals,

102   ʒyt be war of that weddyng, for witty is treuthe.

103   And Conscience is of [his] conseil, and knoweth ʒo*u* echone,

104   And yf he fynde ʒo*u* in defaute, and *with* the fals holden,

105   Hit shal be sette to ʒour soules wel sore at the laste.'

106   Her-to assenteth Cyuyle, ac symonye ne wolde

107   Til he hadde syluer for h*is* seales and for h*is* seignes.

108   Thanne fet fauel forth florynes ynowe

109   And bad gyle faste goo, and ʒeue gold*e* aboute,

110   And namelich to notaries, that hem non faile,

111   And feffe fals *with*nesse *with* fele faire nobles,

112   For thei may mede maistren & maken hire at here wille.

113   Tho this gold*e* was y-gyuen, grete was the thonkyng*e*

114   To fals & to fauel for hire faire ȝeftes,
115   And comen and conforted fro care the fals,
116   And saiden, 'for certeyn, ceese ne sholde we neuer
117   Tyl mede be thi weddid wyfe thorgh witt of vs alle,
118   For we haue mede maistried with oure mery spech,
119   And that she graunted with vs to goo with a goode wille
120   To londoun to loke yf that lawe wolde
121   Iugen ȝou to-gedre ioyntly in ioye for-euere.'
122   Than was fals ful faynn and fauel ful blythe
123   And lete sumpne al the scysoures aboute in sheres;
124   And also bonde men, beggeres, and other,
125   To wenden with [hem] to westmynster to wittnesse that dede.
126   Thanne careden thei forth caplis to carie hem thider;
127   Thanne fette fauel forth folys of the beste
128   And sette mede on a shereue y-schod al newe,
129   And fals sat on a sysour that fetusly trotted,
130   And fauel vp on a faire spech, quentely atirude.
131   There hadden notaries noon hors; anoied thei were
132   That Cyuyle and symonye scholde a-fote gange.
133   Than swore Cyuyle & saide by the roode
134   That sompneres scholde be sadeled and seruen hem echone,
135   'And let aparaile these prouysourus in palfraies wyse.
136   Syre symonye hym-self sat vpon hire bakkes;
137   Al the Officiales and denes, as destreris hem dyghtte,
138   For thei scholden bere the bischepis & brynge hem at reste.
139   Paulynes peple, for pleyntys in the [constorie],
140   Shullen serue my-self that Cyuyle hatte.
141   And cartsadyl oure comysorye, oure cart shal drawe,
142   And fette forth oure vitailes fro fornycatouris;
143   And maketh of lyȝere a-long carte to lede al these otherre,
144   As foolys and faytours that on hire fete trotten.'

---

114 to (2)] *om.* BmBo — **116** ne] he Bm — **117** witt of] *ms. damaged* Bm — **120** lawe] þe lawe
BmBo — **125** hem] BmBo; hym Cot — **126** forth] for BmBo — **130** a] *om.* BmBo — **139**
constorie] BmBo; concistorie Cot — **141** comysorye] comyssarie BmBo — **144** *line om.* Bm.

145	Fals & fauel faren forth bothe to-gyder,
146	And mede in myddys, and al this mayny after.
147	I haue no tome to telle the tail that hem folwid
148	Of many man*re* of men that in this world*e* libbeth.
149	[Ac] gyle was forgoere and [gied] hem alle.
150	Sothenesse sey hym wel and sayde but lytyl,
151	And p*ri*ked forth on his palfray and passed hem alle,
152	And com*m* to the kynges court and conscience tolde,
153	And conscience to the kyng carpid hit aftyr.
154	❡ 'Now, by cryst,' *quod* the kyng, 'and y myghtte caicche
155	Fals other fauel or eny of his ferys,
156	I wolde be wroken of thyse wrocches that worcheth hem so ille,
157	And hange hem by the hals and alle that hem manteyneth.
158	Shal ther neuer man of molde meynp*ri*se the leste,
159	But ryght as the lawe lokiþ let falle on hem alle.'
160	And com*m*awndid a constable that com at the ferste
161	To atache these tirauntes, 'þat for no catel 3e ne lette
162	Y hote 3o*u* to fetere falsnesse faste for eny [skynnes] 3yftes,
163	And gerde of gylours heede let hym go no ferther;
164	And bryngeth mede to me maugre hem alle.
165	Symonye and cyuyle, I sende hem to warne
166	That holicherche for hem worth harmed for eu*re*more;
167	And if 3e [lacche] ly3ere lete hym nat a-scape
168	Er he be pyt on the pyllery, for eny p*ra*iere, I hote.
168a	And therto, I charge 3o*u* and bidde that he nat a-scape.'
169	That herde drede at the dore ther*re* he stode al that hard*e* dome,
170	And wytelich hym went to warne fals;
171	And bad hym flee for ferd*e* and his feris alle.
172	❡ Thanne falsnesse for ferd*e* fledde to the freris,
173	And gyle doth hym to goo agast for to deie.
174	Ac marchauntyse mett w*ith* hym & made hym abyde;

---

149 Ac] BmBo; and Cot; gied] BmBo; grayed Cot — **152** tolde] *ms. damaged* Bm — **162** hote
ho*u*] how hote Bm. skynnes] kynnes Cot — **167** lacche] Bm; kacche CotBo — **168** Er] þat Bm.

175   And shetten hym in hire shoppes to shewe hir ware;
176   Aparaileden hym as a prentis, the peple to serue
177   Lythlich ly3ere lepe a-way, lurkyng thorgh lanes,
179   He was nower welcome for his many talis,
180   Oureal he was hunschid and yhote trusse,
181   Til pardoners had of hym pite and putten hym to house,
182   Weischen hym & wyped hym & wonden hym in clothes,
183   And senten hym on sonedaies with seales to chirche,
184   And 3af pardoun for pans pound-mel aboute.
185   Ther of hirde a leche and lettris hym sente
186   Forto wonye *with* hym, and wateres to looke.
187   A spicer spak *with* hym to aspie hem here ware,
188   For he couth on hire crafte and knew many gum*m*es.
189   And mynstrel[is] and messangeris metten *with* hym ones,
190   And withhelden hym *with* hem the terme of hire lyues,
190a To ben of hire consail whan thei carieden aboute.
191   Freris *with* faire spech fetten hym thennys;
192   For knowyng of komers copeden hym as a frere.
193   Ac he hath leue lepen out as ofte as hym lyketh;
194   And is welcom*m* whan he wole and woneth *with* hem ofte.
195   Alle fledden for fere and flowen in-to hernes;
196   Saue mede the mayde noman durst abyde.
197   Ac trewely to telle she tremblid for drede,
198   And weepe and wrang whan she was atached.

Passus 3

1   Now is mede the maide, nomen of hem alle,
2   W*ith* bedels & baylyues ybrought to the kyn*g*e.
3   The kyng called to hym a clerk — I can nat tell his name —
4   To take mede the maiden and make hire at ayse.
5   'I wul Asay hire my-self, and sothly apose

185 Ther] Ter Bm — **188** gum*m*es] gumnes Bm — **189** mynstrelis] BmBo; mynstrel Cot —
1 nomen] na mo Bm — **3** his] is Bm.

6	What man of this worlde that to hire were leuest;
8	I wole for3eue hire the gylt, so me god helpe.'
9	¶ Curteislich the clerk thanne, as the kyng hym hyghtte,
10	Took mede by the myddil and brought hire to chaumbre.
11	And ther was myrth and mynstrecye mede for to plese;
12	That woneth at westmynster worschipeth hire alle;
13	Ful gentilly with ioye the iustyses sone
14	Boskid hym to the boure ther as the berde dwelleth,
15	And conforteth hire kyndely by clergies leue,
16	And seyde, 'morne nat, mede, ne mak thou no sorwe,
17	For [we] wullen [wisse] the kyng and thi wey make
18	For alle conscienses cast a craft as I trowe.'
19	¶ Myldelich mede than mercied hem alle
20	Of here goodis & hir grete 3iftis.
21	Coupes of clene golde and pecis of sylure.
23	The lest man of hire mayne hadde a motoun of gold.
24	Than took thei hire leue, thise lordes of mede,
22	With rynges, with rubies, and richesses manye.
25	Tho comm these clerkes to conforte hire thanne,
26	And bidden hire blithe to be, 'for we ben thyn owne
27	Forto workyn thy wille while oure lyf lasteth.'
28	Ful hendly than she hyghtte hem the same,
29	To loue hem leely and lordes to make,
30	And in the [constorie] at the court do calle 3our names.

---

11 And] Ac Bm — **16** nat] no Bm — **17** we] BmBo; *om.* Cot; wisse] BmBo; kisse Cot — **18** a] and Bm — **29** hem] hym Bm — **30** constorie] BmBo; concistorye Cot.

Appendix

BmBoCot Comparative Dialect from *LALME* Questionnaire

	Item	Bm	Bo	COT
2	THESE	þise	þise	these, ((thyse))
4	SHE	she	she	she
5	HER	hire	hire	hire, (here)
6	IT	it	hit	hit
7	THEY	þei, ((þey))	þei	thei
8	THEM	hem	hem	hem
9	THEIR	here, (her), ((hire))	her, (here)	hire, ((here)), ((hir))
12	EACH	ech-	ech-	ech-
13	MANY	many, (meyne)	many, (meyne)	many, (mayny), (mayne)
14	MAN	man	man	man
15	ANY	eny	eny	eny
19	IS	is	is	is
21	WAS	was	was	was
22	SHALL, sg.	shal, schal	shal	shal
22	SHALL, pl.	chulle, shullen	shullen, shulde	shullen, sholde
23	SHOULD, pl.	shulden, shullen	shulden, ((shulde)), ((shullen))	sholde, scholde, scholden, shullen
24	WILL	wole, wille	wille	wille, wole
25	WOULD	wolde	wolde	wolde
28	FROM	fro	fro	fro, fro
29	AFTER	aftir	aftir	after, (aftyr)
30	THEN	þanne	þanne	thanne, (than)
32	THOUGH	þo	þo	tho
33	IF	ȝif, if	if, ((ȝif))	yf, (if)
38	ERE	—	er	er
40	YET	ȝit	ȝit	ȝyt
44	WH-	wh-, ((w-))	wh-	wh-, ((w-))
45	NOT	not	not	nat

	Item	Bm	Bo	COT
48	WORLD	world	world	worlde
50	WORK	worch-, (werk-)	werk-, (worch-)	worch-, werk-, ((work-))
51	THERE	þere, (þer)	þere, ((þer))	there, therre, ther
52	WHERE	wher	-wher	-wer
53	MIGHT	myȝte, myȝtte	myȝte, myette	myghtte
54	THROUGH	þurgh	þourgh, þurgh	thorgh
55	WHEN	whanne, wan, whan	whan, ((whann))	whan
56	SUB. PLUR.	-is, (-es)	-is, (-es)	-es, (-is), ((-ys)), (((-us)))
57	PRES. PART.	-yng	-yng, -ynge	-ynge
85	BOTH	boþe	boþe	bothe
91	BUT	ac, but	but, ac	but, ac
94	CAME	comm	com	comm
98	CHURCH	chirche, (cherche)	chirche	cherch, cherche, chirche
103	DIE	deye	deye	deie
106	DREAD	drede	drede	drede
125	FIRST	first	firste	ferste
137	GIVE	ȝeue	ȝeue	ȝeue
138	GO	go, (goo)	go, (goo)	goo, ((go))
139	GOOD	gode, god	goode	goode
141	HANG	hange	hange	hange
142	HAVE	haue, han	haue	haue
144	HEAR	herde, (harde)	herde, (harde)	herde, harde, hirde
154	HOLD	holden	holden	holden
158	I	y	J, y	I, (y)
159	KIND	kynde	kynde	kynde
165	LEAD	lede	lede	lede
167	LET	let, ((lette))	let, ((lete)), ((lette))	let, (lete), ((lette))
170	LITTLE	litil	litil	lytyl
171	LIVE	libbiþ	libbiþ	libbeth
210	SAY	seeide, saide	seiden, seide, sayde	saiden, saide, sayde

	Item	Bm	Bo	COT
211	SEE	sei (saw)	sei (saw)	sey (saw)
213	SELF	-silf	-silf, (-silue)	-self, (-selue)
215	SILVER	siluer	siluer	syluer
234	THENCE	þennis	þennys	thennys
235	THITHER	þider	þider	thider
238	TOGETHER	to-gedre, (to-gidir)	to-gredre, to-gedre, to-gidir	to-gedre, (to-gyder)
248	WENT	went	wente	went
257	WITEN	wot, weten,	witen	wyten
278	-LY	-liche, -li, -ly	-liche, -ly	-lich, -ly

THE SCRIBE OF BODLEIAN LIBRARY, MS DIGBY 102 AND THE CIRCULATION OF THE C TEXT OF *PIERS PLOWMAN*

Simon Horobin

This essay offers an identification of the scribe responsible for copying one of the best manuscripts of the C text, Oxford, Bodleian Library, MS Digby 102, as a clerk working for the Brewers' Guild during the opening decades of the fifteenth century.[1] Despite the scribe's connection with the Brewers' Guild he makes no attempt to respond to *Piers Plowman* C's stringent criticism of brewers. However, even though this identification does not provide insights into the scribe's personal response to the poem, it does substantially increase our understanding of the circulation and production of the C version in fifteenth-century London. For while Russell and Kane assumed that MS Digby 102 and other textually related copies of the C version were produced in a copying centre, the scribe's employment by the Brewers' Guild make such an assumption unlikely.[2]

---

[1] For the high quality of the text of *Piers Plowman* preserved in this manuscript see A. V. C. Schmidt's description of Y as 'potentially the best copy of C but for lacking, through loss of leaves, the first 600 lines' (*William Langland: Piers Plowman; A Parallel-Text Edition of the A, B, C, and Z Versions*, ed. by A. V. C. Schmidt, I: *Text* (London: Longman, 1995); II: *Introduction, Textual Notes, Commentary, Bibliography and Indexical Glossary* (Kalamazoo: Medieval Institute Publications, 2008), II, 174).

[2] *Piers Plowman: The C Version*, ed. by George Russell and George Kane (London: Athlone; Berkeley and Los Angeles: University of California Press, 1997).

Simon Horobin (*simon.horobin@magd.ox.ac.uk*) is Reader in the Faculty of English and a Fellow of Magdalen College, University of Oxford.

Abstract: This essay identifies the scribe of an important manuscript of the C version of *Piers Plowman* as a clerk working for the London Brewers' Guild during the early fifteenth century. Following a presentation of the palaeographical evidence upon which this identification rests, the essay considers its implications for our understanding of the production and reception of this copy of *Piers Plowman*, its relationship with other texts within the manuscript, and the light it sheds upon the transmission and circulation of this recension of Langland's poem among London scribes and readers during the first quarter of the fifteenth century.

Keywords: manuscripts, scribes, William Langland, *Piers Plowman*, Oxford, Bodleian Library, MS Digby 102, Brewers' Guild.

10.1484/J.YLS.1.102110

The close textual affiliations between Digby 102 and other members of the *i*-group of C manuscripts does, however, suggest that these copies were produced in close proximity to one another.[3] The institutional and geographical localization of the Digby 102 scribe offered here thus helps to situate the production of these and other copies of the poem. Digby 102 is unusual among copies of *Piers Plowman* C in containing a number of other texts, raising further questions about the relationship between these items and the manuscript's intended audience.

Digby 102 contains the following items: *Piers Plowman* C.2.159–22.386, a sequence of political and religious verse, Richard of Maidstone's metrical paraphrase of the *Seven Penitential Psalms*, and *The Debate between the Body and the Soul*.[4] It seems likely to me that a single scribe was responsible for copying the entire manuscript, although Russell and Kane attributed the work to two or three different hands. Russell and Kane report 'an unmistakable change of scribe at folio 128a after the end of *Piers Plowman*', clearly a typographical error since they had just recorded, correctly, that *Piers Plowman* concludes on folio 97^v.[5] That folio is followed by a blank leaf, with the following text beginning at the head of folio 98^r. But there is certainly no change of hand at this juncture; the use of individual letterforms, the distinctive aspect, and the size of the script remain constant across this break in texts. There is, however, a marked change in ink colour on folio 128^r, where the *Seven Penitential Psalms* begin. This switch to a dark black ink from a much lighter colour lends a superficial difference to the appearance of the hand-

---

[3] The '*i*-group' consists of San Marino, Huntington Library MS Hm 143 (X), University of London Library, MS S.L. V.88, *olim* Ilchester (I), the Holloway fragment, now Oslo, Schøyen Collection, MS 1953 (H), London, British Library, MS Additional 35157 (U), Oxford, Bodleian Library, MS Douce 104 (D), and London, British Library, MS Additional 34779 (P^2). This large textual group is identified by the presence of 132 variant readings; within this group MS Digby 102 is most closely affiliated with MS Hm 143 and the Ilchester manuscript, a group attested by thirty-three agreements in erroneous readings. Although this is a relatively small number of shared readings, Russell and Kane argued that one of these, a misdivision at 11.71–79, seems too extensive to be coincidental. They also note that the lack of persistent agreement in erroneous readings may be indicative of accurate transmission, or of correction. The implication of these comments is that these three manuscripts shared a single common ancestor. Within this group of three manuscripts there are no clear subgroups. XY agree in thirty-eight readings, XJ share twenty-four agreements, and YJ have seventeen agreements. Further variants led Russell and Kane to suggest the following relationship between these manuscripts: [(XY)J]. On this presumed inter-relationship the editors comment: 'If that indication is correct the likeliest explanation of the conflicting agreements here is sporadic consultation and "correction" in a single copying centre' (p. 44).

[4] For a full list of contents see *The C Version*, ed. by Russell and Kane, p. 16.

[5] *The C Version*, ed. by Russell and Kane, p. 16.

writing. There is also a change in the size of the script, resulting from the scribe's difficulty in assimilating the greater amount of Latin in this text to the layout employed through the manuscript. In this text the scribe maintains his earlier practice of using a larger format and more formal script for the Latin lemmata, but their increased frequency, coupled with the introduction of more pronounced *litterae notabiliores*, creates less space on the page and results in the adoption of a smaller module for the vernacular text. The use of the dark black ink at the beginning of this text clearly indicates a break in copying at this point, but need not necessarily be indicative of a lengthy interruption, given that this was clearly a natural point at which to pause. The more familiar lighter ink appears once more in the last three lines of folio 130[r] and is used for the remainder of the manuscript. The change in layout demanded for the final text, *The Debate between the Body and the Soul*, allowed the scribe to revert to his more familiar and more comfortable module; in general aspect and size the final folios are remarkably similar to those at the beginning of the manuscript.

A further piece of evidence that points to the conclusion that the manuscript is the work of a single scribe is the appearance of a rebus in the scribe's hand following the end of *Piers* on folio 97[v], which Russell and Kane read as 'HERON', while Hunt and Watson read it as 'R A E O (?) and I (?)'.[6] The same rebus is also found at the end of the manuscript on folio 139[v]. If this is understood to be a scribal signature, then it might well imply that the book is the work of a single scribe.[7] But it is unclear whether this is the scribe's own mark or rather that of an owner or patron. This rebus, and the large initial *R* in the top margin of folio 128[r], might be the scribe's initial, a possibility to which I will return later in this essay, but this conclusion is by no means certain.

The Digby scribe writes a small anglicana hand employing a number of letter forms typical of this variety of script.[8] Characteristic anglicana graphs include 8-shaped *g*, but here with a projecting spike to the right of the lower bowl similar to that found in the hand of Adam Pinkhurst.[9] The scribe employs the anglicana

---

[6] See *Bodleian Library Quarto Catalogues*: IX, *Digby Manuscripts* (Oxford: Bodleian Library, 1999), pp. 116–17.

[7] *A Linguistic Atlas of Late Mediaeval English*, ed. by Angus McIntosh, M. L. Samuels, and Michael Benskin, 4 vols (Aberdeen: Aberdeen University Press, 1986), LP 7770, describes the manuscript as the work of one hand (III, 561).

[8] For a facsimile of this manuscript see Plate 23 in M. B. Parkes, *Pause and Effect: An Introduction to the History of Punctuation in the West* (Aldershot: Ashgate, 1992).

[9] For this and other characteristic features of Pinkhurst's handwriting see Linne R. Mooney, 'Chaucer's Scribe', *Speculum*, 81 (2006), 97–138.

long *r*, which here descends considerably lower than is common (see Fig. 2, line 6, *to gyderes*). Unusually, long *r* is also used at the beginnings of words (see line 6, *ryt*). The scribe's *w* graph is the anglicana form, here with wide looping approach strokes (see line 4), and he uses 2-compartment *a* with a distinctively pointed upper compartment that rises above the height of neighbouring minims (see line 6, *maystre*). His form of *y* has a tail that sweeps back towards the right and is often dotted (see line 1, *tyme*), while the limb of *h* curls towards the left (see line 4, *with*, and the exaggerated tail on the final line: *he*); frequent use is made of round *e* (see line 1, *sette*). A larger and more formal bastard anglicana is employed for Latin text, written in rubric, which includes variant graphs such as 8-shaped *s* in preference to the sigma *s* used within the English text. While this combination of letter forms is typical of anglicana of this period, it is the way that the letters are formed, what is termed the 'duct' or 'aspect' of the hand, that is particularly distinctive of this individual scribe. Duct and aspect are features of handwriting that are not easily categorised, but which comprise the size, spread, and slant of the individual letter forms. The writing of Digby 102 is distinguished by its small module, a tendency for words to appear crammed into a restricted space, a slight lean to the right, and a pronounced tremulous or spiky appearance.

The manuscript is also unusual among copies of *Piers Plowman* in setting out verse lines as prose, rather than using separate lines. The employment of this layout for all the constituent texts demonstrates that it must have been the scribe's decision to introduce it, rather than a feature of his exemplar. The scribe was clearly aware that the texts he was copying were in verse, and he is careful to employ punctuation marks to indicate line divisions. Individual lines are distinguished by the inclusion of a virgule highlighted in rubric at line ends, and the first word of the following line begins with a *littera notabilior*. The hemistichs of each verse are separated by a distinctive form of the *punctus elevatus* in which the pes is formed by an s-shaped stroke. This unusual choice of layout is hard to explain; it is unlikely to have been motivated by considerations of space, given that the manuscript is not significantly narrower than other copies of *Piers*. A. S. G. Edwards's observation of the frequency of the adoption of this layout in books intended for female readers, especially in Books of Hours and lives of saints, may be relevant for our understanding of the audience of Digby 102, especially given its inclusion of Richard Maidstone's *Seven Penitential Psalms*.[10]

---

[10] A. S. G. Edwards, 'Fifteenth-Century English Collections of Female Saints' Lives', *Yearbook of English Studies*, 33 (2003), 131–41.

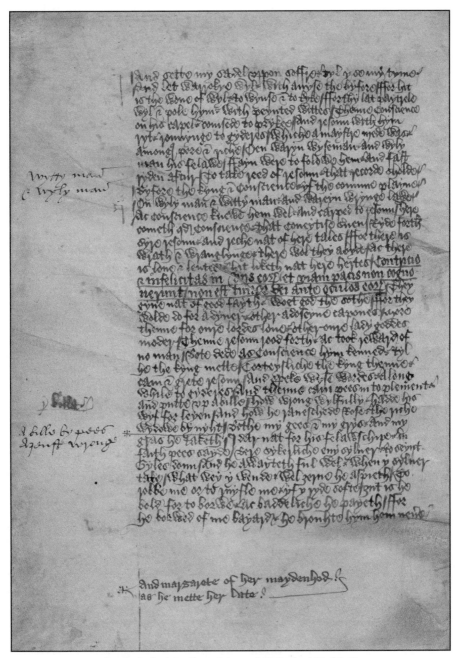

Fig. 2. Oxford, Bodleian Library, MS Digby 102, fol. 9ᵛ.
Reprinted by permission of the Bodleian Library.

A different, yet contemporary, hand has included three additions to the text of *Piers* in the bottom margin, with the place of insertion marked by a cross with four dots (see Fig. 2). There is one further addition to a text other than *Piers* in this hand: a single line supplied to the opening stanza of *The Debate between the Body and the Soul* on folio 136ʳ. These additions and corrections will be discussed further below. A later hand, probably of the sixteenth century, is responsible for an extensive series of marginal glosses that have been transcribed and discussed by Tanya Schaap.[11]

The same hand that writes the main text in Digby 102 is also found in the Memorandum Book of the London Brewers' Guild. This book is a compilation of accounts, petitions, memoranda, and ordinances relating to the Brewers' Guild. It was begun in 1418, during the mayoralty of William Sevenoke, by the Brewers' common clerk, William Porlond, appointed on the death of the previous clerk John Moroy, who was granted a dwelling for himself and his family in the Brewers' Hall on Addle Street. The records continue until 1441, although a payment of a pension to his late wife in 1440 indicates that Porlond died sometime in the spring of that year. He was succeeded by a Robert Cokat, payment of whose wages begins in the same year. While the main hand in the Brewers' book is that of William Porlond, there are several others that make contributions throughout the book.[12] The earliest entries in the Brewers' Minute Book are in French; however in 1422 the Brewers decided to keep their records in English, although there are some occasional entries in Latin and French subsequent to this decision to switch to English. A number of the entries by different hands are clearly later additions, inserted into spaces left blank by the original compilers. Their status as later additions is clear from the manner of their insertion and the fact that they have not subsequently been crossed out, as was the practice with all original contributions. This practice enables us to distinguish later additions easily and clearly, such as the English entries inserted into blank spaces in different hands and inks before folio 69ᵛ, which marks the transition from French to English.

---

[11] Tanya Schaap, 'From Professional to Private Readership: A Discussion and Transcription of the Fifteenth- and Sixteenth-Century Marginalia in *Piers Plowman* C-Text, Oxford, Bodleian Library, MS Digby 102', in *The Medieval Reader: Reception and Cultural History in the Late Medieval Manuscript*, ed. by Kathryn Kerby-Fulton and Maidie Hilmo, Studies in Medieval and Renaissance History, ser. 3, 1 (New York: AMS, 2001), pp. 81–116.

[12] For a facsimile of William Porlond's hand and a brief description of its contents and dating see P. R. Robinson, *Catalogue of Dated and Datable Manuscripts c.888–1600 in London Libraries* (London: British Library, 2003), Plate 98.

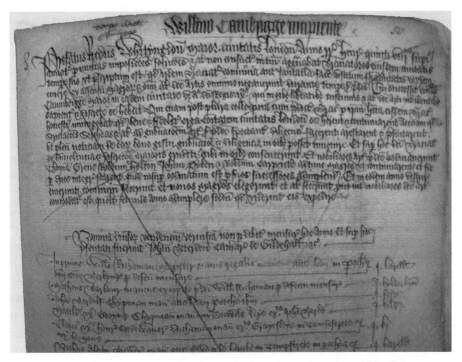

Fig. 3. London Metropolitan Archives, CLC/L/BF/A/021/MS05440, fol. 50ʳ.
Reprinted by permission of the Brewers' Company and the City of London Corporation.

In addition to these later additions by supplementary hands, there is also another hand, contemporary with that of Porlond, which is identical to that found in Digby 102. Figure 3 is an extract from the Brewers' book in the hand of the Digby 102 scribe. Most distinctive is the reappearance of the tremulous, or spiky aspect, although the hand is larger than that found in Digby 102, presumably a response to the increased size of the writing space. Despite the larger module adopted in the Brewers' book, the same combination of letter forms, with the same distinctive features, can also be observed. The 2-compartment *a* with pointed upper-compartment (see Fig. 3, line 3, *aut*); the *W* with wide looping approach strokes, the *y* with a tail that sweeps to the right; the 2-compartment *g* with projecting spike (see Fig. 3, line 1, *Whityngdon*); the low-descending long *r* (Fig, 3, line 2, *Braciatores*); the *h* with a tail that curls to the left (see Fig. 3, line 16, *Gildehall*); the round *e* (Fig. 3, line 5, *ciuitate*). The first entry in Figure 3 is written in a more formal grade of anglicana than the subsequent entries, closer to the bastard anglicana of the Latin rubrics in Digby 102, seen in the scribe's frequent use of 8-shaped *s* instead of sigma *s* (cf. line 1, *ciuitatis*, and line 17, *regalis*). Figure 3 also shows the use of the distinctive form of the *punctus elevatus* with the s-shaped pes (see line 3, following *est*).

Some entries made by the Digby 102 scribe in the Brewers' book could be considered later additions, such as the totalling up of accounts itemized by Porlond, but the majority of his entries appear to have been added at the same time as those by Porlond, while others provide evidence of Porlond adding further details to the Digby scribe's contributions. For instance, on folio 49ᵛ the Digby scribe itemized the members of the guild, a list which was subsequently updated by Porlond with additional names and indications of members since deceased. In Figure 3 (fol. 50ʳ) the Digby scribe has written the main entries but William Porlond has added a title in a larger and more formal version of his hand. Entries like these suggest that the Digby scribe may have been a junior colleague, or perhaps an apprentice, whose work Porlond supervised and updated. The close interaction between the two hands, combined with the fact that the Digby scribe's entries are found over a protracted period, suggest that, like Porlond and his family, the Digby scribe was also physically located in the Brewers' Hall.

A possible identification of the Digby scribe is a Robert Lynford, whose name appears a number of times in the entries in Porlond's Minute Book and who was clearly a junior colleague.[13] Payments for a lock and staple and three keys for the chamber door of Robert Lynford indicate that he, like Porlond himself, was resident in the Brewers' Hall. There are records of payments to both Lynford and Porlond for carrying out basic housekeeping duties, such as sweeping the Hall: 'Item, for ale [...] to Robert lynford and to William porlond, yn þe tyme of Swepyng of þe seide place jd.'[14] Robert Lynford is included in the list of members of the Brewers' Guild submitted by the masters to the Mayor in 1420, in response to Richard Whittington's attempt to enforce an earlier ordinance regulating the measures and prices at which the Brewers sold their ale.[15] Lynford is also mentioned in the Feet of Fines for Middlesex in 1413–14, as owner of a property in Hendon, along with John Clerk and Joan his wife.[16] Like Lynford, William

---

[13] Chambers and Daunt describe Lynford as 'apparently some minor official resident at the Brewers' Hall' (*A Book of London English, 1384–1425*, ed. by R. W. Chambers and Marjorie Daunt (Oxford: Clarendon Press, 1931), p. 258).

[14] *A Book of London English*, ed. by Chambers and Daunt, p. 158.

[15] *Calendar of Letter-Books Preserved among the Archives of the Corporation of the City of London at the Guildhall*, I: *1400–1422*, ed. by Reginald R. Sharpe (London: Guildhall Corporation, 1909), pp. 231–43.

[16] *A Calendar to the Feet of Fines for London & Middlesex*: I: *Richard I–Richard III*, ed. by W. J. Hardy and W. Page (London: Hardy & Page, 1892), pp. 169–77.

Porlond was also engaged in property transactions involving other members of the Brewers' Guild, as in the gift of a brewhouse known as 'le Faucon on the Hoop' situated in the parish of St Botolph, which he and Robert Smyth had received as a gift from members of the guild; they subsequently quitclaimed the property to William Belle who then gifted it to Porlond and two other members of the guild in April 1432. Porlond was also recipient, along with other members of the guild, of a demise by Richard Gretham and others of a tenement in Ware, Hertfordshire, on 12 August, 1 Henry VI. Porlond's close relationship with members of the guild is further witnessed by his serving as executor for the will of John Mason, along with Mason's wife and John Broke, in 1431. In addition to being charged with distributing Mason's wealth for the good of his soul, Porlond was the recipient of a gift of 40s., for his 'counsel', as well as five yards of black cloth costing 4s. a yard.[17] It may be worth recalling the large initial R in the top margin of folio 128[r] found in Digby 102, reported above, which could possibly stand for the first name 'Robert', though this is far from conclusive.

Whether the Digby scribe can be identified as Robert Lynford or not, the identification of his hand working alongside that of William Porlond in the Brewers' Memorandum Book makes clear that he was working in London, not in the West Midlands, as was suggested by M. L. Samuels on the basis of the dialect of Digby 102.[18] The Digby scribe's entries show him as an active copyist for the period from 1418 to 1441, providing a framework for dating his work on Digby 102, though it is of course possible that his copy of this *Piers* manuscript pre-dates or post-dates these entries. If my suggestion that the Digby scribe was acting as Porlond's junior partner is accepted then it would follow that the Digby manuscript was written towards the end, or after, this period of apprenticeship. The professional nature of the production, including the high level of its textual accuracy, suggests that the scribe was relatively experienced when he took on the commission, although the ordinatio of the texts, including the unprecedented decision to lay *Piers Plowman* out as prose rather than as long lines, might imply a lack of familiarity with the copying of literary texts.

What remains unclear from this identification is whether the production of Digby 102 was connected in any way with the Brewers' Guild itself, or whether

---

[17] *Parish Fraternity Register: Fraternity of the Holy Trinity and SS. Fabian and Sebastian (Parish of St Botolph without Aldersgate)*, ed. by Patricia Basing (London: London Record Society, 1982), pp. 38–68.

[18] M. L. Samuels, 'Langland's Dialect', *Medium Ævum*, 54 (1985), 232–47 (repr. in *The English of Chaucer and his Contemporaries: Essays by M. L. Samuels and J. J. Smith*, ed. by J. J. Smith (Aberdeen: Aberdeen University Press, 1988), pp. 70–85).

it was an entirely separate commission. The dates for the scribe's contribution to the Brewers' Minute Book fit with the conventional dating of Digby 102 to the first quarter of the fifteenth century, although it suggests that the latter part of that period is more likely than earlier, and possibly even later still. In her recent edition of the twenty-four lyric poems that appear on folios 98^r–127^v of this manuscript, Helen Barr reports the view of Ralph Hanna that the manuscript is no later than 1430 and '"possibly a good deal earlier" (i.e. as early as 1400–10 potentially, and certainly there is no problem about it being second decade of the fifteenth century)'.[19] The Digby poems were first edited by Joseph Kail in 1904, in which edition he presented them as a chronological sequence, stretching from 1401 to 1421.[20] The dating of the individual poems was based upon Kail's identification of specific political allusions which allowed him to link them with particular parliaments or historical events. Earlier datings of the Digby manuscript have placed its production in the first quarter of the fifteenth century, although it seems likely that these were influenced to a certain extent upon Kail's sequence.[21] In her new edition Barr has convincingly demolished the basis for these datings, arguing that the few genuine historical allusions fit better with the early years of the reign of Henry V, especially the period 1413–14.[22] Barr's revised dating of these poems fits with the later date that is suggested by the evidence of this scribe's work for the Brewers' Guild.

Research into the identities and professional associations of the scribes responsible for copying literary texts in early fifteenth-century London has uncovered a number of prominent scriveners with connections to the London guilds. Adam Pinkhurst, the copyist of important Chaucerian and Langlandian manuscripts mentioned above, was employed by the Mercers' Guild to copy their

---

[19] Helen Barr, *The Digby Poems: A New Edition of the Lyrics* (Exeter: Exeter University Press, 2009), p. 1 n. 1.

[20] *Twenty-Six Political and Other Poems*, ed. by Joseph Kail, Early English Text Society, o.s., 124 (London: Kegan Paul, Trench, Trübner, 1904).

[21] See, for example, R. H. Robbins's discussion of the collection of political poems, which he considers to be a 'closet' production by a single author. Robbins dates the manuscript itself to the first quarter of the fifteenth century but does not include any discussion of the other texts within the manuscript, nor does he provide any basis for his dating. See *A Manual of the Writings in Middle English, 1050–1500: Volume V*, ed. by Albert E. Hartung and others (New Haven: Connecticut Academy of Arts and Sciences, 1975), pp. 1416–22. R. W. Hunt and A. G. Watson provide the dating 's. xv in.' in their revised edition of the catalogue of the Digby manuscripts. See *Bodleian Library Quarto Catalogues*, pp. 116–17.

[22] See Barr, *The Digby Poems*, p. 18.

accounts and their petition of 1387/88.[23] He was also involved in several property transactions with members of the guild, and may have been physically located in their meeting place, the hospital of St Thomas of Acon. Jeremy Griffiths identified the scribe of the Petworth House manuscript of the *Canterbury Tales*, who also copied deluxe manuscripts of Nicholas Love's *Mirror of the Blessed Life of Jesus Christ*, Gower's *Confessio Amantis* and other works, copying entries in the records of the London Skinners' Guild.[24] Thomas Usk, a professional scribe with literary interests, was employed as a scrivener by John of Northampton and by the Goldsmiths' Guild to copy their account book.[25] How formal these associations between scribes and guilds were in this period is as yet unclear. It is likely that full-time professional scriveners like Pinkhurst and Usk would have taken on a variety of copying tasks for customers from a diversity of backgrounds and affiliations, although it seems plausible to assume that prospective patrons who were members of a particular guild would turn to their own clerk when commissioning a manuscript copy of a particular work.

The similarity in the professional profile of these scribes might help to explain the textual affiliations between certain copies of the C text. I noted above Russell and Kane's view that the close textual relationship between these copies of the *i*-group implied their being copied in a 'centre.' However, in their seminal analysis of the London book trade in the early fifteenth century Doyle and Parkes found little evidence for the existence of centralized scriptoria.[26] Their view of the book

---

[23] For the identification of scribe B as Adam Pinkhurst and his work for the Mercers' Guild see Mooney, 'Chaucer's Scribe'. For the attribution of a copy of the B version of *Piers Plowman* to this scribe see Simon Horobin and Linne R. Mooney, 'A *Piers Plowman* Manuscript by the Hengwrt/Ellesmere Scribe and its Implications for London Standard English', *Studies in the Age of Chaucer*, 26 (2004), 65–112.

[24] This identification is discussed by A. I. Doyle in 'The Study of Nicholas Love's *Mirror*, Retrospect and Prospect', in *Nicholas Love at Waseda: Proceedings of the International Conference, 20–22 July 1995*, ed. by Shoichi Oguro, Richard Beadle, and Michael G. Sargent (Cambridge: Brewer, 1997), pp. 163–74.

[25] Caroline Barron announced the identification of Usk as a scribe for the Goldsmiths' Guild in a paper entitled 'New Evidence of Usk' delivered to the Fifteenth International Congress of the New Chaucer Society on 29 July 2006 at Fordham University, New York City. On the implications of this identification see Marion Turner, 'Usk and the Goldsmiths', *New Medieval Literatures*, 9 (2008), 139–77.

[26] A. I. Doyle and Malcolm Parkes, 'Production of Copies of the *Canterbury Tales* and the *Confessio Amantis* in the Early Fifteenth Century', in *Medieval Scribes, Manuscripts and Libraries: Essays Presented to N. R. Ker*, ed. by V. J. Scattergood and Andrew G. Watson (London: Scolar, 1978), pp. 163–210.

trade as operated by freelance independent professionals is supported by my identification of the scribe of Digby 102, who was evidently not a member of a commercial scriptorium or bookshop. However, the similar professional associations shared by a number of professional scribes active in the early fifteenth century help to explain the patterns of textual affiliation which would emerge from the sharing of exemplars among neighbouring colleagues. The Brewers' Hall was situated close to the halls of many other London Guilds, such as those occupied by the Bowyers, Barbers, Pinners, Curriers, and Girdlers, while the hospital of St Thomas Acon and the Mercers' Hall were just a short walk in the direction of Cheapside.[27] In the midst of this area stood the imposing Guildhall, with its impressive library founded under the terms of the bequest of the mercers Richard Whittington and William Bury.[28] The entries in the Brewers' book record numerous transactions between the guild and the Guildhall, and its various officers, particularly with the chamberlain, Sir John Bederenden. Such transactions meant that the guild clerks would have needed to make regular trips to the Guildhall and would have been familiar with the clerks employed there to record the business of its meetings. Among these clerks was the scribe who copied San Marino, Huntington, MS Hm 114, containing a copy of the B text of *Piers Plowman* with additions from A and C, as well as a copy of Chaucer's *Troilus and Criseyde* and Mandeville's *Travels*.[29] This scribe was evidently closely involved in the copying and circulation of vernacular literary works in this period; his hand is also found in another copy of Chaucer's *Troilus and Criseyde*, now London, British Library, MS Harley 3943, as well as a miscellaneous volume containing the *Siege of Jerusalem*, the *Prose Brut*, and other texts, now London, Lambeth Palace, MS 491, Part I.[30] This scribe can be located at the Guildhall through his association with the city's Common clerk, John Carpenter, who assembled the city's own memorandum book, known as the *Liber Albus*, and who was the principal executor of Richard Whittington and a leader in the establishment of the Guildhall library.

---

[27] See the map in Caroline M. Barron, *London in the Later Middle Ages* (Oxford: Oxford University Press, 2004), p. 410.

[28] On the foundation of the Guildhall library see Nicholas Orme, *Medieval Schools: From Roman Britain to Renaissance England* (New Haven: Yale University Press, 2006), p. 84.

[29] On this scribe and his copying career see Ralph Hanna III, 'The Scribe of Huntington HM 114', *Studies in Bibliography*, 42 (1989), 120–33.

[30] The Hm 114 scribe copied fols 2–7ᵛ, 9–56ᵛ, 63–67ᵛ of Harley 3943. For a description of Lambeth Palace, MS 491 see *The Siege of Jerusalem*, ed. by Ralph Hanna and David Lawton, Early English Text Society, o.s., 320 (Oxford: Oxford University Press, 2003), pp. xx–xxiii.

The entries in this volume were copied by a variety of different hands; the hand of Hm 114 appears in an organizational capacity, adding marginalia, running heads, and a table of contents.[31] The interaction between the scribe of Digby 102 and that of Hm 114, and other clerks employed by the various London guilds at the Guildhall, may well explain the close relationship between the early copies of the C text observed by Russell and Kane. Rather than being based in a scriptorium or copying centre, a more plausible scenario would see these scribes engaging in a policy of sharing of exemplars, perhaps through connections between the various guilds and especially via contacts at the London Guildhall.[32]

I suggested earlier that it may have been the practice for members of a guild to engage their own clerks when commissioning a manuscript. Unfortunately there is no evidence in Digby 102 as to its early provenance. One prominent member of the Brewers' Guild can be connected indirectly with a copy of the poem owned by William Palmere, rector of St Alphage, Cripplegate, which he bequeathed to Agnes Eggesfeld in his will of 1400. Palmere's will also includes a bequest of a breviary to William, chaplain to John Hore; Hore was a brewer and a prominent parishioner in the parish of St Alphage. In 1379 Hore was appointed a collector of the subsidy of the poll tax for the ward of Cripplegate and he served as Common Counsellor from 1384 to 1388. He owned substantial property in the parish of St Alphage and he left money to the Brewers' Guild and to the parish church, where he was buried on his death in 1413.[33] Although Palmere's will does not include a bequest to John Hore, Hore's close connection with the church of St Alphage, and thus with its parish priest, means that the two men must have known each other well. Given the close proximity of the parish church of St Alphage and the Brewers' Hall, Hore was probably not the only member of the Brewers' Guild to be a member of the parish church of St Alphage and thus known to its parish priest William Palmere.[34]

---

[31] The identification of this scribe's hand in the *Liber Albus* as well as in the Corporation of London Record Office, Letterbook I is reported by Ralph Hanna in *London Literature, 1300–1380* (Cambridge: Cambridge University Press, 2005), pp. 28–29.

[32] My analysis of the corrections found in the a copy of the B version of *Piers Plowman*, now British Library, MS Additional 35287, which I attributed to the hand of Adam Pinkhurst, is also suggestive of collaboration and cooperation among the earliest copyists of the B version. See Simon Horobin, 'Adam Pinkhurst and the Copying of British Library MS Additional 35287 of the B text of *Piers Plowman*', *YLS*, 23 (2009), 61–83.

[33] Robert A. Wood, 'A Fourteenth-Century London Owner of *Piers Plowman*', *Medium Ævum*, 53 (1984), 83–89 (p. 88).

[34] See the map printed in Barron, *London in the Later Middle Ages*, p. 410.

Piers Plowman makes a number of references to brewers and would have been of considerable interest to members of that guild, although one wonders what they would have made of Langland's depiction of their trade. In a passage in passus 3 Langland accuses the Brewers, and other victualling guilds, of getting rich through the practice of *regraterye*, buying up goods cheaply and selling them at a substantially increased price, a practice specifically condemned in guild ordinances:

> Bothe Schyreues and seriauntes and suche as kepeth lawes,
> To punischen on pilories and on pynyng stoles
> As Bakeres and Breweres, Bocheres and cokes;
> For thyse men don most harm to þe mene peple,
> Rychen thorw regraterye and rentes hem beggeth
> With that þe pore peple sholde potte in her wombe[35]

In addition to this accusation of overpricing of goods, the passage goes on to associate these tradesmen with charging inflated prices while providing short measures: 'thei fillen nat ful þat for lawe is seled' (C.3.88). There has been no attempt to edit or revise this passage in the Digby manuscript, despite the clear attack on the retail practices of the brewers. A further reference to brewers later in the same passus is equally unflattering in blaming them for the frequent fires that destroy people's houses:

> Al this haue we seyn, þat som tyme thorw a breware
> Many burgages ybrent and bodies þerynne
> And thorw a candle clemynge in a cursed place
> Ful adoun and forbrent forth alle þe rewe
>
> (C.3.104–07)

Once again the Digby scribe simply reproduces the passage without comment or any attempt to mitigate its criticisms of the brewers' trade. It may be that such accusations were of only secondary interest to the scribe and his readers; perhaps of greater relevance was the subsequent appeal to the Mayor which follows this passage. Here Langland specifically admonishes the Mayor to take great care to ensure that userers and regraters are not allowed to become freemen, in spite of the bribes that they offer:

[35] *The C Version*, ed. by Russell and Kane, 3.78–83. All quotations of the C Version are taken from this edition.

> Forthy mayres þat maketh fre men, me thynketh þat ȝe ouhten
> For to spyre and to aspye, for eny speche of suluer,
> What maner muster oþer marchandise he vsed
> Ar he were vnderfonge fre and felawe in ȝoure rolles.
> Hit is nat seemely, forsothe, in Citee ne in borw toun
> That vsurers oþer regraters for eny skynes ȝeftes
> Be yfranchised for a fre man and haue a fals name.

(C.3.108–14)

In this passage the focus turns to the Mayor and various city officials, who are urged to resist the allure of bribes offered by Lady Meed despite the 'riche handes' of these 'regraters'. Here it is the mayors that become responsible for suppressing and punishing illegal trade practices rather than the individual guilds themselves. This transfer of responsibility from the brewers on to the mayors is made apparent by the quotation from Job 15. 34 at line 3.124: 'Ignis deuorabit tabernacula eorum qui libenter accipiunt munera', in which those who accept bribes become the cause of the fires that destroy their homes. This call upon the Mayor to behave fairly and appropriately would have certainly appealed to the Brewers' Guild, for whom the Mayor was a figure of considerable authority and significance. Many of the entries in the Brewers' book register their attempts to remain on friendly terms with the Mayor and to ensure election of a candidate who was sensitive to their interests. An especially bleak period for the brewers was the third term of office of Richard Whittington (1419–20), who was particularly draconian in his attempts to regulate the price of ale and the measurements by which it was sold.[36] The lowly status of the brewers and other retailers of food and drink, and the suspicion with which they were treated by the civic authorities, is apparent from their treatment in the *Liber Albus*. Brewers are among the group of tradespeople that are specifically excluded from holding civic office, and are subject to stringent legislation. Under city legislation infringements of the assize of ale could be interpreted as an act of rebellion, while a refusal to maintain an appropriate supply of ale could be seen as a deliberate attempt to withhold victuals from the city.[37]

Even during periods out of the mayoral office Whittington is directly blamed for the mistreatment of the Brewers' Guild and their masters, as is well illustrated

---

[36] Anne F. Sutton, 'Whittington, Richard (*c.*1350–1423)', *Oxford Dictionary of National Biography* (Oxford: Oxford University Press, 2004), <http://www.oxforddnb.com/view/article/29330> [accessed 14 September 2009].

[37] See Helen Carrel, 'Food, Drink and Public Order in the London *Liber Albus*', *Urban History*, 33 (2006), 176–94.

in an entry on folio 69ᵛ, dated 1422. On 30 July of this year, during the mayoralty of Robert Chichele, the masters of the Brewers' Guild were summoned to appear before the Mayor at the Guildhall. On their appearance they were accused of overcharging for their ale, given the low prices at which malt was currently being sold. The guild members were also accused of deliberately inflating the price of malt by creating a shortage by riding throughout the country and buying up all available stocks: 'men seyden atte that tyme that Breweres wer cause of the derthe of malt, with her riding yn to diuerse Contrees to bie malt'. Richard Whittington himself specifically accused the Brewers of forestalling: 'And be mocion of Richard Whityngton, ther beyng present, he seid to the Breweres that they had reden yn to the Contre and forstalled malt, wher-fore hit caused malt to be soo dere.' Despite the overall authority of the Mayor, who was also present at this hearing, it is clear that the Brewers attributed this shameful mistreatment to the machinations of Richard Whittington. At the very beginning of the account, they note that the Mayor sent for the brewers 'at a Suggestion made be Richard Whityngton'. The Mayor commanded the clerk of the Guildhall, John Carpenter, to read an ordinance drawn up during the mayoralty of Richard Whittington, obliging them to pay a bond of twenty pounds towards the upkeep of the Guild-hall. As a result the Mayor commanded that the masters of the guild should be imprisoned by the Chamberlain until they pay the sum required in full. However, once the Mayor and the aldermen left, the Chamberlain and John Carpenter released them without charge because the charges had only been made to please Whittington, 'for he was cause of alle the forsaid Juggement.' John Carpenter was a favourite of Whittington's, as shown in his appointment as chief executor of Whittington's will; it was his diplomacy that mitigated the harshness of Whit-tington's attitude towards the brewers during his third term of office.

This account is of interest for a number of reasons. Firstly it witnesses to the seething animosity between Whittington and the brewers, and the importance of good relations between the guild and the Mayor for the success of the trade and their members. Secondly, the accusations made against the brewers, the practice of forestalling, or *regraterye*, is precisely that which Brewers and other trade guilds are accused of in *Piers*, C.3.82. Given the Brewers' animosity towards Whitting-ton, and the importance of amiable relations between the guild and the Mayor, it may be that it was Langland's exhortation of the Mayor that was of primary interest in this passage. Yet there is an irony here, given that other entries in the Brewers' book make regular reference to their practice of offering bribes to newly appointed mayors. On folio 113ʳ there is a record dated to 1423 noting that Mayor William Crowmer refused their offer of gifts or rewards but yet thanked them profusely and promised to look after their interests: 'And also he thanked hem as meche as thow he hadde receyued hem, and he made promys to be good Frende to hem be all his ȝer, and so he was.'[38] Other mayors were more susceptible to the charms of Lady Meed: William Waldere, having treated the brewers well throughout his reign began to cause trouble during the final weeks before his retirement in 1422. The Brewers responded by presenting him with a bear and an ox, worth 20s and 17s respectively, thus ensuring better treatment.[39] On his appointment to the mayoralty in 1425, the Brewers presented John Michell with an ox and a boar, thereby protecting their interests throughout his reign: 'To þe wheche John Michell, be a comon assent of þe craffte of Brewers, after þat þe seide John was chosen Mair of london, aforn þat he dede take his Oth at Westmonster, we dede ȝeve hym an Ox, pris xxjs. ii d., and an Bore, þe pris of xxx s. j d. And so, yn þe ȝere of þe same John Mair of london, he dede no harme ne desese to þe seide Craffte of Brewers.'[40]

Elsewhere in the poem brewers are generally portrayed negatively, as in the depiction of Covetyse's wife, who combines her business as a webber with brewing, in which she employs a number of the tricks of the trade specifically outlawed in the city's ordinances. She dilutes the strongest ale with the weaker 'peny ale' (C.6.226) and keeps the best quality brew in her own bedchamber. She is named 'Rose þe regrater' (C.6.232), further linking brewers with the practice of *regraterye*. While this was not an illegal practice, it was legislated against in detail in the city and guild ordinances. She is also linked with the practice of *hokkerye*: employing hucksters to sell her ale on the doorstep, another practice outlawed by the city's trade regulations.

However, in spite of this negative depiction of the brewers trade, members of the guild may have taken comfort from the poem's vision of a community where the honest practice of trade forms a valid and valuable contribution to the commune. Where earlier depictions of the ideal community are posited upon an agrarian model, in passus 21 we see a validation of urban traders as acceptable members of the Christian community. Here Grace distributes favour to a variety of trades and professions, not simply those belonging to the traditional model of

---

[38] *A Book of London English*, ed. by Chambers and Daunt, p. 182.

[39] Brewers' Memorandum Book, fols 72ᵛ–73ʳ.

[40] Brewers' Memorandum Book, fols 120ᵛ–121ʳ; printed in *A Book of London English*, ed. by Chambers and Daunt, p. 189.

the three estates. Langland's vision here is of a community where craft guilds are in harmony, loving one another and eschewing discord:[41]

> And al he lered to be lele, and vch a craft loue oþere,
> Ne no boest ne debaet be among hem alle.
> 'Thouh somme be clenner then somme, 3e sen wel', quod grace,
> 'That all craft and connyng come of my 3efte
> Loke þat noen lacke oþere bute loueth as bretherne
> And ho þat moest maistries can be myldest of berynge.'
>
> (C.21.250–55)

The importance of harmony and the resolution of strife between the members of different craft guilds is also a recurrent theme of the the poems found on folios 98ʳ–127ᵛ. In keeping with the poems' universal appeal, specific guilds and disagreements are not mentioned, but it seems likely that the poet's cautioning against disputes between guilds would have had a particular relevance to the members of the Brewers' guild in this period. For instance, Poem 3, titled 'Treuth, reste and pes', urges peaceful resolution of craft disputes:[42]

> Whan craft riseþ a3ens craft,
> In burgh, toun, or cite,
> Þey go to lordes whan lawe is laft,
> Whoche party may strengere be,
> But wyse men þe sonere se.
> By witles wille þey gedre pres,
> Or lordis medle in foly degree.
> Let lawe haue cours in reste and pes.
>
> (ll. 33–40)

Poem 16, which enumerates the 52 follies of Flanders, includes a reference to the foolishness of violent disputes between crafts:

> Flaundres was þe richest land and meriest to mynne,
> Now is it wrappid in wo and moche welþe raft,
> For defaute of iustice and singulere to wynne,
> Þey were rebell to ryse craft a3en craft.
>
> (ll. 57–60)

---

[41] James Simpson has discussed the relevance of the model outlined here for the craft disputes of the 1380s; see '"After Craftes Conseil clotheth yow and fede": Langland and London City Politics', in *England in the Fourteenth Century: Proceedings of the 1991 Harlaxton Medieval Conference*, ed. by Nicholas Rogers (Stamford: Tyas, 1993), pp. 109–27.

[42] These poems are quoted from Barr, *The Digby Poems*.

Part of the solution to inter-craft disputes is for those in positions of authority to remain impartial in their treatment of individual crafts, to 'loue al crafty folk yliche' (Poem 14, l. 35). This vision of a harmonious society must begin with harmony within the household; the poet's image of a household where 'Trouþe is worschiped at euery des' (Poem 3, l. 6) might have functioned as an idealized image for the Brewers of their own hall.

The Digby poems are repeatedly concerned with stressing the value of corporate unity over the self-seeking desire for 'synguler profyt'. The poet's desire to see concord between men is intimately linked to the need for concord between man and God, symbolized more fully in the sacrament of the Eucharist:

> 3e haue resceyued 3oure God of my3t;
> Ayþer in oþer 3oure wille is on.
> 3oure hertys were heuy; þey may be li3t:
> Glade in God — 3e ben at on!
> (Poem 11, ll. 77–80)

This emphasis on personal spirituality highlights a theme that unites all of the texts found in Digby 102, especially prominent in Richard of Maidstone's metrical paraphrase of the *Seven Penitential Psalms*, a poem which meditates on the penitential psalms and on the cycle of penitence and redemption. Some twenty-seven copies of the work survive, a number of which were owned by members of religious houses and parish priests, while others were owned by laymen. Maidstone's text is most commonly accompanied by the *Prick of Conscience* and other orthodox devotional texts, such as the works of Richard Rolle, the *Lay Folk's Mass Book*, and Lydgate's *Life of our Lady*.[43] The highly conventional and orthodox nature of Maidstone's rendering of the Psalms, with its simple message urging the personal recognition of sin and the need for salvation, serves to accentuate such themes in *Piers Plowman*, playing down its engagement with theologically and socially challenging issues. Maidstone's tendency to render the Psalms in terms that focus on Catholic sacraments, such as Psalm 37, which is presented as a straightforward confession and plea for mercy, or Psalm 50, a sinner's call for God's grace, further narrows the interpretative framework within which the Digby texts may be read. The allegorical reading of Psalm 101, in which the poor man petitioning God in his hour of need becomes Christ on the Cross reassuring the sinner through an account of his sacrifice, distances the text from a literal interpretation. This

---

[43] For brief descriptions of the manuscripts and their patterns of ownership see *Richard Maidstone's Penitential Psalms*, ed. by Valerie Edden (Heidelberg: Carl Winter, 1990), pp. 11–20.

rendering of the psalm forms a natural continuation to *Piers Plowman*, passus 20, with its account of the Crucifixion and the dreamer's response in which he calls his wife and daughter to Mass.

Personal faith and salvation are central to *Piers Plowman* too, but their prominence in the Digby 102 copy of this text is accentuated by two substantial additions to the text. The first of these additions appears after 14.193 and reads as follows:

> Iob was a paynym & plesede god at prys
> And arystotle also sewed þe same secte
> And ful holy lyf ladde after lawe of kynde
> Wherfor it semeth soþely by sondry skeles to schewe
> That he is saf as was Iob y can not wete þe soþe
>
> (fol. 53ᵛ)

This interpolation comes in the midst of a learned debate between Will and Imaginatif concerning the salvation of heathens. At this stage in the debate Imaginatif remains agnostic about the fate of learned pagans like Socrates and Aristotle, although Will's response is less open to the possibility of their salvation. The addition found in Digby 102 weights the argument in favour of the salvation of the heathen, giving greater support to the view that Aristotle's learning and righteous living was pleasing to God, despite his paganism. These lines are additions in the sense that they do not belong in the archetypal text as far as that can be reconstructed, but they are also physical additions to Digby 102 in that they are written at the foot of the page in a different hand. Comparison with other manuscripts of the C version reveals that the same lines appear in four other copies: Cambridge University Library, MS Additional 4325 (Q); Cambridge, Corpus Christi College, MS 293 (S); Oxford, Bodleian Library, MS Bodley 851 (Z); and Duke of Westminster's MS (W).[44] The appearance of these lines in these four manuscripts may be explained by the fact that there is a clear genetic relationship between these copies of the C text, as outlined by Russell and Kane.[45] But what is less apparent is how the lines should have been transmitted to Digby 102. Two of these manuscripts have been localized to the South-West Midlands: CUL, Add. 4325 has been localized to North-West Gloucestershire, Corpus 293 to South Herefordshire, while the C addition found in Bodley 851 has been written in an East Anglian dialect consonant with its associations with Ramsey

---

[44] This manuscript is now York, Borthwick Institute, MS Additional 196.

[45] See *The C Version*, ed. by Russell and Kane, pp. 49–50.

Abbey in Huntingdonshire.[46] The Duke of Westminster's manuscript, however, shows signs of a London origin. Ian Doyle likened the 'elegant set secretary' script of its main hand to those used by Privy Seal and other official scribes of the beginning of the fifteenth century, leading him to conclude that it may have been 'commissioned and executed in that milieu'.[47] The appearance of these additional lines in Digby 102 does not, of course, mean that they were added from the Westminster manuscript itself. However, it is clear that they have been added after the copying of the text, presumably by comparison with another witness. The Westminster context suggested by Doyle for the production of W fits well with the London guild associations I have already noted for Digby 102 and its associated manuscripts, and would help to explain how a scribe came to access a copy of the poem containing these additional lines and include them in Digby 102.

There is a further supplementary passage which has also been added to Digby 102 in a different hand after 16.89:

> And þou3 þe pore wolde holde eneuye in his herte
> He may not greue no gost so gretly as hymsulue
> For his eneuye may do non harm to hye ne to lowe
> Bote his owen carful cors he croneth neyh to deþe
> Wherfor pore pacient may no puyre enuye haue
> Bote eneuye mot fle hym fro for his pacient herte
>
> (fol. 59ᵛ)

These lines differ from the previous addition in that they are not found in any other copy of the poem. They also reveal a different focus from the concern with trade practices and London city politics that we have been discussing so far, emphasizing the theme of patient poverty. Here the concern is to reinforce the poem's call for the poor to remain strong and spiritually firm, despite the weakness of poverty in the face of the combined strength of Covetise and Avarice. The emphasis is upon a personal response and the need to remain pure in heart for the good of one's body and soul. Here the added lines foreground a penitential focus that provides a central theme for the contents of the manuscript as a whole. The

[46] On the dialects of these manuscripts see Samuels, 'Langland's Dialect'.

[47] A. I. Doyle, 'Remarks on Surviving Manuscripts of *Piers Plowman*', in *Medieval English Religious and Ethical Literature: Essays in Honour of G.H. Russell*, ed. by Gregory Kratzmann and James Simpson (Cambridge: Brewer, 1986), pp. 35–48 (p. 46).

appearance of these additions in the margins of the manuscript indicates that the second scribe worked after the first had completed his copying of the text of *Piers*.

The presence of a third brief addition to the final text, *The Debate between the Body and the Soul*, on folio 136ʳ is of a different kind in that it makes good an omission of a line accidentally missed by the main scribe: 'and litil had serued god to pay.' There is one correction of this kind in *Piers Plowman*, where the second scribe has added the omitted line 'And margarete of her maydenhod as he mette her late' at the foot of folio 9ᵛ (see Fig. 2). These two corrections of errors in copying imply that the second scribe checked the work of the main hand against an exemplar, and that he oversaw the entire production process and not just that of *Piers Plowman*. This might be taken to suggest that the manuscript remained close to the place of copying for some time. But the evidence does not require this interpretation. The presence of the correcting scribe's hand at both the beginning and the end of the manuscript indicates that he was involved in overseeing the entire production process, but this could have been done immediately following the main scribe's completion of his work rather than at a later date. The presence of just two such corrections of the text by this hand implies a much more casual approach to the process of overseeing, or supervising the work than is suggested by the modern terms *corrector* or *supervisor*. Indeed the missing line restored by this correcting hand at the opening of *The Debate between the Body and the Soul* could have been added from memory rather than by collation against the exemplar. Any reader who knew the opening stanza by heart would have readily noted the omission and been able to supply the missing line.

The penitential theme highlighted by the unique addition to *Piers* is well expressed in the collection of lyrics first edited by Kail and recently re-edited by Helen Barr. While Kail sought to read these poems as direct responses to political events of the early fifteenth century, Barr notes the emphasis on the values of individual spirituality and support for the institutional church and its sacraments. Vincent Gillespie has written of how meditational lyrics like those of Digby 102 'provided the lexical groundswell that carried many moral and penitential commonplaces out into the devotional and didactic mainstream'.[48] The revised dating offered by Barr and the dates of the Brewers' accounts suggest that the poems had not travelled far before they were included into Digby 102. Although there is no indication of authorship, Barr argues that the author's awareness of parliamentary business and international affairs, combined with his support for Henry V, sug-

---

[48] Vincent Gillespie, 'Moral and Penitential Lyrics', in *A Companion to the Middle English Lyric*, ed. by Thomas G. Duncan (Cambridge: Brewer, 2005), pp. 68–95 (p. 71).

gests that he was based in the King's household. The authorial dialect is a mixed variety which further suggests a London origin, although the presence of a number of South-West Midland forms might indicate that the author was originally of provincial origins, like Langland himself. Numerous parallels between the Digby lyrics and a series of macaronic sermons in Oxford, Bodleian Library, MS Bodley 649, written by a Benedictine monk trained at Oxford, are suggestive of Benedictine authorship, and Barr offers two possible candidates: John Paunteley, monk of St Peter's Gloucestershire, owner of Oxford, Bodleian Library, MS Laud misc. 706, which contains several of the sermons in Bodley 649, and Hugh of Morton, Abbot of St Peter's Gloucestershire and a receiver of petitions at the 1416 Westminster parliament.

The support for the new monarchy apparent from this reading of the poems is consonant with the pro-Henrician attitude revealed in the Brewers' book. This is most evident in their decision in 1422 to switch from French to English as the language of their records, a determination made in direct response to the use of the vernacular by Henry V for his royal missives. This decision is recorded in Latin on folio 69ᵛ of the Brewers' book where it marks a definite switch to English in the records, with occasional lapses into French or Latin.[49]

In addition to the penitential focus offered by the Digby poems, the frequent use of accounting imagery in the treatment of sin and restitution may have held a particular relevance for the scribe who was also responsible for maintaining the Brewers' accounts. Poem 8 describes the accumulation of sin as 'rerage' (l. 100), while Poem 9 instructs the reader to 'Rekene, er þu renne in rerage' (l. 103). This image is elaborated most fully in Poem 11:

> Thow nost how sone be after sent
> To ȝelde rekenyng of Goddis lon.
> The rolles of rerage þe fendis han brent;
> For God and man is wel at on.
>
> (ll. 109–12)

More specific references to malpractice engaged in by those involved in trade would have had a particular resonance for the Brewers' guild, especially as here it is coin-clippers, drapers, and lawyers who are singled out for castigation (see Poem 9, ll. 49–56).

---

[49] For the Latin text see *A Book of London English*, ed. by Chambers and Daunt, p. 16; an English translation is included on p. 139.

Although it remains unclear whether my identification of the scribe of Digby 102 as a clerk working for the Brewers' Guild indicates that the manuscript was commissioned by a member of that guild, it is apparent that its contents would have had considerable relevance for its members and their clerks. Despite the uncertainty that remains concerning the manuscript's commissioning and readership, this identification makes clear the London provenance of its production and consumption, and helps to suggest connections between its scribe and those responsible for contemporary copies of *Piers Plowman*. This essay has also highlighted the importance of the identification of the scribes of our extant witnesses as an index to the poem's early readership, an importance also recognized by John Bowers: '[W]e would indeed like to know more about these copyists, where they worked, what were their institutional affiliations (if any), to what larger communities their efforts might have been directed, and what significances they attached to their texts.'[50] The lack of centralized scriptoria in London during the early fifteenth century means that scribes occupied a prominent role in the organization of the various process involved in producing copies of vernacular literary works and are thus central figures in the literary culture of late medieval London.[51]

[50] John M. Bowers, 'Piers Plowman and the Police: Notes Towards a History of the Wycliffite Langland', *YLS*, 6 (1992), 1–50 (p. 20). See also his more recent remarks in *Chaucer and Langland: The Antagonistic Tradition* (Notre Dame: University of Notre Dame Press, 2007), p. 130.

[51] Research for this article was carried out as part of a project entitled 'The Identification of Scribes Responsible for Copying Major Works of Middle English Literature', currently being undertaken by the author, Professor Linne Mooney, and Dr Estelle Stubbs of the University of York. The project is supported by a four-year grant from the UK Arts and Humanities Research Council and aims to examine all the manuscripts containing the works of Chaucer, Gower, Langland, Hoccleve, and Trevisa. I am grateful to both Professor Mooney and Dr Stubbs for helpful comments on a draft of this essay. I am also indebted to Dr Lawrence Warner and Professor Michael Calabrese and Roger Nicholson for detailed criticisms and suggestions for improvement.

Commentary on an Unacknowledged Text: Chaucer's Debt to Langland

Anne Middleton

In street, in tavern, happening would cry:
'I am myself, but part of something greater;
Find poets what that is; do not pass by.
For feel my fingers in your pia mater.
I am a cruelly insistent friend;
You cannot smile on me and make an end'.

—Thom Gunn, 'A Mirror for Poets'

I t is a truth universally acknowledged that Chaucer owes to Langland nothing of fundamental or systematic importance for his own poetic practice. Haunted and defined by his relations to 'olde bokes' written anywhere but England, Chaucer became the father of English poetry by working through his debts to Ovid, Virgil, the *Romance of the Rose*, Dante, Boccaccio, and other Continental predecessors and contemporaries, and it is the tracing of these debts and squaring of these accounts that have until recently virtually defined Chaucer studies — and chiefly as 'source' studies.

But Langland? While for George Kane Chaucer and Langland are 'an obligatory conjunction', and he rightly finds several shared imaginative and constructive practices, notably including artfully enigmatic poetic self-presentation, the terms of discussion connecting the two poets have chiefly taken the form of suggestive

Anne Middleton (*middletona@berkeley.edu*) is Professor Emerita of English, University of California, Berkeley.

Abstract: This essay examines Chaucer's formal and ideational tribute to his older contemporary in the figure and performance of the Pardoner, a tribute enacted not primarily in local adversions and echoes, but in the sustained appreciation of the poetics of Langland's enterprise, and of its dilemmas of literary form and modes of address. Chaucer also displays, in the improprieties of gender, age, and vocation that characterize this virtuoso of penitential rhetoric, his anatomy of the structural as well as affective hazards of Langland's complex literary project, and its implications for his own, perhaps equally unfinishable, long poetic fiction.

Keywords: Geoffrey Chaucer, William Langland, the Pardoner's Prologue, the *Pardoner's Tale*, *Piers Plowman*, literary influence, literary history, penitential rhetoric, gender, sexuality.

10.1484/J.YLS.1.102111

analogies of this sort, which testify to a 'spirit of the age' in which both participate, without, so to speak, the mediation of human hands, craft-knowledge, or
intentions — without, in other words, a historical syntax.[1] I want to argue here
that Chaucer learned late, but deeply, from Langland — and that what he
learned did not merely suggest or enable certain details of the Canterbury project
(and it is such local aspects of the influence that have most often been remarked),
but ultimately gave to that project a clear vision of its limits. Langland represents
the return of the repressed in Chaucer's career, and his mark in the *Canterbury
Tales* is as deep as it is unacknowledged openly by Chaucer. It has stood un-
remarked for all these centuries largely because of the success of that repression as
realized in the way we do literary history in English.

In the larger project of which this paper is no more than a sample, I have two
main tasks in demonstrating Langland's impact on Chaucer's production and the
form of his literary career: crudely put, I divide my attention between the 'how'
of that impact and the 'why' of it. Under the first heading, which will occupy most
of my attention here, I examine one indicative instance of where and in what
forms, and to what effects, Langland's enterprise is registered in Chaucer's; under
the second, I consider why, if my sketchy account of the nature of Langland's
influence on Chaucer is even partly plausible, did it take the form it did, as what
is still one of the best-kept secrets of early English literary history? I will attempt
to offer some very tentative and brief answers to the second question in conclusion.

In apportioning my labours between the 'how' and the 'why' of this literary
relationship, I have already begged or finessed the question of 'whether': I have
elided from the start the logically prior task of demonstrating, in the face of
almost complete critical silence on the topic, *that* such a relation exists. I believe
I am justified in doing so by the several claims of borrowing, allusion, suggestion,
or other forms of local intertextuality that have already been made over the
decades. I take it as axiomatic, however, that no literary artist merely appropriates
local bits and pieces, magpie-like, from an antecedent work unless that work exerts

---

[1] George Kane, 'Chaucer and Langland: An Obligatory Conjunction', in *New Perspectives in
Chaucer Criticism*, ed. by Donald M. Rose (Norman, OK: Pilgrim, 1981), pp. 5–19 (repr. in
Chaucer and Langland: Historical and Textual Approaches (London: Athlone; Berkeley and Los
Angles: University of California Press, 1989), pp. 123–33); also, in the latter volume (pp. 134–
49), 'Chaucer and Langland II'. For a recent exploration of this conjunction, see John M. Bowers,
Chaucer and Langland: The Antagonistic Tradition (Notre Dame: University of Notre Dame
Press, 2007), chaps 2, 4.

some broader fascination, unless it also answers questions and offers formal and modal examples to the appropriating poet that are available to him in no comparably compelling form and synthesis anywhere else. Only relatively recently have several critics begun to identify some of the key materials and bearings of those larger acts of translation.

This essay adds little to the documentation of local literary resemblances between these two poets: much of what follows has been noticed before, and with special salience within the same narrow span of years (the early 1990s) in which the original version of this essay was first presented, when several simultaneous ventures in this vein were proceeding largely without direct reference to any of the others.[2] Instead, this thought-experiment is meant to illustrate an important

---

[2] Among these, perhaps the most germane, albeit different not only in scope and emphasis but in critical aims, is David Aers's important account of two counterposed imaginative formations in later medieval religious thought and devotion. First presented in condensed form in *YLS*, 8 (1994), 107–25, as 'Christ's Humanity and *Piers Plowman*: Contexts and Political Implications', a fuller version of his analysis occupies two chapters in David Aers and Lynn Staley, *The Powers of the Holy* (University Park: Pennsylvania State University Press, 1996), pp. 15–76, where it forms the first two of a trio of essays by Aers (the third is on Julian of Norwich) on 'the humanity of Christ'. Aers's contribution remains required reading for its justly influential delineation of issues of method in the study of religious culture that demand the attention of scholars of English medieval literature. The present essay pre-dated both published forms of Aers's argument, however, and despite his salutary observation (*The Powers of the Holy*, p. 74 n. 82) that Langland's representation of the humanity of Christ in the male figure of Piers (rather than in the *tunica humanitatis* of Mary, as argued by Caroline Bynum), is 'a topic not yet explored', I have left this essay's main point of tangency with his work relatively undeveloped here. Yet it will be apparent that while my main objective is quite different from his, my account does not wholly corroborate his view that the two forms of medieval devotion he discusses constitute the prevailing binary of the era's religious and political imagination (whether as 'orthodox' vs. 'Wycliffite' or heterodox, or as a 'dominant' formation and its opposite); nor does my exploration of the socially gendered aspects of these two poets' self-depictions align with the gender binary he assigns to these. Instability of gender and age proprieties, as well as of vocational identifications, are featured in both Langland's and Chaucer's fictive depiction of the unsanctioned social role and affective character of poetic production, which remains for both poets at best either tractable or transgressive 'play'. My concern here is the difference between Langland and Chaucer on this point, and the impact of Langland's fictive portrayal on Chaucer's embodiments of reformative religious rhetoric; Lynn Staley examines the latter more fully in her essay 'Chaucer and the Postures of Sanctity', in *Powers of the Holy*, pp. 179–259. As she notes (p. 180 n. 2) I presented a sequel to the present paper, concentrating on the broader issues of method implicit in this exploration, at the 1992 New Chaucer Society meeting, as 'Changing the Subject: Chaucer, Langland, and the Problem of Character'. It was infeasible for reasons of length to incorporate its reflections here; it is forthcoming elsewhere in revised form, as is a third comparative essay on

general principle of source-and-influence studies, demonstrated anew in every specific venture in this kind pursued to critical rather than 'merely' historical conclusion: that the most profound results of such literary relations are those that are most fully and deeply metabolized by the appropriating poet. The result of deep assimilation of the work of another is not simply 'allusion' or reference (an act nearly meaningless in itself), but the kind of achieved formal and semantic reintegration of intention, and clarification of design, that is more often recognized among poets than among exegetical expositors. It offers one kind of response to George Kane's austere resistance to any suggestion that claims about the transmission and reception of the poem can have some bearing on the 'meaning' of the 'text'.[3] My counterclaim here is that distinguishing what is external to the 'work' from those semantic and mimetic features that render it fully intelligible as a complex intentional act involves philological reasoning akin to that of an editor, but operative on several different scales of magnification — and that ascertaining authorial 'meaning' is a product of all of them in concert.

Jill Mann has suggested that Chaucer's schematization of the figures of estates satire, in the form of persons depicted largely through their own professional terms, idioms, and positionalities, in a narratorial perspective that in part mimes their own self-valuations, owes something to Langland's example in the Confession of the Sins, in which the sins in effect represent themselves in first-person speech. She has also proposed that it was Langland's example in the opening panorama of the field of folk that prompted Chaucer to include a Pardoner in the Canterbury company — one who, like Langland's, purposefully undertakes to 'blear the eyes' of the people to whom he preaches.[4]

Lee Patterson has gone significantly further, arguing that these two sites of Langlandian innovation are joined imaginatively in a single invention by Chaucer

---

Chaucer, Langland, and literary history (see n. 25 below), 'Playing the Plowman: Legends of Fourteenth-Century Authorship'.

[3] See George Kane, 'Reading *Piers Plowman*', *YLS*, 8 (1994), 1–20, for one instance among many exemplifying his insistence that 'meaning' is fully (and only) internal to the text, while the behaviours of copyists and other intermediaries exemplify almost without exception 'the response of mediocrity to genius'. In practice, this austere position was more often displayed in ad hoc direct response to others in correspondence than in his own editorial performance; in both roles he was at once a deeply illuminating reader and a shrewd, if sometimes minimally respectful, diagnostician of how other readers work. For other examples see Ralph Hanna, 'George Kane and the Invention of Textual Thought: Retrospect and Prospect', in the present volume.

[4] Jill Mann, *Chaucer and Medieval Estates Satire* (Cambridge: Cambridge University Press, 1973), pp. 145–52, 208–11, 277.

in the *Canterbury Tales*.[5] He suggests that the example of Langland's Confession of the Deadly Sins offers the most telling analogue to date for Chaucer's exploration of a peculiar general paradox of confessional self-representation, and of what might be called the precarious psychology and therapy of confession; Chaucer represents this pattern most fully in the character and performance of the Pardoner. This paradox, he shows, lurks at the heart of all confessional self-disclosure: a sin cannot sincerely confess itself without at the same time unmaking itself, and a human being in the process of confessing thereby attests not true self-knowledge but the impossibility of such a state. The Pardoner, Patterson argues, manifests in his performance the self-destructive despair that is at once the antitype and the demonic twin of the scouring contrition from which self-reformation begins; but he also, through the Old Man, voices the habitual return of repressed cultural as well as personal knowledge, his deepest desire to assimilate himself not to the paternal deity through penitential self-reformation but to the forgiving body of maternal earth through self-annihilation. In this way, the Oedipal story of incest and fratricidal warfare (the Theban fate of repetition without edification that haunts Chaucer's career from the first, as Patterson shows, and was assimilated in medieval legend to the life story of Judas as well) is the cultural equivalent to that individual cycle of fatalism and despair that always threatens to swamp penitential contrition in self-consuming nostalgia and regret, emotions so closely allied that the individual subject may at any time mistake the one for the other.

Schematically considered, the Pardoner is 'made of' two key components that are found together in none of the other posited models or analogues for this complex figure, except in Langland. In generic and formal ancestry, he is a version of the false and cynical preacher of much anticlerical satire and vernacular comedy, represented as he is regarded by others. Although this figure may be described as a spiritual minister with a hollow centre, it is not normally his own subjective condition that is the focus of interest in such representations, but his sheer rhetorical power and skill, his breathtaking ability to make his 'gaude' work again and again, even (perhaps especially) on those who ought logically to be proof against it, either through their own knowledge or his own open and boasting disclosure of his intentions. His audience's strange and malleable will to believe,

---

[5] Lee Patterson, 'Chaucerian Confession: Penitential Literature and the Pardoner', *Medievalia et humanistica*, n.s., 7 (1976), 153–73 (repr. in Patterson, *Chaucer and the Subject of History* (Madison: University of Wisconsin Press; London: Routledge, 1991), chap. 8, pp. 374–97).

not his own intentionality, becomes the primary matter for reflection in the more profound versions of such figures: one thinks of Boccaccio's preaching charlatans and lugubriously phony deathbed confessors, as well as Jean de Meun's Faus Semblant in this tradition. The second component of the Pardoner, however, is drawn from the heart of the vast late medieval literature of confession and examined interiority. Chaucer complicates the comic figure of the master-deceiver of others, the enabling premise of anticlerical satire, by shifting it into the first person, depicting from the inside the subjective problematic of self-deception that is more encompassing than any individual's malicious motive, however enigmatic, and lies at the heart of the society's chief procedures for self-reformation; he thus transforms a comic figure into a tragic and pathetic one. Within the regimen of self-scrutiny prescribed by the more sophisticated confessional literature of the period, boasting of one's own treacherous schemes and then trying to work them on others is no more elusive to motivational understanding than the regular if vertiginous uncertainties that attend the effort to renounce a *habitus* by rehearsing it. Chaucer thus renders a figure of political and social evil as simultaneously a subjective abyss, the main victim of his own cynical fictions who stands accused by the very truths they embody. In turning this stock figure of political satire and anticlerical comedy to face himself, Chaucer exposes not only a newly complex problem in representing human intentionality, but at the same time a profound problem in poetics. He embodies the subjective danger that confronts all makers of fictions, benign as well as cynical: the possibility that his own designs are hidden even from himself.

It is this combination of two much-discussed practical problematics of preacherly and confessional utterance, both with a widely attested separate discursive life in late medieval literature and practical instruction, that gives the Pardoner his strange 'edge', his aura of tragic subjective depth. I know of no other place in which the characterological dilemma of public penitential suasion undergoes in development this same thorough reversal, to become an anatomy of the poet's own position and responsibility — in effect a massive subjectification of what began as a satirical anatomy of the commune — except in Langland's work. The following analysis extends Patterson's suggestion that this figure comes to embody for Chaucer a pivotal recognition that turned out to be critical for the late work of his career, and for the form of closure of the *Canterbury Tales*. I would argue that Langland's work is the direct inspiration, not merely a suggestive analogy, for this complex and haunting Canterbury pilgrim. In the Pardoner, Chaucer registers his understanding of Langlandian poetics, and their dark implications for his own.

I have already suggested elsewhere (in an article on John But's improvised ending to Langland's A-version, originally written for a Festschrift in honour of George Kane) that one of the most fundamental structuring 'ideas' of Langland's years of making and revising his *sui generis* masterpiece was precisely this perception of the treacherous doubleness of the call to penitential reflection.[6] Here I propose that Langland makes his literary self-depiction, and his repeated acknowledgment of the near-indefensibility of his own literary project, a test case in his broadly Augustinian anatomy of the enterprise of 'roming in remembraunce' as the misdirected pursuit of reconstructive grace. The elusiveness and obscurity of the 'maker's' own vocational motives and position among those of others on the field present in especially acute form the broader grounds for despair of the commune's reconstruction through its own penitential labours alone: the poetic persona's eloquence, argumentative ingenuity, and 'clergial' mastery are exposed dialogically as inert and inefficacious substitutes for the love that alone can animate them to good ends. In brief, Langland's poem pervasively represents his own literary 'making' as the demonic double of penance: an enterprise that defers and deflects the inner resources of the self into merely nostalgic and self-aggrandizing pursuits, while it is also a literal waste of time, the finite earthly span lent to human beings for the working-out of their salvation.

Even the desire to shame wrongdoing, to be a truth-teller to a commune in need of reform, is exposed repeatedly as simply another form of pride, as Will's quest repeatedly reveals new depths of obscurity about the motives at the heart of both self-scrutiny and reformative eloquence. This anatomy of Will's work, metonymic of Langland's broader analysis of the world's ills and the always-receding means of its rectification through its own efforts alone, is what I think underlies Chaucer's representation of the Pardoner as an unrepentant professional caller to penance. The Pardoner is in some sense Chaucer's depiction of Langland, not as biographical fact or historical being, but as an influential, idiosyncratic, and almost unassimilable poetic premise and presence. In his fatal eloquence as preacher, in his pride in his deceptive and ultimately self-deceptive craft, in his opportunistic appropriation of every occasion to use his guilt-inducing skills to evoke in his audience a mordant recognition of their world as a scene of ever-renewed opportunity for sin and self-deception, Chaucer's

---

[6] Anne Middleton, 'Making a Good End: John But as a Reader of *Piers Plowman*', in *Medieval English Studies Presented to George Kane*, ed. by E. D. Kennedy, R. Waldron, and J. S. Wittig (Woodbridge: Brewer, 1988), pp. 243–63.

Pardoner embodies a central and durable Langlandian recognition, that the self is ultimately resourceless to effect its own restoration by either knowledge or craft. As the pivotal recognition of the *Confessions*, this Augustinian perception (cited in Latin at C.11.287; B.10.461)[7] is given its most exhaustively staged examination in the 'inward journey' at the centre of Langland's poem, and dramatized in its most acute form by the repeated bafflement of the persona's sustained flights of reformative rhetoric, and the shaming and rebuke of his putatively laudable enterprise of 'makyng'.[8]

Yet the devil's advocate must have a hearing. It is conceivable, even if not in my view probable, that Chaucer and Langland each arrived independently at this suggestive combination of two spiritual dangers, one to the commune and one to the self, in the art of preacherly eloquence, and made each echo the other. Chaucer is certainly capable of creating this startling characterological chemistry on his own. What is gained by attributing this Chaucerian anatomy of self-deceptive rhetorical professionalism to an encounter with the work of Langland specifically? As with any demonstration of the significance of an absence — in this case an absence in Chaucer of any unambiguous mention of or allusion to Langland's poem as such — the hypothesis can only be tested by the quality of readings or explanations of otherwise inscrutable features of the text that it makes accessible. What aspects of the Pardoner, and of the effect of his performance and placement in the Canterbury project, make more sense (and what kind of sense) if we posit that they have Langland's work as their direct inspiration?

The most conspicuous one, unmotivated by any other source or analogue, is the linkage of the already complex mix of issues of instructive truth and confessional efficacy, self-knowledge, and poetic rectitude with discomfiting ambiguities of gender identity, and the related issue of the proprieties of age. None of the other proposed sources or antecedents for the Pardoner as invention contains and links all of these features — except Langland's massive example, which I suggest implicates them in each other in precisely the ways Chaucer does in the Par-

---

[7] All citations of *Piers Plowman* are from the Athlone editions of B and C: *Piers Plowman: The B Version*, ed. by George Kane and E. Talbot Donaldson, rev. edn (London: Athlone; Berkeley and Los Angeles: University of California Press, 1988); *Piers Plowman: The C Version*, ed. by George Russell and George Kane (London: Athlone; Berkeley and Los Angeles: University of California Press, 1997).

[8] See Rita Copeland, 'The Pardoner's Body and the Disciplining of Rhetoric', in *Framing Medieval Bodies*, ed. by Sarah Kay and Miri Rubin (Manchester: Manchester University Press, 1994), pp. 138–59, especially pp. 149–55.

doner's performance. It is the addition of sexual and gender irregularity, together with an unseemly preference for the styles and desires of youth, to the Pardoner's complexities of motive and identity that in my view secures Chaucer's indebtedness to Langland for this provocative and grotesque figure.[9]

Now on the face of it nothing could be more improbable than this claim: where, you might ask, is the interest in gender and sexuality in Langland?[10] Of all the English medieval writings that might be imagined to lend themselves to illumination through a gender-studies approach, surely at first glance Langland's must seem among the least promising: again, one is in the position of arguing from, and about, an absence. Yet although it has been little remarked, Langland's poem is in many respects unique among late medieval English vernacular works in its orientation to certain of the most characteristic, and most strongly gender-marked, expressions of late medieval religion. It is precisely Langland's avoidance of the deeply inscribed fictive displacement of public and spiritual issues onto a fictive scene of heterosexual (and nugatory) erotics, his refusal to represent spiritual and metaphysical desire in the gendered codes that pervade the work of Chaucer and virtually all of his other major poetic antecedents, that marks

[9] One of the most generative earlier accounts of the Pardoner's several physical and psychological grotesqueries in relation to his rhetorical project (and an important influence on this essay) remains that of Donald Howard, 'The Pardoner: Actor and Martyr', presented 11 May 1974 at a meeting of the Medieval Academy of America, Kalamazoo, and published in *The Idea of the 'Canterbury Tales'* (Berkeley and Los Angeles: University of California Press, 1976), pp. 339–63. Judson Allen and Theresa A. Moritz, in *A Distinction of Stories* (Columbus: Ohio State University Press, 1981), pp. 163–79, discuss its Medieval Academy version at appreciative length; Monica McAlpine, 'The Pardoner's Homosexuality and How it Matters', *PMLA*, 95 (1980), 8–22, offers an astute account of this topic, on which there were several provocative contributions in the 1980s. Alastair Minnis, 'Chaucer and the Queering Eunuch', *New Medieval Literatures*, 6 (2003), 107–28, provides a valuable overview of three decades of critical discussions of the grotesque character and sexuality of the Pardoner; he sees the primary significance of this depiction as residing chiefly in the unsettling oddity of this figure, manifested in a perverse will to eloquence and the uneasy responses to him by other pilgrims, rather than in specific attributes of his enigmatically represented psychological or physical condition. See also Alastair Minnis, 'Moral Fallibility: Chaucer's Pardoner and the Office of Preacher', in *Fallible Authors: Chaucer's Pardoner and Wife of Bath* (Philadelphia: University of Pennsylvania Press, 2008), chap. 2 (pp. 98–169), which subsumes his essay of the same title in *Intellectuals and Writers in Fourteenth-Century Europe: The J. A. W. Bennett Memorial Lectures, Perugia, 1984*, ed. by Piero Boitani and Anna Torti (Tübingen: Narr, 1986), pp. 88–119.

[10] Helen Cooper, 'Gender and Personification in *Piers Plowman*', *YLS*, 5 (1991), 31–48; *YLS*, 12 (1998) is a special issue devoted to gender criticism of the poem.

Langland's position in fourteenth-century literature as unique, and more than a little ... well ... *queer*.[11] In fact, it is precisely his strong tropism toward regulatory religious discourses rather than figurations that are more characteristic of the devotional or meditative writings of the period that has led to the critical perception of Langland's representational strategies as 'unliterary'. The sign of the 'literary', in other words, inscribed in Chaucer's and the *Pearl*-Poet's work but not, it is thought, in Langland's, is taken to be precisely the courtly/erotic figure of heterosexual courtship and procreation as a key figure for the relation of the soul to God.

Though it is by no means now confined to such enquiries, gender criticism in literary studies was initially forged chiefly in the study of writings about, for, by, or prominently representing women — and Langland's poem appears to be none of the above. And that, I shall argue, is precisely the point: this is a distinctly remarkable state of affairs in a poem that so prominently and insistently depicts the characteristic intellectual dilemmas, affective appeal, devotional practices, and spiritual disciplines of late medieval religiosity.[12] It is, on the contrary — and to a degree that is, I would argue, surprising in a vernacular work of the fourteenth century — preoccupied with and steeped in the categorically masculine discursive and practical world of the priesthood, the regular clergy, the university, and the extended court bureaucracy and reward system. It is not their presence, however, but rather the absence of any of the characteristic marks of women, as symbolic or actual force, in the forms, especially the leading fictive forms, of late medieval intellectual and spiritual life that calls for analysis.

[11] For a different sense of the 'queerness' of the Pardoner from the one considered here, see James J. Paxson, 'Gender Personified, Personification Gendered, and the Body Figuralized in *Piers Plowman*', *YLS*, 12 (1998), 65–96, especially pp. 89–92 on the 'queerness' of Elde in *Piers*. See also the discussion of the increasingly masculine gendering of personifications as the poem progresses by Masha Raskolnikov, 'Promising the Female, Delivering the Male: Transformations of Gender in *Piers Plowman*', *YLS*, 19 (2005), 81–105, and her astute concluding remarks (pp. 102–05) on the uneasy relations between feminist and queer readings of the poem.

[12] For a valuable account of some of the meditative themes of the Cistercian devotional tradition upon which the poem draws (while it largely eschews their most vividly gendered language and metaphors), see Caroline Walker Bynum, *Jesus as Mother: Studies in the Spirituality of the High Middle Ages* (Berkeley and Los Angeles: University of California Press, 1982), and *Holy Feast and Holy Fast: The Religious Significance of Food to Medieval Women* (Berkeley and Los Angeles: University of California Press, 1987); the latter is the chief focus of Aers's critical view of Bynum's account of representations of Christ's humanity (*The Powers of the Holy*, p. 74 n. 82).

One may render this absence visible on several levels of the composition, beginning with the gendering of allegorical personifications. Here Langland actually violates the proprieties of grammatical gender, one important basis for a long Latin allegorical tradition of wise tutelary female personifications, to render those personifications who oppose or challenge Will's search for salvation as for the most part feminine, and those that approve and nurture that enterprise as masculine. Lady Holy Church is the first of several personifications to participate helpfully in the serial instruction of the dreamer, but virtually the last of these supportive figures to be gendered female. While other female personifications beyond Holy Church/Ecclesia are involved at critical points in the dreamer's quest for enlightenment, their role is precisely that: critical in all senses of the term. Dame Study and Dame Scripture, for example, each depicted as the wife of a complementary figure also involved in this enterprise (Wit and Clergy, respectively), are depicted as scolds or scorners, their distrustful attitudes toward Will's quest standing in marked contrast to their spouses' readiness to respond without rancour to Will's questions; Meed and Fortune are likewise deflectors rather than furtherers of Will's quest.[13] Yet Langland's Anima, grammatically feminine, is nevertheless referred to consistently by the masculine pronoun (becoming Liberum Arbitrium in C), and Kynde is likewise 'he', though this figure might be supposed equivalent to Natura.[14] One cannot plead ignorance on

---

[13] Ralph Hanna, 'School and Scorn: Gender in *Piers Plowman*', *New Medieval Literatures*, 3 (1997), 213–27.

[14] See Mary Clemente Davlin, 'A Genius-Kynde Illustration in Codex Vaticanus Palatinus Latinus 629', *Manuscripta*, 23 (1979), 149–58. In this valuable contribution to explicating the iconographical as well as grammatical bases for the gendering of personifications in the poem, Davlin demonstrates (pp. 154–58) that the poet's representation of Kynde as masculine (rather than as the expected female figure, consonant with the grammatical gender of Natura depicted in medieval literary-philosophical fictions) is based primarily on pictorial depictions of Nature and Genius common in legal manuscripts, such as the *Decretum Gratiani*, particularly in contexts associated with the laws of marriage (as is Wit's explication of Kynde, beginning at C.10.151; B.9/A.10.25, and occupying in all versions the remainder of the passus, through C.10.307; B.9.210; A.10.218). This iconographic programme, in which a male figure of Nature is accompanied by a diagrammatic tree of consanguinity, is used in canon law to clarify relationships by blood and by marriage, and here corroborates the broader observations of Hugh White and John Alford that the poet's figuration of the inward powers of the soul, particularly in the difficult third vision of the poem, owe much to civil and canon-law notions of natural law, and correspondingly less than often assumed to the literary myths of the Latin poetic tradition. See further Brian Tierney, '*Natura, id est Deus*', *Journal of the History of Ideas*, 24 (1963), 307–22; he

Langland's behalf: a poet who interlards his poem with Latin and uses grammatical analogy within the poem as a tool of explanation is certainly aware of grammatical gender as a formal propriety of language, though as a property of English it was vanishing in the usage of his era. It seems that Langland's gendering system is stronger than grammatical conventions and leads him to depict male rather than female personifications as those who accept Will's visionary enquiry and his qualifications for it as largely valid, and who invariably support his most significant intellectual and spiritual progress toward rectification with the Creator. Imaginatif (*vis imaginativa*) and Kynde are among the most noteworthy, and Piers himself, though not quite a personification, is yet another.

At another level, in his imaginative rehearsal of salvation history, Langland eschews feminized figurations of key events of the earthly life of Christ, even where the religious culture of his era offered peculiarly rich, indeed seemingly all-but-inevitable, opportunities for it. His references to the Incarnation and Nativity generally emphasize the angel's proclamation of the holy birth to the shepherds and magi (and by extension philosophers generally: 'to pastours and poetes appered þe Aungel'; B.12.148; C.14.92), not the Annunciation to the Virgin or the Saviour's vulnerability as infant son of 'a pure pouere maide [...] to a pouere man ywedded' (B.11.249). His sublime antepenultimate vision of the Crucifixion and Resurrection elides all those moments of pathos and pain that were featured in late medieval Eucharistic celebration and gave a place in meditative practice to the three Maries and to the sorrows of the Virgin. In Langland the Redeemer is a conquering hero, a wrestler who struggles with death and wins on the Cross, and wins a second time in a battle of juridical wits with the powers of darkness on Holy Saturday, rather than the willing sacrifice who sheds his blood to feed his people, or a locus of refuge in his wounded side. In one sense, this representational tropism of Langland's merely betrays its discursive affinities (and probably biographical origins) in the poet's deep immersion in the several regulatory discourses of the late medieval church as institution, largely at the expense

notes (p. 317) that a sense of *natura naturans* as signifying both the creator and the 'supreme law of nature', and paralleling the usage of the jurists, is transmitted in the *Speculum Maius* of Vincent de Beauvais, and appears as well in the writings of Bonaventure and Aquinas. A more detailed account of these filiations will appear in my commentary on the third vision of the poem, in the forthcoming Volume III of the *Penn Commentary on 'Piers Plowman'*; there I also examine a few instances in which lectional uncertainties (and concomitant ambiguities in the specification of speakers) arise from the use of 'he[o]' in the poet's South-West Midlands' dialect for the nominative case of the feminine pronoun.

of predominantly meditative or devotional texts, whether for enclosed religious or pious layfolk.[15]

Yet Langland manages to turn these discursive habits to powerfully conscious and ironic structural consequences, exposing the subjective impossibility of the lawful and regulated at the heart of the pursuit of salvation. He depicts the initiation of the quest for human rectitude and rectification in a figure who is indeed lay, but significantly and problematically masculine: Piers Plowman. Piers's role in the poem is structurally surprisingly like that of idealized female figures in the spiritual journeys of other major vernacular poets of the fourteenth century: in his continual vanishings from the desirous view of the dreamer-protagonist, he is reminiscent of no other poetic figure so much as Petrarch's Laura or Dante's Beatrice, or Amant's Rose. As an envisioned ideal of human perfection, already in possession of the kind of knowledge the dreamer seeks, Piers activates desires for self-restoration, and at the same time masks and forecloses the source and force of these desires — unlike other nearly contemporary representations of such pursuits that depict the search for self-identity as driven by a passion and energy that has all the strength and focus of erotic obsession, and (what is significant for Langland's project) the idealized desire for mutual knowledge. In choosing this figurative system for representing the quest for human perfection or salvation,

[15] Langland's major exception to this large-scale figurative tendency of the poem requires mention here, not only because it 'proves the rule' just described, but because it is pivotal to the remaining narrative development of Vision 3. At C.12.50–71; B.11.115–36, the dreamer is driven by Scripture's severe 'teme' (Matt. 22. 14: 'many [*multi*] are called but few [*pauci*] are chosen') to recall the terms under which he was 'underfonged [...] atte font' by Holy Church. Registering the meaning of this sacrament (C.12.53–57; B.11.117–24a) in the words of Isaiah 55. 1 ('O you who thirst, come to the waters'), echoed at Apoc. 21. 6 as denoting the 'water of life' offered as his blood by the sacrificial Lamb (Apoc. 7. 17), he now perceives the terms of his election as expressed in Christ's invitation to all his children freely to 'souke [...] saufte' at his breast, thus imaginatively conflating baptismal and Eucharistic 'bote for bale'. Scripture emphatically approves as 'soth' (C.12.72–74a; B.11.137–39) this identification of the promise of penitential and Eucharistic *restauratio* as implicit in baptism, confirming it with a further dictum generalizing the point: 'His mercy is above all his works' (Ps. 144. 9). As several critics have noted, Scripture's approval of the dreamer's formulation here marks the first time in the poem that his grasp of his nature and condition has been endorsed as 'soth' without reservation by any of his informants. Bynum has emphasized (in *Jesus as Mother*, pp. 110–69) that depiction of the love of God in images of bodily intimacy, especially maternal nurture of the infant, was developed primarily in Cistercian and Carthusian devotion, and that its use within and beyond the cloister was not gender-specific. The further implications of this relatively rare figurative complex in the poem will be examined in my volume of the *Penn Commentary* (see n. 14, above).

Langland simultaneously evokes and rigorously suppresses one of the most useful analogies of his religious culture, heterosexual amatory desire. He locates the imaginative field of his vision instead in the pursuit of earthly labour and the satisfaction of hunger, rather than in the gratification of sexual ardour, while the rich imagery of Christ as nurturing his people with his body and blood is also minimally available. Having foreclosed both erotic longing and the infant's fantasized union with the mother that feeds it as an iconology of satisfaction in the language of the poem, Langland's work is condemned to repeat its depictions of efforts to accomplish this satisfaction through rule and law, the domain of masculine functionaries in medieval ecclesiastical culture — which is also, in the figurative terms of this poem, precisely the location of the wound or lack that this quest seeks to heal.[16]

Langland's aversion to the possibilities of 'feminized' religious as well as courtly imagery thus has far-reaching consequences for the *form*, not simply the figuration, of his poem. It has similarly deep consequences for the poet's representation and valuation of the poetic project itself. The language and posture of heterosexual courtship, of the lover's imploring pursuit of the beloved — which are structurally analogous to the appeal to the great through 'makyng', the social fiction of play, and of suasion by means of charm rather than argument, that underwrite the role of the court poet — has no place in the enterprise of recovering Piers, and hence no imaginary force in invoking that infusion of grace into worldly labour that alone renders it salvific instead of merely disciplinary. Langland's poem works out in utterly uncompromising detail the extremely harsh consequences, for the imagining of man's salvation, of a hypermasculine rhetoric of rectification through law, rather than through affective identifications either pathetic or empathetic. There is no 'fyal/filial' love with this folk, in large part because Langland's figuration of it has made that love largely unspeakable on earth.[17] Langland can represent both Christ's sacrificial love and his earthly

---

[16] Jill Mann, 'Eating and Drinking in *Piers Plowman*', *Essays and Studies*, n.s., 32 (1979), 26–43, discusses the language and metaphors of satisfaction.

[17] For this lection at C.8.215, see *The C Version*, ed. by Russell and Kane, p. 151; also Thomas Hill, 'Green and Filial Love: Two Notes on the Russell-Kane C Text: C.8.215 and C.17.48', *YLS*, 16 (2002), 67–83. Hill rejects the Athlone C-text lection 'fyal', derived from French *feal*; in arguing for 'filial' as the correct reading, he posits that its primary sense here is not the love between brothers as human sons of God, but that of the human son for the divine father. In *Piers Plowman* these two are mutually implicated throughout the poem, in ways most fully explicated in the third vision (see especially B.11.185–269a; C.12.101–54a), where the conquering Christ,

leadership in deeply moving ways by sending him into earthly engagement 'in Piers armes'; what he cannot find a way to represent enduringly in the folk of the field, with himself as poetic persona notably included among these, is the passionate ardour that leads humanity to desire, love, and embrace that model in itself: on earth, Will's love for Piers motivates his occasional wordless swoon, but it is otherwise a love that lacks a conventionally understood expressive language and iconography.

It is at this point that one may begin to consider Chaucer's Pardoner as a profound commentary on the implicit poetics of *Piers Plowman*. The reciprocal desires for confession and penance on the one hand, and for mastery through artful indirection on the other — the twin desires of the writer and performer to tell the truth and to lie — have never been more searchingly exposed than in the figure of Chaucer's Pardoner.[18] The impetus to present such an anatomy is derived, I suggest, largely from the already-raw exposure of these gigantic and unsatisfiable opposed wills in Langland's poem. He also found in Langland's literary self-representation as Will a problematically gendered bodily self-image, framed at once by self-loathing and a grotesque preening, presenting a model of the courtier-poet as a far more alarming kind of *senex amans* than was bodied forth in Chaucer's more genial intertextual byplay with his friends Gower and Scogan. It is one of Chaucer's deepest insights about Langland's enterprise, realized in the Pardoner's self-fashioning on the pilgrimage as a kind of ageing Absalon, that for him the discourse of sin and unsatisfiable acquisitive hunger are the only love-song he knows how to make. In this figure Chaucer saw a mirrored death's-head, Dorian-Gray image of the court poet's ritualized self-presentation.

In an age in which iconically particularized self-representation in the form of performed and inscribed literary signature put the 'maker's mark' upon a poet's work, designating it as 'a work', a unitary enterprise infused with the distinctive

revealed at the resurrection as *Redemptor* (B.11.207; C.12.115) is said thereby to secure the 'gentil' blood-brotherhood of humankind.

[18] For influential accounts of the representation of subjectivity in Langland and Chaucer, respectively, see David Lawton, 'The Subject of *Piers Plowman*', *YLS*, 1 (1987), 1–30; and H. Marshall Leicester, *The Disenchanted Self: Representing the Subject in the 'Canterbury Tales'* (Berkeley and Los Angeles: University of California Press, 1990), especially pp. 35–64, 178–94, 399–417; see also James Paxson, 'Inventing the Subject and the Personification of Will in *Piers Plowman*', in *William Langland's 'Piers Plowman': A Book of Essays*, ed. by Kathleen M. Hewett-Smith (New York: Routledge, 2001), pp. 195–231.

intentionality of a single producer, both Chaucer's and Langland's literary body-images gain a peculiar force in declaring their poetics.[19] We are all accustomed to noting the repeated inscription of roly-poly and doll-like Chaucer in his work: this body image presents him as at once genial, innocuously sensual, a partaker of life's feast, yet always to one side, not a principal player in the love game which is the displaced form of ethical discourse allowed to the court-entertainer to the great, who must please through indirection, and who must keep declaring his 'work' to be only 'play'. Chubby Chaucer thus represents himself as comic male protagonist either as a kind of preadolescent (like the infantile and sweetmeat-loving Sir Thopas, or the speaker of the ballade *To Rosamounde* who depicts his love-longing in culinary terms) or as a man chronologically and biologically past the age of being seen primarily as a sexual contender, as in the rueful comedy of the *Envoy to Scogan*, in which he places himself and Scogan among those 'hoor and rounde of shap' (l. 31) on whom Venus is not likely to exercise her wrath in the form of erotic misfortune, but will instead take vengeance in the form of lack of patronage forthcoming from those who do continue to delight in imaginative representations of themselves as among 'love's folk'.[20] Chaucer thus desexualizes his masculine identity while also allying himself with the central fiction of the courtier poet: that his subject-matter and milieu is a society wholly preoccupied with love-dalliance.

For Langland it is far otherwise: the dreamer's represented body image in the poem, presented initially in wry disavowal, and ultimately in direct self-reference, is in every way the diametric opposite of Chaucer's. Unlike Thought, a 'muche man [...] lik to myselue' (B.8.70), Wit, the dreamer's next informant, is 'long and lene, like to noon ooþer' (B.8.120), yet in the waking episode inserted in the C version between the first two visions, the narrator is self-characterized as too tall to stoop, too weak to work (C.5.23–25), and, if the scriptural text behind this account is recognized, too proud to beg (Luc. 16. 3). From first to last, Langland figures his poetic persona as lean and hungry — always hungry, indeed insatiable;

---

[19] Anne Middleton, 'William Langland's 'Kynde Name': Authorial Signature and Social Identity in Late Fourteenth-Century England', in *Literary Practice and Social Change in Britain, 1380–1530*, ed. by Lee Patterson (Berkeley and Los Angeles: University of California Press, 1990), pp. 15–82.

[20] Geoffrey Chaucer, *The Riverside Chaucer*, ed. by Larry D. Benson, 3rd edn (Boston: Houghton Mifflin, 1987). Citations of the *Canterbury Tales* below are specified by fragment and/or line number in the main text.

this perpetual hunger and sense of deprivation becomes the counterpart of playful courtship/courtiership in Chaucer's work. Insofar as he situates himself imaginatively among the ritual pastimes of the great, those pastimes are not the interpersonal games of 'luf-talking' that mime in the literary register and space of the court those singular bonds of fidelity and trust that, in theory, bind society in intense individual political and patronage relations, games in which the poet speaks, and experiences his affective and imaginative stakes in these relations in Chaucerian fashion, as nugatory surrogate. Langland projects Will instead repeatedly into the chief *collective* rituals, sociopolitical rather than intimate and domestic, that produce solidarity and reinscribe hierarchical and dependency relationships among the great generally: rituals such as councils, feasts, and legal proceedings. In these occasions he is always figured as a desirous and excluded observer, and decidedly in earnest.

Desire in Langland's poem is universalized as hunger rather than personalized as eros: as a sexual body Langland's Will is more desired than desiring. Imagining other sexualized subjects in the first person, in the speaking figures of both Pride and Lechery, Langland gives voice to the truism that the most powerful sexual organ is the mind, as he depicts these figures deriving far more delight from boasting of their own bodily beauty and desirability (Pride) and contemplating and imaginatively staging their own scenes of sexual conquest, past and yet to come, through foreplay that is more overwhelmingly verbal than physical (Lechery), rather than depicting either figure as overcome with pleasure, anticipatory or otherwise, in sexual activity. Representing Will's own masculine identity and potency, however, is a matter of dwelling on the presence or absence of bodily strength for work, of which sexual potency is only a sort of special case; both are asserted as expectations that others have of him, not principles of self-definition and self-projection in the world. In the late C-addition often called the 'autobiography', Will is accosted by Reason and Conscience in an apocalyptic 'hot hervest' while he is still young and able-bodied, and has a wife and a daughter, represented here and throughout as what Jerome called 'hostages to fortune': they are among the reasons he can be held as a layman to the responsibility to labour, rather than the harvest of his own specifically sexual wild oats. The poem's one brief adversion to the charms traditionally wielded by Cupid comes late, in all senses: in the final passus, at B.20/C.22.110–20, where, as earlier in Fortune's 'mirour' (B.11.1–36), amatory dalliance is simply another fleeting temptation of youth and early manhood. Shortly thereafter, Elde strikes Will bald, toothless, deaf, gouty, and finally impotent, but the latter indignity is just that: the disabling of what he calls 'that "lome" [tool or instrument] that my wife loved me for', a wound which makes her, not Will, wish him dead (B.20/ C.22.190–99). For Will himself, it is his condition late in the poetic narrative and his imagined life, finally beyond the demand for either sexual performance or productive labour, that makes it possible for him to renounce his characteristic contentiousness and genuinely to desire assimilation to Unity, and to realize Kynde's most fundamental injunction: 'lerne to love'.

Neither masculine nor feminine, the Pardoner's desires run to acquisition ('moneie, wolle, chese, and whete', as well as 'a joly wenche in every toun'; VI.448, 453), chiefly of goods that can benefit him only as items of exchange or display rather than use. They also thereby run to repetition: one bring-down-the-house performance succeeds another, while the fruits of such virtuoso exercises in 'wynning' consistently fail to satisfy. There will never be enough money, wool, cheese, or wheat — or wenches — to satisfy an appetite that is felt not in the gut or genitals or even in the projective imagination, but in the soul, and is by definition beyond satisfaction by human effort. Nor will the dead body parts in his 'male', however much they 'win' for the performer, supply the fatal lack, or reanimate and edify the body as a potentially decorous dwelling for the spirit that the speaker cannot bring himself openly to invite to dwell therein. Whether in drunken belching or in swearing, the sounds that come out of the mouth of the sinful are equally meaningless, and both are equivalent to the winds that emerge from the nether end of a human body imagined as perpetually unfillable gut ('At either ende of thee foul is the soun'; VI.536). In this sense, the Pardoner's grotesque body — the particular one he inhabits, and the generic human corpus he imaginatively evokes in his preaching as a veritable thesaurus of sinfulness — is a distinctly non-comic version of the poet's speaking and performing body as the drafty dwelling of rumour, as in the early *Hous of Fame*.[21] Exploiting the full potential of the late medieval clergy's highly articulated imaginary economy for the mechanical manipulation of the spirit and its fears, and its quantification of the terms of spiritual reward and punishment, the Pardoner's trade in the imputed spiritual power of relics is a confidence trick largely analogous to those of any poet who uses traditional tropes and figures of salvation history, from the Parables onward, to draw humankind to salvation — or perdition: to the virtuoso it is all one whether their souls go to heaven or 'a-blakeberyed' (VI.406).

---

[21] See Frank Grady, 'Chaucer Reading Langland: The House of Fame', *Studies in the Age of Chaucer*, 18 (1996), 3–23.

The Pardoner as invention stands in contraposition to the Wife of Bath, who also embodies the process of improvising a self out of the shreds of various current discourses, especially those that would condemn her enterprise. But while the Wife exemplifies the endless resourcefulness of such fictive miming, the Pardoner foregrounds its arbitrariness and its suspect motives. If, as Patterson has suggested, the Wife of Bath's improvisatory performance implies that the dilations and deferrals of self-definition are generative in their seductive power, productive of reformative insights that 'prepare the way to herself' as a term of gratification, the Pardoner registers the costs of this deflection, the consequences of separating questions of individual and communal identity.[22] Like the Wife, he represents a general depoliticization of issues of self-definition that Langland if anything repoliticized in his last two passūs: it is against Langland's fictive politics of the dispossessed, his realization of a world in which the lack of money, wool, cheese, and wheat has visible and appalling consequences in many a household by the time the 'hot hervest' rolls around each year is the perpetual condition of humankind in the state of nature, that we can best begin to understand the 'depth of field' behind the Pardoner's atavistic and unsatisfiable acquisitiveness as a powerful figure for spiritual lack.

Chaucer registers his understanding of the implications of this pattern in his portrayal of the Pardoner, not simply as 'lost soul' but as specifically a performer, wholly consumed and defined by performance, caught in a compulsion to repeat the last spectacular deception by yet another, as Donald Howard has eloquently argued. This malign dimension of the will to verbal performance embodies the dark realization that anything that can be improvised or imagined can also be commodified and sold, which is another way of saying that all art can become ideology. The Pardoner can only be rewarded by acquisitions that can be of no use to him except for further manipulation in his symbolic economy, not for gratification of any of his insatiable hungers. For Chaucer the spectacle of a major poetic talent expending itself in repeated articulations of a theme that is 'alwey oon' was not only imposing but cautionary: extended and reworked over at least a decade as an act of poetic self-exploration and self-constitution through antecedent authoritative texts, Langland's lifelong enterprise presented Chaucer with the alarming prospect of a massively, spectacularly unfinished and unfinishable

---

[22] Patterson, *Chaucer and the Subject of History*, chap. 6. For an overview of psychological accounts of the Pardoner, see also Patterson, 'Chaucer's Pardoner on the Couch: Psyche and Clio in Medieval Literary Studies', *Speculum*, 76 (2001), 638–80 (repr. in *Temporal Circumstances: Form and History in Chaucer's Poetry* (New York: Macmillan, 2006), chap. 5).

poem, and of a poetic self depicted as always in process of formation, yet grown old and exhausted by the process.

I have probably already begun to suggest not only what Chaucer learned from Langland, but why it was that, once he finally grasped the implications of Langland's poetic enterprise as one that short-circuited altogether the erotic fictions of the courtly milieu in which he founded his own practice, this became in effect guilty knowledge and began to engender its own pattern of suppression and repetition compulsions in the *Canterbury Tales* itself. Langland exposes, and Chaucer represents in the Pardoner, the corrosive and self-deceptive motive of self-glorification that dwells even at the heart of confession, self-humiliation, and penitential discipline, and hence renders any kind of poetic vocation as an adult masculine profession even more suspect than that of the pliant pet poet. Hence the concluding movements of the *Canterbury Tales* — the Manciple's and Canon's Yeoman's performance, as well as the dialogue over 'sentence and solas' in Fragment VII — represent genuinely reformative insight attained through the exercise of the imagination as an ever-receding possibility. So does the elided verse that follows the Parson's preaching text as exhortation to penance: the theme-text from Jeremiah reads: 'Stop at the crossroads, look for the ancient paths; ask "Where is the way that leads to what is good?" Then take that way, and you will find rest for yourselves'; the following verse, silently elided, reads 'But they said, "We will not"'.

The Parson's declining to 'geste "rum, ram, ruf," by lettre' (X.43) marks not merely a refusal to perform in verse (let alone a particularly despised verse form, for 'rym holde[s he] but litel bettre'; X.44), but specifically a break with the metier in which edifying or historical 'matere' was translated into Middle English before about 1380, and hence with those texts that furnished some of the chief materials and models for Langland's project.[23] By distinguishing his prose homily on

---

[23] Significantly, and not inaccurately, the Parson associates spiritual edification in verse with the northern regions of England. At a conference in March 2010 (at St Hilda's College, Oxford) on Anglo-French literary relations after 1350, Ralph Hanna presented a paper, 'The French Note in English Verse Translation' (quoted here from an unpaginated typescript provided by the author), in which he revisits the often-remarked fact that, in sharp contrast to developments in other medieval vernaculars, it was only after about 1380 that prose became 'the norm for reproducing serious materials' in English. Drawing his examples from the Middle English *Pricke of Conscience* and *Speculum vitae*, Hanna argues that for those who translated Latin and French spiritual and moral edification into English verse, 'whatever the distortions to the *utile*, useful knowledge, that might inhere in verse composition, verse equally provides the *dulce*, a pleasurable, beautiful response that both poets want to stimulate'. 'Encouraging aesthetic sensations will

penance and the deadly sins from the pre-1380 tradition of 'sweet' spiritual edification in English verse, the Parson aligns his 'myrie tale' (X.46) with the more exacting project of prose translation that followed, with its 'compulsive interest in literal reproduction [and] an informed and meticulous fidelity to source materials, at least initially, all Latinate ones'. The filiations of the latter enterprise are familiar; it is these that prompt the Host to scent 'a Lollere in the wynd' (II.1173) in the Parson's animadversions well before his Canterbury performance. Among its other fruits, as Hanna notes, are 'the comments in the Wycliffite pro-logue to Old Testament history, Chaucer's pernickety imposition of Boethius's lexis (after having translated Jean de Meun's French), the carefully signed and set off explanatory notes of Trevisa and Love'. By declaring these intentional parameters of his offering, the Parson divides truth from beauty as spiritually compelling qualities of edifying discourse, and imaginatively collapses the social and vocational heterogeneity of the Canterbury company into the undiffer-entiated category of layfolk that has often been seen by modern readers as the default audience, direct or indirect, of many of the manuals and compilations to which Langland's poem is formally and ideationally indebted. He also thereby draws a firm line between his edifying designs and those of Langland: for the Parson, a company festively convened is for the duration both lay and 'lewed', and imagining their interpellation as devout aspirants to more inward forms of knowing, both more 'kyndely' and 'clergial' than routine fare for the general, is largely beyond his remit as concluding speaker on the Canterbury pilgrimage. For Chaucer, too, the Parson's advertisement is a telling gesture: recasting the final tale as text rather than performance, it brackets the question of enjoyment as outside its canons of merit and redoubles this gesture with the Retractions. (These paired declarations of edifying final intent in turn echo the pilgrim Chaucer's doubled effort to please and instruct, by offering a 'litel thyng in prose' (VII.937) when the Host disrupts and scorns the 'rym dogerel' (VII.925) of his verse romance.) In its last moments as a represented action, the *Canterbury Tales* begins

---

always fall outside the poets' insistence upon dangerous worldliness', he adds, 'because it is protected by the appeal to "reading in/hearing of holy books"'. For these earlier translators, the 'joy of heaven' evoked by the beautiful is part of the intentional design of their enterprise as trans-lators: 'what the *Speculum*-poet calls "swete sauoury knawynge" (SV, 14634); just to turn the screw a little further, he illustrates this "savour", as traditionally both *sapor* and *sapiencia*', an identity-within-distinction that has often occupied readers of *Piers Plowman*; see Jill Mann, 'Eating and Drinking'. Citation of *Speculum vitae* by line number refers to *Speculum vitae: A Reading Edition*, ed. by Ralph Hanna, Early English Text Society, o.s., 331 and 332, 2 vols (Oxford: Oxford University Press, 2008).

to retrace the final moments of Langland's poem: as an unheeded call to unity and penitential self-reform. Chaucer, however, closes his work with the act Langland's poetic persona managed to defer for a lifetime, thereby greatly troubling such readers as John But, who registers his understanding of Langland's visions in a different mode: as a representation of 'Will's' pursuit and end-of-life profession of contrition, and his conclusory penitential rectification in his own person — one that removes his 'werkes', the production of a literary career, from both moral and literary judgement altogether.

Carolyn Dinshaw has convincingly shown that the Host's final scatological curse upon the Pardoner ('I wolde I hadde thy coillons in myn hond | In stide of relikes or of seintuarie'; VI.952–53) draws into the intertextual meanings of this figure that moment in which, and that example through which, Reason in the *Romance of the Rose* exposes the conventional rather than 'natural' basis of all linguistic reference, and hence the arbitrary nature of all poetic metaphor, which, as Reason in good Augustinian fashion goes on to argue, is efficacious — that is to say, most likely to awaken the interpretive faculty, and spur the soul to reflection — precisely where it is most arrestingly contrary to literal sense, where its fictive components behave most 'unnaturally'.[24] It may indeed have been this antecedent text that suggested to Chaucer a way in which a specifically sexual if unspecified 'unnaturalness' might be linked in representation to questions of the kind of truth that is told in fabling, in those 'tales oold' the appetite for which at once stirs the Pardoner's contempt and reawakens his own unsatisfied appetite for further control and acquisition. But I believe that stark suggestion, felicitous as it was, had to be bodied forth more fully in Langland's enterprise before Chaucer could realize it in the invention of the Pardoner as a figure of enormous pathos as well as an incisive ethical exemplum. It is the figuration of gender and sexuality as a problem in poetic self-representation as well as in poetic metaphor that Chaucer learned from Langland rather than Jean de Meun. For whatever the Pardoner's physiological condition, or psychosexual disposition, his character as a desiring

---

[24] Carolyn Dinshaw, 'Eunuch Hermeneutics', *English Literary History*, 55 (1988), 27–51; (repr. in Dinshaw, *Chaucer's Sexual Poetics* (Madison: University of Wisconsin Press, 1989), chap. 6, pp. 156–86). See especially pp. 34–38 on arbitrary and conventional versus 'real' signification, referring to *Romaunt*, ll. 6898–6901, Amant's objection to Raison's use of the word *coilles* (testicles). See also Dinshaw, *Getting Medieval: Sexualities and Communities, Pre- and Postmodern* (Durham, NC: Duke University Press, 1999), chap. 2, especially pp. 113–42, and p. 208 n. 6, on the distinction between 'unspeakable' and 'unspoken'; also the remarks of Minnis (n. 9, above) on Dinshaw's account of the Pardoner.

being (which is to say as a being capable of exercising his worldly talents in imagining and compassing action and work) is realized in a projected *gender* identity that offers a grotesque and cautionary mirror-image of the fictive subject-position of the court poet.

What made Langland's poetic self-presentation as a kind of hunger-artist so compelling to Chaucer — as material to rework, and by reworking, not only to understand but to exorcise — was that it presented a fearful answer to the question always latent in Chaucer's own process of career formation, from at least the *Hous of Fame* onward: suppose the fictively and perpetually post-adolescent male court poet were to be forced to grow up? Who or what would he be become? The courtier-poet's dependent amateurism, the pretense that his performances were provisional, disposable, and tailored to others' pleasures, was a convenient and benign fiction, sustainable only so long as the poetic persona could success-fully depict himself as deferring or suspending any articulated career ambitions or goals of his own beyond beguiling the far more valuable time of others who reward what pleases them. In other words, it required a man to profess wide-eyed adolescence more or less indefinitely, a perpetual deferral of adult male identity in the form of a determinate vocation or settled craft or profession. Chaucer seems to play speculatively with the discontents of this position in his late Envoys to Bukton and Scogan, but Langland presents a far more scathing analysis of the untenability of this posture in his final and fullest representation of Will's vocational self-definition, in the 'autobiography' of C, passus 5. The alternative proposed there to the itinerant maker of unconsidered trifles is to unmake his enterprise of 'making' altogether, to 'grow up' and take on enterprises incumbent on an adult and serious man: the exercise of talent and strength in a determinate vocation on behalf of the commune, as well as the enactment of penitential dis-cipline on behalf of self and world. Langland presents in stark and schematic form the prospect of male adulthood in the world of fiction-making as a kind of verbal masturbation (the 'thief of time' as Oscar Wilde called it), a misuse of the tools and the medium (time itself), and finally a deflection of the desire and will, given to humankind for the sustenance and salvation of the commune and for making an individual wager for immortality.

If even a part of the foregoing analysis has any value as a provocative hypoth-esis, then the first part of my question of *why* Chaucer's debt to Langland's work was occluded and unattributed virtually answers itself. Chaucer may not have known the name of the poet who gave him this cautionary image of poetic bad faith. But the poetic persona he found in *Piers Plowman* embodied a kind of guilty knowledge, a signpost on a road not taken except in the final paragraphs of the Canterbury project, in the form of a Retraction, a text which may stand as one of the most conclusive signs of what Chaucer learned from Langland about infinitely extendable and dilatory poetic projects. Chaucer gave to his understanding of what he learned from Langland a fictive form that rendered that knowledge at once encrypted and manifest, like the heart of the Pardoner's mystery: in the form of a figure who bears in his person an unacknowledged and unspeakable secret that is nevertheless manifest to all.

As a coda, I would like merely to suggest that the repression of Langland's imprint in Chaucer's work has had its counterpart in literary history: we have no way of putting Chaucer and Langland in the same frame and granting the status of specifically literary projects to both of their designs. I think this has to do with our own unwitting accession to the form of literary history that was in fact given to English literature by Chaucer himself. It is the form of his career, a pattern read back from Spenser to Virgil, that gives us our (largely 'humanist') idea of how literary history — or for that matter any history premised upon individual agency as determinative — is made: influence, reverent borrowing, mostly acknowledged or easily recoverable, issuing in mastery figured as coming into one's inheritance.[25] For us, Chaucer's production still traces what we recognize as the gradual realization of 'the literary' in literary history, of others' inventions made one's own and in turn transmitted: it is a matter of paternity, succession, transmissable proprietary rights, and reciprocal gratitude. Langland, who as poet refuses his sire's surname and declines to acknowledge openly the literary aspirations of his work, figures for us the strife of history itself, rather than the genial and uncompetitive Chaucerian model of literary 'development'. While Langland's work has never vanished from view, it has not been viewed under the sign of literary interest until well into this century, and the implications of the conscious choices that informed its literary production are still hard to bring to light, as George Kane has repeatedly observed.[26] We have no way to talk seriously and sympathetically about acts of imaginative analysis as thoroughgoing as Langland's, as unsparing of the craft in which they participate, and fashioned, as most of his are, from essentially non-literary materials. For these reasons, it still seems necessary to deny to his work the literary consequentiality and seriousness of its most

[25] As I argue in my forthcoming essay, 'Playing the Plowman' (see n. 2, above).

[26] Besides Kane, 'Reading *Piers Plowman*', see further Steven Knapp, *Literary Interest: The Limits of Anti-Formalism* (Cambridge, MA: Harvard University Press, 1993).

pervasive and hard-won concerns. But Chaucer registers for us, without anywhere admitting that he is doing so, the magnitude of what his allegedly inartistic predecessor forced into his own vernacular literary consciousness. When we ourselves figure out how to get both Langland and Chaucer into our account of English literary history, as titanic contemporaries in one of the most imaginatively productive periods of English literary achievement, we will have finally discovered how to write a literary history of the era worthy of their efforts.[27]

[27] Presented to a Chaucer session at the December 1991 MLA meeting, this essay was initially designed as a provocative thought experiment rather than a close reading of all the evidence that might be brought to bear on the topic; still less was it meant as a foray into gender studies, a field to which I have remained an appreciative bystander. Like the 1974 Medieval Academy lecture by Donald Howard that was its earliest inspiration, it has in the interim led a kind of half-life in the recollection of others, whose enquiries for details of its (presumed) publication prompted me to revisit it. I have attempted to retain here its original character as an exploratory essay, citing not only those whose work informed the original lecture, but some who have in the intervening years enlarged my understanding of the relations between gender, allegorical representation, and authorial self-representation in these texts. In offering it in memory of George Kane, I mean to acknowledge with gratitude the formative importance of that exacting and provocative scholar, whose kindnesses and stringencies over many years have been of equal value to my thinking about the 'obligatory conjunction' of these two poets. I do not deceive myself that he would wholly approve of these results.

THE SUBJECT OF CANON LAW:
CONFESSING COVETISE IN *PIERS PLOWMAN*
B AND C AND THE *MEMORIALE PRESBITERORUM*

Arvind Thomas

In the course of his confession in the B and C texts of *Piers Plowman*, Covetise admits that he has committed usury. Repentance's response to Covetise's admission, however, is not the same in both the texts. In the B text, Repentance initiates a sustained enquiry into Covetise's remorse for the victims of his usury before insisting that he make restitution. In his initial response to Repentance's questions, Covetise reveals nothing but a ferocious contempt for those he has defrauded, and so Repentance urges him to repent or else risk being forsaken by God:

> 'Lentestow euere lordes for loue of hire mayntenaunce?'
> 'Ye, I haue lent lordes, loued me neuere after,
> And haue ymaad many a kny3t boþe mercer and draper
> That payed neuere for his prentishode no3t a peire gloues!'
> 'Hastow pite on pouere men þat [borwe mote nedes]?'
> 'I haue as muche pite of pouere men as a pedlere haþ of cattes,
> That wolde kille hem, if he cacche hem my3te, for coueitise of hir skynnes!'
> 'Artow manlich among þi ne3ebores of þi mete and drynke?'
> 'I am holden,' quod he, 'as hende as hound is in kichene;
> Amonges my ne3ebores namely swich a name ich haue'.

Arvind Thomas (*arthomas@fordham.edu*) is a PhD candidate in English at Fordham University.

Abstract: In this comparative study of the B and C versions of Covetise's confession to Repentance, I highlight the lateral relations between *Piers Plowman* and the near contemporary penitential manual *Memoriale presbiterorum* on the question of restitution. Examining Langland's revisions to the B version of Covetise's confession through the lens of canon law, I point out that they show the poet's thinking about restorative justice to resonate with that found in the *Memoriale*. By expressing a shared professionally pastoral approach to sins that cause material damage to the community, both Langland and the *Memoriale* stress the confessor's answerability to the canon law of restitution.

Keywords: literary history, canon law, restitution, sacramental confession, William Langland, absolution, penitential rhetoric, anticlericalism.

10.1484/J.YLS.1.102112

'Now [but þow repente þe raþer', quod Repentaunce, 'God lene þee neuere]
The grace on þis grounde þi good wel to bisette',[1]

In the corresponding passage in the C text, Repentance neither enquires into Covetise's 'pite' for his victims nor invokes 'God' to exhort him to repent. Rather, castigating usurers in general, Repentance shifts the emphasis immediately from contrition to restitution. Invoking the papal penitentiary, he asserts that not even the Pope and 'alle his pentauncers' have the 'power' to grant Covetise absolution unless he makes restitution:

'Lenedestow euere eny lord for loue of his mayntenaunce?'
'Y haue lent lordes and ladyes þat louede me neuere aftur,
And haue ymad many a knyht bothe mercer and draper,
Payed neuere for his prentished nat a payre gloues!
That chaffared with my cheuesaunces cheued selde aftur'.
'Now redily', quod Repentaunce, 'and by þe Rode, Y leue,
Shal neuere seketoure wel bysette the syluer þat thow hem leuest,
Ne thyn heyres, as Y hope, haue ioye of þat thow wonne;
For þe Pope with alle his pentauncers, power hem fayleth
To assoyle the of this synne *sine restitucione*:
Numquam dimittitur peccatum, nisi restituatur ablatum'.

(C.6.248–57)

To juxtapose the B and C passages quoted above is to encounter two perspectives from which Langland represents Repentance's adherence to the canon law of penance. In the B text, Repentance follows canon law from the perspective of the penitent insofar as he initially enquires into Covetise's remorse for the victims of his usury and only later demands that he make restitution.[2] In the C text, by contrast, Repentance follows canon law from the perspective of the confessor insofar as he repeatedly clarifies every confessor's obligation to impose restitution

---

[1] *William Langland, Piers Plowman: A Parallel-Text Edition of the A, B, C and Z Versions*, ed. by A. V. C. Schmidt, I: *Text* (London: Longman, 1995), B.5.249–60. All references to *Piers Plowman* are from this edition and are cited by version, passus, and line. The title of my essay deliberately evokes Andrew Galloway's stimulating essay on secular law, '*Piers Plowman* and the Subject of the Law', *YLS*, 15 (2001), 117–28. Unless otherwise stated, all translations from Latin and German are my own.

[2] In the B text, Repentance insists that Covetise make restitution at the end of the confession process; see 5.269–72.

upon the penitent who commits usury.[3] By acknowledging Langland's invocation of the canon on restitution from the confessor's rather than from the penitent's perspective, we can see the extent to which the revised version of Covetise's confession expresses a socio-legal *mentalité* embodied in near contemporary penitential manuals such as the *Memoriale presbiterorum*. Seen through the lens of canon law, Langland's revisions to Covetise's confession are not just local to the B text but also indicative of a lateral relationship between revised poem and penitential manual on the question of restorative justice. By expressing a shared professionally pastoral approach to sins that cause material damage to the community, both Langland and the *Memoriale* offer a vision of penitential reform in which the confessor is bound by the canon law of restitution.

Wrath's Confession in the C Text

Langland's additions to Wrath's confession foreshadow the canon law rendered explicit in the revisions made to Covetise's confession, and so we would be well served to examine briefly this former scene as a prelude to the concerns in the following scene with Covetise. While confessing his role in sowing discord between the secular and mendicant clergy, Wrath identifies fraternal violations of canon law as a cause of the sin that he personifies:

> Freres folewen my fore fele tyme and ofte
> And preuen inparfit prelates of Holy Churche;
> And prelates pleyneth on hem for they here parschiens shryuen
> Withoute licence and leue, and herby lyueth wrathe.
> Thus thei speke and dispute þat vchon dispiseth oþer.
>
> (C.6.118–22)

In these lines, which have no parallel in the B version of the same confession, Wrath explains that he 'lyueth' because the friars who follow in his footsteps shrive parishioners '[w]ithoute licence and leue'.[4] Such friars administer the

---

[3] As Nick Gray notes, the Latin words ('*Numquam dimittitur peccatum, nisi restituatur ablatum*') that Repentance cites comprise a '[c]anon law maxim' ('Langland's Quotations from the Penitential Tradition', *Modern Philology*, 84 (1986), 53–60 (p. 53)).

[4] In the B version of Wrath's confession, although Wrath does not mention the prelates or their complaint about the friars' disregard of canon law, he notes that penitents prefer to confess to friars rather than to their own parish priests — a preference that implicates the friars in the kinds of legal violation of jurisdiction that these C revisions render explicit; see B.5.140–45.

sacrament of penance by violating canon law. The words *licence* and *leue* in the prelates' complaint against the friars point to the legislation embodied in papal bulls of the thirteenth and fourteenth centuries that require friars to secure permission from parish or episcopal authorities in order to hear confessions from parishioners.[5] Discussing such papal decretals, H. A. Kelly observes:

> Dominicans and Franciscan friars who wish to hear confession in a diocese are to present themselves to the bishop, who will licence them; if he refuses to do so, for no good reason, the necessary licence will be supplied by papal authority. The licence does not confer powers greater than those possessed by the parish priests, unless the bishop explicitly says so.[6]

Michael Haren's paraphrase of two such papal bulls (*Super cathedram* and *Dudum*) underscores the requirement of friars to obtain an appropriate licence or leave from prelates in order to hear confessions:

> They [the friars] may not, however, preach in parish churches unless invited by the parish priests and with their consent or licence or unless authorized by the bishop or a higher prelate [...] in the case of the Franciscans [the priors principal or their vicars general] must approach the bishop, in person or by deputy, for a special licence that selected friars may hear confession of such of the bishop's subjects as wish to confess to them, and enjoin penances and absolve them. They shall then present the chosen friars to the bishop for license. The number licensed in this way is to be determined by local conditions and the friars thus licensed shall not hear confessions outside the cities and the dioceses for which they have been commissioned.[7]

Wrath's explicit mention of the terms *licence* and *leue* invokes such papal legislation, and, hence, locates not only the sin of wrath but also negligent fraternal

---

[5] Michael Haren argues that in the thirteenth and fourteenth centuries Canon 21 frequently provided the legal basis for arguments against granting friars the right to hear the confessions of parishioners ('Friars as Confessors: The Canonistic Background to the Fourteenth-Century Controversy', *Peritia*, 3 (1984), 503–16 (p. 505)). The 'licence' or 'leue' resembles the bishop's 'breef' that a friar secures in order to hear the allegorical Contricion's confession in the last passus of *Piers Plowman* (in both texts). As Stephen A. Barney observes, 'In 1300 Pope Boniface VIII issued a bull that required friars to receive bishop's formal licence in order to hear confessions' (*The Penn Commentary on 'Piers Plowman'*, V: *C Passus 20–22; B Passus 18–20* (Philadelphia: University of Pennsylvania Press, 2006), p. 242).

[6] H. A. Kelly, 'Penitential Theology and Law at the Turn of the Fifteenth Century', in *A New History of Penance*, ed. by Abigail Firey, Brill Companions to the Christian Tradition, 14 (Leiden: Brill, 2008), p. 275. See also Haren, who notes that the papal bulls such as the *Super cathedram* and *Dudum* 'provide[d] an effective means for the establishment of ordinary control over the confessional activities of the friars' ('Friars as Confessors', p. 510).

[7] Haren, 'Friars as Confessors', pp. 508–09.

confessors explicitly within the framework of canon law. Presenting wrath as arising from the friars' failure to obtain the appropriate licence(s) to hear confession, Wrath's confession foreshadows Repentance's persistent recourse to canonical legislation in the C revisions to the confession of the subsequent penitent Covetise, to whom we now turn.

Covetise's Confession

It is within the context of Covetise's admission of usury that Repentance frames the sin explicitly as a legal violation and proceeds to enjoin confessors not to disregard the canon law of restitution.[8] While both the B and C versions are alike in identifying Covetise's sin as lending to 'lordes', the two versions differ with regard to how Repentance handles usury and its canonistic remedy.[9] In the B version, Langland foregrounds Repentance's role as that of a diligent and prudent investigator of souls.[10] Repentance endeavours to elicit from Covetise both a

[8] For a general discussion of usury as a sin in the later Middle Ages, see Diana Wood, 'Lesyng of Tyme': Perceptions of Idleness and Usury in Late Medieval England', in *The Use and Abuse of Time in Christian History*, ed. by R. N. Swanson (Woodbridge: Boydell, for the Ecclesiastical History Society, 2002), pp. 106–16, and her two chapters 'The Nature of Usury: The Usurer as Winner' and 'The Theory of Interest: The Usurer as Loser', in *Medieval Economic Thought* (Cambridge: Cambridge University Press, 2002), pp. 159–205. For the canon law on usury, see T. P. McLaughlin, 'The Teaching of the Canonists on Usury', *Mediaeval Studies*, 1 (1939), 81–147.

[9] The prominent place usury occupies in Covetise's confession can be explained in light of Wood's observation that although '[t]he Church prosecuted "manifest" usurers and ordered restitution [...] in practice a lot of the correction was left to the inner forum of individual conscience and to the priest in the secrecy of the confessional. The confessor had to induce the usurer to make restitution before absolution could be given' (*Medieval Economic Thought*), pp. 170–71.

[10] Post-Lateran IV penitential manuals typically portrayed the confessor as a spiritual judge who needed to perform a diligent and prudent enquiry of the sins of penitents. In his influential confessional guide, Raymond of Peñafort mandates that the confessor should know and discern what he has to judge, and, hence, must be a diligent and subtle analyst ('Oportet ut sciat cognoscere quidquid debet iudicare. Iudicaria enim potestas hoc expostulat, ut quod debet iudicare, discernat. Diligens igitur inquisitor, subtilis investigator sapienter et quasi astute interroget a peccatore quod forsitan ignoret, vel verecundia velit occultare'); see 'De paenitentiis et remissionibus', in *Summa de iure canonico; summa de paenitentia; summa de matrimonio*, ed. by Javier Ochoa Sanz and Luis Diez Garcia, 3 vols (Rome: Commentarium pro religiosi, 1975–78), vol. II, 30.827. All citations of Peñafort are from this edition and refer first to the section and then the column. Likewise, the statutes of Exeter postulate that the priest should exercise his spiritual care just as a wise doctor

confession of, and contrition for, his sins. He seeks to know not only whom Covetise has defrauded but also whether or not he feels sorry for his victims. Following procedures for interrogation disseminated by confessional treatises written in the wake of Lateran IV, Repentance asks if Covetise has pity for the 'pouere men þat [borwe mote nedes]' (B.5.253). With sneering contempt, Covetise replies that he has as much concern for them as 'pedlere haþ of cattes, | That wolde kille hem, if he cacche hem myȝte, for coueitise of hir skynnes!' (B.5.254–55). And, when Repentance asks if he is 'manlich among þi neȝebores of þi mete and drynke', Covetise responds that the 'neȝebores' regard him 'as hende as hound is in kichene' (B.5.256-57).[11] In enquiring whether Covetise has 'pite' or is 'manlich', Repentance attempts to determine the presence and nature of Covetise's feeling for the people whom he has presumably defrauded.[12] On

does ('Curet igitur sacerdos ut sapiens medicus et perfectus primum peccata sua diluere et postea aliena tergere et sanare'); see the 'Statutes of Exeter II', in *Councils & Synods, with Other Documents Relating to the English Church*, II: *A.D. 1205–1313*, ed. by F. M. Powicke and C. R. Cheney (Oxford: Oxford University Press, 1964), p. 991. William of Pagula's *Pars oculi* (of his *Oculus sacerdotis*), likewise, stipulates that the confessor or spiritual judge know what he must adjudicate over: 'Iudex enim spiritualis non debet carere munere scientie; oportet ut sciat cognoscere quicquid debet iudicare. Judiciaria potestas hoc expostulat ut quem debet iudicare discernat, igitur diligens inquisitor [...] sapienter [...] interroget a peccatore quod fortisan ignorat [...]. Habeat dulcedinem in affeccione, pietatem in alterius crimine, discrecionem in alterius varietate [...] circumstancias autem peccati quas sacerdos debet precipue attendere in his versibus continentur: Quis, quid, ubi, per quos, quociens, cur, quomodo, quando, quilibet obseruet anime medicamina dando (passages from Pagula's *Pars oculi* are from J. P. Daly's edition of Rolle's *Judica me Deus* (Salzburg: Institut für Anglistik; Amerikanistik Universität Salzburg, 1984), pp. 37–38).

[11] The image of the hound in the kitchen, as one of the anonymous readers of this essay has pointed out, invites comparison with a similar image found in the popular penitential work *The Book of Vices and Virtues* (as well as in its source *Somme le roi*) where contrite tears parallel scalding water and the devil the hound: 'Suche teeres [of contrition] dryuen awey þe deuel, riȝt as þe scolde hot watre makeþ an hound flee þe kychene' (*The Book of Vices and Virtues: A Fourteenth-Century English Translation of the 'Somme le Roi' of Lorens d'Orléans*, ed. by W. Nelson Francis, Early English Text Society, o.s., 217 (London: Oxford University Press, 1942), p. 172).

[12] Repentance's insistence that Covetise inwardly experience and outwardly express 'pite' or heartfelt repentance receives considerable elaboration in *The Book of Vices and Virtues*: 'Repetaunce askeþ grete sorwe and grete ofþenkynge in herte of þat þat we haue wraþþed oure maker, and þe more we haue wraþþed hym, þe more schal be þe sorwe; and so repenteded hym þe kyng Dauid whan he seide in þe Sauter, "I worche and trauaile in my wailynges; and al nyȝt I wasche my beed and my couche wiþ my teeres." Þei þat haue wraþþed God bi dedly synne, þei schulle seye "weilawey" wiþ riȝt deep herte, so þat þe herte mowe melte and brynge forþe alle þe teeres wiþ grete

failing to detect any signs of remorse, Repentance urges Covetise to repent, admonishing him about God's abandonment of him: 'Now [but þow repente þe raþer', quod Repentaunce, 'God lene þee neuere]' (B.5.259). By the end of the confessional process, Covetise is so overwhelmed by the enormity of his sins that he fears damnation and expresses a suicidal impulse. Persisting in his care for the penitent's spiritual state, Repentance hastens to comfort him in order to prevent him from falling into despair.[13]

In the corresponding C lines, by contrast, Repentance digresses from his questioning of Covetise in order to clarify the confessor's obligation to heed the canon law of restitution:

> 'Now redily', quod Repentaunce, 'and by þe Rode, Y leue,
> Shal neuere seketoure wel bysette the syluer þat thow hem leuest,
> Ne thyn heyres, as Y hope, haue ioye of þat thow wonne;
> For þe Pope with alle his pentauncers, power hem fayleth
> To assoyle the of this synne *sine restitucione*:
> *Numquam dimittitur peccatum, nisi restituatur ablatum'*.
>
> (C.6.253–57)

In these revised lines, Repentance shifts the emphasis from enquiring into Covetise's interior feeling of 'pite' (B.5.253) to asserting the confessor's lack of 'power' to absolve a usurious sinner who does not make restitution (C.6.256). It is as if Repentance were asserting to an implied audience of confessors that they need to treat usury as a material sin that cannot be remitted unless the usurer makes material amends to her or his victims.[14]

---

sorwe, and wiþ grete wepynge and sore syȝhing schal crie God mercy as his þef, as his mansleer and murþerour, þat þat haþ deserued to be honged in helle' (p. 172).

[13] 'Thanne weex þe sherewe in wanhope and wolde han hanged hymselue | Ne hadde Repentaunce þe raþer reconforted hym in þis manere | "Haue mercy in þi mynde, and wiþ þi mouþ biseche it"' (B.5.279–81).

[14] Both the B and C versions of Covetise's confession construct usury less as a sin of intention in the mind of the penitent than as a sin of action that affects its victims in concrete socio-economic ways. Focusing on the 'seketoure', the 'syluer', and the 'heyres', Repentance locates Covetise's material gains within the context of misappropriated interest and its transmission to the penitent's heirs, and thereby exemplifies what Wood considers 'the more legalistic' of Gratian's two definitions of usury, namely, 'to expect whatsoever exceeds the principal is usury' ('quodcumque sorti accidit usura est; et quodcumque velis ei nomen imponas, usura est'; Gratian, *Decretum*, II.14.3.3); Wood notes that '[t]wo definitions [of usury] feature in Gratian's *Decretum*, both of them citing patristic texts. They emphasize two different aspects of the question. The first

Deploring the possession and enjoyment of ill-gotten gains, Repentance invokes no ordinary confessors but the Pope and his 'pentauncers' (C.6.256). John Alford explains that a 'pentauncer' 'is a priest appointed by a pope or bishop to administer the sacrament of penance, esp. in cases reserved to the bishop or pope'.[15] Given that Repentance describes the 'pentauncers' as all belonging to the 'Pope', they are in all likelihood *paenitentiarii* who, as W. P. Mueller explains, 'were the principal representatives of the Apostolic Court (Curia) [...] papal confessors [who] counted it among their main duties to hear confessions of contrite pilgrims who had come to Rome (or the pope) to ease their troubled consciences'.[16] Belonging to the highest ecclesiastical court of penance, the papal 'pentauncers' alone possessed the dispensatory power to grant favours such as permission to priests to absolve penitents from those sins that lesser confessors such as bishops and parish priests could not ordinarily remit. In a recent study of the relations between the penitentiary and laity, P. D. Clarke stresses the power of the papal penitentiary by noting that it not only 'issued various kinds of *littere confessionales* by the fifteenth century, including those described as *in forma* "Cupientes" that granted priests special powers to absolve their parishioners from certain grave sins' but also, given the popularity of friars as spiritual counsellors, interpreted the canon law requiring penitents to confess to their own priests so broadly as to 'allow laity [in royal and noble households] to choose them [the friars] and other suitable priests as their confessors'.[17]

As the confessors' powers to grant absolution varied according to their clerical status, Repentance's invocation of the Pope and his 'pentauncers' rather than lesser confessors such as the bishop, the friar, and the parish priest is significant:

---

is "expecting to receive back more than you have given" in a loan, whether of money or anything else, and it underlines the sinful intention of the usurer [...]. The second of Gratian's definitions was more legalistic: "Whatsoever exceeds the principal was usury". This highlighted the familiar idea of balance and equality. It also made the point that although usury applied primarily to money, anything that could be counted, weighed, or measured could be the subject of a loan' (*Medieval Economic Thought*, pp. 159–60).

[15] *'Piers Plowman': A Glossary of Legal Diction* (Cambridge: Brewer, 1988), p. 113.

[16] W. P. Mueller, 'The Price of Papal Pardon', in *Festschrift für Ludwig Schmugge zum 65. Geburtstag* (Tübingen: Niemeyer, 2004), p. 459. For a comprehensive study of the papal penitentiary, see Emil Göller, *Die päpstliche Pönitentiarie von ihrem Ursprung bis zu ihrer Umgestaltung unter Pius V*, 4 vols (Rome: Loescher, 1907–11), and also Kirsi Salonen and Ludwig Schmugge, *A Sip from the 'Well of Grace'* (Washington, DC: Catholic University of America Press, 2009).

[17] P. D. Clarke, 'New Evidence of Noble and Gentry Piety in Fifteenth-Century England and Wales', *Journal of Medieval History*, 34 (2008), 23–35 (p. 29).

it stresses that all confessors are answerable to the canon on restitution.[18] To appreciate Repentance's accent on the limits upon all confessors' powers to grant absolution from usury, it is necessary to read the revised passage alongside its original in the B text, where Repentance cites the canon on restitution to exhort Covetise both to make restitution and repair ties with his victims:

> 'Thow art an vnkynde creature — I kan þee noȝt assoille
> Til þow make restitucion' quod Repentaunce, 'and rekene wiþ hem alle,
> And siþen þat Reson rolle it in þe Registre of heuene
> That þow hast maad ech man good, I may þee noȝt assoille:
> *Non dimittitur peccatum donec restituatur ablatum*'.
>
> (B.5.269–72)

In this passage, Repentance's admonitory words to Covetise occur toward the end of the confessional process at a stage where the confessor would typically decide whether or not to grant absolution to his penitent: if the sinner had committed one of the reserved sins including usury, the confessor would withhold absolution and send the penitent to superior confessors.[19] What occasions Repentance to mention the canon in the B passage is precisely the need to spell out to Covetise the terms of absolution. Repentance explains to Covetise that as 'Reson rolle it in þe Registre of heuene' (B.5.271), the penitent cannot receive absolution without restitution. Addressed solely to Covetise, Repentance's words about restitution make no reference to any confessor's answerability to canon law but solely to the penitent's requirement to abide by the canon for his own spiritual and social good. Specifically, Repentance's words to Covetise exemplify a pastoral rhetoric more suited to penitents who need to be persuaded to repent and make restitution than to confessors who need to be admonished about their canonistic duties. This is probably why Repentance substantiates the canon on restitution by recourse to allegorical figures such as 'Reson' and the 'Registre of heuene', who have a vividly

---

[18] Repentance's concern with the legal limits of papal power invites comparison with Will's assertion of the unconditionality of such power in his reflections upon the efficacy of pardons in the famous pardon scene in passus 9 of the C text: 'ȝut hath þe Pope power pardoun to graunte | To peple, withouten penaunce to passe into ioye, | As lettrede men vs lereth and lawe of Holi Churche: *Quodcumque ligaueris super terram erit ligatum et in celis*' (C.9.324–26).

[19] For instance, Richard Rolle, in his confessional manual, advises the parish priest to send the sinner who commits grave sins such as usury to the bishop, observing that he cannot absolve such a penitent unless he is in danger of death: 'In istis uero casibus non potest sacerdos parochialis absoluere nisi in periculo mortis, sed debet mittere peccatorem ad episcopum seu eius peni-tenciarium, uidelicet, blasfematores, claudestine matrimonium contrahentes [...] usurarius [...]. Hii et huiusmodi ad superiores debent mitti' (Rolle, *Judica me Deus*, p. 66).

dramatic or even demotic appeal rather than, as in the C version, to the concrete figures of the institutional church such as the Pope and his papal confessors, who would appear prosaic — perhaps even a trifle technical — to such a socially marked audience as Covetise typifies. All these examples of Repentance's concentration upon, and care for, Covetise's soul articulate a project of penitential reform directed not at the confessor and the conditional 'power' canon law confers upon him (as in the C version) but at the penitent and the socio-legal obligations owed to his victims.

'Sine restitucione' in the C Version of Covetise's Confession

Just as, in the C version of Covetise's confession, Langland privileges the literal over the allegorical to stress the topicality of canon law and confessors, so he revises the B version of the Latin maxim on restitution in this passage in order to bring it linguistically closer to the formulation typically used by late medieval canonists. Langland adds 'sine restitucione' and replaces 'Non' with 'Numquam' to stress the absolute necessity of restitution for the remission of sin: '*sine restitucione*: | *Numquam dimittur peccatum nisi restituatur ablatum*'. In particular, Langland's replacement of 'donec' with 'nisi' aligns the revised wording closer to that found in legal discourse, as '[n]o parallel from earlier or contemporary texts has yet been reported for Langland's reading of "*donec*"'.[20] Such subtle linguistic differences between the B and C formulations of the canon on restitution are by no means value-neutral. In light of Fiona Somerset's insight into Latin usage in *Piers Plowman*, the revised version of the canon on restitution may be said to exemplify the 'deliberate changes [in Latin] designed to fit the "quotation" [in Langland's poem] to its surroundings'.[21] Taken in the sense of contexts, the 'surroundings' for the citation of the same canon differ in each text. In the B version, Repentance introduces 'deliberate changes' to the Latin wording of the canon solely to 'fit' the curatorial context of exhorting Covetise to make restitution. In the C version, Repentance revises such 'changes' in order to 'fit' the pedagogic context of clarifying restitution to Covetise *and*, by implication, to all confessors. Put differently, in the C version, Langland has Repentance adopt a more legally precise formulation of the canon that would suit an intended audience beyond the immediate physically present penitent Covetise.

---

[20] Gray, 'Langland's Quotations', p. 54.

[21] Fiona Somerset, "Al þe comonys with o voys atonys': Multilingual Latin and Vernacular Voice in *Piers Plowman*', *YLS*, 19 (2005), 107–36 (pp. 108–09).

Repentance's emphasis upon the confessor's accountability to canon law persists in the additions that Langland makes toward the end of Covetise's confession:

> ȝe, þe prest þat thy tythe toek, trowe Y non other,
> Shal parte with the in purgatorye and helpe paye thy dette,
> Yf he wiste thow were such, when he resseyued thyn offrynge.
> And what lede leueth þat Y lye, look in þe Sauter glosed,
> On *Ecce enim veritatem dilexisti*,
> And there shal he wite witterly what vsure is to mene,
> And what penaunce the prest shal haue þat proud is of his tithes.
> For an hore of here ers-wynnynge may hardiloker tythe
> Then an errant vsurer, haue God my treuthe,
> And arste shal come to heuene, by [Hym] that me made.
>
> (C.6.298–307)

With no parallel in the B version of the Covetise's confession, Repentance's added words both introduce a new, albeit absent, referent — the parish priest — and relocate the canon on restitution within the context of parochial administration. Recalling and reinforcing his earlier shift in focus (in the C version of Covetise's confession) from the penitent to the Pope and his penitentiary, Repentance here digresses from hearing Covetise's confession to apostrophizing and admonishing Covetise's own parish priest. He warns 'þe prest þat thy [Covetise's] tythe toek' (C.6.298) about the perils of profiting from the proceeds of usury.

The immediate context for the words directed against Covetise's parish priest is common to both versions of the poem: the clarification of the canon that, in the case of usury, makes absolution conditional upon restitution.[22] The versions differ with regard to the roles assigned to confessor and penitent in the observance of the canon on restitution. In the B version, Repentance does not even mention the confessor's duty to withhold absolution on legal grounds. Instead, he focuses on the penitent's duty to 'make restitucion' and 'rekene wiþ hem alle' (B.5.270). In speaking to Covetise, Repentance continues to express the same interest in Covetise's social obligation to repair ties with his victims that he (Repentance) intimated while interrogating him about 'pite' at an earlier stage of the confessional process (B.5.253). When Repentance's exhortation causes Covetise to fall into 'wanhope' instead of making restitution, Repentance persists in his acute concern for Covetise's spiritual welfare (B.5.279). Ceasing to admonish Covetise,

---

[22] See B.5.269–74 and C.6.294–97.

he hastens to comfort him, advising him to think of divine mercy.[23] In this shift in emphasis from admonishment to encouragement, he again presents himself as immediately concerned with the care of Covetise's soul.

In the corresponding lines in the C text, Repentance no doubt stresses Covetise's need to make restitution but his attention shifts from the penitent's duty to make restitution, on the one hand, to the parish confessor's obligation to ensure that the penitent make restitution, on the other. Repentance handles restitution not so much from Covetise's perspective as from that of the parish priest who would be authorized to receive Covetise's tithes and hear his confessions. This is not to say that Repentance ceases to care for Covetise's soul. Rather, Repentance's spiritual care for Covetise is, and this point is crucial to my argument, expressed in terms of the confessor's accountability to canon law. Just as Repentance earlier on invokes papal confessors in an effort to urge Covetise to make restitution, so he now invokes the parish priest to clarify his [the priest's] subjection to the canon on restitution. In shifting the emphasis from penitent to parish priest, the revised C lines reconfigure Covetise's necessity to make restitution within the *cura animarum* with which his parish priest is entrusted. Repentance's words stress the penal consequences that will befall the parish confessor in the event that he disregarded the canon on restitution during tithe collection. Repentance has the parish priest share Covetise's burden of sin should he have collected tithes that derived from ill-gotten gains. Repentance's point is that the parish confessor who willfully ignores the canon on restitution by accepting tithes from a parishioner who has misappropriated goods is no less guilty of usury than the parishioner himself or herself: both the parish confessor and the parishioner will together have to share and expiate the debt of usury in purgatory.

Repentance's criticism of the parish priest in the C additions bears upon and amplifies the rigour of Canon 21 of Lateran IV.[24] Mandating that all parishioners confess to their own parish priest at least once a year, Canon 21 rested on the assumption that only the parish priest knew the parishioners under his charge best

---

[23] 'Haue mercy in þi mynde, and wiþ þi mouþ biseche it | For [His] mercy is moore þan alle Hise oþere werkes' (B.5.281–82).

[24] Making annual confession to one's proper priest obligatory, Canon 21 of Lateran IV, as Winfried Trusen notes, accelerated and accentuated the legalization of the sacrament of penance: 'Der Einbruch der Jurisprudenz in die Praxis des *forum internum*, den wir zunächst an wenigen Stellen beobachten können, wird nun durch ein Ereignis beschleunigt und intensiviert. Im Jahr 1215 erlässt das 4. Laterankonzil die berühmte Konstitution 21 *Omnis utriusque sexus*' ('*Forum internum* und gelehrtes Recht im Spätmittelalter: *Summae confessorum* und Traktate als Wegbereiter der Rezeption', *Zeitschrift der Savigny-Stiftung für Rechtsgeschichte, Kanonische Abteilung*, 57 (1971), 83–126 (p. 90)).

and that an intimate knowledge of their activities was integral to hearing and interpreting their confessions:

> Omnis utriusque sexus fidelis, postquam ad annos discretionis pervenerit, omnia sua solus peccata saltem semel in anno fideliter confiteatur proprio sacerdoti, et iniunctam sibi poenitentiam propriis viribus studeat adimplere, suscipiens reverenter ad minus in Pascha eucharistiae sacramentum, nisi forte de proprii sacerdotis consilio ob aliquam rationabilem causam ad tempus ab huiusmodi perceptione duxerit abstinendum, alioquin et vivens ab ingressu ecclesiae arceatur, et moriens Christiana careat sepultura. Unde hoc salutare statutum frequenter in ecclesiis publicetur, ne quisquam ignorantiae caecitate velamen excusationis assumat. Si quis autem alieno sacerdoti voluerit iusta de causa sua confiteri peccata, licentiam prius postulet et obtineat a proprio sacerdote, quum aliter ipse illum non possit absolvere vel ligare.[25]

> (All faithful members of both sexes, after having reached the age of discretion, should confess their sins faithfully at least once a year to their proper priest and should try to fulfil the imposed penance with their own strength, receiving reverently at least during Easter the sacrament of the Eucharist, unless perhaps, with the counsel of the proper priest for some reasonable cause, they are directed to abstain from receiving the sacrament at the time; otherwise, while living, they would be at a distance from the entrance of the church and, dying, would lack a Christian burial. Hence, this statute is published frequently in the churches lest anyone with the blindness of ignorance should assume the veil of excuse. However, if anyone, with just cause, should wish to confess his sins to another priest, he should first request and obtain a licence from his proper priest, since the other priest cannot absolve or bind him.)

In light of Canon 21, Repentance's ascription of penalties to Covetise's parish priest may be construed as a salutary canonistic admonition to the parish priest who ceases to express spiritual care for his parishioners by ignoring and profiting from their usurious activities. What Repentance demands is that the parish priest follow the canon law of restitution not only within the internal forum of confession but also within the context of tithe collection.[26] In mandating that the priest acquire an intimate knowledge of his parishioners' activities not only from their confessions, but also from his verification of the sources of their tithes, Repentance's additions can be seen as supplementing Canon 21 in the Derridean sense of the supplement: as juridical elaborations and glosses of Canon 21, they not only enrich what is full but also replace what is deficient.[27]

---

[25] *Liber extra*, 5.38.12, in *Decretalium collectiones*, ed. by Aemilius Friedberg, Corpus iuris canonici, 2 (Leipzig: Tauchnitz, 1881), p. 887.

[26] For the major role of the secular clergy in Langland's vision of penitential reform, see Lawler's essay 'The Secular Clergy in *Piers Plowman*', *YLS*, 16 (2002), 85–117.

[27] Helen Barr succinctly explains Derrida's 'supplement' in her reading of the 'Piers Plowman Tradition'. Such 'poems can be seen to supplement institutionalized discourse in the Derridean

Among the C additions that I have discussed so far are those that refer to clerics such as the pope, the papal confessors, and the parish priest. Absent from the corresponding B lines, these confessors are mentioned as answerable to canon law: no matter what the rank of the confessor, his power of granting absolution, in Repentance's view, is circumscribed by the canon on restitution. My point is that with the additions of the pope, the 'pentauncers' and the parish priest, the C revisions highlight a hierarchy of confessors (representing different kinds of clergy) in order to present their subjection to the same canon law of restitution. In other words, as one moves from the C revisions invoking the most powerful papal penitentiary to those invoking the least powerful parish clergy, one retrospectively discerns the unfolding of the entire clerical chain of penitential command that canon law governs.

Subtle as the revisions to the C version of Covetise's confession may appear, they nevertheless frame Repentance's treatment of restitution more explicitly and securely within the institutional church's legal discourse than do the comparable B lines that address the same matter of restitution. When taken independently, each of C's revisions discussed so far may not contain compelling evidence of a strategy of reform grounded in canon law. When, however, considered cumulatively in light not only of the invocations of confessors but also of a more historically specific or linguistically legal register that Langland introduces, the C revisions to Covetise's confession suggest a motive to reach out to an audience beyond and behind Covetise himself — an implied audience of confessors whom he deemed wanting in the *cura animarum* and in whose interests the canon law of restitution is explained and reinforced.

Restorative Justice in 'Piers Plowman' and the 'Memoriale presbiterorum'

By juxtaposing the B and C versions of Covetise's confession, I have thus far been arguing that in the C version Langland has Repentance sharpen the focus on the canon law of restitution in order to present confessors with the contingency of absolution upon restitution. Repentance's running concern with confessors and

---

sense of "supplement": that which is simultaneously both an enrichment of something already full and a replacement of something which is deficient' ('*Piers Plowman* and Poetic Tradition', *YLS*, 9 (1995), 39–64 (p. 47)). See also Jacques Derrida, *Of Grammatology*, ed. and trans. by Gayatri Spivak (Baltimore: Johns Hopkins University Press, 1978), pp. 144–45.

with their accountability to the canon law of restitution exemplifies contemporary traditions that sought to reform confessors indifferent to, or even complicit with, usurious penitents. I would now like to argue that *Piers Plowman* and the *Memoriale presbiterorum* are strikingly similar on the question of restorative justice, which demands that the usurious penitent make appropriate material reparations to his or her victims.

Recent scholarship on Langland has highlighted anticlerical polemics as a source for understanding the poet's treatment of restitution in the C text. Wendy Scase, Traugott Lawler, and Michael Haren among others have demonstrated the extent to which Langland treats restitution within the context of polemical battles between the mendicant and secular clergy.[28] Scase reads the C additions on restitution in Covetise's confession as an extension of the anticlerical scope of the B text to include not only friars but also parish priests as objects of censure for their neglect of canon law.[29] She sees in Repentance's attack on Covetise's parish priest (in additions with no parallel in the B text) evidence of a 'new anticlericalism' that transforms the antifraternal polemics spearheaded by contemporaries of Langland such as Richard FitzRalph.[30]

Drawing upon Scase's discussion of the extended anticlericalism inherent in the C revisions, Lawler observes that the C text, on the whole, attaches greater significance to restitution than does the B text. Explaining the differences among the versions of *Piers Plowman* on the basis of their treatment of the 'redde quod debes' principle, Lawler argues that 'the subject [of restitution] grew in

[28] Wendy Scase, *'Piers Plowman' and the New Anticlericalism* (Cambridge: Cambridge University Press, 1989); Traugott Lawler, 'Harlots' Holiness: the System of Absolution for Miswinning in the C Version of *Piers Plowman*', *YLS*, 20 (2006), 141–89.

[29] For the additions on restitution in the C text, see 6.298–307; commenting on the additions, Scase writes that '[i]n *Piers Plowman* an anticlerical development of this antifraternalism is apparent: antifraternal still, but with its implications for other priests brought out too [...] especially (typically) in the C text revision where Repentaunce warns that any priest who knowingly accepts tithes from ill-gotten gains can discover from the gloss of Ps. 51:8 "witterly what vsure is to mene" (C.VI.304)' (Scase, *'Piers Plowman' and the New Anticlericalism*, p. 29).

[30] Scase notes that '[t]his example [Repentance's attack on Covetise's parish priest] is typical of how in *Piers Plowman* the reference of the polemical language is often wider, and its implications more developed, than in FitzRalph's writings. What in FitzRalph's polemics was a language for addressing the limited problem of the friars' dominion became a language in which the dominion of all clerics might be discussed, when later political developments made this the more pressing question' (Scase, *'Piers Plowman' and the New Anticlericalism*, p. 29); see also pp. 25–28 of Scase's book for a reading of Repentance's admonition to Covetise's parish priest concerning the canon on restitution.

importance in Langland's mind as he wrote the B version, to the point that he made it the subject of the final scene [...] and in the C version expanded it still further'.[31] Commenting on Repentance's sharpened focus on the same principle of *redde quod debes* in the C version of Covetise's confession, Lawler makes it abundantly clear that '[t]he whole last part of the scene of the confession of Covetise, then, from line 286 to 349, has focused on the system, implicating in it lords, usurers, and retailers on the one hand, and friars, priests, and bishops on the other'.[32]

Mentioning moral and satirical affinities between the *Memoriale presbiterorum* and *Piers Plowman*, Haren provides the extra-textual penitential context for Langland's handling of restitution.[33] In his unpublished dissertation on the *Memoriale*, Haren discusses in detail the *Memoriale*'s recurrent concern with the canon law of restitution, a concern strikingly similar in its insistence on justice to that of the revised version of Covetise's confession.[34] Although Haren does not argue for the *Memoriale*'s influence on the handling of restitution in *Piers Plowman*, he does indicate enough similarities between the penitential work and the poem to lead to the assumption that it is a 'possible source for Langland'.[35]

Enriching such studies, I shall now draw attention to the penitential discourse that provides the larger extra-poetic context within which Langland revises Covetise's confession. That is, I shall attempt to demonstrate that the C revisions discussed so far exemplify a thinking about restorative justice best clarified in

---

[31] Lawler, 'Harlots' Holiness', pp. 142–43.

[32] Lawler, 'Harlots' Holiness', p. 154.

[33] Michael Haren, *Sin and Society in Fourteenth-Century England* (Oxford: Oxford University Press, 2000). Haren follows W. A. Pantin, who long ago identified the *Memoriale presbiterorum* as one of a cluster of penitential works underlying *Piers Plowman's* vision of reform. For an overview of such works contemporary with the *Piers Plowman*, see Part III of Pantin's *The English Church in the Fourteenth Century* (Cambridge: Cambridge University Press, 1955).

[34] Michael Haren, 'A Study of the *Memoriale presbiterorum*, a Fourteenth-Century Confessional Manual for Parish Priests' (unpublished doctoral dissertation, University of Oxford, 1975). All citations of the *Memoriale presbiterorum* throughout this essay derive from Part II of Haren's dissertation and, in light of his advice, have been repunctuated (with a few spellings emended) to aid reading. I thank him both for permission to cite from his dissertation and for advice on the citations. See also his *Sin and Society in Fourteenth-Century England* where he notes that 'the [*Memoriale*'s] author's contribution [to the subject of restitution] is considerable and he reveals a marked zeal for his subject. It is a trait which is shared by other moralists of the middle and later part of the century, notably Richard FitzRalph, Thomas Brinton, and William Langland' (p. 75).

[35] Drawing upon Haren's insight into the kinship between the poem and the penance manual, Lawler makes such an assumption in his 'Harlots' Holiness', p. 144.

a number of late medieval penitential treatises.[36] Largely inspired by Lateran
IV's educational reform of the secular clergy, such treatises include Thomas of
Chobham's and John of Freiburg's *Summa confessorum* as well as the more contemporary William of Pagula's *Oculus sacerdotis* (especially *Pars oculi*, which is
devoted to confessional procedure), Richard Rolle's *Judica me Deus*, John de
Burgh's *Pupilla oculi* (which 'was largely dependent upon the *Oculus sacerdotis*'),[37]
the anonymous *Memoriale presbiterorum*, and the *Book of Vices and Virtues*.[38]
What I propose is to uncover the presence of a shared socio-legal *mentalité* of
restorative justice in both poetic and penitential discourses. I choose the historicizing term *mentalité* because I want to suggest a lateral relationship between
Piers Plowman and various penitential manuals, between Repentance's handling
of restitution and the penitential writer's clarification of restitution. In other
words, I wish to argue that Langland is not simply reflecting the concern with
restitution articulated in the penitential tradition but is shaping it along with
contemporary canonists and theologians. Implicit in the B version of Covetise's

---

[36] Such penitential treatises are best introduced in Leonard Boyle's essay '*Summae confessorum*', in *Les Genres Littéraires dans les sources théologiques et philosophiques médiévales* (Louvain-
la-Neuve: Institut d'études médiévales de l'Université Catholique de Louvain, 1982), p. 234; see
also his *Pastoral Care, Clerical Education and Canon Law* (London: Variorum, 1981) for a general
historical background to late medieval *pastoralia*. See also Leonard Boyle, 'The *Summa* for Confessors as a Genre, and its Religious Intent', in *The Pursuit of Holiness in late Medieval Renaissance
Religion*, ed. by Charles Trinkaus with Heiko A. Oberman (Leiden: Brill, 1974), pp. 127–30.

[37] These words are Leonard Boyle's and are found in the opening chapter of his dissertation,
'A Study of the Works attributed to William of Pagula: With Special Reference to the *Oculus
sacerdotis* and *Summa summarum*' (unpublished doctoral dissertation, University of Oxford,
1956), p. 1.

[38] See William of Pagula's penance manual (embedded in the *Oculus sacerdotis*) in Daly's
parallel edition of Rolle and Pagula's manuals in *Judica me Deus*. For the *Memoriale presbiterorum*
see Haren's unpublished edition of the text in 'A Study of the *Memoriale presbiterorum*'. For the
early scholarship on late medieval confessional manuals, see Michaud-Quantin's *Sommes de
casuistique et manuels de confession au moyen âge (XII–XVI siècles)* (Louvain: Nauwelaerts, 1962).
For more recent comprehensive accounts of the procedural features of post-Lateran IV penitential
manuals, see Maria Giuseppina Muzzarelli's *Penitenze nel Medioevo: Uomini e modelli a confronto*
(Bologna: Patron, 1994). For a nuanced history of the practice of late medieval confession, see
Peter Biller's 'Confession in the Middle Ages: Introduction', in *Handling Sin: Confession in the
Middle Ages*, ed. by Peter Biller and A. J. Minnis, York Studies in Medieval Theology, 2 (York:
York Medieval Press, 1998), pp. 3–33. For the latest historiography on the penitential literature
following Lateran IV, see Joseph Goering, 'The Internal Forum and the Literature of Penance and
Confession', *Traditio*, 59 (2004), 175–227.

confession, this *mentalité* is reinforced and rendered explicit in the C revisions that offer a reformist admonition to all confessors.

To begin with, all the Latin penitential treatises mentioned above single out and treat restitution as a matter that confessors must enjoin as a condition for the remission of sins personified by Covetise. In insisting upon restitution, the treatises express what John Bossy has identified as 'the social dimension of the sacrament'.[39] Pointing out that 'restitution had formally speaking no part in the sacramental process at all', Bossy explains that it was given an 'inordinate space [...] in confessional manuals' because it fulfilled the social claims of restorative justice:

> [T]he priest could not absolve a person from his sins, if he proposed to remain in a state of social hostility with a neighbour [...] but abandoning such hostilities was not purely a matter of the heart; the commentators were clear that a man was required to show forgiveness by performing the social acts of recognition and salutation which the relation of charity implied, to accept a proffer of hospitality if made.[40]

Post-Lateran IV penitential treatises frequently mandate such 'social acts of recognition and salutation' by invoking the same canon law maxim on restitution that Repentance spells out in *Piers Plowman*.

Indeed, in diction and emphasis, poem and penitential treatise are alike in clarifying the confessor's obligation to ensure that penitents guilty of ill-gotten gains make or intend to make appropriate reparations to their victims as best they can. For example, having defined theft in Questio IIa of his *Summa confessorum*, Chobham specifies that penitents guilty of such a sin cannot be absolved unless they make appropriate reparations, if at all possible:

> Et est regula generalis in omni furto et in omni rapina quod nunquam *dimittitur peccatum nisi restituatur ablatum*/ si potest restituere ille qui abstulit, et si non potest restituere, lugeat et doleat et sciat se obligatum esse ad restitutionem faciendam si unquam habuerit facultatem restituendi.[41]

[39] John Bossy, 'The Social History of Confession in the Age of Reformation', *Transactions of the Royal Historical Society*, ser. 5, 25 (1975), 21–38 (p. 26). Commenting on Bossy's scholarship on the social history of confession, Peter Biller notes that '[s]uch a word as "social", according to Bossy, should not be used in a sense other than the sense it generally held in the past period about which the historian is writing' ('Confession in the Middle Ages', p. 37).

[40] Bossy, 'The Social History of Confession', p. 25.

[41] Thomas de Chobham, *Summa confessorum*, ed. by Frederick Broomfield, Analecta mediaevalia namurcensia, 25 (Louvain: Nauwelaerts, 1968), p. 488.

(And it is a general rule that for every theft and every act of plunder that sin is never remitted unless restitution is made, if he is able to restore what he misappropriated, and if he is not able to do so, then he should grieve and bemoan and know himself to be obliged to make restitution, if ever he had the ability to do so.)

It is this 'regula generalis' that Chobham returns to and elaborates upon in his discussion of usury in a subsequent section of his *Summa*:

Quia vero regula canonica est quod nunquam *dimittitur peccatum nisi restituatur ablatum, patet quod fenerator nunquam* vere potest penitere nisi totum restituat quod per usuram extorsit. (p. 505)

(Because it is a canonical rule that sin is never remitted unless restitution is made, it is clear that the money-lender can never truly repent unless he makes a full restitution of that which he extorted through usury.)

Here, Chobham makes abundantly clear the legal basis of restitution: the canon ('regula canonica') was already included among the synodal statutes of Salisbury 'that appeared shortly after the Fourth Lateran Council' and constituted 'some of the most important diocesan legislation of medieval England'.[42] Presented under the title *De restitutione rerum ablatarum*, the statute decrees that absolution is contingent upon restitution:

In furto, rapina, usura, fraude, caveant sibi sacerdotes ne iniungant penitentias, videlicet, missarum, elemosinarum, pro talibus peccatis, set iniungant (primo) restitutionem, quia non dimittitur peccatum nisi restituatur ablatum.[43]

(In cases of theft, acts of plunder, usury, fraud, priests shall take heed lest they, on account of such sins, impose penances, namely, of [saying] masses, [performing] works of charity, but they should first impose restitution, because sin is not remitted unless restitution is made.)

This 'regula canonica' that both Chobham and the statute enunciate is no different from the Latin canon on restitution ('*Numquam dimittitur peccatum, nisi restituatur ablatum*') invoked and expounded by Repentance in *Piers Plowman* and thus illustrates the larger historical basis for his concern with restorative justice.[44]

---

[42] See 'Statutes of Salisbury I', in *Councils & Synods*, ed. by Powicke and Cheney, p. 57.

[43] 'Statutes of Salisbury I', p. 74.

[44] Other statutes such as those of Exeter include a similar ruling on restitution: 'In rebus nephariis adquisitis sacerdotes iniungant parochianis penitentibus ut dampnum passis omnino si supersint ablata restituant; alias autem in elemosinarum quarumque largitiones ablata huiusmodi nullatenus convertantur' ('Statutes of Exeter II', p. 994).

Both John of Freiburg in his *Summa confessorum* and John de Burgh in his *Pupilla oculi* reinforce the same 'regula canonica' within their sections of restitution. John of Freiburg, as Kelly observes, 'set about updating Penafort's work, and in 1298 he produced his *Summa confessorum*, at the last minute taking into account the new collection of canon law compiled by order of Pope Boniface VIII, the *Liber Sextus* or *Sext*, issued earlier that year'.[45] '[A] mixture of practical theology and canon law', Freiburg 'follow[s] the plan of Raymond's *Summa de casibus* [...] reproduces the chapter-headings in Raymond [...] breaks each chapter into *quaestiones* [...] [a]nd where Raymond often discussed several subjects under a single heading, John gives each new subject a special *rubricella*, without, however, disturbing the consecutive numeration of the *quaestiones*'.[46] In the 'rubricella' devoted to restitution, Freiburg cites the same canon law maxim that Repentance in Covetise's confession invokes: '*non dimittatur peccatum nisi restituatur ablatum*' (sin is not remitted unless restitution is made).[47]

In his *Pupilla oculi*, John de Burgh 'makes use of Freiburg's *Summa confessorum*' and 'summarize[s] and systematize[s]' William de Pagula's *Oculus sacerdotis*.[48] John's *Pupilla oculi* distinguishes itself from its source with regard to a treatment of restitution that surpasses John of Freiburg's in length and detail.[49] Within the section concerning satisfaction and its parts ('de satisfactione et partes eius') John de Burgh advises the priest to impose upon the penitent the 'fundamental' of satisfaction, namely to abstain from sin and to make restitution, as well as to impose the 'substance' of satisfaction, namely to fast, keep vigils, to give alms, and to go on a pilgrimage ('sacerdos quedam iniungit penitenti ad satisfactionis fundamentum sicut abstinere a peccato et restituere ablatum quedam iniungit ad satisfactionis substantiam sicut ieiunare vigilare, dare elemosynam, peregrinari').[50] After discussing the 'substance' of satisfaction in five columns, John devotes over twenty-one columns to the 'fundamental' of satisfaction under

---

[45] Kelly, 'Penitential Theology', pp. 242–43.

[46] Boyle, *Pastoral Care*, p. 249.

[47] *Die 'Rechtssumme' Bruder Bertholds: Eine deutsche abecedarische Bearbeitung der 'Summa confessorum' des Johannes von Freiburg; Die handschriftliche Überlieferung* [Lyon, 1518], ed. by Helmut Weck, Texte und Textgeschichte, 6 (Tübingen: Niemeyer, 1982), fol. 65ʳ.

[48] Kelly, 'Penitential Theology', p. 243.

[49] In the Appendix to his essay 'Penitential Theology', Kelly conveys considerable insight into John de Burgh's handling of restitution.

[50] Johannes de Burgo [John de Burgh], *Pupilla oculi [...]* (Paris: Wolfgang Hopyl, 1510), fol. 31ᵛ; all citations of *Pupilla oculi* refer to this edition.

the extended section on restitution ('de forma restitutionis'). Interestingly enough, John, like his predecessors Freiburg and Chobham, opens the section on restitution with the same canon law maxim on restitution that Repentance cites:

> Non dimittitur peccatum nisi restituat ablatum si restitui potest [...]. Oportet igitur ut de omnibus damnis et rebus iniuriose acquisitis fiat restitutio. Vel ad minus habeat firmum propositum restituendi siquid ab alio iniuriose ablatum est antequam valeat satisfactio sacramentalis.[51]

> (Sin is not remitted unless one makes restitution of the misappropriated thing, if it [the thing] can be restituted [...] therefore, it is necessary that restitution be made concerning damages and things wrongly acquired. Or, at least, one must have the firm intention of making restitution, if something is wrongfully taken from another before sacramental satisfaction can have force.)

In the confessional manual embedded in his penitential treatise *Judica me Deus*, Richard Rolle, likewise, devotes close attention to the question of restitution, distinguishing it from mere satisfaction. Among the four tracts that make up Rolle's *Judica me Deus*, the tract 'B2', which 'consists almost entirely of selected quotations on confessional practice from the first section [of Pagula's] *Oculus sacerdotis*, the *Pars oculi*', makes clear that confessors must enjoin penitents to 'satisfy' whomever they have injured because they are bound to make restitution:[52]

> Pro periuriis et mendacio debet sacerdos iniungere penitenti quod satisfaciat illi quem lesit, quia tenetur ad restitucionem omnium dampnorum. Similiter pro rapina, furto, fraude, et usura debet restitucio plena iniungi.[53]

> (For perjuries and mendacity the priest must enjoin the penitent to make satisfaction to whom the penitent injures, because he [the penitent] is held to make restitution for all damages. Similarly, for rape, theft, fraud, and usury full restitution must be imposed.)

More than any of the penitential manuals discussed so far, the *Memoriale presbiterorum* comes closest to the C revisions to Covetise's confession not only because it is contemporary with *Piers Plowman* but also because it draws upon the canon law of restitution in the interests of reforming the *cura animarum*: '[A]s a manual for confessors, the treatise is a thoughtful application of the continental tradition to the mid-fourteenth English scene by a puritanical though sensitive

---

[51] John de Burgh, fol. 31ʳ.

[52] Daly, 'Introduction', in Rolle, *Judica me Deus*, p. viii.

[53] Rolle, *Judica me Deus*, p. 65.

observer.'[54] The *Memoriale* expresses what Haren terms 'a strong legalism in its approach to confessional technique [...] by a punctilious, remorseless concern for abstract justice, as is particularly evident in its burning preoccupation with restitution'.[55] Treating restitution as central to the *cura animarum*, the sections on restitution in the *Memoriale* further illuminate the larger social context for the C revisions' admonishment to confessors to heed the canon on restitution. Indeed, to read such C revisions in light of the *Memoriale*'s handling of restitution is to confront more clearly than ever the *mentalité* of restorative justice central to the revised poem's reformist vision of penance.

Describing the *Memoriale*'s approach to restitution, Haren writes that the 'two outstanding characteristics of the *Memoriale* are its puritanical and legalistic approach to penance — as evidenced principally by the author's emphasis on the canonical penances and on the overriding necessity of restitution as a prerequisite of absolution in cases where the obligation has arisen'.[56] In one of the sections on restitution in the *Memoriale*, the author not only enjoins penitents to make reparations to their victims but also deplores the confessors' granting of absolution to such penitents as have not made restitution:

> Tenentur eciam ad restitucionem faciendam dampnum passis, in quantum dampnum dederunt per se vel familiam suam directe vel occasionaliter. Set quicquid hic vel alibi scribatur de materia ista, vix/ reperitur aliquis qui de hoc peccato confiteatur, et si aliquociens forsan hoc contingat, plerique tunc confessores moderni et maxime de ordinibus mendicancium ceci et duces cecorum, nullam penitus talem peccatorem in hoc casu absolvendi potestatem habentes, data sibi aliqua parte huiusmodi prede, vel re alia, predonem et alios sibi adherentes absolvunt de facto, de restitucione prout ius exigit facienda | penitus non curantes.[57]

> (They are also held to the making of restitution concerning the damage done insofar as they perpetrated the damage themselves or through their people [servants] directly or occasionally. But [despite] whatever is written here or elsewhere concerning this matter, hardly is anyone found who confesses concerning this sin, and if perhaps at times the confession touches upon it [this sin], then many confessors modern and mostly those belonging to the mendicant orders, blind and leaders of the blind, have the power of absolving no such sinner at all in this case; gifted with some part of the booty or some other thing, they absolve the predator and his accomplices de facto, caring not at all that justice demands that restitution be made.)

---

[54] Michael Haren, 'Confession, Social Ethics and Social Discipline in the *Memoriale presbiterorum*', in *Handling Sin*, ed. by Biller and Minnis, pp. 109–22 (p. 111).

[55] Haren, *Sin and Society*, pp. 4–5.

[56] Haren, *Sin and Society*, p. 77.

[57] *Memoriale presbiterorum*, pp. 219–20.

In its relentless critique of 'many confessors modern and mostly those belonging to the mendicant orders', the *Memoriale* author participates in the same reformist spirit that animates Repentance's equally relentless critique of all confessors who disregard the canon on restitution.

Nowhere is such a reformist spirit of restorative justice more apparent in the *Memoriale* than in the treatment of usury in the section 'De usurariis'. Accentuating the focus on the blindness of 'modern' confessors' and on their resultant abuse of the powers of absolution, the *Memoriale* author treats usury with an urgency and clarity that Repentance expresses when handling the same sin in Covetise's confession:

> Hic scire debes quod usura singulis diebus, aliquando occulte, aliquando manifeste, exercetur a plerisque, tam clericis quam laicis, qui, recipiendo aliquid ultra sortem in hoc non credunt se peccare, nec in foro penitenciali de hoc peccato confitentur nec confessores moderni aliquid inquirunt de hoc peccato. In foro vero iudiciali, iusticia contra usurarios non redditur, eo quod omnes iudices moderni in exequenda iusticia circa hoc peccatum tepidi sunt et remissi nec aliqualiter volunt punire hoc peccatum. Caveas igitur tibi, o confessor, ut consideres condiciones cuiuslibet persone tibi quoad hoc confitentis, videlicet, utrum fuerit mercator, sive fuerit clericus sive laicus, et utrum consuevit mutuare peccunias suas vel blada seu alia bona sua aliquibus gravatis, nichil penitus recipiendo a suis debitoribus ultra sortem, et si sic, tunc mutuans non est in culpa. Quod si taliter mutuans aliquid ex convencione receperit vel spem habuerit recipiendi ultra sortem, et postea quicquid ultra recepit, usurarius est censendus [...]. Multe sunt et alie species usure, quas hic omitto scribere causa brevitatis. Tenebis igitur pro summa quod omnes et singuli usurarii tenentur ad restitucionem usurarum, hoc est enim omnium bonorum illorum que pacto vel alio modo illicito receperunt ultra sortem [...] quia usurarii raptores dicuntur, et secundum quod raptor tenetur ad restitucionem, sic et usurarius, qui secundum canones exercendo usuras infamia notantur, et gravi pena a iure statuta puniuntur, prout superius est scriptum suo loco.[58]

> (You should know that each day usury is perpetrated by the majority, sometimes secretly, and sometimes openly, both by clerics and by lay folk who do not believe themselves to sin when they receive more than their due; neither do penitents confess this sin in the penitential forum nor modern confessors enquire into this sin. In the judicial forum [i.e., the external forum], justice against the usurers is not rendered because all modern judges are tepid and remiss concerning the justice to be done concerning this sin, and they do not wish in any way to punish this sin. You shall advise yourself, O confessor, so that you [in the internal forum of confession] consider the circumstances of the person confessing to you, namely whether he is a merchant, or cleric or a layperson, and whether he is accustomed to lend his money on interest or grain or other goods to those oppressed, by receiving nothing beyond the due from his debtors; and if this is so, then the one lending

---

[58] *Memoriale presbiterorum*, pp. 247–50.

is not to blame. But if the one lending in such a manner should by agreement receive or have hope of receiving something beyond what is due, and afterwards receives whatsoever extra [beyond what is due], he must be regarded as an usurer [...] and there are other species of usury that I omit to mention on account of brevity. You will require therefore that all and each of the usurers be bound to the restitution of the gains of usury — that is, all those goods which by pact or any other illicit mode they received beyond their proper share [...] because usurers are called plunderers, and just as a plunderer is held to make restitution, so are the usurers, who, according to the canons, are infamous for practising usury and are punished by a grave penalty by the established justice, as mentioned above.)

In at least four ways, such a passage can help uncover the conceptual apparatus of restorative justice underlying Repentance's treatment of restitution in the C revisions.[59] First, the passage deplores the modern confessors' indifference to the sin of usury; second, it enjoins confessors to enquire into the circumstances of the penitent and sins confessed in order to determine whether or not usury is committed; third, it treats the sin of usury as requiring correction in accordance with the rigour of established justice; fourth, it regards restitution as the appropriate response to usury not merely because it might help the penitent gain salvation but, significantly, because it serves the social claims of restorative justice. The *Memoriale*'s continual insistence that usury cannot be expiated without restitution resembles Repentance's repeated emphasis upon the letter of the canon law of restitution that makes absolution for usurers dependent upon restitution. That is, just as restitution in the *Memoriale* is viewed as a kind of justice (*iusticia*) against usurers (*usurarios*) so, too, is it viewed in the C revisions as necessary for justice to be done to those victimized by the usurers. In a later section discussing restitution as exemplifying the social dimension of justice, the *Memoriale* writer urges confessors to persuade penitents both to feel contrite over ill-gotten gains and to return them to their rightful owner(s) whenever they are able to do so:

> Ex quo supra vidisti de quibusdam personis que ad restitucionem male adquisitorum et satisfaccionem dampnorum datorum de iure obligantur, pro eo quod sic inique agendo mortaliter peccaverunt, quia peccatum proprie est voluntas consequendi vel retinendi quod iusticia vetat, et peccatum dicitur breviter mali perpetracio, consequenter restat videre quam formam debes observare et tenere, quando iniungere te contingit in casu tibi a iure permisso, restitucionem seu satisfaccionem fore faciendam. Et/ primo debes semper iniungere quod penitens satisfaciat, de bonis male adquisitis vel de dampnis per ipsum

---

[59] In addition to this and other passages on restitution cited from the *Memoriale presbiterorum*, it would be worthwhile to consider the passages transcribed and translated by Haren in his 'The Interrogatories for Officials, Lawyers and Secular Estates of the *Memoriale presbiterorum*', in *Handling Sin*, ed. by Biller and Minnis, pp. 123–63.

datis, personis spoliatis vel dampnum passis aut eorum heredibus aut executoribus si poterunt inveniri.[60]

(From what you have seen above concerning the persons who are obliged by law to make restitution of things acquired wrongly and to make satisfaction of damages caused, on account of this, they sin mortally by acting wickedly, because the sin is specially the will of pursuing and retaining what justice proscribes, and the sin is defined briefly as the perpetration of evil; consequently, it remains to be seen what form you ought to observe and hold, when it pertains to you in a case authorized by law to impose restitution or satisfaction to be done. And first you must always enjoin that the penitent make satisfaction concerning goods acquired wrongly or concerning damages done through him to those persons despoiled or those who have suffered damage or to their heirs or executors, if they can be found.)

For both the poem and the penance manual, to make restitution is to restore the social ties impaired by the commission of usury, in sum, to fulfil the claims of restorative justice — claims that, if left unanswered, could result in the vitiation of the Christian community.

Deploring the clerical ignorance of canon law, the *Memoriale* holds confessors culpable for not prescribing restitution to penitents guilty of usury. In a substantial section on the clerical neglect of the canon on restitution ('De restitucione male adquisitorum, et dampnorum datorum iniuste'), the *Memoriale* author castigates 'modern confessors' for leaving their penitents in a state of spiritual sickness:

Circa istam materiam a diversis doctoribus tractatur varie et diffuse, et pauci sunt confessores qui considerando advertunt quid vel qualiter consulte agere debeant in hoc casu, cum quia pro maiori parte confessores moderni sunt iuris ignari, tum quia experti in iure, scripta/ doctorum circa materiam huiusmodi in diversis voluminibus sparsa non habent, nec unquam respexerunt, et sic obumbrata acie sue mentis de facili errant in dando consilium salubre taliter delinquentibus, et letalia eorum vulnera/ nonnunquam relinquunt/ penitus incurata. Et licet soli episcopi et eorum penitenciarii de peccatis huiusmodi se debent intromittere de iure et nullus alius nisi auctoritate apostolica sibi fuerit specialiter hoc commissum, in casu tamen necessitatis tu presbiter parochialis poteris confessionem taliter delinquencium audire, et vel consilium dare de modo restitucionis seu satisfaccionis faciende, vel restitucionem seu satisfaccionem confitentibus fore faciendam iniungere, considerata condicione cuiuslibet persone tibi confitentis, et criminis commissi qualitate.[61]

---

[60] *Memoriale presbiterorum*, p. 269; for the rest of the section, see the Appendix below, item 1.

[61] *Memoriale presbiterorum*, pp. 195–96. For the rest of the section, see below, Appendix, item 2.

(Concerning this matter [restitution] different doctors have treated it in varied ways and few are the confessors who attend to it by considering how they ought to handle [it], partly because, for the most part, modern confessors are ignorant of the law — and partly because experts in law [i.e., specialized canonists and commentators] do not have the scattered texts written by doctors on this matter in diverse volumes of this kind. [As a result] they [confessors and canonists] do not ever reflect [on it] and, with restitution obscured from their mental view, they err easily in giving proper council to those erring and they (the penitents) never get entirely cured of their lethal wounds. And although only bishops and their confessors ['penitenciarii'] ought to intervene by law concerning sins of this kind, and no other without apostolic authority should take up this commitment; in case of necessity, however, you the parish priest could hear the confession of those erring thus, or give [them] counsel concerning the mode of restitution or of satisfaction to be made, or impose upon those confessing restitution or satisfaction to be done, having considered the condition of the person confessing to you, and the quality of the crime committed.)

Recalling the *Memoriale's* complaint that 'modern confessors are ignorant of the law', the C additions to Covetise's confession not only clarify the canon on restitution but also reinforce it by prescribing penalties to the parish priest who profits from tithes that derive from usury. In light of the *Memoriale's* insistence that the usurer make restitution for the cause of justice, the C revisions' ascription of penalties to the parish priest may be read as expressive of *iusticia*, of the claims of restorative justice. Covetise's 'prest þat [his] tythe toek' (C.6.298) and the *Memoriale's* modern confessors (*confessores moderni*) or modern judges (*iudices moderni*) are thus presented as suffering from the same vice of neglecting the claims of justice.

The clarification of the canon law of restitution, expressed more explicitly and insistently in the C version of Covetise's confession than in the corresponding B version, bears out the theory that in the later Middle Ages confession, focusing more on the seven deadly sins than on the Ten Commandments, pointed up 'the dominance of sinners in relation to neighbours'.[62] It is this 'horizontal relationship' — between penitents in a parish community — that both the C-text passage and the *Memoriale* seek to preserve and reinforce in their common critique of confessors who disregard the canon on restitution.[63] To both Langland and the *Memoriale* writer, sins such as usury require not merely a correction of inner intentions but a performance of appropriate material actions that would reconcile sinners to their victims. Thus, both writers seek to reform the errant handling of penitents guilty of usury by clarifying that they can obtain spiritual liberation

[62] Biller, 'Confession in the Middle Ages', p. 29.

[63] The expression is Biller's; see his 'Confession in the Middle Ages', p. 29.

from it (usury) only if they perform physical acts of restitution to all those materially injured by the penitent. It is this apparatus of restorative justice, which is at once material and spiritual, that explains why both writers single out only the canon on restitution as the basis of their reformist critique of confessors: for this canon, more than any other, impacts not just upon the intention of pentitents to make amends but, more significantly, upon their action of doing so in materially concrete ways. Hence, in the C additions that target Covetise's parish priest, Repentance invokes canon law precisely to address the material basis of the negligent priest's livelihood (the tithes that provide for his livelihood) and warns him of the penal consequences of living off ill-gotten gains.

All this is to say that the C revisions to Covetise's confession insist upon the indispensability of the canon on restitution in the interests of the 'horizontal' social-economic ties that bind sinner and victim, penitent and confessor within the Christian community. Repentance's subjection of all confessors to canon law must thus be read as an attempt to ensure that such communal ties are protected by a systematized legislation that does not privilege any partisan interests that might jeopardize them. It is in this sense alone that the C revisions can be seen as a privileging of law over the subjects of law, of the canon on restitution over all confessors.[64]

Appendix

Further Passages on Restitution from the *Memoriale presbiterorum*

1. From 'De forma restitucionis faciende penitenti iniungenda': 'Quicquid igitur aliquis in preiudicium alterius adquisivit, utputa aliquid furatus fuerit, vel quia rapuit, vel per metum extorsit ab aliquo vel per iniuriam commisit in preiudicium illius vel dampnum dedit aliter qualitercunque vel quia interest alicuius quod sibi fieri debet restitucio seu satisfaccio, verbi gracia, aliquis defloravit

---

[64] I dedicate this essay to Helen Barr and Joseph Goering, both of whose intellectual generosity and painstaking mentorship enabled me to substantiate Langland's dialogue with canon law in the C text. I am especially grateful to Bridget Anderson, Robert Lemkin, Tara Devi Roy, and the Oxford Vegan Society for providing the intellectual and material support for revising the essay in the summer of 2008. For their feedback on the essay, I thank Eve Keller, Paul Strohm, W. P. Mueller, Maryanne Kowaleski, Jay Gundacker, Katherine Little, and the three anonymous readers for *YLS*. Special thanks are due to Andrew Cole and Lawrence Warner for their editorial comments on the final draft.

virginem, quo casu deflorator de iure tenetur eam ducere in uxorem, vel dotare si habeat unde, et de iure eam ducere non poterit, vel quia interest alicuius quoad famam suam, verbi gracia, aliquis falso et maliciose diffamavit statum alterius, quo casu tenetur ad restitucionem fame quantum in ipso est et in quantum facere poterit, quilibet talis peccator tenetur in solidum restituere omnia illicite percepta et de dampnis datis competenter satisfacere dampnum seu iniuriam passis, ex quo novit personas quibus restitucio seu satisfaccio fuerit facienda. Set si ignoraverit illas personas, tunc debet totum illud quod fuerit restituendum, auctoritate episcopi, dari pauperibus pro animabus illorum quibus de iure foret restitucio facienda, et precipue in villis/ in quibus morabantur illi quibus restitucio deberet fieri. Quod si ignoretur vel eciam dubitetur de villis in quibus debet fieri talis distribucio, tunc sufficit quod distribuatur inter pauperas illius diocesis, de consensu diocesani episcopi, et si alibi preter voluntatem et consensum episcopi vel ipso contradicente fuerit ista restitucio et bonorum distribucio facta, taliter restituens et distribuens non liberatur a peccato, quia in tali restitucione facienda necessaria est auctoritas episcopi, eo quod nullus episcopo inferior potest regulariter aliquem a tali peccato absolvere. Et in hoc casu pessime errant et animas multorum decipiunt confessores mendicantes, qui alia bona sibi ipsis appropriant, consensu diocesani penitus irrequisito. In symonia tamen, doctores quidam tenent quod symoniacus habet restituere diversimod<o> pecuniam symoniace receptam. Dicunt enim quod si totum capitulum vel collegium circa hoc deliquerit, quod tunc debet fieri resti/tucio illi qui pecuniam dedit. Set si unus vel duo de capitulo vel forsan aliquis extraneus, seu quevis singularis persona circa hoc deliquerit, tunc debet fieri restitucio illi ecclesie in cuius iniuriam pecunia data fuit. Secundum aliquos tamen doctores legitur quod non debet fieri restitucio illi qui dedit pecuniam, si voluerit in seculo omnino remanere, et istam opinionem tenent plures/ moderni, quia conferens debet puniri in eo in quo noscitur deliquisse. Set si voluerit intrare religionem, tunc debet fieri restitucio illi monasterio quod ingreditur, ne sibi sit onerosus. Alii tenent quod huiusmodi pecunia symoniace recepta debet converti in usus pauperum iuxta arbitrium diocesani, eo quod taliter donans ex causa illicita et a iure reprobata dedit, unde non debebit de eo sentire com<m>odum, saltim temporale, pro quo meretur penam sustinere. Sufficere igitur sibi debet, si pecunia taliter data pro redempcione peccati sui in usus pauperum convertatur, secundum ipsos. De istis oppinionibus eligas cui dicas: 'Tu michi sola places.' De prelatis autem qui singulis diebus extorquent peccuniam ab ecclesiis sibi subiectis, debes tenere quod si aliquid extorserint per symoniam, debent illud reddere dupplicatum ecclesiis sic gravatis. Si vero per impressionem vel concussionem hoc fecerunt, debent illud reddere in quadruplum. Et intelligas quod ille crimen concussionis dicitur committere, qui, pretextu officii sibi commissi, comminando aliquid extorquet ab invito.Tenetur igitur male adquirens et eciam dampnum dans, ad restitucionem in solidum, si habeat unde. Set si nichil omnino poterit reddere, quia nota est paupertas sua, tunc sufficit sibi contricio cum alia penitencia sibi iniungenda, et voluntas reddendi quando ad uberiorem pervenerit fortunam, et quod omni tempore donec plene satisfecerit restituere satagat, in quantum hoc com<m>ode poterit, quia talis pauper notorius non debet excommunicari, nec aliqua pena pecuniaria multari secundum iura. Set si poterit aliquid reddere, non tamen in totum com<m>ode, absque periculo sustentacionis sue et uxoris vel familie sue, tunc tu confessor ipsum inducere quod restituat, in quantum com<m>ode facere potest; set si nichil voluerit restituere, tunc debes ipsum inducere ad contricionem et veram penitenciam peragendam, et sibi in confessione hoc modo dicere: 'Fili, ecce quod graviter peccasti, unde necesse habebis unam de duabus viis eligere, aut restituere in quantum potes et sic penam inferni evadere, et salvari eternaliter, vel si nolueris restituere pro posse tuo set penes te retinere quod iniuste adquisisti, in perpetuum cum diabolo cruciari.' Et si talis tibi dicat quod magis vult pati tormenta in futuro quam aliquid restituere, tunc debes ipsum inducere ad contricionem et ostendere sibi vias per quas possit salvari. Et si nullo modo poterit ad hoc induci, constat quod omnino impenitens est, et sic non poteris sibi dare penitenciam aliquam quo ad salutem, set tantum consilium penitendi. Si vero a principio vel eciam ex postfacto poterit induci ad restituendum id quod potest com<m>ode et videris ipsum contricionem veram habere de peccato, tunc debes sibi dicere statim vel infra certum tempus per te sibi limitandum, emendet quicquid poterit commode emendare, et quod de reliquo humiliter petat veniam et devote ab eo cui dampnum dedit, et si veniam et remissionem invenire poterit, satis tutus erit quantum ad restitucionem plenius faciendam. Set si non potest habere remissionem de residuo, tunc debet componere cum illo cui tenetur satisfacere, quod particulatim poterit sibi satisfacere per annos vel per mensem vel per alia tempora vel quod assignet sibi de redditibus vel bonis suis aliquod certum particulatim recipiendum, quousque fuerit sibi plene satisfactum' (pp. 269–72).

2. From 'De restitucione male adquisitorum, et dampnorum datorum iniuste': 'Ut igitur tu confessor circa materiam huiusmodi restitucionis et satisfaccionis faciende lucidius instruaris, scire debes quod quilibet qui iniuste aliena invadit, occupat, consumit, alienat, seu alias de eisdem disponit illicite preter domini

voluntatem seu cuidam iniuriose dampnum dedit tenetur ea restituere seu de eisdem satisfacere illis a quibus illa bona extorsit vel alias qualitercunque maliciose ledit seu dampnum dedit, si vixerint et sciatur quales fuerint et ubi/moram traxerint. Set si mortui fuerint, debet ea restituere heredibus suis sive executoribus vel successoribus, si poterint inveniri. Set si ignoretur ubi morentur quia forsan morantur in locis remotis vel regionibus longinquis, tunc restitucio seu satisfaccio huiusmodi debet fieri ad arbitrium episcopi loci, prout hoc/ infra dicetur. Preterea si ille qui dampnum dedit aliquibus, ut dictum est, decesserit antequam restituerit modo debito omnia restituenda vel eciam satisfecerit integre de dampnis per eum datis, eius heredes vel execu-tores tenentur pro defuncto satisfacere dampnum passis, in quantum bona defuncti ad ipsos pervenerunt. Ille tamen qui dampnum dedit, tenetur ad restitucionem in solidum faciendam si tantum habuerit in bonis unde de hiis competenter/ satisfacere poterit. Alioquin frustratoria erit sua penitencia quia sibi non dimittetur peccatum, nisi restituerit integre sic ablatum, secundum Augustinum' (pp. 195–96).

'BEATUS QUI VERBA VERTIT IN OPERA':
LANGLAND'S ETHICAL INVENTION
AND THE TROPOLOGICAL SENSE

Ryan McDermott

I can conceive him (like his own visionary William) to have been sometimes occupied in contemplative wanderings on Malvern Hills [...]. Sometimes I can descry him taking his staff, and roaming far and wide in search of manners and characters; mingling with men of every accessible rank, and storing his memory with hints for future use. I next pursue him to his study, sedate and thoughtful, yet wildly inventive, digesting the first rude drafts of his Visions, and in successive transcriptions, as judgment matured, or invention declined, or as his observations were more extended, expanding or contracting, improving and sometimes perhaps debasing his original text.[1]

William Langland has never needed a Charles Muscatine to rescue him from critical exaggerations of his originality. While *Chaucer and the French Tradition* proposed to debunk the 'post-Victorian [...] notion of Chaucer's "revolt" from "outworn" convention',[2] one of Langland's most important Victorian-age readers was J. J. Jusserand, whose Langland was largely oblivious to — not in conflict with — classical and recent Continental poetic traditions.[3]

---

[1] Thomas Dunham Whitaker, *Visio Willi de Petro Plouhman* (London: John Murray, 1813).

[2] Charles Muscatine, *Chaucer and the French Tradition: A Study in Style and Meaning* (Berkeley and Los Angeles: University of California Press, 1957), pp. 3–4.

[3] 'Never, assuredly, would it occur to our visionary [Langland] that when approaching the threshold of God's paradise, the thing to say is: "Apollo! Now that the hour has come for the last

Ryan McDermott (*rjm95@pitt.edu*) is Assistant Professor of English, University of Pittsburgh.

Abstract: How are we to understand an invention that neither copies its source texts in a servile manner, nor competes to displace them? *Piers Plowman* defies the categories of primary and secondary translation. Instead, Langland adopts non-competitive habits of invention from the theory and practice of tropological exegesis in order to embody ethical and literary sources in the invention of 'heretofore unseen phenomena'. In the Pentecost episode, Will joins 'many hundret' in inventing the 'Veni Creator Spiritus', a hymn given to them by the Holy Spirit. The nascent church invents something completely new even as it conforms as closely as possible to its source, the Holy Spirit.

Keywords: William Langland, *Piers Plowman*, ethics, invention, tropology, exegesis, literary influence, Pentecost, liturgy.

10.1484/J.YLS.1.102113

When it comes to originality and that sprightliness of creative thought the Victorians called 'invention', Langland appears an anomaly, at least viewed alongside Chaucer. There is little evidence of his striving with agonistic, paternal literary traditions against which one might assess originality, but at the same time readers throughout the nineteenth and twentieth centuries remarked on his lively knack for invention.[4] Readers have always found Langland to be just as inventive as Chaucer. The critical challenge has been to explain how they can both be so inventive despite their drastically different habits of invention and disposition to their sources.

Despite the deep theological, philosophical, liturgical, and political backgrounds illuminated by the last fifty-odd years of research, Anne Middleton's 1988 assessment of the critical heritage is still true today, with important qualifications: '*Piers Plowman* yields to "sources and analogues" study little trace of its immediate *literary* antecedents and possible models: it appears that what Chaucer called "alle poesie" played little part in Langland's conception of his "making".'[5] However many quotations, images, or topoi we might identify, they

---

of my tasks, fill me with the breath of thy inspiration" [Dante, *Paradiso*, I.1.13–15]' (J. J. Jusserand, *'Piers Plowman': A Contribution to the History of English Mysticism*, trans. by M. E. R. (London: Unwin, 1894), p. 211).

[4] Even when Langland was taken as the Ricardian *vox populi*, he was deemed 'as much entitled to the credit of originality' as Thomas Jefferson, 'who has best expressed the passions and emotions of men in the shifting scenes of the drama or of song' (G. P. Marsh, *Origin and History of the English Language* (1862), qtd. in *The Vision of William Concerning Piers the Plowman, in Three Parallel Texts*, ed. by Walter W. Skeat, 2 vols (London: Oxford University Press, 1961), II, p. xlviii). And as the mouthpiece of the *commune*, 'the man in whom Catholic faith and national feeling are fused in a single flame', Langland has struck modern readers such as Christopher Dawson as original, one-of-a-kind, productive of some rare and protomodern vision ('*The Vision of Piers Plowman*', in *Medieval Essays* (New York: Sheed & Ward, 1954; repr. Washington, DC: Catholic University Press of America, 2002), pp. 206–34 (p. 207)). Dawson not only finds Langland more inventive than Chaucer, but opposes Langland's 'realism', by which he implies modernity, to Chaucer's 'classicism' (p. 214). I do not cite these critics snidely, but to emphasize that whatever attention Langland has enjoyed beyond English literary studies has been sustained in large part by a sense — right or wrong — that he was particularly *inventive* of innovative social and cultural configurations. David Matthews observes that Thomas Dunham Whitaker, cited in the epigraph, characterizes Langland 'as a protomodern poet' in much the same way Renaissance and Victorian writers talked about Chaucer (*The Making of Middle English, 1765–1910* (Minneapolis: University of Minnesota Press, 1999), p. 91).

[5] Anne Middleton, 'Introduction: The Critical Heritage', in *A Companion to 'Piers Plowman'*, ed. by John A. Alford (Berkeley and Los Angeles: University of California Press, 1988), pp. 1–28

always stand in oblique relation to the poem, functioning less as 'background' or 'source' than as fodder for a remarkably fecund organic process that incorporates, metabolizes, and transforms them into something new.[6] In this respect, Langland's 'invention' seems closer to the modern sense of the word, with its emphasis on original creation, than to that offered by the handbooks of classical rhetoric, which stress the discovery of ready-to-hand *materia* that need only be disposed and possibly amplified or otherwise turned — and all of this in a poem whose *modus agendi* often is that of commentary, ostensibly the most derivative of inventional habits.[7]

(pp. 19–20); my italics. We have suffered no shortage of work on *Piers Plowman*'s literary antecedents, especially on the genre of dream visions. But this type of criticism often ends up in an apophatic mode, calling our attention to similarities between Langland and other poets only to identify Langland's ever greater dissimilarity. See, for example, David Aers, '*Piers Plowman' and Christian Allegory* (London: Edward Arnold, 1975), pp. 42–51; and J. A. Burrow, *Langland's Fictions* (Oxford: Clarendon Press, 1993), pp. 6–27 and pp. 113–18, both of which argue for Guillaume de Deguilleville's influence on Langland while drawing sharp contrasts between Deguilleville's heavy-handed, static allegories and Langland's 'imaginatively powerful and satisfactory' disposition of dreams and salvation history (Aers, '*Piers Plowman*', p. 102).

[6] Compare Mary Carruthers's exemplary remark about the meaning of *Dowel*: 'No outside source can possibly tell us what the word really means; the concept is being created by the text of the poem itself' (*The Search for St. Truth: A Study of Meaning in 'Piers Plowman'* (Evanston, IL: Northwestern University Press, 1973), p. 20).

[7] Recent scholarship has made up for the paucity of literary models primarily by mining the rhetorical and homiletical traditions for clues to Langland's craft of thought. As early as 1963, A. C. Spearing noted how some of the *artes praedicandi* envisioned the kind of free invention apparent in Langland's 'willingness to conceive of better beginnings and impose them on the emerging structure of the work', as D. Vance Smith more recently observed (*The Book of the Incipit: Beginnings in the Fourteenth Century* (Minneapolis: University of Minnesota Press, 2001), p. 73); A. C. Spearing, 'Verbal Repetition in *Piers Plowman* B and C', *JEGP: Journal of English and Germanic Philology*, 62 (1963), 722–37. See also Elizabeth Salter, '*Piers Plowman': An Introduction*, 2nd edn (Cambridge, MA: Harvard University Press, 1969), pp. 24–57; and A. C. Spearing, *Criticism and Medieval Poetry* (New York: Barnes & Noble, 1964), pp. 68–95. In some of the earliest research on medieval rhetorical theory as literary theory, Judson Boyce Allen suggests that *Piers Plowman* is a 'book about its own making [...] a text in which the *modus agendi* [the mode of making] and the *forma tractatus* [the structure of the work] are the same' (*The Ethical Poetic of the Later Middle Ages: A Decorum of Convenient Distinction* (Toronto: University of Toronto Press, 1982), pp. 92–93). Smith elaborates on this point in *The Book of the Incipit*, pp. 104–06. On theories of *modi* and *formae*, see *Medieval Literary Theory and Criticism, c. 1100–c. 1375: The Commentary Tradition*, ed. by A. J. Minnis and A. B. Scott, with David Wallace, rev. edn (Oxford: Clarendon Press, 1992), pp. 198–203; Alastair Minnis, *Medieval Theory of Authorship: Scholastic Literary Attitudes in the Later Middle Ages*, rev. edn (Philadelphia: University of Pennsylvania Press, 1988), pp. 28–29.

If *Piers Plowman* is 'a commentary on an unknown text', then it is a remark-ably inventive one.[8] But since Rita Copeland's study of the creative potential of commentary, this should not surprise us.[9] And we have learned from Mary Carruthers to interpret monastic meditational and exegetical theories and practices as crafts of rhetorical invention.[10] So Langland's harnessing of scriptural and liturgical commentary habits, like Piers's yoking of the four exegetical 'stottes' (plow horses), should make sense to us as a productive means to 'tulye [cultivate] treuthe' and 'verba Scripturae vertere in opera' — to turn the words of Scripture into ethical and literary works, as Liberum Arbitrium proposes in passus B.15/C.16, citing Bernard of Clairvaux.[11] Langland's habits of tropology extend beyond an imagined conversion of the will to influence even his own acts of composition. In *Piers Plowman*, tropology works not as an exegetical key to unlock the ethical secrets of the text; rather, habits of tropological *interpretation* translate into habits of tropological *invention*. On this reading, Langland is concerned not only with readers' ethics and the ethics of reading, but with the ethics of invention: with habits that make writing itself meaningful action and submit the invention of new literature to the high standard of the 'law of love'.[12]

---

[8] Morton W. Bloomfield, *'Piers Plowman' as a Fourteenth-Century Apocalypse* (New Bruns-wick, NJ: Rutgers University Press, 1962), p. 32. Cf. Friedrich Nietzsche's remark about the 'physiological process' that produces moral judgements: 'all our so-called consciousness is a more or less fantastic commentary on an unknown, perhaps unknowable, but felt text' (*Daybreak: Thoughts on the Prejudices of Morality*, ed. by Maudemarie Clark and Brian Leiter (New York: Cambridge University Press, 1997), p. 120). Nietzsche's argument is the obverse of the account I give here of Langland's invention: the narrative consciousness of *Piers Plowman* — if we can call its *forma tractatus* that — is a more or less fantastic commentary on the complexity of moral judgement and action.

[9] Rita Copeland, *Rhetoric, Hermeneutics, and Translation in the Middle Ages: Academic Traditions and Vernacular Texts* (Cambridge: Cambridge University Press, 1991).

[10] See Mary Carruthers, *The Craft of Thought: Meditation, Rhetoric, and the Making of Images, 400–1200* (New York: Cambridge University Press, 1998) and *The Book of Memory: A Study of Memory in Medieval Culture*, 2nd edn (New York: Cambridge University Press, 2008).

[11] '"*Beatus*," saith seynt Bernard, "*qui scripturas legit | Et verba vertit in opera* emforth his power"' (*Piers Plowman: The C Version*, ed. by George Russell and George Kane (London: Athlone; Berkeley and Los Angeles: University of California Press, 1997), 16.222–23). Cited here-after in the text by passus and line number. For the scene of plowing scripture, see C.21.262–73a.

[12] Another name for this essay could be 'Will as Writer', which would echo James Simpson's important enquiry into the ethics of interpretation. James Simpson, 'Desire and the Scriptural Text: Will as Reader in *Piers Plowman*', in *Criticism and Dissent in the Middle Ages*, ed. by Rita Copeland (New York: Cambridge University Press, 1996), pp. 215–43. There Simpson argues

I turn to tropology because we currently do not have adequate theories to explain how Middle English writing can seek harmony with its literary and ethical models and simultaneously strike readers as 'wildly inventive'.[13] According to the Roman theorists in Copeland's account of translation-as-invention, *Piers Plowman* would have to displace its sources in order to be truly inventive, yet Langland has no intention of doing so. And according to some recent theories of exemplarity as a mode of ethical literary invention, *Piers Plowman*, in order to achieve the characteristic aesthetic of Middle English exemplary texts, would have to 'invalidate the very norms [it] invoke[s]'.[14] These theories assume that to be creative, an author must violently overthrow a model or break a law.[15] They consequently risk occluding habits of literary and ethical invention that are not motivated by competition and, rather than displacing their models, harmonize with them.

Piers Plowman invites us to rethink these assumptions — not only for medieval literature, but for prevailing theories of literary invention and ethics. When Jacques Derrida meditates on the conditions of invention by reading Cicero, he appreciates the great orator's inventiveness in disguising the violence of his own invention.[16] For Derrida, nothing less than the appearance of the absolute Other — the first condition of ethics — is at stake. The Other cannot appear unless all norms and expectations are shattered. If this is true, then rhetorical invention always implies ethics — an insight that has recurred in studies of literary ethics over the past two decades. With the rise of the 'new ethics' in literary studies, we

that Langland 'often represent[s] Will, as the human will, as a readerly model being moved from within the text, and being moved through his encounter with scriptural texts' (p. 219). This essay looks within the text not primarily for models of interpretation, but for models of invention.

[13] Thomas Dunham Whitaker, 'Introductory Discourse', in *Visio Willi de Petro Plouhman*, in *The Vision of William*, ed. by Skeat, II, pp. xxxix–xlv (p. xli).

[14] Elizabeth Allen, *False Fables and Exemplary Truth in Later Middle English Literature* (New York: Palgrave Macmillan, 2005), p. 23. Allen is glossing Wolfgang Iser, *The Act of Reading: A Theory of Aesthetic Response* (Baltimore: Johns Hopkins University Press, 1978), pp. 218–25.

[15] Or in the words of Derek Attridge, one of our most incisive theorists of invention and ethics in modernity, 'To be original [...] is to create something that marks a significant departure from the norms of the cultural matrix within which it is produced and received' (*The Singularity of Literature* (New York: Routledge, 2004), p. 35). This view of originality is common because it holds true for so much literature, especially modern literature.

[16] See Jacques Derrida, 'Psyche: Invention of the Other', trans. by Catherine Porter, in *Psyche: Inventions of the Other*, ed. by Peggy Kamuf and Elizabeth Rottenberg, 2 vols (Stanford: Stanford University Press, 2007–08), I, 1–47.

have become open to literary moments where a genuine encounter with the Other might occur, so long as 'ethics' does not involve specific moral injunctions. Yet Emmanuel Lévinas argues that 'only the ritual law of Judaism' with its 'austere discipline that strives to achieve [...] justice [...] can recognize the face of the Other'.[17] Does genuine invention break *this* law, too? Do Dowel, Dobet, and Dobest threaten the invention of the Other?

While Langland does not require us to pit one high theorist against another, he does invite us to notice that Cicero does not have a monopoly on ancient theory of invention. We find different theories of invention in the Jewish tradition, with its strong emphasis on law as a fruitful and empowering grace, and the Christian tradition, with its Trinitarian model of how to think about likeness and difference at the same time. In Langland's hands, these traditions also give us a vital link between rhetoric (the words we invent to get people to do things) and ethics (the responsible action we actually undertake). We can enquire about Langland's 'ethical invention' only if we are willing to entertain the notion that invention extends beyond rhetoric to action. For Langland, rhetoric and hermeneutics are incomplete without an active response, just as in exegetical theory it is not enough to perceive by allegorical interpretation that the gift of tongues at Pentecost recapitulates and redeems the confusion of tongues at the Tower of Babel if we do not also tropologically take the event to include ourselves and kneel to sing a hymn of praise in unity with our fellow Christians. Even the best-intentioned rhetorical inventions are only pre-ethical, and they will come to naught if not borne out in a praxis that copies in action what the invention modelled in words and ideas. At the same time, Langland is striving to conceive and practice a kind of writing, of making, that will count as action, and he draws on tropological theory to do so. For tropology is never simply an analysis of one text, but an invention of another — fruitful activity, acted out in production of new literature, even of profane literature.[18]

My argument is cumulative, but throughout it traces what are most helpfully thought of as model-copy relationships: the play of similarity and difference between literary or ethical models and the texts and patterns of action that derive from those models. In Langland's poetics of exemplarity, likeness between model and copy does not obliterate the copy's freedom, individuality, or originality. Because they are not in competition, the copy's adherence to the model can

---

[17] Emmanuel Lévinas, 'A Religion for Adults', in *Difficult Freedom: Essays on Judaism*, trans. by Seán Hand (Baltimore: Johns Hopkins University Press, 1990), pp. 11–23 (p. 18).

[18] I am grateful to Ashley Faulkner for this felicitous way of putting it.

actually intensify its individuality. For this reason, the classical account of rhetorical invention as a competition for mastery between generations needs to be
supplemented with non-competitive models of invention in order to understand
Langland's irenic relationship to his literary and intellectual sources. In Langland's treatment of Pentecost, the literary centrepiece of this essay, we see how a
literary text can conserve its biblical and liturgical models, yet nevertheless invent
previously unseen phenomena. Medieval theories of biblical exegesis provide the
fullest articulation of how this happens because they emphasize the continuity
between rhetoric, interpretation, and action, and they rest on a robust doctrine
of analogy that allows readers and writers to copy the Bible as a model even as they
participate in the history of salvation by inventing previously unforeseeable
phenomena. But before I propose that tropological theory can best articulate
Langland's ethical invention, we need to see how the discourses of exemplarity
and classical rhetoric give alternative but overlapping accounts of ethics and
invention.

Exemplarity at Pentecost

At perhaps the climax of *Piers Plowman*, Will and his guide Conscience show up
at the scene of Pentecost just as the Holy Spirit is descending on the apostles.
Langland gives us a mere sketch of the Acts narrative:

> and thenne cam, me thouhte,
> Oen *spiritus paraclitus* to Peres and to his felawes.
> In liknesse of a lihtnynge a lyhte on hem alle
> And made hem konne & knowe alle kyne langages.
> (C.21.200–03)

These details suffice to import the episode from Acts into Will's dream as a live,
interactive exemplum continuous with Conscience's sermon on the economy of
salvation, which paused just two lines earlier. As exempla go, this one is particularly participatory, an extreme case of an exemplum 'set in a pragmatic situation
that is inconclusive and demands a decision'.[19] Indeed, Will, distinctly perceiving

[19] Karl-Heinz Stierle, 'Story as Exemplum — Exemplum as Story: On the Pragmatics
and Poetics of Narrative Texts', trans. by David Henry Wilson, in *New Perspectives in German
Literary Criticism: A Collection of Essays,* ed. by Richard E. Lange and Victor Amacher (Princeton:
Princeton University Press, 1979), pp. 390–417 (p. 398). Stierle is commenting on Dante's use
of exempla.

the action's inconclusiveness, has to nudge Conscience and ask for an interpretation: 'Y wondred what þat was and wagged Consience' (C.21.204). And the
situation certainly demands a decision, exacted by Conscience's none-too-subtle
command, 'Knele now [...] and yf thow canst synge, | Welcome hym and wor-
schipe hym with *veni creator spiritus*' (C.21.209–10). As befits an exemplum, the
coming of the Holy Spirit opens up a range of meanings even as it closes down the
range of proper action.[20]

Yet the Pentecost narrative as it occurs in Acts is not originally an exemplum;
it only becomes one by a complex process of translation, beginning with the
collation of eye-witness accounts and developing through Greek manuscript
recensions, Old Latin translations, Jerome's Vulgate, evolving theological
exegesis, Middle English oral paraphrases in sermons, and finally Langland's rendering here. These translations form the back-story to any exemplary citation
of Scripture. This exemplum not only invites an audience's interpretation and
response — that is, not only posits inventive activity as its final cause — but also
presumes a prior history of invention.

I mean this in a very modern way: this exemplum was not just discovered in
and excised from Acts, then plopped into *Piers Plowman*, 'isolated from a context
and placed in a new context', as J. D. Lyons characterizes early modern exempla.[21]
Rather, it had to be *made into* an exemplum. Exempla like this one are just as
much made as they are found. But it is easy to miss this point. The collections of
exempla that were made in the later Middle Ages, if interpreted as the natural
habitat of exempla, can belie the vibrant novelty that the mode can convey even
as late as *Piers Plowman*.[22] At Pentecost with Will and Conscience as they join

---

[20] 'The nature of the exemplum', according to J. Allan Mitchell, 'is to be open-ended or
expansive with respect to the meaning of the moral terms, and closed or reductive when it comes
to determining action' (*Ethics and Exemplary Narrative in Chaucer and Gower* (Cambridge:
Brewer, 2004), p. 19). On the historical development of exempla away from the purpose of
motivating determinative action, see Stierle, 'Story as Exemplum', pp. 389–417.

[21] J. D. Lyons, *Exemplum: The Rhetoric of Example in Early Modern France and Italy* (Princeton: Princeton University Press, 1989), p. 31.

[22] One of the greatest 'exempla collections' of the age, John Bromyard's *Summa praedi-
cantium*, displays the two competing tendencies of exempla. On the one hand, it presents itself
as a collection or encyclopedia of exempla alphabetically organized by topic and cross-referenced.
On the other hand, potted exempla are few and far between, interspersed amidst densely
associative, analogical meditations that deploy concrete, 'exemplary' situations to speculate on the
mysteries of vice, virtue, and the human and divine natures. The preacher on deadline would be
hard pressed to follow, much less re-create the series of agile analogies that get Bromyard from here

'many hundret' in singing the 'Veni Creator Spiritus', we are quite far from an exemplarity that pretends to transcendent moral authority, regardless of its local context.[23] Langland desires no such thing. Granted, the meaning of Pentecost does transcend time and place — hence Will's apparent time travel — but not in order to achieve an absolute identity across the temporal, situational, and perspectival lines that might otherwise separate author and reader, source text and translation, model and copy. The exemplum of Pentecost connects Will's and the readers' time to the early church, allowing them to participate in Pentecost, but without collapsing the two times. Will's bewilderment — 'Y wondred what þat was' (C.21.204) — signals his and the reader's persistent sense of distance and difference from what is happening, even as he gets to take part.

Indeed, an animating doctrine of Pentecost is that unity does not necessarily entail identity, that difference does not preclude likeness — and never less so than in the Trinity, which is really only first given, in its full economic manifestation, at Pentecost. Nicholas of Lyra can thus report in his own words 'what the Gloss says here: The apostles were not only speaking and understanding every language, but while they themselves spoke in one language, whatever that was, all of those listening, however different their languages, understood by the power of God in their own language, whatever that was'.[24] The Pentecostal vision of unity amidst

to there. I have consulted a microfilm of San Marino, Huntington Library, MS 85691: Bromyard, *Summa predicantium* (Nuremberg: [n. pub.], 1485). For the subfield-changing argument for the historical complexity of the exemplum's narrative simplicity, see Larry Scanlon, *Narrative, Authority, and Power: The Medieval Exemplum and the Chaucerian Tradition* (New York: Cambridge University Press, 1994), pp. 25–36.

[23] Allen argues that the exemplary mode is 'ostensibly dedicated to the fantasy that, if a story can remain unchanged as it is imported into a new set of circumstances, then so too can its meaning be fixed, transcending time and place, and that it can thereby perpetuate clear and immutable social and moral principles as well' (Allen, *False Fables*, p. 21). On this view, the exemplary mode is disingenuous in its pretensions to authority (because its authority is not *actually* clear and immutable). Scanlon's account of exemplary authority better fits Langland's exemplary mode in the Pentecost episode. Exempla such as this do not make claims to transcendent authority; rather they 'persuaded by appealing to heroic figures and *auctores* the audience *already* venerated. This appeal was never static because it was precisely the capacity to produce moral authority which the figures being appealed to embodied' (*Narrative, Authority, and Power*, p. 33; my emphasis). The Holy Spirit, Piers, and his 'felawes' embody the capacity to invent moral authority and to invent actions in accord with these morals.

[24] Nicholas of Lyra, *Postilla super totam bibliam*, 4 vols (Strasbourg: [n. pub.], 1492; repr. Frankfurt: Minerva, 1971), vol. IV: '*Et c[o]eperunt loqui variis linguis*, secundum quod dicitur hic glossa: Apostoli non solum loquebantur et intelligebant omnia idiomata, sed ipsis loquentibus in

diversity accentuates humans' individuality. Far from promoting 'the fantasy of moral imitation [...] as [...] the creation of an exact correspondence between the two versions',[25] Pentecostal unity as imagined in *Piers Plowman* assumes a diversity of tongues without assuming primal conflict between the One and the Many. A Wycliffite can thus write, '[I]t is licly þat þes pilgrimes conseyveden þe same langage þat þei knewen moost of alle, and þe witt of þis langage; and so ech man hadde his owne miracle, and God movede apostlis as he wolde. And þis figuride oonesse of herte.'[26] Pentecostal translation intensifies individuality while at the same time fostering 'oneness'; each man could have his own miracle because although he experienced the same Holy Spirit as every other man, his experience was not in competition with the others'.

While medieval cultural discourses, including literature, were often concerned with the translation of authority in order to conserve or assimilate ideological, symbolic, religious, and political power, these competitive objectives are not the only factors that motivated translation or governed the relationships between religious or literary models and copies.[27] Never complacent about linguistic and cultural disparities, Langland seeks to reconcile his culture's heteroglossia in what Katherine Zieman, drawing on the theory of choral communities, has called heterophony, 'the experience of different voices sounding in unison'.[28] At Pente-

---

uno idomate quodcumque esset illud omnes audientes quantumcumque essent diversorum idiomatum intelligebant quilibet idioma proprium virtute divina hoc faciente, sicut enim per rebellionem ad deum divise sunt lingue (Genesi xi) ita per infusionem spiritus sancti sunt unite.' Cf. the Venerable Bede's citation of Gregory of Nazianzus by way of Rufinus on Acts 2. 6 in *Commentary on the Acts of the Apostles*, trans. by Lawrence T. Martin (Kalamazoo: Cistercian, 1989), p. 30.

[25] Allen, *False Fables*, p. 21.

[26] *Select English Works of John Wyclif*, ed. by Thomas Arnold, 3 vols (Oxford: Clarendon Press, 1868–71), II (1871), 307.

[27] For an example of genuinely political translation motivated by power and competition, see Lynn Staley, *Languages of Power in the Age of Richard II* (University Park: Pennsylvania State University Press, 2005), pp. 75–164. Writing of Charles V's translation programme as 'the prime example of the arts of translation', Staley observes, 'If *texts* were the objects of *translatio*, they had to be transplanted into the soil of the vernacular with the apparatus of the academy, the culture to which and out of which they were meaningful, still somehow intact. Academic culture was one of privilege and power; to relocate it in a vernacular sphere was to transfer or "give" wisdom to its patron, usually a prince. What is, in fact, moved from one place to another is privilege, power, a set of meanings now singled out and given new and protected life' (p. 77).

[28] Katherine Zieman, *Singing the New Song: Literacy and Literature in Late Medieval England* (Philadelphia: University of Pennsylvania Press, 2008), p. 160.

cost Langland imagines a harmony of the many servant voices conforming to the voice of their master, the Holy Spirit, even as they achieve their individuality — points to which I will return near the end of the essay.

Competitive Invention in Classical Rhetoric

In *Rhetoric, Hermeneutics, and Translation in the Middle Ages*, Copeland demonstrates how medieval exegetes of classical literature assimilated the *auctoritas* of classical texts to their own rhetorical performances of commentary, serving their 'master' texts, but also supplanting them.[29] The analogy of master and servant derives from classical rhetorical theory, and its recognition of hierarchical power relations is apt. Copeland identifies a centuries-long struggle for primacy among the disciplines, waged in a competition between the discourses of grammar, rhetoric, and commentary. The key distinction is between 'primary translations', which 'exhibit a close alliance with the aims and methods of exegetical practice, and like exegesis define their purpose in terms of service to a source text', and 'secondary translations', which 'derive their essential methods and motive from exegesis, but [...] define themselves [...] through rhetorical models of invention, that is, discovery of one's own argument or subject out of available topics or commonplaces'.[30]

Copeland also demonstrates that translation and commentary are fundamentally practices of invention, even of creative originality. Cultural rivalry with Greece leads Roman translators to opt for an agonistic theory of imitation. The inheritance of a Greek literary tradition incites 'a historical agenda of conquest and supremacy through submission, or in Horace's famous words, "Graecia capta ferum victorem cepit et artis | intulit agresti Latio" (captive Greece captured the savage victor and brought the arts into rustic Latium)'.[31] For Horace and the subsequent *Ars poetriae* tradition that was so influential in medieval poetics, the copy's inventive difference from the model, not its lineal continuity, comes to constitute its excellence. 'Horace proposes a theory of rhetorical imitation where the force of invention intervenes between model and copy, just as Quintilian

---

[29] Copeland, *Rhetoric*, p. 3. An early, and in some ways more theoretically explicit, version of this argument appears in Copeland, 'The Fortunes of "Non Verbum pro Verbo": Or, Why Jerome Is Not a Ciceronian', *The Medieval Translator* (1989), 15–35.

[30] Copeland, *Rhetoric*, pp. 6–7.

[31] Copeland, *Rhetoric*, p. 31, citing Horace, Epistle 2.1.156.

remarks that "nothing grows from imitation alone".[32] While translation always to a certain extent preserves the text or culture translated, what is valued in the translation may be the copy's competitive striving to displace the model text. For the Roman rhetorical theorists, likeness to the model is the norm and difference is a desirable departure by which copies attain to individuality, vitality, and excellence.

This distinction holds true enough for the classical rhetorical traditions, and it goes a long way toward explaining how Chaucer and, to a lesser extent, Gower vie with their classical forbears and literary contemporaries in order to 'make it new' and assimilate *auctoritas* and originality to their own texts. But the only model of invention by translation and commentary that Copeland explores is the classical rhetorical model animated by generational competition between model and copy. The question remains open whether literature motivated by *non-competitive* exegesis, 'in service to a source text', cannot be just as inventive as, say, Chaucer's *Legend of Good Women*, the featured text of Copeland's discussion of Chaucer.[33]

The Pentecost episode in *Piers Plowman* gives us just one reason to theorize a literary ethics that can explain how a product of invention might be non-competitive, non-totalizing, 'original', and ethically demanding all at the same time. Too often Copeland's early work on translation is cited as a comprehensive account of medieval literary translation and its potential for rhetorical invention. The master-servant model that structures translation and commentary *in the rhetorical tradition* from at least the time of Horace down to Chaucer and Gower

---

[32] Copeland, *Rhetoric*, p. 29.

[33] Copeland, *Rhetoric*, pp. 184–203. In recent essays on devotional writing, Atsushi Iguchi has proposed alternatives to Copeland's models for understanding vernacular difference from Latin sources: 'Copeland's theoretical framework of medieval vernacular translation, based on those writers who [...] are conscious of what they are doing in the vernacular in contestation with Latin, is not directly applicable to devotional translation, where the chief aims are replicative [...]. In such a context, the subversive aspect of translation is less apparent.' In what could be seen as a dilation of Copeland's category of 'primary translation', Iguchi accounts for difference between model and copy in devotional translations in terms of the 'new purposes, different effects and, as often as not, [...] different audience', rather than competition to displace the model ('Translating Grace: The *Scala Claustralium* and *A Ladder of Foure Ronges*', *Review of English Studies*, n.s., 59 (2008), 659–76 (p. 661)). See also Atsushi Iguchi, 'The Visibility of the Translator: The *Speculum Ecclesie* and *The Mirror of Holy Church*', *Neophilologus*, 93 (2009), 537–52. In my view, Langland is much more innovative than the devotional texts on which Iguchi focuses, so that neither Iguchi's expanded category of primary translation nor Copeland's category of secondary translation is adequate to *Piers Plowman*.

is not the only way of construing the relationship between text and commentary — but it has dominated scholarship on the topic.[34]

Model and Copy: The Image on the Coin

Langland's conception of ethical and rhetorical invention, though it relies on the classical rhetorical topos of the imprinted coin, construes the relationship between model and copy differently by introducing the element of false intentions in the politically charged practice of counterfeiting:

> Me may now likene lettred men to a loscheborw oþer worse
> And to a badde peny with a gode printe:
> Of moche mone þe metal is nauhte
> And ȝut is þe printe puyr trewe and parfitliche ygraue.
> And so hit fareth by false cristene: here follynge is trewe,
> Cristendoem of holy kyrke, the kynges marke of heuene,
> Ac þe metal þat is mannes soule of many of this techares
> Is alayed with leccherye and oþer lustes of synne
> That god coueyteth nat þe coyne þat crist hymsulue printede
> And for þe synne of þe soule forsaketh his oune coyne.
> Thus ar ȝe luyþer ylikned to lossheborwe sterlynges
> That fayre byfore folk prechen and techen
> And worcheth nat as ȝe fyndeth ywryte and wisseth þe peple.
> (C.17.73–85)

Likening 'lettred men to a loscheborw oþer worse | And to a badde peny with a gode printe', Conscience observes that 'here follynge is trewe, [...] Ac þe metal þat is mannes soule [...] Is alayed with leccherye and oþer lustes of synne' (C.17.73–74, 76–80). Like *lossheborwes* — the counterfeit English coins imported from the Low Countries (or Luxembourg, as the name suggests)[35] — the souls of false

---

[34] Take for example Douglas Kelly's blanket statement about literary translation: 'infidelity to source, and thus unfaithful translation, is what we must expect and, in all its intertextual implications, what we must look for and study' ('The *Fidus interpres*: Aid or Impediment to Medieval Translation and *Translatio*', in *Translation Theory and Practice in the Middle Ages*, ed. by Jeanette Beer (Kalamazoo: Medieval Institute Publications, 1997), pp. 47–58 (p. 58)).

[35] *Lusshebournes* were counterfeit English pennies manufactured from cheap alloys in the Low Countries to piggyback on the strength of the English coinage, on which Edward I built one of the most reliable monetary systems in Europe. Edward III's Statute of Treasons of 1352 makes

Christians are alloyed with sin, so that, although they bear the image of Christ impressed in baptism (*follynge*), 'god coueyteth nat þe coyne þat crist hymsulue printede | And for þe synne of þe soule forsaketh his oune coyne', refusing to recognize them as legal tender (C.17.81–82). By contrast to later Lancastrian discourses of counterfeiting, which rhetorically linked the crime to heresy and treason, Langland is more concerned here with everyday moral orthopraxis than with orthodoxy. But the discourse of true and counterfeit coinage activates a symbolic complex not easily contained: 'between seeming and being, outer and inner, counterfeit and real, material and ineffable, heretical and orthodox, illegitimate and legitimate'.[36]

Langland's awareness of this semiotic richness is reflected in his C-text revisions, where the theory of imitation evolves from concerns about rhetoric to concerns about ethics. In B, Anima counsels 'alle cristene to conformen hem to charite'.[37] Where C locates the corruption of the coin in 'false cristene' who have received the mark in baptism, B does not mention baptism and locates the 'defaute' in the discrepancy between the 'fair speche' of 'som folk now' and their actual failure to love (B.15.347, 351): 'Boþe lettred and lewed beþ alayed now wiþ synne, | That no lif loueþ ooþer, ne oure lord, as it semeþ.' According to this theological anthropology, baptism imprints the soul with the image of God, making it a Christian soul. The Christian then bears out the image in 'fair speche', rhetorically conforming to the image of God. As in the sequence of the Incarnation, where the *Logos* exists first only as Word but then takes on flesh, the

---

counterfeiting 'the king's [...] money' an offence of the same gravity as plotting his death or violating his wife since it 'extends to our lord the king and his royal majesty' (*English Historical Documents*, IV: *1327–1485*, ed. by A. R. Myers (London: Eyre and Spottiswoode, 1969), p. 403). See Diana Wood, *Medieval Economic Thought* (New York: Cambridge University Press, 2002), pp. 127–28. For other treatments of the image of God and the image of the coin in *Piers Plowman*, see Barbara Raw, 'Piers and the Image of God in Man', in *'Piers Plowman': Critical Approaches*, ed. by S. S. Hussey (London: Methuen, 1969), pp. 143–79; and Margaret E. Goldsmith, *The Image of 'Piers Plowman': The Image on the Coin* (Cambridge: Brewer, 1981).

[36] Paul Strohm, *England's Empty Throne: Usurpation and the Language of Legitimation, 1399–1422* (New Haven: Yale University Press, 1998), p. 146. Strohm does not discuss *Piers Plowman*, and his case study of William Carsewell's confession of counterfeiting involves a different kind of counterfeiting from the racket run in the Low Countries. Instead of passing off cheap metals as real coins, Carsewell claimed to have been recruited by the outlawed fugitive Lollard John Oldcastle to melt down silver clippings from genuine coins and to cast them as groats with the proper markings.

[37] *Piers Plowman: The B Version*, ed. by George Kane and E. Talbot Donaldson (London: Athlone, 1975), B.15.344; hereafter cited in the text.

rhetorical image of God precedes the deeds that incarnate the word of God in an ethical life.

The C text further develops the movement from rhetoric to ethics, explicitly drawing on invention theory. Bad clergy now take the brunt of the criticism in the C text, and they are at fault not just because of common hypocrisy, but because they 'fayre byfore folk prechen and techen | And worcheth nat as ʒe fyndeth ywryte' (C.17.84–85). Hypocritical clergy elevate the hypocrisy of the 'lewed' in B to a sin made graver because they practice it in the institutionally authorized rhetorical office of the preacher. They not only fail to match actions to words, but also betray the *character* impressed on them in ordination, 'a particular imprint on the soul, which indicates that those in holy orders are marked off to perform certain spiritual functions'.[38]

The ethical errors of the clergy therefore follow from rhetorical errors, namely errors of invention. Scripture, what is 'ywryte', supplies ample models and topics both for speaking and action. These preachers apparently find the material sufficient for the invention — the *finding* (C.17.85) — of elaborate sermons, but insufficient for the invention of works. They do not act according to what they discover written and what they invent homiletically. The hypocritical preachers manage to interpret and invent according to the ethical sense of Scripture, but their invention realizes only its rhetorical potential without proceeding to practical ethical invention, the invention of actions. Because their invention is not an invention of works, Liberum Arbitrium observes, it cannot persuade and they fail truly to teach the people ('nat [...] wisseth þe peple'; C.17.85). Liberum Arbitrium's analysis suggests that interpretation and rhetorical performance are irreducibly ethical; if invention is not borne out in practice, even its rhetorical dimension will come to naught.

For Langland, then, the goal of rhetorical invention is rhetorical imitation, which should issue in practical, concrete ethical imitation. Because of original sin, the model and the copy are originally different. Baptism restores — indeed, perfects — the similarity between model and copy. But sin persists, and even with the clear imprint of baptism, the total form of the soul, the complete image, remains different from the model. Thus difference between model and copy is the norm, and similarity is a desirable departure from the norm. People achieve excellence by closing the gap between model and copy.

---

[38] Alastair Minnis, *Fallible Authors: Chaucer's Pardoner and Wife of Bath* (Philadelphia: University of Pennsylvania Press, 2008), p. 67. On the moral responsibility of preachers, see Minnis, ibid., pp. 36–54.

This logic of invention and imitation should be familiar from the cult of the saints and the theology of Christ's and Mary's exemplarity that animates much late medieval monastic piety and transfigures the agonistic violence of classical rhetoric as a positive, reconciling force. Horace's violent images of invention come strikingly close to twelfth-century Cistercians' and Carthusians' images of sin as Caroline Bynum describes them, but with the goals reversed: 'fragmentation, rupture, assertion of one's differentness from the image of God that one is in the process of becoming. The idea of Christ as nursing or pregnant mother is for Cistercians one among a host of images that articulate a process of return through love of others to true dependence, a return made possible by the breaking of false dependence on the difference and otherness of the world.'[39] Whereas for Copeland's Romans 'the force of invention intervenes between model and copy',[40] for Langland the force of invention should conform the copy to the model. And while this relationship is figured by Horace with the violent imagery of battle, in the later medieval discourse of the imitation of Christ, as expressed in the devotion to the Sacred Heart and in theological explanations of the stigmata, the wounds of Christ 'were regarded as places of refuge, spiritual remedies, and wells or fountains of life, pity, mercy, comfort, grace'.[41] That is, the copy conforms to the model by suffering violence, but this is seen as salutary and reconciling, rather than as martial and hegemonic. If invention does indeed entail violence, why should we not understand it as the violence of repair, instead of rupture?[42]

---

[39] Caroline Walker Bynum, *Jesus as Mother: Studies in the Spirituality of the High Middle Ages* (Berkeley and Los Angeles: University of California Press, 1982), p. 166.

[40] Copeland, *Rhetoric*, p. 29.

[41] Giles Constable, *Three Studies in Medieval Religious and Social Thought* (Cambridge: Cambridge University Press, 1995), p. 225. This represents a further application to bodily suffering of an enduring interpretation of imitation as the reconciling participation in Christ's divinity and the closing of the gap between humans' intact *imago Dei* and their obliterated ethical and ontological likeness (*similitudo*) to God. On participation, see Constable, ibid., pp. 150–55 and pp. 164–65; on ethical and ontological image and likeness, pp. 166–68.

[42] The 'violence of repair' could suggest one path for thought about Langland's own chronic revisionism, here on display in the transition from B to C. Humans may achieve excellence by closing the gap between model and copy, but *Piers Plowman* never depicts life with the gap closed. This is not to say that Langland avoids imagining rightly ordered lives and communities, just that he reserves visions of fulfilment for his most allegorical moments, one of which I discuss at the end of this essay when I raise the question of how Langland's anagogical imagination relates to his tropological imagination. Besides issues of eschatological fulfilment, there are other reasons copies will never be *the same* as their models. In kinship models, for instance, the child will never be *the*

Tropology and the Ethics of Making

For texts such as *Piers Plowman*, we need a more supple theory of invention and exemplarity than a dyadic account according to which imitation produces alterity, not sameness. If I am right that the rhetorical traditions, as they have been used to explain Middle English literary invention, cannot provide such an account, then perhaps other intellectual sources will serve us better. I suggest that we turn to the highly developed theories of ethics and invention that emerge from the theology and practice of biblical exegesis and overlap with homiletic theory. Let me sketch the rationale behind such a shift in our critical perspective.

In 1215 the Fourth Lateran Council intervened in debates about the relationship between nature and grace by succinctly defining the doctrine of analogy in terms that should be familiar from the foregoing discussion: 'One cannot note a similarity between Creator and creature — however great — without having to note an ever greater dissimilarity between them.'[43] The doctrine of analogy expressed here carefully secures the transcendence of the absolutely other God while allowing creaturely participation in and imitation of God. Such a dynamic, tensile theory of analogy can contemplate the sameness and difference entailed in every invention without reducing literary and ethical action to a zero-sum economy of struggle between old and new, model and copy.

Such a theory can help us understand a peculiar aspect of readers' responses to exemplary texts: while readers are often inspired to convert words into works, they seldom do exactly what their models did. Some kind of translation occurs between

---

same as its father or mother, no matter how close the resemblance. D. Vance Smith has shown how, in the genealogy of sin that *Piers Plowman* runs through the curse of Cain, human paternity threatens to displace divine paternity, positing 'an irredeemable gap between material making and divine creation' (Smith, *The Book of the Incipit*, p. 138; on paternity and beginnings, pp. 113–39). However, other gaps — such as the non-contrastive gap between God's being and human beings — are built into creation and so not in need of redemption or violent recuperation (see 'The Invention of Peace', below, pp. 187–92, especially pp. 191–92 n. 97).

[43] For this translation, see John R. Betz, 'Beyond the Sublime: The Aesthetics of the Analogy of Being (Part One)', *Modern Theology*, 21 (2005), 367–411 (p. 374). Betz, in turn, is translating the German of Erich Przywara, whose work on analogy has inspired a new wave of creative work on the analogy of being in philosophical theology. See Erich Przywara, *Analogia entis, Metaphysik: Ur-Struktur und All-Rhythmus* (Einsiedeln: Johannes, 1962). The Lateran IV formulation occurs in a defence of Peter Lombard's Trinitarian definitions against Joachim of Fiore's criticisms: 'inter creatorem et creaturam non potest similitudo notari, quin inter eos maior sit dissimilitudo notanda' (*Enchiridion symbolorum, definitionum et declarationum de rebus fidei et morum*, ed. by Heinrich Denzinger and Adolf Schönmetzer (Barcinone: Herder, 1973), p. 806).

the represented action and the action readers feel inspired to perform. The theology of exegesis helps to explain how this process happens because, in Gilbert Dahan's words, '[I]t is the passage from the letter to the spiritual or mystical senses that sets in motion the mechanisms of *translatio* [transfer of meaning].'[44] In the exegetical theory of Bonaventure, for example, the translation of a text (or any created datum) into a reader's ethical action is built into the fabric of creation itself: 'Because the way to God is through faith, hope, and love, every creature is a suggestion of what we should believe, expect, and do. And parallel to this, there is a threefold spiritual meaning: the allegorical concerning what we should believe, the anagogical concerning what we should expect, and the moral [tropological] concerning what we should do, for love leads to action.'[45] But every imitative action, as Lateran IV insists, evinces an ever greater dissimilarity from the model for the action — not because imitation subverts the model, but because the model itself transcends any possible likeness it inspires. Like Gregory of Nyssa's Moses, who chases after the back of God for all eternity, the nearer the copy approaches its model, the farther it finds it has to go.[46]

Imitation does indeed produce alterity, but it also produces sameness — or, more accurately, correspondence. The challenge of interpretation is not to determine whether ethical inventions reflect literal or figural modes of interpretation, but how — since invention is never the *same* — to be sensitive to the diverse renditions models undergo as they are reinvented in unforeseeable copies. In other words, saints in hagiographies and literary characters such as Will and Conscience are not just models, but models of how to be copies. Built into these texts is the understanding that ethics is always translation, and translation always entails invention; and texts like *Piers Plowman* give examples — represent models — of people struggling to turn words into works, inspired not merely by responsibility to the Other, but the very specific possibility of participation in the history of redemption on the way to contemplation of a God who is always ever greater.

---

[44] Gilbert Dahan, *L'Exégèse Chrétienne de la Bible en Occident médiéval: XIIᵉ–XIVᵉ siècle* (Paris: Cerf, 1999), p. 55.

[45] Bonaventure, *Collations on the Six Days*, in *The Works of St. Bonaventure*, trans. by José de Vinck, 5 vols (Paterson, NJ: St Anthony Guild, 1960–70), v (1970), 13.11.

[46] 'Certainly whoever pursues true virtue participates in nothing other than God, because he is himself absolute virtue. Since, then, those who know what is good by nature desire participation in it, and since this good has no limit, the participant's desire itself necessarily has no stopping place but stretches out with the limitless': Gregory of Nyssa, *Life of Moses*, ed. by Abraham J. Malherbe and others (Mahwah, NJ: Paulist, 1978), Prol. 7.

The theory of tropological interpretation can help us attend to these translations in at least two important ways. First, tropology helps us to see writing as ethical action. If Liberum Arbitrium is right about the blessedness of the one who turns words into works, then Langland can defend his practice of making because writing qualifies as labour, as *opera*. Imaginatif, sometimes a critic of literary making, approves Spirit-inspired copying: 'Although men maden bokes God was here maystre | And seynt spirit þe saumplarie and said what men sholde write' (C.14.46–47). He imagines the making of the Bible in a monastic scriptorium, where God (the Father) superintends the scribal work and the authors of Scripture copy from the 'saumplarie' (the exemplar) that is the Holy Spirit. Imaginatif uses the image to prove a point much larger than the inspiration of the Bible, namely, that books are an appropriate and necessary medium for knowledge of God: 'For as a man may nat se þat misseth his yes, | No more can no clerk but if hit come of bokes' (C.14.44–45). It is noteworthy that Imaginatif does not here defend the teaching office of the church, *sacra doctrina*, philosophy, or even learning in general. Instead he defends 'bokes', which metonymically comprehend all disciplines, even the 'makyng' he earlier criticized.

Bonaventure draws an analogy between the two terms of Imaginatif's metonym — the Bible and 'bokes' — dividing all the arts on analogy to the four senses of Scripture. All knowledge concerned with practical action falls under the tropological sense of Scripture. And he extends the analogy according to Aristotelian causal analysis: everything relating to efficient causation (which corresponds to practical action) also falls under the tropological sense. For example, in the mechanical arts, the allegorical sense corresponds to the 'mediating similitude' the maker has in mind; the tropological sense to the manner, quality, and activity of making; and the anagogical sense to the delight in the finished product.[47] Bonaventure can thus 'reduce' — lead back — all making to the divine illumination of Scripture because all making already proceeds from the same source as Scripture. Imaginatif, who has accused Will of meddling with makings,[48] can approve of a kind of making that can be led back to Scripture by an analogical reduction. Tropological making, then, is not merely writing about ethical themes or even for the purpose of inspiring ethical action, but a habit of invention that translates idea into action with a 'reductive' momentum leading back to Scripture

---

[47] Bonaventure, *De reductione artium ad theologiam*, in *Works of St. Bonaventure*, ed. by Emma Thérèse Healy, 2nd edn, 14 vols (Saint Bonaventure, NY: Franciscan Institute, 1955–2008), I (1955), 12–14.

[48] '[Þ]ou medlest þee wiþ makynges' (B.12.16).

and (at the same time) forward toward full correspondence with its model, toward the soul's mystical union with God and the Church's fulfilment in the Kingdom of Heaven. That is to say, tropological making happens between the letter of Scripture (the literal sense), the truth of salvation history (the allegorical sense), and their eschatological fulfilment (the anagogical sense).

Second, tropological theory helps us to recognize those moments when Langland specifies ethical action and the good as, precisely, participation in Christian salvation history as made available in the Bible, the liturgy, and the sacraments. For example, Christ's exemplarity is given a tropological cast when it becomes the means by which the disciples on the road to Emmaus recognize him:

> Cleophas ne knewe hym nat þat he Crist were
> For his pore parail and pilgrimes clothes
> Til he blessed here bred and brake hit hem bitwene.
> So by his werkes thei wisten þat he was iesu
> Ac by clothyng they knewe hym nat, so caytifliche he 3ede.
> And al was ensample, sothly, to vs synfole here
> That we sholde be low and louelich and lele vch man til oþer
> And pacient as pilgrimes for pilgrimes are we alle.
>
> (C.12.124–31)

Cleophas and his companion recognize Christ not by his words or appearance, but by his works. This is 'al' an example — first to the disciples in Emmaus who recognized Christ by his actions, and then to 'vs synfole here', who must recognize Christ in poverty, meekness, and love, so conforming ourselves to his pilgrim ethic. The 'here' functions as a tropological deictic, locating the example's intended audience in the present place and time, and by those coordinates identifying the reading subject as the hermeneutical object of Christ's ethical intentionality.

This hermeneutics requires conversion. The poverty that is commended as a good at the end of the quotation actually distracts the disciples from Christ's identity at the beginning of the episode, requiring their interpretive conversion along the way. In order to do the good, they have to recognize the good, and in order to do that they have to interpret Christ's poor rags as signs of his divinely humble identity. But the interpretation is not complete until Christ *acts*, making himself known in the breaking of the bread: 'So by his werkes thei wisten þat he was iesu.' The act allows the disciples to read the situation aright, and when they do so, they (and perhaps we) discern a call to be 'low and louelich [...] and pacient as pilgrimes'.

In Luke's telling of the story, their act of interpretation results in their conversion: they turn back from Emmaus and return to Jerusalem (where Jesus had already instructed the disciples to wait). This literal turn is a reminder of why early Christians appropriated the classical definition of tropology (dealing with turns of phrase, figures of speech) to name the ethical sense: the Greek root *tropos* means both 'turn' and 'way of life'. This moral use of *tropologia* was a Christian innovation, for in classical rhetoric the root was taken much less literally; our modern sense of a trope as a 'turn of phrase' is nearly identical to the ancient usage. In the words of Robert de Melun, '*Tropologia* means speech that turns (*sermo conversivus*), because (*eo quod*) it designates a deed of such a sort that it is necessary for us to be converted to it with respect to the establishment of moral edification.'[49] Alain de Lille, in perhaps the most widely known etymology of the later Middle Ages, significantly draws his example of tropology from the life of Christ: 'It is called tropology when through some act it is understood what we ought to do; whence also it is called tropology as if [it were] a word turned toward us, like this: by Christ having his hands affixed to the Cross, it is signified that we ought to restrain our hands from the guilt of sin.'[50]

On the road to Emmaus, Christ gives the example of the ideal unity of interpretation and invention, having himself 'expounded to them in all the Scriptures the things that were concerning him' (Luke 24. 27). Christ presents himself as the ideal copy of the Old Testament model (the Law), but at the same time he reverses the relationship, establishing himself as the model in which Law and Love are summed up. As Langland's subsequent discourse on poverty suggests, the same Christ who rightly expounds the Scriptures becomes the prototypical exemplar

---

[49] Cited in Henri de Lubac, *Medieval Exegesis: The Four Senses of Scripture*, trans. by Mark Sebanc and E. M. Macierowski, 3 vols to date (Grand Rapids: Eerdmans, 1998–), II (2000), 129.

[50] He continues, '*Tropus* means conversion. It is also a figure, as when a word is converted from its proper meaning, whence the phrase, "it is said *tropica*", that is, figuratively' (Tropologia dicitur [...] quando per aliquod factum intelligitur quod a nobis sit faciendum; unde et tropologia dicitur quasi sermo conversus ad nos, ut per hoc quod Christus habuit manus affixas cruci significatur quod manus debemus cohibere a reatu peccati. Tropus dicitur conversio. Est etiam figura quando dictio a propria significatione convertitur, unde locutio dicitur tropica, id est figurativa): Alain de Lille, *Distinctiones dictionum theologicalium*, s.vv. 'tropologia' and 'tropus', in PL, CCX, 981A–B). On the migration of this etymology from early lexicons into the homiletic aids and sermons of the later Middle Ages, see Riccardo Quinto, 'Peter the Chanter and the "Miscellanea del Codice del Tesoro" (Etymology as a Way for Constructing a Sermon)', in *Constructing the Medieval Sermon*, ed. by Roger Andersson, Studies on Patristic, Medieval, and Reformation Sermons, 6 (Brepols: Turnhout, 2007), pp. 33–81.

of poverty. Mary herself was 'a puyre pore mayde and to a pore man ywedded' (C.12.135), copying the model of her son.

For Langland, it is not enough to see Christ, or even to hear him interpreting Scripture Christologically; Christians must also be enabled by the Spirit to practise spiritual exegesis on the Scriptures themselves and invent 'in our own tongues the wonderful works of God', which is what Luke says of the glossolalic apostles at Pentecost (Acts 2. 11). The ethical invention modelled in *Piers Plowman*, then, should be considered tropological because it situates ethical activity — especially Langland's activity of making *Piers Plowman* — between the Christian-historical narrative of allegorical or figural reading and the mystical union of the anagogical sense. Tropological invention is a pilgrim invention, always underway between doctrine and fulfilment, between model and perfected copy, and realized only in 'low and louelich and lele' relations 'vch man til oþer [...] for pilgrimes are we alle' (C.12.130–31). That is, tropological invention according to *Piers Plowman* situates the ethics of alterity within a dynamic, circulating movement between moral law, free action, and final goods.

Ethical Invention and the Event of Beginning

How do final goods rate in a lifetime of chronic revision? On the one hand, there is the Langland who revises in a dogged, faithful pursuit to understand and experience the ultimate goods of the Christian faith that are 'out there'.[51] On the other hand, there is the Langland whose search for St Truth is an 'exploration' without 'a fixed, previously known referent', in which 'the concept is being created by the text of the poem itself'.[52] Surely Langland invents both by transcendent and immanent impulses.[53] But we have more trouble understanding how final goods, how ethical teleologies, can coexist with free invention, free action, and the ethics of alterity. Literature involves, in Derrida's words, 'the invention of the other'.[54] In his influential account, invention is an ethical act, first, because it requires breaking the norm and, second, because it allows the Other to come into view,

---

[51] Along these lines, I appreciate how Pamela Raabe argues for the coherence of Langland's project and the attainability of faithful understanding and final goods (*Imitating God: The Allegory of Faith in 'Piers Plowman' B* (Athens: University of Georgia Press, 1990)).

[52] Carruthers, *The Search for St. Truth*, p. 10; p. 20.

[53] As Raabe and Carruthers both recognize, each in her own way.

[54] See Jacques Derrida, 'Psyche'.

and as Lévinas teaches, 'access to the face [of the Other] is straightaway ethical'.[55] But the origin of this encounter with the Other is, tellingly, an act of inventive violence: 'An invention always presupposes some illegality, the breaking of an implicit contract; it inserts a disorder into the peaceful ordering of things, it disregards the proprieties.'[56]

In the so-called 'new ethical theory', the conflict that Derridean invention imposes between the Same and the Other orders the social ethics of literature.[57] As his work has been digested and applied by literary theorists, Derrida stands for an agonistic ethic of reading in which literature facilitates ethical experience when '[t]he reader experiences the free play of his or her imagination as produced through a power struggle with a social other [...] who, in turn, binds him or her'.[58] For literary studies proponents of the new ethics, literature invents ethical experience when it troubles 'certainty by an apprehension that comes through surprised feeling',[59] when it upsets the rigid absolutes of morality with the contingencies and irresolvable tensions of (the new) ethics.[60]

But this distinction between an underdetermined, immanent, non-teleological *ethics* and an absolute, extrinsic, teleological *morality* smuggles in a Kantian opposition between heteronomy and autonomy that may only awkwardly be applied to the concrete moralities we encounter in *Piers Plowman*. For a poem in which a central character is a personified Conscience, a simplistic opposition between loving, open-ended concern for the Other and the prescriptive morality of law will not suffice. 'Hoso lyueth in lawe and in loue doth wel', counsels Wit, adducing matrimony as a prime example of love for others, but also warning married couples, 'worcheth nat out of tyme' (C.10.203, 288). The 'lawe' forbids 'loue'

[55] Emmanuel Lévinas, *Ethics and Infinity*, trans. by Philippe Nemo (Pittsburgh: Duquesne University Press, 1985), p. 85.

[56] Derrida, 'Psyche', p. 83.

[57] For a survey of the 'new ethics' in literary studies, see Dorothy J. Hale, 'Aesthetics and the New Ethics: Theorizing the Novel in the Twenty-First Century', *PMLA*, 124 (2009), 896–905. On the first wave of the new ethics, see Lawrence Buell, 'In Pursuit of Ethics', *PMLA*, 114 (1999), 7–19.

[58] Hale, 'Aesthetics and the New Ethics', p. 902.

[59] Hale, 'Aesthetics and the New Ethics', p. 903.

[60] J. Allan Mitchell contrasts 'the immanent particularity of ethical practices or patterns of behaviour (Hegelian *Sittlichkeit*) and normative rules of morality regulating behaviour (*Moralität*)' in order to argue that 'ethics is situated in the factical event prior to congealing into abstract morality' (*Ethics and Eventfulness*, p. 24).

during menstruation and pregnancy. Is this a paradox? Wit does not think so. He does not admit a choice between autonomous practical reason and heteronymous moral law; loving couples must use their practical reason to cooperate with and participate in the natural and moral laws governing fertility, with the understanding that their love and their offspring (their inventions) will be the better for it.

This ethical conception is underwritten by what Rémi Brague, intending to short-circuit the heteronomy-autonomy binary, calls 'cosmonomy', according to which 'it is in fact the insertion into the cosmos that enables the moral subject to be truly himself, to be truly an *autos*. This conformity in no way consists in bending to an exterior law, an other (*heteros*). [...] It is only our insertion into the *kosmos* where it is most fully itself [...] that confers authentic freedom upon us.'[61] According to Wit, men and women are most fully and freely able to exercise their love when they reserve 'bedbourde' (bed play) for the right 'tyme' (C.10.288–91). Just as a copy need not displace its model in order to be freely itself, the law of creation is not in competition with creaturely becoming.[62]

At Pentecost, Will and Conscience are inserted into one of those points where the *kosmos* is most fully itself, a signal event in the history of salvation. By sleight of dream and the *ductus* of Conscience's sermon, they achieve what Margot Fassler identifies as the goal of Victorine sequence hymns: 'to draw the singing clergy into the world of the primitive Christian church'.[63] But however primitive this intense experience of cosmonomy might be, the old does not efface the new. Will's subjective perspective — 'and thenne cam, me thouhte, | Oen *spiritus paraclitus*' (C.21.200–01) — tethers readers to the *now*, even as he assimilates himself to the *then*. Just as the Wycliffite exegesis of Pentecost envisions the simultaneous diversity of language and unity of understanding, so does Langland's treatment of this episode conserve the new and the old, the model and the copy. The 'Creator Spirit' comes 'In liknesse of a lihtnynge' and 'ouerspradde[s]' the apostles 'in fuyres liknesse', counterintuitively adopting the role of copy to his creatures' models, as the language of likeness suggests (C.21.202–06).

---

[61] Rémi Brague, *The Wisdom of the World: The Human Experience of the Universe in Western Thought*, trans. by Teresa Lavender Fagan (Chicago: University of Chicago Press, 2003), p. 153.

[62] In Rémi Brague's phrase, 'human action [is] in phase with cosmological realities' (*The Law of God: The Philosophical History of an Idea*, trans. by Lydia G. Cochrane (Chicago: University of Chicago Press, 2007), p. vii).

[63] Margot Fassler, *Gothic Song: Victorine Sequences and Augustinian Reform in Twelfth-Century Paris* (Cambridge: Cambridge University Press, 1993), p. 269.

Similarly, Langland casts the episode in the likeness of the Acts narrative, but in doing so he also invents it. Exploiting the combinatory, imaginative privileges of a maker, Langland makes a quasihistorical aetiology of the invention of the Church and part of the liturgy.[64] The scene is both interpretive — encountering a historical 'source' that comes before it — and inventive. Langland represents an act of literary-liturgical invention even as he himself innovates. In the interpretive mode, like the bystanders in the Acts narrative who 'wondered [...] "what meaneth this?"' (Acts 2. 12), Will 'wondred what þat was and wagged Consience' to interpret the tongues of fire; Conscience explains their meaning as the 'spiritus paraclitus', whose name is Grace (C.21.204–08). And in the inventive mode, with the 'many hundret' they can kneel — 'Knele now'! (C.21.209) — and sing the song of praise, a response to the Holy Spirit's advent.

Here we glimpse the invention of the 'Veni Creator Spiritus' — a Pentecost sequence hymn — at the foundation of the liturgy, which Langland envisions simultaneously with the foundation of the Church. En masse, as if at Mass, the crowd kneels and creates a hymn of praise to the Spirit of creation. Inspired like Peres's 'felawes' (C.21.201), who instantaneously 'knowe alle kyne langages' (C.21.203), Will and the congregation find that they know a hymn in the language of the Church, the universal language, Latin.[65] The hymn pre-exists their singing — or so Conscience presumes — but it could not have pre-existed Pentecost. They sing it for the first time, but it comes before them, comes to them,

---

[64] On imagination as a combinatory faculty, see Alastair B. Minnis, 'Langland's Ymaginatif and Late-Medieval Theories of Imagination', Comparative Criticism, 3 (1981), 71–103. For an excellent discussion of Langland's imagination, including a current survey of relevant research, see Michelle Karnes, 'Will's Imagination in Piers Plowman', JEGP: Journal of English and Germanic Philology, 108 (2009), 27–58 (pp. 43–53).

[65] Fiona Somerset has recognized a similarly demotic use of Latin in the B-prologue, where MS F prefaces Latin lines from a summa for preachers with, 'Thanne cryeden alle þe comonys with o voys atonys' (B.Prol.143). This line asserting lay unity takes the form of a Latin leonine hexameter, melding conventions from both languages and 'accomplish[ing]' on the level of form the assertion of commonality, exchange, or even fusion between Latin and the vernacular that [...] is foregrounded by the passage's insistence that the "commune" speaks a "vers of latyn". [...] There is no firm boundary between Latin and English [...] : words or phrases may be used effectively by both the fully fluent, and those with the most limited functional literacy' ('"Al þe comonys with o voys atonys": Multilingual Latin and Vernacular Voice in Piers Plowman', YLS, 19 (2005), 107–36 (pp. 135–36)). What Somerset identifies from a sociolinguistic perspective Langland approaches theologically in the Pentecost episode, addressing the pneumatological and ecclesial conditions under which linguistic unity and diversity need not conflict.

ready-made. They invent it because they discover it, and they discover it in singing it. The hymn is a gift, but no less, for that, an invention.

Read in light of Derrida's analysis of invention, the Holy Spirit breaks through the horizon of history to reinterpret the Jewish holiday, thus inventing a new event that issues in a call — signalled by the incipit of the hymn '*Come* Creator Spirit' — with which the nascent church responds by its own participatory 'come'. Invention of the other breaks through history as an *event*, the event of a call, to which the inventor answers, 'come in'.[66] Here the ethical comes into view: how to say 'come' and to answer the call of the other.[67] But can Derrida's construal of the event of invention comprehend Langland's invention? If Langland's invention does not disturb the peace but *makes* it, if the highest aim of his copies is to conform to their models, then either *Piers Plowman* is an 'invention of the same' — limiting itself to the realm of the possible, inventing only what already exists, and so, in effect, inventing nothing and foreclosing the advent of the other — or we need to question whether Derrida's account of invention is comprehensive enough. In Derrida's thought, because 'invention of the other' is predicated on the impossible, invention structured on a model-copy relationship can only be 'invention of the same'. Invention of the other must always involve the overthrow of all models, and so some kind of originary violence. In Derrida's terms, the event of invention must interrupt every possible horizon (every possible model). But what if the event comes before all horizons, if the copy precedes the model? This is the crucial question that Jean-Luc Marion has introduced to phenomenology, and it opens a perspective on Langland's invention and ethics not afforded by the new ethical theory.[68]

---

[66] 'This invention of the entirely other is beyond any possible status; I still call it invention, because one gets ready for it, one makes this step destined to let the other come, *come in*. [...] To get ready for this coming of the other is what can be called deconstruction. [...] To invent would then be to "know" how to say "come" and to answer the "come" of the other' (Derrida, 'Psyche', p. 39).

[67] The possibility of the other's call is implied by the temporality of texts. Because a text is also an event, it participates in the event-ness of history. 'Never does an invention appear, never does an invention take place, without an inaugural event. Nor is there any invention for the future of a *possibility* or of a *power* that will remain at the disposal of everyone. Advent there must be, because the event of an invention, its act of inaugural production [...] must be valid *for the future* [l'avenir]' (Derrida, 'Psyche', pp. 5–6).

[68] To give a brief genealogy of Marion's innovation in phenomenology: Edmund Husserl limited phenomenality — what it is that phenomenology studies — to sensory objects. Martin Heidegger redefined phenomenality to include all beings and Being. Marion further stretches

In the phenomenology of agonistic invention, invention is violent because it breaks a 'horizon', a prior condition of possibility. But Marion sidesteps violence by sidestepping horizons. In Marion's thought, the event of invention does not interrupt horizons; rather, it happens, or *comes*, without horizon or before any horizon. The event is always a gift, a phenomenon that comes without being called, before there is even language with which to call: 'The gifted does not have language or *logos* as its property, but it finds itself endowed with them — as gifts that are shown only if it regives them to their unknown origin.'[69] In a similar manner, Will and the crowd at Pentecost are endowed not with just any language of praise, but with the sequence hymn that, at least in the liturgies of York and Hereford, accompanied the procession of the gifts of bread and wine, the works of human hands, to the altar before the Eucharistic canon.[70] They give the gift of the hymn back to its origin, the Creator Spirit who, as the hymn says, swells the neck with speech.[71] But does this not cancel out the singers' originality? 'How can anything be the origin of what it must take as its own premise?' asks Jean-Louis

phenomenality to define it as anything that shows itself, effectively conceptualizing the phenomenon before or without any horizon. So mental states that have no existence, such as boredom or expectation, as well as phenomena without being (understood as *ens commune*), such as God, would now be objects of phenomenological enquiry. For the original manoeuvre in this direction, see Jean-Luc Marion, *God Without Being: Hors Texte*, trans. by Thomas A. Carlson (Chicago: University of Chicago Press, 1991). A helpful conspectus of these issues may be found in Kevin Hart, 'Of Love and How', *Journal of the American Academy of Religion*, 77 (2009), 712–33.

[69] Jean-Luc Marion, *Being Given: Toward a Phenomenology of Givenness*, trans. by Jeffrey L. Kosky (Stanford: Stanford University Press, 2002), p. 288. In Marion's work, the language of 'the given' and 'givenness' take over the conceptual work that 'event' performs in Derrida's thought. It may be that the concepts are interchangeable in the most fundamental issues of phenomenology, such as the definition of phenomenality and the possibility of phenomena without being. At some crucial moments, especially when speaking of temporality, Marion crosses into the language of event, and at these moments his thought is completely consistent with other moments when the language of gift dominates. See, for example, *Being Given*, pp. 131–39.

[70] Stephen A. Barney, *The Penn Commentary on 'Piers Plowman'*, V: *C Passus 20–22; B Passus 18–20* (Philadelphia: University of Pennsylvania Press, 2006–), p. 132.

[71] 'Sermone ditans guttura' (l. 12). The possessives in the first stanza underscore the Spirit's intrinsic cooperation with human creativity: 'Veni, creator spiritus, | Mentes tuorum visita, | Imple superna gratia, | Quae tu creasti pectora' (Come, Creator Spirit | Visit your minds, | Fill with supernal grace | The hearts you have created); *Hymnographi latini: Lateinische Hymnendichter des Mittelalters*, ed. by Guido Maria Dreves, Analecta hymnica, 38, 52, 2 vols (Leipzig: Reisland, 1905–07; repr. New York: Johnson, 1961), II, 193–94, ll. 1–4.

Chrétien.[72] How can makers possibly bear out the work of the Holy Spirit so that neither are they merely Spirit-*possessed* ('These men are full of new wine'; Acts 2. 13), nor does their making conflict with and eventually displace the Spirit's agency?

Marion answers this question by differentiating between sameness and correspondence. For Marion, as for Derrida, the structure of the event is one of call and response. But Marion inverts the order: although the call (or the gift) is absolutely prior to the response, the response is phenomenologically prior because 'only the response performs the call, and the gifted renders visible and audible what gives itself to it *only by corresponding to it* in the act of responding'.[73] While in Derrida invention is predicated on rupture, Marion bases invention on correspondence. The response's correspondence to the call, what Derrida might call its 'sameness', is not an optional choice (as the invention of the same is for Derrida), but the very condition of the call showing itself at all. How, then, does Marion escape the tyranny of the same? He does so just as Langland does: by refusing the dichotomy of likeness and difference. The given, for Marion, is like Langland's *spiritus paraclitus*: its single source 'In liknesse of a lihtnynge' (C.21.202) in a single movement 'ouerspradde hem alle' (C.21.206) in order to produce the diversity of 'alle kyne langages' (C.21.203). Since all that one has (the grace of the Holy Spirit) has been given, and the given only appears when the gifted one makes it appear in a response ('Veni, creator spiritus!'), the call and the response (the given and the gifted) always correspond without ever being the same because the response is always a completely new, unforeseen event. The call 'shows itself only if the gifted *converts* it into a phenomenon (responsal) where from now on it has a visibility'.[74] We find here in Marion the fundamental tropological movement that Liberum Arbitrium expresses in the words of Bernard: '"*Beatus* [...] *qui* [...] *verba* vertit *in opera*"' (Blessed is the one who *converts* words into works; C.16.222–23). The call (the text) never shows itself, is never activated (was never a call at all) unless it first receives a response in the form of *conversion* into a new action, an event, a phenomenon. And while that phenomenon is nothing more than the call of the Holy Spirit made audible in choral response, it is also nothing less than a completely new, previously impossible, unforeseeable phenomenon.

---

[72] Jean-Louis Chrétien, *The Call and the Response*, trans. by Anne A. Davenport (New York: Fordham University Press, 2004), p. 5.

[73] Marion, *Being Given*, p. 288, my emphasis.

[74] Marion, *Being Given*, p. 299, my emphasis.

The Pentecostal image of ideal model-copy relationship — reconciling individual to communal voice, Latin to vernacular, local parish to universal church — breaks down in subsequent action. Beginning with Grace's sermon on the crafts, where the vagaries of daily economic life defy neat summary according to estates theory, the breakdown culminates in the capitulation of the Barn of Unity to vicious complacency. The only reason we should not read this collapse as the undoing of the work's cumulative ambitions is that *Piers Plowman*'s vision of ethical invention is not necessarily a vision of ethical progress. Indeed, as Nicolette Zeeman has observed, '[A]lthough the poem has its visionary climax, it does not cease to produce narratives of failure, rebuke, suffering and desire.'[75] As the gap between model and copy reopens, as the Christian community disintegrates and Piers disappears from the narrative, the resultant lack instigates desire, which translates into more writing, more passūs or, at end of the work, into Conscience's new quest for Piers, presumably 'solicit[ing] the reader to enter into this process'.[76] *Piers Plowman*'s ultimate beginning shifts the onus of invention onto the reader, joining 'the reader with the text's "I" and carr[ying] an imperative of performance, a demand that this text [...] be embodied and put into action'.[77] This imperative, I would suggest, is best considered as *tropological* because instead of taking the form of a raw command, it invites readers to participate in a narrative that has been represented (allegorically) as salvific. Just as allegorical interpretation recognizes Christ in the Old Testament history of Israel's redemption and by tropological interpretation readers daily depart from Egypt in their own personal exodus, so does *Piers Plowman* invite its readers to participate in its salvific narrative (copied from the biblical model) and invent new beginnings.[78]

Such an account of invention as the response to a tropological imperative allows us to elaborate D. Vance Smith's explanation of how invention begins 'in

---

[75] Nicolette Zeeman, *'Piers Plowman' and the Medieval Discourse of Desire* (Cambridge: Cambridge University Press, 2006), p. 263.

[76] Zeeman, *'Piers Plowman' and the Medieval Discourse of Desire*, p. 19.

[77] Nancy Bradley Warren, 'Incarnational (Auto)biography', in *Oxford Twenty-First Century Approaches to Literature: Middle English*, ed. by Paul Strohm (New York: Oxford University Press, 2007), pp. 369–85 (p. 380).

[78] The daily recapitulation of Israel's history is a prominent tropological theme. For example, the pseudo-Remigius writes, 'For that which was prefigured there once is fulfilled in each believer at the end of the age by means of the Church's daily mournings; for Israel departs from Egypt daily, when one of the faithful spiritually departs from this world' (*In Psalmos* [113], PL, CXXXI, col. 721A; cited in Lubac, *Medieval Exegesis*, II, 359 n. 42).

the act of living itself. A well-ordered life, an exemplary life, constructs the mind as a well-ordered place in which to store the knowledge acquired to live properly. It is for this reason that the Middle Ages connects poetry with ethics'.[79] And it is for this reason that *Piers Plowman* begins again and again, seeking to make up for the brute reality that, as Marion puts it, 'the responsal will always be suspected of having poorly or partially identified the call, of not having perfectly accomplished its injunction, of not having exhausted all its possibilities. [...] Each advance remains a beginning, and the responsal never finishes beginning (like desire).'[80] Langland's new beginnings emerge (more often than not) from a desire to keep the law, not to break it, as Derridean invention would have it. But these beginnings are not oblivious to Derridean invention. Indeed, Conscience sets out on his ultimate quest at the end of passus B.20/C.22 not only 'to seke Peres the Plouhman', but so that friars, who currently 'for nede flateren | And countrepledeth me', might have an alternative 'fyndynge' (C.22.382–84) — not just an endowment (*MED*, 5c), but a better mode of ethical invention, as the Wycliffite Bible translates the Latin *adinventio* in Wisdom 14. 12: 'The bigynnyng forsothe of fornycacioun is the outseching of maumetis, and the finding of hem is corupcioun of lyf.'[81] Conscience, poised at the beginning of his final journey, desires to respond to the call issued at Pentecost, to undertake the responsibility and let the call manifest itself. He hopes his new beginning will create, in turn, other calls that in their inevitable inadequacy will demand interpretation and invention, forming a circuit for what Marion has called the 'invention of heretofore unseen phenomena'.[82] To revise Liberum Arbitrium's citation of Bernard: blessed is the one who converts these words into heretofore unseen phenomena.

If allegory, according to Augustine of Dacia, deals with the content of belief, and anagogy with the substantial fulfilment of things hoped for, then tropology fittingly falls between them, measuring and traversing the distance between ideas and their fulfilment.[83] The ethical imperative to invent words and actions, to

---

[79] Smith, *The Book of the Incipit*, p. 68.

[80] Marion, *Being Given*, p. 303.

[81] *The Holy Bible [...] by John Wycliffe and his Followers*, ed. by J. Forshall and F. Madden, 4 vols (Oxford: Oxford University Press, 1850), vol. III. Cited in *MED*, s.v. 'finding', 3b.

[82] Jean-Luc Marion, '"Christian Philosophy": Hermeneutic or Heuristic?', in *The Visible and the Revealed*, trans. by Christina M. Gschwandtner and others (New York: Fordham University Press, 2008), pp. 66–79 (p. 74).

[83] 'Littera gesta docet, quid credas allegoria, | moralis quid agas, quid speres anagogia' (The letter teaches what happened, allegory what you should believe, | tropology what you should do,

enact ideas, occurs in the gap between copy and model. Langland, for this reason, is never in danger of succumbing to the Joachist heresy, which holds that the New Testament fulfilment of the Old Testament types would in turn be ful-filled — and superseded — in a new Age of the Spirit inaugurated by St Francis. The 'spiritual' Franciscans, by reading their own age as the anagogical referent of biblical prophecy, especially the Apocalypse of John, collapsed the tropological sense into the anagogical sense. No longer was human activity to be thought of as an ethical passage between the doctrine of the Church (allegory) and the Parousia (anagogy); rather they believed that right now, immediately, they, the spiritual Franciscans, were making the Kingdom of Heaven on earth.[84] It is true that for Langland and orthodox exegetes the tropological age corresponds to the age of the Church (a correspondence Langland signals in the Pentecost episode), but *Piers Plowman* leaves no room for Joachim of Fiore's pre-millennial Age of the Spirit. Langland everywhere rejects such triumphalism, replacing progress, in the Joachist sense, with making — that paraliturgical craft, the practitioners of which live hand to mouth and have no place to lay their heads. If Langland apologizes for making by 'short-circuit[ing] the binary opposition between clerical and lay performance and identity', then Will's notoriously unsettled, unbeneficed, and economically uncertain clerical identity, as described in the C text, passus 5 vita, corresponds to an equally unstable, non-progressive form of making.[85]

The Invention of Peace

Despite these challenges, Langland does imagine the closing of the gap between model and copy in the debate between the Four Daughters of God, where their reconciliation in songs of praise achieves in the poem's narrative what Christ's sacrifice and resurrection have achieved offstage. I turn to this episode as a

anagogy what you hope for): Augustine of Dacia, *Rotulus pugillaris*, ed. by A. Walz, in 'Augustini de Dacia, O. P., "Rotulus pugillaris"', *Angelicum*, 6 (1929), 253–78 (p. 256).

[84] Lawrence M. Clopper notes 'how profoundly different Langland's historical scheme is from Joachist ones' (*Songs of Rechelesnesse: Langland and the Franciscans* (Ann Arbor: University of Michigan Press, 1997), p. 279). For a summary of the Joachist heresy in the context of exegetical theory, see *Nicholas of Lyra's Apocalypse Commentary*, ed. by Philip D. W. Krey (Kalamazoo: Medieval Institute Publications, 1997), pp. 1–30. See also Henri de Lubac, *Exégèse médiévale: Les Quatres sens de l'écriture*, 2 vols (Paris: Aubier, 1959–64), II, pt II (1964), 325–67.

[85] Zieman, *Singing the New Song*, p. 177.

counterpoint to Nicolette Zeeman's powerful exploration of how *Piers Plowman* sublimates frustrated desire in a discourse constituted by the failures of theology and systematic thought in general in order to 'hint at the presence of a divinity whose workings are veiled but who can still be glimpsed in the interstices of events'.[86] To be sure, the reconciliation of the Daughters of God could be read as yet another of 'the "episodic" narratives of the poem', where 'what appears to be progress always leads directly back to reiterative experiences of failure, rebuke, and loss'.[87] This climax of B.18/C.20 is followed in quick succession by the Pentecost episode and prompt collapse of the Church. But these vicissitudes never actually cancel out the Daughters' reconciliation; it remains a beacon of hope, which is not necessarily the same thing as desire.[88] If Langland spends much of the poem in the tropological mode (especially passūs B.8–13, where Zeeman situates her study), tracing and retracing 'a recurring beneficial pattern operating in creation according to which human desire can be turned, through a natural experience of sin and suffering, to good',[89] he also sustains an anagogical mode through B.18–19/C.20–21. By placing this vision of eternal reconciliation in Hell, and imagining it as a debate, Langland can maintain the gaps and tensions that drive *Piers Plowman*'s plot and thematic development. At the same time, he is able to demonstrate *in literary terms* how the gap between model and copy might be closed. In Peace's final reconciliation with her sisters, the logic of exemplarity functions not only as an ethical theory placing public and private rhetoric under the normative practices of baptism and conversion, as in the counterfeiting passage. Here the logic of exemplarity also underwrites Langland's disposition of wisdom traditions, Scripture, and liturgy as he inventively converts them into verse and, at times, song. Peace closes the gap between model and copy by an act of literary invention. In Peace's invention of a reconciling song, Langland depicts how the gap between

---

[86] Zeeman, *'Piers Plowman' and the Medieval Discourse of Desire*, p. 36.

[87] Zeeman, *'Piers Plowman' and the Medieval Discourse of Desire*, p. 18.

[88] Zeeman distinguishes between Will's fearful desire of despair and 'tentatively positive' desire of hope (*'Piers Plowman' and the Medieval Discourse of Desire*, p. 226; see also pp. 85–89), but hope as an infused theological virtue 'is not a passion, but a habit of the mind'. See Thomas Aquinas, *Summa theologica*, II–II.17.1, *ad* 1. I quote from *The 'Summa theologica' of Thomas Aquinas*, trans. by the Fathers of the English Dominican Province, 22 vols, 2nd edn (London: Burns, Oates & Washbourne, 1915–36); online edition ed. by Kevin Knight, <http://www .newadvent.org/summa/> [accessed 2 December 2010].

[89] Zeeman, *'Piers Plowman' and the Medieval Discourse of Desire*, p. 19. For Zeeman on the network of interpretive and inventive ethics I am associating with tropology, see especially pp. 173–87; pp. 201–26.

model and copy might be closed — and why 'closure' does not adequately describe the new beginnings opened up by ethical invention.

When Peace 'piped [...] of poesie a note' to resolve the soteriological dispute over justice and mercy among the Four Daughters of God, she cites the most exemplary of texts, a proverb from the easiest section of a standard elementary Latin 'textbook': '*Clarior est solito post maxima nebula phebus*; | *Post inimicicias Clarior est & Amor*' (C.20.451*a–b*). She then goes on to translate and amplify the distich:

> 'Aftur sharpe shoures', quod pees, 'most shene is þe sonne;
>
> Is no wedore warmore then aftur watri cloudes;
>
> Ne no loue leuore ne leuore frendes
>
> Then aftur werre and wrake when loue and pees ben maistres.
>
> Was neuere werre in this world ne wikkedere enuye
>
> That loue, and hym luste, to lauhynge ne brouhte;
>
> And pees thorw pacience alle perelles stoppeth.'
>
> (C.20.452–58)

Although the *Liber parabolarum*, or *Parabolae*, is probably the work of Alain de Lille, it did not circulate under his authority; instead, it gained widespread adoption as part of a primary-education curriculum bundle that modern scholars refer to as the *Auctores octo* or *Liber catonis*, the 'Catoun' that Chaucer's John the Carpenter 'knew nat' (I.3227).[90] The 'poesie' Peace cites had currency not as the clerkly wisdom of classical antiquity, nor as the work of a theological pioneer of the late twelfth century, but as a school text that nearly every young pupil across western Europe learned by 'memorizing the text so that it entered into his very

---

[90] Geoffrey Chaucer, *The Riverside Chaucer*, ed. by Larry D. Benson, 3rd edn (Boston: Houghton Mifflin, 1987); cited by fragment and line number. See Alain de Lille (Alano di Lilla), *Liber parabolarum (Una Raccolta di Aforismi)*, ed. by Oronzo Limone (Lecce: Congedo Editore, 1993). The distich Peace cites is lines 33–34 (also edited in PL, CCX, cols 579–94C). The *Liber parabolarum* is translated and introduced in *Ten Latin Schooltexts of the Later Middle Ages*, ed. by Ian Thomson and Louis Perraud (Lewiston, NY: Edwin Mellen, 1990), pp. 283–325. For a good survey of the *Liber catonis* tradition, see Jill Mann, '"He Knew Nat Catoun": Medieval School-Texts and Middle English Literature', in *The Text in the Community: Essays on Medieval Works, Manuscripts, Authors, and Readers*, ed. by Jill Mann and Maura Nolan (Notre Dame: University of Notre Dame Press, 2006), pp. 41–74. On the ethical evolution of the primary curriculum, see Nicholas Orme, *Medieval Schools from Roman Britain to Renaissance England* (New Haven: Yale University Press, 2006), pp. 98–105, which cites the fourteenth-century statutes of the university of Oxford that instructed schoolmasters 'to teach only "morals or metaphors or honest poetry"' (p. 100).

bones'.[91] The distich seems indeed to have become part of Peace, for when she goes on to amplify the text in English, she makes it about the divine attribute *she* personifies, peace. Peace obviates competition with her model because she has already assimilated it to herself, so that her song can express both the model and her own invention in a seamless development. Her copy (translation, amplification) has the difference that her identity is now central to the theme of the proverb, but this extends the proverb's vitality rather than confuting it.

Peace's song is a kind of autobiography, describing her own role in the reconciliation of conflict, and inscribing her identity into a traditional proverb that previously spoke only allegorically of peace. At the same time, her song actively consolidates the peace that the entire episode has worked toward. She speaks it or sings it in dialogue with her sisters, Righteousness, Truth, and Mercy — and it was their original disagreement that opened the episode to conflict. Her invention is very much her own, extremely innovative, but it works to confirm and renovate, rather than to surpass, the elementary wisdom that children learn from parents and teachers. The success of Peace's song depends, then, not only on her conformation to the model inculcated through a primary-school text, but on the grownup's confirmation by experience that what she was taught as a child is indeed still true. As Jill Mann aptly remarks, 'one of the best things about the Redemption is finding out that one's schoolbooks are true'.[92] If Peace's poetics of invention aimed to outdo and displace her model, she likely could have done so — indeed, an eleventh-century grammarian rated the *Liber catonis* 'tin' or 'lead' on an aesthetic scale, far below the gold of Virgil and silver of Plautus.[93] Instead, Peace's invention is oriented not toward rivalry, but toward action, toward securing the happiness of reconciliation.

At the same time, Peace's vision of reconciliation runs on comparatives: reconciliation ushers in not only brightness, warmth, friendship, and laughing, but comparatively *more* brightness, warmer weather, dearer friendship, more laughing. The new peace *does* surpass whatever détente obtained before 'werre and wrake', just as the personified Peace's amplification of 'Cato's' distich goes beyond the original. To close the gap between model and copy, to supply the object of desire (Zeeman), to reconcile individual to communal in choric heterophony (Zieman) — none of these anagogical operations in *Piers Plowman*

---

[91] Mann, '"He Knew Nat Catoun"', p. 42.

[92] Mann, '"He Knew Nat Catoun"', p. 66.

[93] Mann, '"He Knew Nat Catoun"', p. 49, citing Harry F. Reijnders, 'Aimericus, *Ars Lectoria*', *Vivarium*, 9 (1971), 119–37; *Vivarium* 10 (1972), 41–101, 124–76.

halts the poem's momentum or forecloses its possibilities or effaces its previous exertions. At this moment of reconciliation, Peace and *Piers Plowman* do not require a catastrophe in order to go on singing. Instead, they can enter the register of praise with Truth, who sings the liturgy's highest canticle, '*te deum laudamus*' (C.20.465). Reconciled and already partaking of Easter joy, 'Til þe day dawed thes damoyseles caroled' (C.20.467). Only Will's waking — not some further fall — silences their strains. While the grand *visio* of spiritual progress disintegrates over the following two passūs, this anagogical vision remains intact.

If *Piers Plowman* owes its multiplying beginnings and episodic pulse to 'a distinctive dynamic of failure, rebuke, and renewal', as Middleton, Smith, and Zeeman have argued, it also envisions more beginnings and more writing on the other side of reconciliation.[94] If Langland's primary mode of invention is tropological, always struggling to convert ideas into words and words into actions, always situated *between* ideal and fulfilment, then he also has a secondary anagogical mode. That is, sin and its consequent suffering and lack are not the only spurs to desire; frustration and sublimation are not the only psychic causes of invention. Especially where *Piers Plowman* rises to the register of praise, it reveals a positivity that is the source even of its negativity.

This is in part, I think, what Smith is getting at in his recent meditation on Langland's *via negativa* when he writes, 'It is precisely because negation has a kind of presence, because it continues to do something, that the poem's theory of reference is so complex.'[95] Driving every pseudo-Dionysian negation is an affirmation of negation.[96] But while many moments of academic disputation and theologizing seem to display Langland's investment in the apophatic tradition, he is at least equally invested in the complementary discourse of analogy — not only logical and grammatical analogy of the kind Smith illuminates in *The Book of the Incipit*, but the analogy of being.[97] The soul journeys to God by analogy because

[94] Zeeman, '*Piers Plowman' and the Medieval Discourse of Desire*, p. 22. See Anne Middleton, 'Narration and the Invention of Experience: Episodic Form in *Piers Plowman*', in *The Wisdom of Poetry: Essays in Honor of Morton Bloomfield* (Kalamazoo: Medieval Institute Publications, 1982), pp. 91–122; and Smith, *The Book of the Incipit*, pp. 82–86.

[95] D. Vance Smith, 'Negative Langland', *YLS*, 23 (2009), 33–59 (p. 48).

[96] And that is why, as Smith points out, the pseudo-Dionysius follows up his rigorously apophatic *Mystical Theology* with *The Divine Names* ('Negative Langland', p. 55).

[97] Smith, *The Book of the Incipit*, pp. 157–70. Smith does argue that Langland's analogical extension of grammatical relation to metaphysical relations 'discloses his attempts to anchor human and divine institutions in stable beginnings' (*The Book of the Incipit*, p. 170). But the

analogy is a created good, the fitting means by which the soul is led back to God. The soul encounters the 'ever-greater dissimilarity' from God in every creaturely similarity as a step toward union with God rather than as frustration and failure.

We must distinguish between moral failures, disorders, frustrations on the one hand, and, on the other, the analogical intervals across which humans approach God. Although Smith is attuned to the affirmations involved in pseudo-Dionysius's and Thomas's *triplex via*, 'failure' is the word that rings out at key moments throughout his discussion of apophaticism.[98] But as Aaron Riches has argued, Thomas recruits the pseudo-Dionysius in order to splice together 'the cataphatic-*exitus* and apophatic-*reditus*' in a third movement beyond cataphaticism and apophaticism, the movement of union by which the created soul participates in God's likeness through its own difference.[99] In this third way, 'the otherness of the creature — its difference — becomes integral to how it participates in God and how it analogously signifies God's goodness'.[100] That is to say, the ever-greater dissimilarities that all naming encounters, and to which Langland is so sensitive, need not frustrate, need not result in failure. It is not calamitous that the gap between model and copy never closes, nor is the 'gap' always a constitutive lack, a guilt that gets sublimated into mystical desire, as Freudian or Lacanian theory would have it.[101] We can discern a positive momentum of *reductio* in the episodes of Pentecost and Peace's song, and even of Conscience's final, hopeful quest. The final passus has plenty of ethical and institutional failure, to be sure, but the gap between tropological making and anagogical fulfilment retains an analogical interval that invites hope.

---

analogia entis is quite a different animal from a foundationalist 'great chain of being' because the epectastic 'ever-greater dissimilarity' slips anchors and destabilizes beginnings (see Betz, 'The Aesthetics of the Analogy of Being', and n. 43, above).

[98] 'Within Studie's critique of theology [...] is an affirmation of a negative way, an affirmation of the necessity and inevitability of the failure of systematic thought. [...] We discern the causes of things in the failure of the terms we use to designate them: their failure to designate both the referent that would give their phenomenal nature substance and real existence *and* to designate their likenesses to each other in ways that would verify their own existence is a failure to designate their ultimate likeness to the divine nature. [...] The failure of Theology continues [...] where the poem returns to the necessary failure of theology to comprehend beginnings' (Smith, 'Negative Langland', pp. 54–56).

[99] Aaron Riches, 'Being Good: Thomas Aquinas and Dionysian Causal Predication', *Nova et vetera* (English edition), 7 (2009), 439–76 (p. 476).

[100] Riches, 'Being Good', p. 468.

[101] Zeeman, *'Piers Plowman' and the Medieval Discourse of Desire*, pp. 31–37.

REVIEWS

David Aers. *Sanctifying Signs: Making Christian Tradition in Late Medieval England*. Notre Dame: University of Notre Dame Press, 2004. Pp. xiii + 281.

David Aers. *Salvation and Sin: Augustine, Langland, and Fourteenth-Century Theology*. Notre Dame: University of Notre Dame Press, 2009. Pp. xv +284.

For at least thirty years, in ten bracing, trenchant books and many strikingly memorable articles, David Aers has been a decisive figure in Middle English studies. Where his work has gone, waves of inspired scholars have followed. That would imply that Aers has been a 'leader', and so he has, consistently. The word *leader*, however, fails to position Aers accurately. Aers's favoured posture is less that of leader speaking for a profession from its front. His position is rather that of advocate of the unheard speaking against a profession from its side, calling the profession, as from the wilderness, to its deeper senses. Aers's favoured form is the essay (almost all the books are compilations of essays), since the essay permits Aers to occupy an often embattled position on the edge of a debate, driving the new position against a consensus usually represented by a single, well-chosen target. His challenge is to centre the politically incorrect but profound truth. Reading Aers is always exhilarating, since one derives three pleasures for the price of one: one read produces the reward of new directions; the performance of courage; and the pleasure of spectacular combat. (It's exhilarating unless of course, I should add, one happens to be the chosen target of Aers's resourceful, ethically driven, wholly fearless offensive.) Aers is a leader, in short, in the way Jeremiah was a 'leader'.

Because Aers consistently moves always to the side of the debate, his interventions constitute a map across large territories. His earlier work set religious and gender ideology in the context of its political and material culture. His later work has preserved the ideal connection between religious and material culture, but the politicized material culture is now marginal. This newer work, of which the two

10.1484/J.YLS.1.102114

titles here under review are examples, pays sustained attention to specifically theological and ecclesiological questions. It pays especially sustained attention to *Piers Plowman*. Aers is driven by the ideal of a material church militant, set against the world, animated as much by a Christocentric, profoundly communitarian and ecclesiological tradition as by an Augustinian anthropology. What are the positions staked out by these books? And, if Aers is indeed always moving, do these two books each stake different positions?

Let me summarize each book in turn. *Sanctifying Signs* is principally focused on 'sanctification and signs'. For the most part these signs are sacramental. Aers focuses in particular on differences of views about the Eucharist in the period 1370 to 1420 or so (thus Chapters 1–4). Chapter 1 adumbrates orthodox accounts (by Roger Dymmock and Nicholas Love) of the identity of sacrament and divine presence. Chapter 2 is ambitious: Aers argues not only that the Eucharist is central to Langland's Christocentric ecclesiology (a major advance), but also that for Langland reception of the Eucharist 'belongs to a long process in which Christ's presence and the sacrament of the altar are *not yet*, a *not yet* which is at the heart of the poet's sacramental theology' (p. 44). Wyclif's Eucharistic theology is the subject of Chapter 3, wherein we understand how identification of sign and sacrament is a kind of idolatry. In the upsurge of interest in Lollardy, most scholars reasonably shy away from the austerities and turgidities of Wyclif's Latin; it is, therefore, refreshing to have a clear exposition of such a work. Chapter 4 ends the sequence devoted to the Eucharist by offering refreshing access to the understudied, subtle, proto-Reformation Eucharistic theology of the 'Latinate layman and Herefordshire farmer' Walter Brut, drawn from his 1380s heresy trial records. This chapter also explicates the Eucharistic theology of William Thorpe, for whom the Eucharist is the 'decisive confirmation of Christ's choice of non-violence' (p. 85), even if that theology leads Thorpe to a Donatist ecclesiology of the predestined.

Chapters 5 and 6 shift attention from sacramental questions, and focus on signs in a much looser sense of that word. Chapter 5 is an extended meditation of poverty in *Piers Plowman*, in which Aers, through patient explication of the dialectic of Langland's poem, concludes that Langland finally distances himself decisively from a Franciscan account of poverty. Poverty, for Langland, is not a sign, and certainly not sanctifying. This is a major essay. Chapter 6 may be about sanctification (by domestic praxis), but I don't see that it is about signs at all. Aers looks to the representation of the home in *Dives and Pauper*, Nicholas Love's *Mirror*, Lollard trial records, and, passingly, *Piers Plowman*. The Aersian heat of the chapter derives from the way Love's cosy account of domesticity occludes the more egalitarian and scriptural households of those under charge of heresy.

The chapters that convincingly break the new ground here are 2–5 inclusive. Both chapters on *Piers Plowman* (2 and 5) are exceptionally searching, sustained, and illuminating. Both are, in my view, utterly convincing in their main theses. And Chapter 4, particularly the material on the much less well known figure of Walter Brut, is also new and arresting.

It will be obvious that *Sanctifying Signs*, for all the power of three essays in particular, is, though nearly a book, more a collection of essays. *Salvation and Sin: Augustine, Langland, and Fourteenth-Century Theology*, published five years after *Sanctifying Signs*, is, by contrast, a book, with a grand structure. It begins with an account of conversion and agency in Augustine (the *Confessions* and the *City of God* especially). Each chapter thereafter marks the reception, or the failed reception, of Augustinian theology and anthropology by fourteenth-century English writers.

Against those who stress only the inwardness of Augustine's representation of conversion, Aers argues that for Augustine conversion is a profoundly social and historical event; God 'acts through a dense network of mediations, a veritable cornucopia of interlocutors' (p. 13). And conversion leads into 'the city of God in its historical form' (p. 12), not into an invisible True Church of the unknowable, predestined elect. Chapter 1 sketches this social Augustinianism, with a visible church at its centre, and the Eucharist at the centre of that visible church. This church, like Christ, does not, ideally, compel its adherents, given its complex distribution of grace, its complex dialectic of agency.

The remaining chapters take one English writer at a time, and measure them against this Augustinian standard. Ockham, Bradwardine, Langland, and Julian of Norwich are the subjects of Chapters 2–5 respectively. All except Langland fail to match up to Augustine, even those who think, as Bradwardine thinks, that they are committed Augustinians. Ockham and Julian fail especially because they have a 'frivolous', non-Augustinian anthropology, and in particular a non-Augustinian conception of human sinfulness. Apart from Langland none of these authors acknowledges, as Aers says about Julian of Norwich, 'the way we form habits that enslave us in the earthly city, individual and collective habits of will that bind us in iron fetters composed out of practices we have chosen, making for us a law from "the violence of habit"' (p. 155). So Ockham's semi-Pelagianism produces a superficial, extrinsic account of grace that marginalizes Christology (Chapter 2). Bradwardine's imagined defence of Augustinianism against the 'Pelagians' of his time turns out to undo itself, insofar as Bradwardine, in Aers's reading, produces a no less superficial account of agency as wholly from without, wholly unmediated by merit of any kind. Humanity is 'absent, as it were, from her own conversion' (p. 72). Bradwardine's ecclesiology is, accordingly, marginal to his monopolistic account of divine agency. Surprisingly, Bradwardine is revealed systematically to replicate the extrinsic, non-Christological theology and ecclesiology of the 'moderns' he thinks he is opposing. These chapters open clear paths into very significant theological territory.

Aers habitually works within explicitly declared sets of champions pitched against losers. With Ockham and Bradwardine out for the count, this book is badly in need of a champion. Enter William Langland, but wearing the mantle of the semi-Pelagian, by which he has been invested over the last twenty-five years. The chapter devoted to Langland is a patient, well tempered reinvestment of fighter Langland with the mantle of Augustinian. The argument derives its especial force from the account of the semi-vif, wholly unable to raise himself, rescued by the Samaritan. This, like Chapters 2 and 5 of *Sanctifying Signs*, is a major intervention in Langland studies. I find it deeply satisfying. I stand in part corrected by it myself, in all but the moments where it fails to answer to its own subtle understanding of the dialectic of Langland's poem. For the most part, that is, Aers attends with extraordinary patience to Langland's complex dialectic of semi-Pelagian positions repudiated one way or another through the increasingly Augustinian reaches of the poem in its later, more psychologically profound and ecclesiologically explicit reaches. So it seems to me that sentences like this one fall somewhere short of Aers's own patient exploration of that very dialectic: 'Like Trajan, Ymagenatyf is content to invent, at this point, a form of salvation without Christology, a readiness quite alien to Langland's theology as it unfolds in *Piers Plowman*' (p. 129). Precisely because Trajan's soteriology, like all the other semi-Pelagian moments of the poem, is *part* of the 'unfolding' of Langland's theology, it is by definition *not* 'quite alien' to 'Langland's theology'.

Chapter 5 turns back to losers. Aware that his treatment of Julian may be regarded as 'wretchedly unappreciative' (p. 167), Aers nevertheless lays the ground of an argument whose conclusion runs as follows: 'Julian systematically ignores our freedom to disobey the covenant offered by the source of life, to destroy others and ourselves, individually and collectively, as we strive to shore up the power of the earthly city we inhabit' (p. 170). Julian does not take Augustinian anthropology on board.

Thus an account of these two powerful books. What, though, of my second question: if Aers is indeed always moving, do these two books each stake different positions? Certainly the anti-semi-Pelagian position of the second book is retrospectively perceptible in the first. A very significant difference does, however, distinguish the two books. This consists of the different communities addressed by them. The first is addressed to a community of scholars prepared to take theology seriously. The second is addressed to a community of Augustinian Christians. The symptom of this significant change is the use of the first-person personal pronoun, as in the representative passage cited in the previous paragraph. The 'we' of that paragraph is no fictional 'we' designed to invoke Langland's original readers. That 'we' is instead 'us'. Many of 'us' will feel unwilling to pay up to an anthropology that has it that 'we' are enslaved 'in the earthly city', by 'individual and collective habits of will that bind us in iron fetters composed out of practices we have chosen, making for us a law from "the violence of habit"' (p. 170). Many of 'us' will also feel uneasy about all of 'us' who are not Christians at all being implicitly corralled in or out of that pronoun, and implicitly in or out of these texts. Many of us feel deeply instructed by an account of whether or not Julian was Augustinian; we feel less instructed by discussion of the question of whether or not Julian was right.

In sum, these are remarkable books, grand contributions to Aers's life-long passion, *Piers Plowman*, and utterly serious accounts of late fourteenth-century theology. I hope, however, that Aers will do the following: not write any more about Nicholas Love (don't kick a man when he's down); write shorter paragraphs (almost all are long, but some are whoppers); give a lot more dating and contextualization for the texts he discusses (the effect is often myopic); and situate this scholarship within a larger, trans-Reformation chronology as it opens out to a broader, earthly community. Above all, I look forward to much, much more from this great scholar.

JAMES SIMPSON
Harvard University
jsimpson@fas.harvard.edu

Andrew Cole. *Literature and Heresy in the Age of Chaucer*. Cambridge: Cambridge University Press, 2008. Pp. xx + 297.

Literature and Heresy is not a systematic study of the period in question, but rather a series of telling snapshots of English intellectual life in the late fourteenth and early fifteenth centuries. Andrew Cole ranges much further than 'The Age of Chaucer', offering chapters on Hoccleve, Lydgate, and Margery Kempe in the second half of the book. Nor, despite forming the subject of one self-contained

10.1484/J.YLS.1.102115

chapter, does Chaucer loom terribly large in its first half: rather, Langland is the dominant literary presence here, and indeed the trajectory of English literary history, as imagined throughout this study, is distinctly Langlandian rather than Chaucerian in character. It is, however, another age, 'the age of Wycliffism' (p. 159) that really concerns Cole. His intention is to 'posit the necessity of Wycliffism to the English literary canon' (p. xiv), and he proceeds to argue how, in various ways, the creativity of late medieval English writers was indelibly affected by their responses to the intellectual climate created by the Wycliffite controversies. Kathryn Kerby-Fulton's recent study, *Books Under Suspicion*, was an attempt to find Continental and other kinds of prophetic and dissenting company for the 'lonely' narrative that posits Wycliffism as the most important influence on intellectual life in late medieval England. Cole, however, attempts to re-establish it as the most important point of reference in this period, taking on both Kerby-Fulton and James Simpson in his declaration, in the book's epilogue, that 'the presence of other kinds of reform in medieval England only makes Wycliffism more prominent as it rhizomatically moves through a variety of genres and modes' (p. 188).

Cole is not particularly concerned with the way in which the controversies surrounding Wyclif's thought evidently made life extremely difficult for a separate tradition of English thinkers, from Brinton to Gascoigne, who saw his ideas either as poisonous, or as part of a much bigger picture of reformist potential. And Cole's nod to 'other kinds of reform' comes late in a book that is far more heavily invested in the redefinition of an altogether more problematic keyword. *Literature and Heresy* is a supremely self-conscious study, allusive and bristling with scare quotes, addressed very much to the coterie rather than to the novice. And the word that most often appears in scare quotes is 'lollard', as Cole makes a timely attempt to cleanse it of its status as a 'curse word' (p. 72). In his study of Wycliffite 'Fellows and Helpers' (1999), Jeremy Catto argued that the term 'lollardy' was 'effectively meaningless' in the period under investigation. Cole treats the term's lack of stable semantic content positively and attempts its wholesale rehabilitation, enterprisingly reassigning it to a host of experimental subjectivities. Thus, he does not merely narrate what he sees as the 'reinvention of lollardy' in texts from *Piers Plowman* to *The Boke of Margery Kempe*: he deliberately furthers that reinvention by providing fresh glosses for the term, heavily invested as he is in keeping it in critical circulation.

It could be argued that Cole's reinvented 'lollardy' is an umbrella term for what was in fact merely reformist thinking; but he is far less enamoured of terms such as 'reformist' or 'dissenting' and more concerned with arguing for the existence in this period of a distinctive, self-conscious, and positively-defined 'lollardy' which, as the study develops, is defined as an extension of fraternal ideals to the laity, resulting in a new and provocative concept of Christian discipleship whose influence may be traced across a wide variety of texts, whether explicitly 'Wycliffite' or not. He thus argues robustly (and, in this reviewer's view, persuasively) for an uncoupling of the terms 'Wycliffism' and 'lollardy', reserving the latter for modes of writing and thought that in other studies might attract the broad label 'reformist' rather than being identified as narrowly and specifically 'Wycliffite' (though it is made rather less clear in this study where corresponding boundaries around the word 'Wycliffite' should be drawn). His central claim is that 'the "lollard" typology opened up [...] a space within which to articulate alternative and newer models of lay piety that became prominent during the age of Wycliffism' (p. 159). And thus, *Literature and Heresy* depends for its success on the reader's acceptance of Cole's claims that this 'lollard typology' subsisted throughout this period as an experimental mode of thinking, writing, and behaviour that was continually available for reinvention. This allows Cole to claim — via an elaborate argument that cannot be summarized here — that Langland shows distinctively 'Lollard sympathies' in the C text of *Piers Plowman*. It allows him to revisit texts such as Clanvowe's *Two Ways* and thereby to reinvigorate the hoary subject of the 'Lollard knights'. And it allows him to claim that *The Boke of Margery Kempe* 'uses the social typology of the "lollard" to offer a new perspective on late medieval religiosity' (p. 155).

Although Cole's discussions of crucial 'lollare' passages from *Piers Plowman* run the risk of reducing Langland's crafty poetry to discourse, more often in this study the focus on not only 'lollard' but actually heretical typologies yields valuable critical insights. It was hard to imagine any more interpretative juice being squeezed out of Hoccleve's 'Address to Sir John Oldcastle', but Cole succeeds in writing freshly about the poet, presenting him as resourcefully and ambitiously manipulating the modes of advocacy available to him here and in the *Regiment of Princes*. And his focus on the significance of shame in the chapter on Kempe sheds new light on the *Boke*, not least in his welcome focus on the significance of Philip Repingdon as Kempe's arguably most significant ecclesiastical interlocutor. The necessity of scrutinizing the workings of Repingdon's charisma in the *Boke* and elsewhere leads Cole to ask some extremely productive questions concerning the place of recanted heretics in English ecclesiastical self-understanding, and the reader might well wish for more on this topic than the space of this study permits. There are other moments at which the analytical narrative needs more room to breathe. The reader would benefit from more context on the subject of pardons in general in relation to Cole's specific claims about Hoccleve's uses of them, and in the Lydgate chapter, a good deal of extremely complex material relating to the history and terms of Eucharistic controversy is presented in necessarily compressed fashion. At times here, Cole's analytical lexicon buckles under the pressure of loaded terms such as 'figure' and 'form' and it is difficult, as a result, to judge just how singular Lydgate's vernacular treatment of the Eucharist really was. Likewise, in a study so attentive to semantic nuance in relation to 'lollard', it is strange to see other terms taken on trust: notable in this context is the problematic, unglossed 'literary censorship', while 'orthodoxy' is similarly in need of parsing — only gradually, as the argument evolves, is 'juridical orthodoxy' (p. 159) helpfully separated from the broader spectrum of discourses and affiliations that might be described as 'orthodox' *tout court*.

Some of the most fascinating voices in this study are the less familiar and anonymous, surfacing even more often in the endnotes than they do in the main text: they are, chiefly, those of preachers, poets, and polemicists writing on (or against) Wycliffism or, in the case of the Lydgate chapter, on the Eucharist. There is a thrilling moment in which the anonymous author of one of the tracts in Cambridge University Library, MS Ii.6.26 precisely anticipates John Audelay's complaints about the use of the word 'lollard' as a term of abuse. In this hinterland of unedited or simply less studied texts, such as *The Fyve Wyttes*, Cole has identified a field that deserves much fuller exploration.

MISHTOONI BOSE
Christ Church, Oxford
mishtooni.bose@chch.ox.ac.uk

Mary Clemente Davlin. *A Journey into Love: Meditating with the Medieval Poem 'Piers Plowman'*. Robert B. Lawton, S. J., Studies in Faith, Culture, and the Arts. Los Angles: Marymount Institute Press, 2008. Pp. x + 170.

Like the Long Text of Julian of Norwich's *Showings*, *Piers Plowman* is 'begun but not yet performed'. Its radical and demanding performativity remains one of the stimuli that drive scholars and readers to seek to understand its various versions and to comprehend the complex trajectories of Will's story. In this unusual but stimulating book, Sister Davlin, whose scholarship and thoughtful engagement

10.1484/J.YLS.1.102116

with the poem have left generations of scholars in her debt, offers short translated extracts from the B version of the poem, rearranged into a topical sequence that covers the arc of human existence and the trajectory of salvation history. In a short but thoughtful Preface, Theresia de Vroom describes the inception of the book in a seminar at Loyola Marymount University, held to explore the relevance of older texts to modern spiritual and ethical discussions. She well observes that the poem explores 'the human struggle to live justly and well across the span of time, spirituality and culture' (p. 1). And Davlin's extracts offer a *cursus* (or series of micro-*passūs*) across this span, beginning with abstracts like Truth, Love, and Kynde, before embarking on capsule accounts of the persona of *Piers Plowman*; Sin, Contrition, and Forgiveness; How We Do Well; and The Poor and the Rich. The final sequence of extracts addresses core Christian concepts and events: Three Lovely Persons (The Trinity); The Life of Christ; The Great Joust; The Great Trial (Who Can Be Saved), and Easter Morning. Certain key sections of Langland's poem provide the core of the extracts: passūs 1, 5, 12, 16, 18, and 19 are the most widely excerpted in her attempt to present a new taxonomy of the poem's themes. These are, she says, to be read 'slowly, in any order you find attractive, and in small "bites" savoring the ones which appeal to you' (p. 7). In other words, like a monastic *compilator*, she is encouraging new readers to subject these passages to the process of para-monastic *lectio* and *ruminatio*.

The book has been carefully and elegantly designed to assist this process. The *ordinatio* has been planned to encourage meditative rather than linear, sequential reading. Each opening is divided between the translated text (on the recto) and Davlin's simple, short but intensely distilled explanations (on the verso). These explanations often serve as stimuli to further thought and reflection: 5.481–87 provokes the challenging thought that 'sin is sickness, even though we choose it' (p. 78), while 9. 97–104 is glossed by 'speech and time are magnificent gifts' (p. 118). In addition, most passages are provided with pastoral and socio-ethical *quaestiones* that could work as prompts to discussion in parochial or private medi- tation, but would, in many cases, also work as starting points for class discussion in pedagogic contexts. Thus, for example, B1.130–33 provokes the question 'In what ways can people be Godlike?' (p. 23); 9.26–29 invites 'Does it seem natural to you to be kind?' (p. 43); 20.199–208 leads to 'In what way is love a craft?' (p. 55); 19.387–99 provokes 'Why do we need to pay what we owe?' (p. 91); and 14.108–19 leads to 'Do you think that every creature has a natural right to joy?' (p. 115). The opening of each of the book's thematic sections is marked by a carpet page, here a series of luminous photographs of South-West Midland scenes, mostly from Gloucestershire (especially the extraordinary cathedral in

Gloucester). These moody images are the work of fellow Langlandian Stephen Shepherd, and they provide gathering points and reflective images on the stages of the journey constructed by Davlin's extracts.

The translations are Davlin's own, though she provides in an appendix a short checklist of her principal citations, and of her borrowings from and coincidences with earlier editions and translations (pp. 167–68). There is also a brief list of further reading, including some important recent studies (Nicolette Zeeman, 2006), and a well-chosen selection of the best and most accessible scholarship of the last half century, as a starting point for those who want to explore the text further.

Davlin's view of the poem is affirmative and optimistic: 'Neither romantic nor unduly idealistic, *Piers Plowman* is a hopeful poem in which the promise of salvation is extended to every person' (p. 5). For many modern scholars and critics of the text, this may feel as if it overstates the tranquillity of the poem's epistemology and ontology, and perhaps understates the anxiety and restlessness of Will's searching. But Davlin is passionate about the 'nourishing power and extraordinary beauty' (p. 5) of the text, and repeatedly shows her profound and sustained engagement with the poem in her comments opposite the extracts, drawn from a text she calls 'straightforward yet invitingly complex' (p. 7). Of course little of the poem's unfolding psychodrama can survive in such a reordering, and little sense of interactions between the extraordinary cast of personifications and abstractions survives into her gobbets. Most of the political and intellectual allegories of the first twelve passūs are not represented, nor are the difficult theological discussions of the middle-teen passūs preserved, and most of the documentary and sociopolitical dimensions are omitted. So many of the complications and contradictions of the poem's tortured progress get elided here. Instead, Holy Church's passus 1 speech is extensively quarried, and understandably provides the foundation for the unfolding sequence of meditations. But its truisms, generalizations and scripturally supported abstractions, though fuelling the whole text, are, of course, the source of Will's initial dissatisfaction and his search for 'kynde knowyng'. Davlin, who has written so well on that very concept, presumably hopes to provoke a similar search in her new readers.

But it is Will's attempt to negotiate and understand the tortured interface between contemporary reality and the scriptural ideal that is arguably the grit in *Piers Plowman*'s oyster. And this interface with the contemporary is one of the central ways in which Langland's poem is different from Julian's text (or those of Catherine of Siena, also mentioned in the notes). Contemplative and mystical writing invariably strives to rise above the contingency of its contemporary circumstances. Inevitably, in its attempt to address 'the relevance of pre-modernity' (which was the title of the Loyola Marymount seminar that stimulated this volume) this reshaping of Langland's text, aimed at a readership whose knowledge and understanding of these issues is assumed to be denuded, has to go for the Big Picture, however much Langland (and Will) seem suspicious of panoramic answers. As Harold Pinter famously said, 'If you get a simple answer, you must be asking the wrong question'.

Davlin sees this book as an attempt 'to make the poem available to the audience for which it was originally written, ordinary people' (p. 6). Whether it is really still possible to characterize the original target audience of Langland's text in this way, I found that her imaginative exploration and thoughtful focusing in on key passages, to which as critics we may sometimes become blinded by our familiarity with the complexity of the larger picture, worked surprisingly well in stimulating me to begin the poem anew and perhaps perform it differently. This little handbook merits the judgement that Davlin bestows on the whole poem: it is 'a work of deep wisdom' (p. 5), even if the modern world may find that wisdom every bit as hard to accept as Will did.

VINCENT GILLESPIE
Lady Margaret Hall, Oxford
vincent.gillespie@ell.ox.ac.uk

Raskolnikov, Masha. *Body Against Soul: Gender and 'Sowlehele' in Middle English Allegory*. Columbus: Ohio State University Press, 2009. Pp. 225.

Masha Raskolnikov's stimulating investigation of personification in body and soul debates reveals this allegorical tradition to be rather more challenging than previous readers have acknowledged. Despite her belief that allegory always risks 'totalising and simplifying' (p. 69), the book in fact illustrates that medieval allegorical narrative is a variable, fragmentary and problem-posing form, often turning up only when required, either in short texts or as part of longer, not necessarily entirely allegorical, works. Although the book concludes with a reading of *Piers Plowman*, Raskolnikov is not laying claim to any particular teleology for body and soul debates in the fourteenth-century poem; and yet the result of this juxtaposition is a good one, situating this famously heterogeneous and anomalous allegory in relation to a longer tradition of heterogeneous and anomalous allegories.

10.1484/J.YLS.1.102117

In the course of an exciting book, Raskolnikov offers what she describes as a 'literalising' reading (p. 13) of features of the body and soul debates that some readers have taken to be of no interest, or merely dead metaphors. Why are certain phenomena personified rather than others? (Body? Soul? Will? Reason? Liberum Arbitrium?) What does it mean to make matter — in particular dead matter — 'speak'? (What is the speaking body? What is its relation to the speaking subject? Can these debates only happen after death?) And, above all, what work does gender perform in these contexts? Like a number of other critics, Raskolnikov believes that a term's grammatical gender in a given language plays a role in determining the gender of its personification, and she rigorously tracks the implications of this for personifications in Latin, Old French, and then Middle English, where grammatical gender has disappeared. She starts with the familiar paradox of texts such as Boethius's *Consolation of Philosophy*, where the traditional male/female gender hierarchy is subverted when a grammatically feminine term (*philosophia*) is personified as a woman and lectures a man ('Boethius'). We might think that misogyny has never had a problem with such sublime exceptions to its own rule. And yet Raskolnikov reveals that this is not, in fact, quite the case. A discussion of Hildebert of Lavardin's *Liber de Querimonia* reveals the contortions that Hildebert has to go through in order to make 'his' dialogue with Anima (feminine) accord with the acceptable gender hierarchy, so that she is in due course re-described as a 'husband' to Hildebert, himself now the unruly 'wife' (pp. 58–60). Raskolnikov goes on, moreover, to show that as soon as authors are writing in Middle English, feminine personifications of Latin *caro* and *anima* (both grammatically feminine) give way to the masculine dyads such as those of the poems 'In a thestri stude' and 'Als I lay in a winteris nyt'. While I was not convinced of the proposed queering effect of these same-sex masculine dyads, I was totally persuaded by the overriding homosociality of these texts. I also felt this was the right context in which to see Langland's seemingly masculinist allegorical spectrum — not only the misogyny of Lady Meed and his masculine Nature, but also, as Raskolnikov argues, his use of the figure of marriage mainly to characterize the relations between personifications, rather than the personifications themselves, and even the ultimate supersession of the Four Daughters of God by the masculine personification Love (p. 171; see also p. 196).

And Raskolnikov complicates this picture further. She explores how the Middle English *Sawles Warde* (addressed to a female audience) reworks its Latin source (which bears no marks of being addressed to women) by 'populating' the text with a lively array of female personifications and personifying the wayward Will in the 'household' of the soul as female and under instruction from a masculine Wit (Chapter 4). It even apparently genders as feminine nouns such as *deaþ* and *hus*, masculine and neuter in OE (though the last point is made misleadingly at p. 156, and without clear reference to line 8 and its note in Wilson's edition of *Sawles Warde*). The book culminates with a provocative discussion of Anima and Liberum Arbitrium in the B and C texts of *Piers Plowman*. Despite the fact that Langland refers to Anima as 'he', Raskolnikov cites the feminine grammatical gender of the Latin term and draws on James Paxson's observation that Anima is both a *thing* and a strange, seemingly feminine orifice, 'oon withouten tonge and teeth' (B.15.11–14): is Anima partly feminine? She then proceeds, again despite Langland's use of the pronoun 'he' (C.16.161), to argue that Liberum Arbitrium, the C-text replacement of Anima, is neuter, again as a result of Latin grammatical gender. According to Raskolnikov, Liberum Arbitrium represents Langland's solution, a 'perfect balance' of the endless dialogue of the masculine and feminine (pp. 190–95). However tenuous these arguments, what they do draw attention to is the lack, or the amorphousness, of the evidence either way: given this minimal gender-marking, how important is gender-marking to Langland? This question is, of course, interesting in itself.

This book is full of intriguing close readings of little-studied debate texts, and Raskolnikov is at her best when getting to grips with their detail. She is insightful on texts ranging from Prudentius's *Psychomachia* and Boethius's *Consolation* to the Latin and Middle English debate poems and *Sawles Warde*. The observation that personification may circumscribe a term, for instance, leads to the striking remark: 'allegorical characters do not have free will, but they often exist as a way of thematizing the limits of the will's freedom' (p. 46). She certainly is right to note a distinctively new emphasis on the mutual love of the body and soul that characterizes the Middle English debates, though she might also have noted that this is also the case in Guillaume de Deguileville's French version of the debate in the *Pelerinage de l'ame*. Each chapter uses a different contextual or theoretical framework to approach its texts, and her comparative method allows her to show important variations between texts that look superficially alike. Sometimes, however, this same comparative method leads up blind alleys — what do we really learn from the observation that *Sawles Warde* has no personification of the soul, or that Wit, here masculine, is feminine in *Hali Maiþhede* (pp. 149–52)? And what is the purpose of a comparison of the *Sawles Warde* 'Four Daughters of God' with the more common 'Four Daughters' (Truth, Mercy, Justice, and Peace), when the *Sawles Warde*'s 'Four Daughters' are clearly a different quartet altogether, the cardinal virtues (pp. 158, 161)? Occasionally there seems to be too much such cross-referencing — maybe the book's reiterative emphasis on its larger argument is a reaction to just this.

A central element in the argument is the puzzle about exactly what part of the moral subject is being represented by the personifications — whether the 'speaking' body, or the soul that addresses it. Raskolnikov is worried at various points by the absent will. She claims that while we cannot always define what phenomena are being personified in these debates (and she also indicates that this is part of their point), they all allegorize the self struggling to understand itself and to locate the sources of its own moral power and culpability. She claims, surely rightly, that these texts dramatize a non-rigid and 'playful' dualism, and that the hypothesized union of body and soul may do violence to both. In these texts, she says, 'the abstraction being embodied is that of the split self itself' (pp. 4, 102). Her larger thesis is that, whether in Latin, French, or English, these debate texts constitute a form of *sowlehele*, 'soul-health', or medicine for the soul; they are practical and performative texts that enable the lay reader to see and reenact the inner workings and divisions of the moral subject. She argues that their narrative form subverts and challenges simple didacticism. Working under the mentorship of Anne Middleton, she claims, as Middleton does for *Piers Plowman*, that these texts are addressed to an audience that is not clerically or philosophically learned, but no less sophisticated for that: 'works of *sowlehele* cross the artificially constructed boundary between the academic discipline of psychology and the cultural studies of quotidian understandings of the self' (p. 10). Raskolnikov notes, interestingly, that the Vernon manuscript, London, British Library, MS Additional 22283, which contains both a Middle English body and soul debate and *Piers Plowman*, describes this last as 'a book of sowlehele' (p. 169).

Raskolnikov is less persuasive when dealing directly with the spectre of medieval 'philosophy' and 'faculty psychology'. She does not need these to produce her own textual analyses, but she repeatedly returns to them, only to pronounce their irrelevance, or, worse, to trash them. On pages 15–19, for instance, she offers schematic versions of Aristotelian, Galenic, and Augustinian descriptions of the relationship between body and soul, but then pronounces them too 'technical and complex' (p. 18); she goes on to discuss later medieval pastoral writings, but finds these 'delimiting' and 'normative', and concludes with 'the fascinating but necessarily limited rubric of medieval faculty psychology' (p. 19; cf. pp. 144–45). How do we know that readers of psychological allegory 'would find the more formal tools and tropes in academic treatments of the self excessively abstract or irrelevant' (p. 67)? And what evidence is there that 'if "In a thestri stude" were a debate written by philosophers [...] if, in other words, this was an orthodox work of philosophy — the speaking parts would be almost endlessly multiplied' (p. 91; also pp. 88–96)? In fact, Raskolnikov herself shows that, just like the authors of the body and soul debates, the later scholastics also thought that the relationship of the body and soul was highly complex — and the two very difficult to prise apart. From St Paul, Augustine, and Gregory the Great through to later medieval scholastic, spiritual, pastoral and encyclopedic writers, after all, medieval spiritual psychology constantly acknowledges the frictional and interpenetrative nature of the soul's various powers, and describes them in dynamic, dialogic, and even narrative terms: 'So these two wills within me, one old, one new, one the servant of the flesh and the other of the spirit, were in conflict and between them they tore my soul apart [...]. I was in each of them' (Galatians 5. 17; see my *'Piers Plowman' and the Medieval Discourse of Desire* (2006), Chapter 2).

And indeed, elsewhere, Raskolnikov is prepared to praise one debate for its philosophical 'coherence' and to connect it to the pleasures of school disputation (p. 133); she even claims that 'philosophy and what we now call psychology were no more separate in medieval thought than allegory was from either of the other two' (p. 35). Robert Ackerman's view (cited by Raskolnikov, p. 90 n. 21) that these poets were so unlearned as to be relying entirely on 'common sense' is laughably irrelevant. These poems perform, as Raskolnikov shows so persuasively, sophisticated and moving analyses of the inner life of the subject. She observes that 'the body of body/soul poetry seems to be born at the moment of death, at the moment of rupture from the soul', but also that it always involves 'the turning of the self upon itself:' 'the body's existence [...] requires the presence of the soul, its *failed attempt* at discipline' (pp. 136–38). Of 'the body's slowly rising head' in 'Als I lay' she adds poignantly, 'why detail that it raised its head "upon its neck" if not to slow down the process of its rising?' If this 'returns the reader forcibly to the horror of dead things speaking', the poem nevertheless also describes the subject 'engaged in an uncertain process of becoming' (pp. 117–18).

NICOLETTE ZEEMAN
King's College, Cambridge
nz202@cam.ac.uk

Nicole Rice. *Lay Piety and Religious Discipline in Middle English Literature.* **Cambridge Studies in Medieval Literature, 73. Cambridge: Cambridge University Press, 2008. Pp. xv + 247.**

Nicole Rice's recent study of rules and forms of living written for or read by laypeople in the late fourteenth century significantly advances the study of the religiosity of the period, turning a fresh eye towards the mixed relationships, sometimes agonistic, sometimes cooperative, between professional religious

10.1484/J.YLS.1.102118

(monks, hermits, and secular priests) and the laity. It also brings to welcome attention a small canon of religious prose works still little known except by specialists — *The Abbey of the Holy Ghost, Fervor amoris* (sometimes called *Contemplations on the Love and Dread of God*), *Life of Soul, Book to a Mother*, and Walter Hilton's *Mixed Life* — situating them in relation both to their great poetic contemporaries, Chaucer and Langland, and to their more radical counterpart, vernacular Wycliffism.

The Introduction maps the terrain of the argument. The well-known phenomenon of translation and adaptation of monastic religious materials for lay use is profitably understood, Rice suggests, as a desire on the part of socially powerful laypeople to share in the 'spiritual capital' previously regarded as exclusively connected to the ascetic life of enclosed religious. Laypeople, especially those who could afford books and the time for advanced religious practice, came increasingly to desire versions of the structured, 'disciplined' life of monastics, and texts like those analysed in the book are addressed to this emerging audience. Importantly, it emerges, laypeople pursued not only monastic but also 'clerical privilege': lay versions of the knowledge and pastoral authority associated with the secular clergy. In the book as a whole, it is this latter, secular identity that, organized as it is around an 'active' life in the world, emerges as the more generative and empowering model for lay appropriation.

Chapter 1 argues that when texts originally produced for enclosed religious are adapted for lay readers, the emphasis on stability, constitutive of monastic vows and modes of living, is translated into an internal, spiritual state that Rice identifies as a penitential and potentially oppressive subjection to clerical control. In the English *Abbey of the Holy Ghost,* a translation of a fourteenth-century French text in which the reader creates an inner, 'spiritual abbey' in order to 'withdraw' from the everyday lay world, a religiosity of spiritual advancement is replaced by an emphasis on self-regulation and the internalization of clerical law. Similarly, *Fervor amoris*, a Middle English adaption of a spiritual rule for an anchoress (Richard Rolle's *Form of Living*), replaces a model of meditative ascent with the penitential internalization of clerical rule. The chapter ends with a reading of Chaucer's *Shipman's Tale*, suggesting that the merchant's desire for 'discipline' is akin to the lay ambition addressed by these lay spiritual rules and is presented sympathetically, despite the tale's critique of the object of lay desire, monastic living as represented by the lax Monk.

Chapter 1 perhaps never quite resolves the tension between the lay desire for subjection to a quasi-monastic penitential obedience and its own valorization of the spiritual ascent models featured in works like *The Form of Living*, making what may be a too easy negative argument that such works are more concerned with the consolidation of clerical prerogative than with their lay readers. In turning to the religious model Rice finds conducive to lay empowerment, that represented by the secular cleric, however, Chapters Two and Three move into innovative and more positive scholarly territory. Indeed, these exciting chapters are the heart of the book.

Chapter 2 argues that the explicitly or implicitly dialogic form of three texts, *Life of Soul*, *Book to a Mother*, and *Mixed Life* opens a discursive space that imagines a substantial level of lay autonomy, offering 'clerical knowledge' and privilege to their lay readers through their textual aid. Lay study of these books as supplements to Holy Writ enables not only *imitatio Christ* but *imitatio clerici* (p. 69), 'bringing techniques of reading, emendation, and writing into alignment with embodied efforts to reform the self and imitate Christ' (p. 62). This is a process conducted in concert with clerical guidance: neither overwhelmed by self-promoting clerical agendas nor, as in many contemporary Wycliffite texts, inclined to refuse clerical supplementation by insisting on the self-sufficiency of the Bible studied 'in defiance of clerical authorities' (p. 69). The emphasis on dialogic participation in these texts has strong echoes in passus 17 of *Piers Plowman*, in which Will is instructed 'for life and for soule' not only through Bible study but in dialogue with Christ.

Chapter 3 extends the previous argument, focusing on Hilton's *Mixed Life*, a text that also promotes the embodied practise of religious values, encouraging laypeople to follow Christ's (and, ideally, the secular clergy's) 'medeled' life in 'cooperation with rather than in submission to the priestly advisor' (p. 67). For Rice, Hilton's text constitutes a new phenomenon: an attempt at a 'reformist translation of professional religious discipline' (p. 83) for lay living. Hybridity (of prelate and lay lord; of active and contemplative lives) is a positive ideal in Hilton's text, in contrast to contemporary Lollard views, which condemn the 'hermaphroditic' intermingling of secular and spiritual authority (p. 83). While Wyclif and Langland, in various but complementary ways, understand the worldly orientation of the prelacy as breeding disordered charity and corruption, for Hilton 'temporal lordship is precisely the element that links the lay lord to bishop and thus to Christ's own example of charity' (p. 89). The lord's 'souereynte' and 'lordschipe' rightly can extend to pastoral authority over other laypeople, if 'covetise' of material goods and secular power is correctly reoriented into spiritual ambition and fulfilment.

Chapter 4, a study of *Book to a Mother*, continues the exploration of late fourteenth-century reformist models of lay pastoral authority, now with respect to that most difficult case, female preaching. In a manner evocative of Lollard writings and the views expressed by Chaucer's outspoken Wife of Bath, *Book to a Mother* suggests that, because all Christians descend from the original apostolic community around Christ, laypeople should 'preche with oure goode liuinge' (p. 130). In telling contrast to both Lollard and the Wife's opposition to vowed chastity, however, it is chaste widowhood and spiritual marriage to Christ that is the exemplary mode of lay living for the *Book* author. '[S]teer[ing] a course between convent and conventicle' (p. 124), the *Book* author interprets two scriptural narratives, that of the annunciation and the Book of Tobias as offering useful orthodox models of lay evangelism. The Virgin Mary teaches 'the reader both to embody and teach virtuous conduct within the confines of female community' (p. 124), while the model of paternal instruction offered by elder Tobias is extended and regendered in association with his daughter-in-law Sara's desire for chaste spiritual marriage. The *Book* author thus imagines his lay reader's potential evangelical agency as complement rather than opposition to clerical authority.

In conclusion, Rice provides an illuminating sketch of the immediate afterlife of her key texts, looking at the contents and traces of ownership of four manuscript miscellanies produced in the fifteenth century. In London, British Library, MS Harley 5272, *Abbey of the Holy Ghost*, despite its carefully generalized lay address, is recontextualized with other contemplative texts back into the 'rarefied, meditative realm' (p. 136) of an elite female audience. In Lincoln Cathedral, MS 91 (the Thornton MS), *Mixed Life* does indeed seem to have found a gentry reader searching for the best way to live a 'medeled life', although in Oxford, Bodleian Library, MS Ashmole 751 a clerical compiler has revised the text to excise Hilton's inclusive address, reclaiming mixed life as a prerogative of professional religious. In Oxford, Bodleian Library, MS Laud misc. 210, finally, *Book to a Mother* and *Life of Soul* find themselves 'with a range of controversialist texts' that enlarge and expand the works' 'lay preaching and teaching imperatives' (p. 136).

The Preface to *Lay Piety and Religious Discipline* (pp. xi–xii) implicitly offers the book as a sequel to David Aers and Lynn Staley's *The Powers of the Holy*, the study that taught us so much about the intricate relation between theology and cultural politics in late fourteenth-century England. With its carefully contextualized and fine-grained analysis of a group of important texts, and especially in the attention it draws to the lay appropriation of pastoral, as distinct from monastic, authority (*imitatio clerici*), this book will also stimulate considerable new interest, and new work, in the field.

AMY APPLEFORD
Boston University
applefor@bu.edu

A. V. C. Schmidt, ed. *William Langland, Piers Plowman: A Parallel-Text Edition of the A, B, C, and Z Versions*, II: *Introduction, Textual Notes, Commentary, Bibliography and Indexical Glossary*. Kalamazoo: Medieval Institute Publications, 2008. Pp. xiii + 948.

This completes a spectacular project: a full introduction, annotation, and glossary for a parallel critical edition of *Piers Plowman* in the Z, A, B, and C versions — and accomplished by one editor in a period of about two decades rather than a half-century or more. The achievement as well as the form does homage to W. W. Skeat, and Schmidt has some of Skeat's brilliant attention to language as well as efficient economy of presentation. A complete and definitive *Piers Plowman*, as any editor would acknowledge, is also spectacular in the sense of a mirage, so mercurial and elusive the poet and so participatory the copyists; and it does not help new users that Schmidt's first volume with his edition of the texts has long been out of print (MIP promises a reprint of Volume I, regrettably dropped by its first publisher, Longmans). But this second volume, though inevitably charged with justifying the texts presented in the first volume of 1995, does excellent service for use with any edition of the poem, presenting exceedingly thoughtful and wide-ranging introductions to the manuscripts, editorial history, principles of editing, and more generally pitched presentation of the poem and author, as well as a terse but densely detailed commentary and textual notes. Though the commentary is necessarily highly selective, and the textual notes limited by the choices and evidence displayed in the first volume, this volume is an invaluable handbook for considering the textual and editorial history and (an ultimate if always more spectral goal) the poem's or poems' peculiar literary achievement.

The consistency of so large a quantity of material, and of its principles and interpretations, is remarkable. Users of Schmidt's first volume will know that he added the controversial Z text to his parallel edition, and given the debate about authenticity stirred by Rigg's and Brewer's claims, its mere presence would mean that Schmidt's justification of and commentary on Z were bound to be exceedingly careful, and they are. The section on all the 'versions' of the poem closes with 'objections to the authenticity of Z'; yet from the sifting of just what can justify including that version emerge the guiding ideas of the whole edition and commentary, the 'authenticating features of language, metre and style' (pp. 220–21) from the other versions that can justify presenting Z as reflecting Langland's own early (though possibly not the earliest) 'draft' of the poem. The testing of Z turns out to generate a number of the norms for the 'core-text' drawn from all versions of the poem, which are then (with careful attention to the possible circularity of

10.1484/J.YLS.1.102119

this) applied back to the process of editing and distinguishing Langland's *echt* poetics. Those seen as emerging from Z range from 'juxtaposition of clerkly and colloquial motifs' to particular 'use of macronic lines' to homophonic wordplay on (merely) 'grammatical lexemes serving as stave-words' (metrically stressed words) in the alliterative metre, to the use of an 'allegorical "command name"' (like 'Bileue-so-or-þow-best-not-ysaued', a device that Schmidt notes is otherwise unique to Langland).

Such crucial use of Z might seem risky in a massive edition making authorita- tive claims and designed for the wide range of readers and users that this text and commentary is. But Z's contribution to positing 'core-text' ideas about Langland's poetry is strictly preliminary to the bulk of supporting evidence from the other versions. The proposition of multi-versional 'core' features and 'core' lines is reasonable, given all the emphasis on lexical and historical detail and argumen- tation, and on the difficulties yet necessity of subjective judgement in using this principle for editing the poem's stages of development (in, say, distinguishing the poet's very rare return to phrases revised out of earlier versions from the much commoner scribal conflation from several versions). The categories of the 'core- text' that Schmidt infers are complex, numerous, and worth continued scrutiny in theory and practice; to the one element of metrical stave use already mentioned that helps admit Z, Schmidt adds eleven others when defining the full range of 'core-text' features (pp. 257–60). He claims to differentiate his certainties about what constitutes the 'core-text' in decreasing probabilities based on increasing percentages of his data: 530 lines are shared by all four versions, a further 598 by three, a further 3020 by two. These then are said to be subjected to linguistic, stylistic, and literary 'acceptability' as norms. All these are carefully displayed props for reaffirming the view of linear revision ZABC as well as the range of habits deemed most distinctively Langlandian, thus the bases for scrutinizing the exceptions as likely cases of archetypal error.

The procedure is neither mechanical nor invisibly high-handed. Like the Athlone editions, it is all dedicated to pursuing and displaying 'the poem's qualities as a great work of medieval literature', a goal modestly articulated in a footnote but evident throughout (p. 302 n. 78). But whereas the Athlone editors, in their notoriously vast introductions but notoriously elusive explanations for their countless emendations, seemed to use the goal of pursuing Langland's 'genius' as a means to paint a rogues' gallery of errant scribes, Schmidt's textual and commentary volume much more centrally focuses on pursuing and accumu- lating Langland's distinctive metrical, rhetorical, and stylistic elements. Previous editors come in for more criticism than scribes. But apart from a now-predictable though fully respectful criticism of how egregiously the Athlone editors departed from the ABC archetypes in their emendations, and a few sustained disagreements in the notes on others' glosses, Schmidt lacks the zeal for invective that seems to impel some editorial monuments. Instead of the boldly revelatory style of the Athlone editions or the keen literary sensitivity and flashes of wit in Derek Pearsall's editions, Schmidt offers balance, thoroughness, explicit reasoning, accuracy, and — at many intellectual as well as all presentational levels — the principle of 'economy' (pp. 242–44), a principle not ironically guiding all of this large tome and project.

In keeping with the principle of economy, the limits of this volume are mostly clear and reasonable. Those limits show up perhaps most in the commentary. The commentary (and the 'textual notes', which should also be read by everyone interested in the issues of Langland's language, revision, and poetics) features fine distinctions of phrases, shrewd comments on small particulars (especially lexical ones), and careful assessment of revision based on the 'linear postulate'. But it explicitly includes only sparing discussion of criticism, restricted mainly to studies where sources or lexical interpretations are at stake, and only a few notes pursue wider relevant historical or literary horizons. Those that do are often helpful or at least intriguing. Particularly full notes appear on religious iconography and selected exegetical traditions (e.g., pp. 543–45, 548a), and on some details of historical *realia* invoked, as in the unparalleled elucidation of Avarice's and his wife's fraudulent clothing and ale operations (pp. 531b–532a). It is a pity that there is no separate index to the commentary; as a consequence, some 'big notes' defining figures like Reason, Meed, and Conscience must be fished out from the index of proper names or sought, but not always exclusively found, when the figures first appear (thus, for Conscience, see p. 476b but also p. 545b; for Reason, p. 517a but also 611b, etc.). Some intriguing historical information is mentioned with no references. In cases like Humphrey de Bohun's glazing of windows at the London Austin Friars' church this may be resolved with a little research (p. 499b), but the glancing mention that 'certain medieval manuscripts' illustrate the feat of performative farting (p. 634a) may leave one wanting more assistance. Criticism published after 2005 is explicitly not incorporated into the introductions or commentary, though the bibliography includes more recent works like manuscript facsimiles in the *Piers Plowman Electronic Archive* and the two published volumes of the *Penn Commentary on 'Piers Plowman'* (though the volumes of the *Penn Commentary* are, in fact, written not 'edited' by Stephen Barney and myself, and those are not participants in the 'Athlone enterprise' (p. 83 n. 5, p. 10) but projects of their own, with a different scope of interpretive commentary than

Schmidt's, and fashioned to be useful for his parallel-text edition as well as any other).

The Athlone editors would likely have argued that they needed no commentary, since their text itself made their boldest and tersest case for what they thought of as the revelation of Langland's poetic essence. Schmidt's Everyman B text (1995), after whose model the full parallel-text presentation was designed, has long implied a different outlook, one more explicitly introductory and more textually conservative. As users of Schmidt's Volume I and the (textually identical) 1995 B already know, apart from the presence of Z his editorial choices were restrained. He emended the ABC archetypes far less readily than the Athlone editors, especially the notorious B archetype against which Kane and Donaldson executed so many scarring thrusts and parries. Schmidt even allowed the final two passūs of B and C to differ continuously in small ways. This is notable. For the Athlone editors George Russell and George Kane, Langland died before finishing C and never got far at all in making B.19–20 into C.21–22, apart from the small distinct sets of new lines inserted in C, which they imagined as left, like most of the C revisions, on separate scraps marked for insertion (and sometimes, they felt, inserted at the wrong points). Thus, in editing C's last two passūs, they emended back to Kane's and E. T. Donaldson's edition of B wherever — apart from those distinct sets of insertions — appeared minute changes between the archetypes of B.19–20 and C.20–21.

Even when Russell and Kane were most conservative, therefore, they were radically so, offering features alarming as well as exciting to those following the epic Athlone venture. Schmidt's response to situations like the end of the poem seems less daring but no less plausible and productive. We now learn that Schmidt finds the most 'economical' theory to be that Langland's revision of B into C proceeded first up to B.19 which he had copied into a new holograph scribal fair copy, to which he attached his revision copy of B.19–20 that he had lightly revised throughout (pp. 166–67, 123–24). Even this fleetingly offered hypothesis shows Schmidt's willingness to posit the poet's care for his poem's details, and this attitude gives new interest to how, in Volume I, Schmidt followed the B and C archetypes so much more closely than did Kane and his co-editors. Schmidt's poet is a nearsighted rather than farsighted reviser, comparable (as he repeatedly declares) to Rembrandt in attention to fine detail (pp. 277, 302 n. 80). In contrast, the Athlone editors' Langland is either not often able to be attentive or has had such attentiveness so profoundly betrayed by his copyists and death that only radical solutions can save him from them. His gaze, like those editors', is often focused beyond the texts on some more perfect ideal.

Schmidt leans toward finding in the data all possible signs of poetic attentiveness, generating, for instance, a proliferation of 'acceptable' categories of metrically significant words, such as the 'mute' staves that alliterate but are not stressed (p. 254), which constitutes one kind of the twelve species of staves Schmidt identifies in *Piers Plowman*: like 'Bischopes and bachelers, *bothe* maystres and doctours' (C.Prol.85). A sub-species of this is the 'small-word' stave, a 'grammatical morpheme that may appear in either half of the line as a full [i.e., stressed and alliterating] or a mute stave' (p. 259). This is a relatively well-established category; as Schmidt notes, Kane and Donaldson mention it, and indeed refer it back to J. P. Oakden (K-D, p. 135). Schmidt has gradually developed his commitment to this feature, finally making it into a major marker of the real Langland at work. In his editorial application, however, mute staves, small word or other, remain generally non-controversial: a feature to store up in his valued 'core-text' elements that rarely leads him to purely conjectural insertion where it does *not* appear (I consider a partial exception, however, to that restraint below).

In contrast, Kane and his co-editors, though they do not dwell long on the theory of this metrical element, have the courage of a conviction in it far exceeding their articulation of its principles. At B.18.389, for instance, where the reconstructed archetype, followed by Schmidt (his line 390), reads, 'I may do mercy þoru3 rightwisnesse, and alle my wordes trewe', Kane-Donaldson emend to 'I may do mercy þoru3 *my* rightwisnesse, and alle my wordes trewe' (my emphasis for their brackets), adding another layer of microlexical mute-stave alliteration by purely conjectural emendation. Since no B manuscript has the first 'my' there, one might suppose they had in mind the small-word mute stave principle — although it is also true that they are there using C's line to emend the B archetype, a point that, unfortunately typically, they do not mention in the B apparatus just as they do not articulate their metrical principles for that emendation.

Cross-versional editing is a principle for the Athlone editors no less than for Schmidt, but he proceeds much more openly, and generally on more directly attested evidence. In the example just mentioned, there is little doubt that if Z and A presented text there and if they agreed with C against B, Schmidt would have followed the majority reading, inserting 'my' into B (indeed, he follows C when the 'my' appears). In the event, B.18.389/390 against C's archetypal evidence presents balanced options, and editors' choices are revealing both of judicial temperament and of assumptions about Langland's poetic modalities. Kane and Donaldson's editorial boldness there may deny the poet a display of gradual improvement in subtle alliteration from B to C, but may also save the poet from the roguish scribes who demonstrably corrupted B. On the other side, Schmidt's restraint from fully applying his own range of possible metrical theories to emend B may reveal reluctance to tamper with empirical evidence, but also presents a poet constantly improving his craft in minute ways. At small levels of texture like this, one confronts not simply different degrees of editorial hubris but also different views of just what kind of poetic genius the texts display, how finely developed and when.

Schmidt does, of course, conjecturally emend (or as he prefers, 'reconstruct') when he sees clearer reasons to do so, and with the second volume we can now follow his thinking in those cases more closely than we ever could the Athlone editors'. Metrical issues remain the main reason for this, but even now, those issues are not as clear as the major efforts that Schmidt and many others have devoted to studying Langland's metre suggest they should be. B.18.392 just following, for instance, shows him following Kane-Donaldson's repair of $aa|xx$ alliteration but with a different conjectured word to produce a different, and in fact metrically bolder result. The majority line — describing those Jesus will send to Purgatory — reads, 'Thei shul be clensed clerliche and wasshen of hir synnes.' K-D, with a brash lexical change, emend to 'and *keuered* of hir synnes', evidently to correct scribal substitution of a hard word and to recover a basic $aa|ax$ alliterative pattern. Schmidt, however, emends to 'and [clene] wasshen of hir synnes'. Based on his other habits of emendation, this is surprisingly bold. He heels closer to the archetype in the sense that it all remains visible in the main text, but he lengthens the line considerably and remakes it into a 'mute stave' line. Schmidt's note on this emendation (p. 452b) now suggests the bases for his choice but also some of the risks and lingering doubts. He justifies inserting 'clene' rather than replacing 'wasshen' partly because of a similar 'ywasche | Clene' at C.10.228–29, and partly by what he takes to be the easier hypothesis of loss of 'clene' through mechanical error. Yet though the emendation boldly inserts a mute stave, his note approaches the metrical consequences of his emendation cautiously, even distantly. As emended, Schmidt notes, the line could be scanned as 'type IIa' ($aaa|xx$; see p. 256) or 'Ia' with 'muted key stave'. His tentativeness about how to scan his own emendation suggests that he has not sought out emendation on clear metrical grounds — or at least by Volume II would no longer condone having done so — but instead begun with the lexical and mechanical possibilities while positing then reconsidering the metrical consequences.

However it happened that second thoughts filled that gap between textual decision and later explanation, the caution looks more like wisdom than failure of nerve, though it leaves his own metrical theories in a rather subordinate practical role. This may be the best outlook to adopt in emending Langland's poetry on metrical grounds, even after one has carried that out, since it shows the need for continued thought about the extraordinary variety of metrical effects of which Langland, in contrast to all other alliterative poets, seems capable. Even the archetypal line at B.18.392 (with its flickering internal alliteration between 'wasshen' and 'synnes') might in the end be metrically justifiable. And to all this it can be added that one B manuscript, Cambridge University Library, MS Gg.4.31 (G), here reads 'Thei shul be wasshen clerliche and clensed of hir synnes', suggesting that scribes' theories and doubts about metre could produce early emendations of their own. Schmidt's critical apparatus, however, lacks G's unique reading here, which I take from Kane-Donaldson (on other grounds, Schmidt considers G 'the most significant' witness to the major branch of B manuscripts known as gamma (pp. 135, 127)). Though it is impossible to imagine using the Athlone editions without fully considering everything Schmidt has made of them and the poem, the narrower evidence of his apparatus should always be kept in mind, especially when continuing the enquiry into Langland's metre, a topic presenting the most important open questions of Schmidt's edition, made still more significant by his many considerations detailed here.

Another, oddly less energized, question left open is the value of Z. With the dust of the earlier conflicts between Kane and Brewer and those following their views having settled, if not some general conclusion having been accepted, Schmidt seems free to explore doubts. This willingness to be sceptical and critical is very useful, though it arouses a more qualified kind of interest in that version than the authenticity debate engendered. Since Schmidt takes Z to be a 'draft' of the poet's work, he routinely describes its poetic features in much more negative terms than the other versions ('superfluous', 'redundant' lines and all); yet he also fairly praises some Z-only text, producing some balance of critical scrutiny and respect for their consistency with later passages, such as the (too-elusively) 'ironic' praise of bishops in Z.Prol.53–58 (p. 474a), or the strange passage on divine and human verbal 'wind' at Z.5.34–40, which he finds more depth in than probably most readers would (p. 520b). On balance the comments on Z do not read as special pleading for its inclusion in the parallel text as part of Langland's development, apart from the constant theme that it is an early 'draft' version. Instead, Schmidt's running remarks leave a sense of Z's strange yet not entirely controlled intellectual power, and present as a whole and in relation to the other versions some of the best arguments I have encountered for Z's status as *somehow* connected with Langland's early writing of *Piers Plowman*. Its claim to 'draft' status depends on these judgments of inferior but associated poetic craft. But just how we are to delineate the concept of a circulating 'draft' version of such an unending yet never fully 'private' or fully finished poem is a further question to keep in mind, if only to resist the dulling effects that the frequent mentions of Z as a mere 'draft' produce. Indeed, since Z is so often seen in the notes as improved on by the later versions, the question may now arise how and why Z will continue to be of interest. Its effect in pressing Schmidt to codify his 'core-text' principles is salutary, but once this has been achieved — then superseded by the much fuller enquiry into how those principles may be developed in the other versions — Z's attractions may prove less strong. Unless, that is, it can prove to be of further interest not as revealing 'a great work of medieval literature', to which Schmidt dedicates all these efforts, but as a contribution to understanding the other kinds of history that he declares are secondary to his real concerns: 'the text, context, background, and theological and political ideas' in *Piers* and its world (p. 302 n. 78).

The limits and edges of the thought and materials in this massive project are worth continued pondering, but its fulfilment of its central goals is masterful. The volume is stunningly free of simple errors, apart from a very few, most inconsequential. A minor clump of misleading or wrong cross-references appear in the notes to the last chapter of the introduction, 'The Poem in Time', which offers a succinct and generally approachable introduction to the poem. Thus in the note for remarks in the commentary on connections to the alliterative English *William of Palerne*, which shares an intriguing number of phrases with *Piers Plowman*, a number of the references do not actually have notes in the commentary (that is, not C.13.148, 16.174, A.3.251, 12.73, Z.3.158, 159, 160), though the passages themselves may be pertinent (p. 298 n. 14). Perhaps this issue emerged late in Schmidt's interests, or lost impetus. A similar number of references to commentary notes on London locales — an issue of continued importance in assessing the poem's urban vision — are also dead ends, though they too indicate relevant places in the poem to look (pp. 298–99 n. 16).

Slightly more troubling is the date of 'the 1390s' given for *Richard the Redeless* (p. 274), a poem that most scholars think post-dates 1399. This advancement of that poem's dates may be related to Schmidt's view that Langland died in 1386 or 1387, the date asserted by John But's comments in A.12.99–105, but somewhat earlier than many critics have recently suggested (p. 276). So too is linked to that dating the view that the *Testament of Love* by Thomas Usk († 1388) is a witness to and can provide a terminus ante quem for the date of *Piers Plowman* C. The connection has been doubted by more scholars than John Bowers, whose essay in this journal Schmidt cites and disagrees with ('Dating *Piers Plowman:* Testing the

Testimony of Usk's *Testament*', 13 (1999), 65–100), but Schmidt finds two parallels that convince him of Usk's knowledge of the poem (p. 276). The claim remains more speculative than Schmidt's insistences on it suggest (pp. 165, 274, 276, 281, 285, 299 n. 28, 525b, 659b). Moreover, the date Schmidt gives Usk's composition of the *Testament*, 1385–87, which derives from Skeat, whose 1897 edition is the only one Schmidt cites, is slightly at odds with the views of the most recent editor of that work, Gary W. Shawver (Toronto: University of Toronto Press, 2002), who argues from a range of evidence for the period 1384–85 (pp. 24–26). Though there are many reasons to hope to find interest by London writers in a poem that was itself so interested in London, Shawver's date would make allusions to C by Usk much less plausible to most scholars.

The only significant error that I discerned, in fact, was in the glossary, and even this is more intricately thoughtful than it looks. Under *slepen*, Schmidt defines 'don [...] to slepe' as 'prevent from sleeping' (p. 875a). Since this unlikely sense for auxiliary *don* (which, as an auxiliary, invariably conveys a causative force) is not in the *MED* (or Kane's *Glossary* (London: Continuum, 2005)), one wonders whence Schmidt derived it. The answer seems to be the one place where he thinks it appears: C.19.306, where if smoke comes in a man's eyes, 'Hit doth him worse þen his wyf or wete to slepe'. The note is consistent with the glossary: he translates, 'It mars his sleep even worse than his wife or the wet' (p. 680a). The glossary entry thus misleads in the first instance simply by omitting 'worse' in the ellipses, an extreme of economy. But the interpretation itself is probably wrong; it connects 'doth' to the infinitive 'to slepe' across too many units of thought and grammar, conflating the scene into an insomniac's multiple torments. Instead, the sense of 'doth him worse' follows 'be beneficial [or adverse] to someone' (see *MED*, s.v. 'don', 1e (b)), not the auxiliary sense of *don* with an infinitive; the context confirms that 'wete to slepe' should be taken alone, as glossed by Pearsall: '(than) to sleep in the wet' (*Piers Plowman: A New Annotated Edition of the C-Text* (Exeter: University of Exeter Press, 2008), p. 320). A chiding wife, a dripping roof at night, and smoke in the eyes and throat are all irksome, and, separately understood, will all drive a man from his house, just as fleshly desires, bodily illness, and 'covetousness and unkindness' all drive grace from the heart. Only the dripping roof, capped by 'reyne on his bedde' (p. 303), is at night. That scenic detail unfolding the idea of bodily illness is Langland's own unprompted and wonderful addition to a topos (from Innocent III's *De miseria*), as Schmidt's nearby note reveals. But Schmidt's glossary and commentary take Langland's apt detail too broadly, conflating the three analogies for how grace is driven away — which actually generate three miniature scenes in *Piers Plowman* — into a single nocturnal tableau. This once at least, the poem's mercurial and idea-driven variegation defeats the standards of more unified Rembrantian realism, even under Schmidt's brilliant attention to the poem's scenic and poetic original-ity, an editorial and literary attentiveness that shines luminously throughout this volume.

ANDREW GALLOWAY
Cornell University
asg6@cornell.edu

ANNUAL BIBLIOGRAPHY, 2009

David Adams, Andrew Cole,
Fiona Somerset, and Lawrence Warner

The annual bibliography attempts to cover the year's work on *Piers Plowman* and other didactic or allegorical poems in the alliterative tradition (e.g., *Winner and Waster, Parliament of Three Ages, Death and Life, Mum and the Sothsegger, Pierce the Ploughman's Crede, Richard the Redeless, The Crowned King*) but not alliterative romances or the works of the *Gawain*-poet. Authors should send abstracts of their books (800 words) and articles (250–400 words) to the editors.

1. Aers, David, *Salvation and Sin: Augustine, Langland, and Fourteenth-Century Theology* (Notre Dame: University of Notre Dame Press, 2009).

A very thorough reconsideration of L's supposedly 'semi-Pelagian' or 'Augustinian' salvation theology is the centerpiece of this book: Chapter 4, 'Remembering the Samaritan, Remembering Semyuief', provides a new account of salvation, sin, and agency in *PPl* C. Aers focuses on L's version of the parable of the Samaritan in C.19, which he compares with the interpretations of Aquinas, Nicholas of Gorran, Nicholas of Lyra, Denis the Carthusian, and Augustine. But he also addresses episodes in the poem that this one 'correct[s] and supersede[s]': Will's encounter with two friars in C.10, Piers's attempt to advise the pilgrims in C.7, the confessions of Gluttony and Sloth in C.6–7, Piers's attempt to build a Christian polity in C.8, the pardon of C.9, Will's encounter with Reason and Conscience, in C.5, the failure of Eucharistic unity in C.21, and the Crucifixion and Harrowing of Hell in C.20. Finally, Aers reconsiders whether the episode of Trajan in C.12 demonstrates L's 'semi-Pelagianism', as has been claimed. It does not: 'the episode of Trajan should be understood as pointing beyond itself to the later christological and Trinitarian narratives' (p. 126). Chapters 1, 2, and 3, on Augustine, Ockham, and Bradwardine respectively, develop an account of the theologies amongst which L is working, while Chapter 5 on Julian presents and critiques her alternative account of salvation and sin: 'Her hollowing out of the language and theology of sin, together with her treatment of human agency, has a series of consequences that unravel central strands of the Christian doctrine of reconciliation' (p. 170).

10.1484/J.YLS.1.102120

2. Barney, Stephen A., 'A Revised Edition of the C Text', *YLS*, 23 (2009), 265–88.

This revision of Pearsall's student-oriented edition of the C text (1978) updates an excellent original. The footnotes are the glory of the work; they now judiciously consider the explosion of scholarship of the last three decades. New features are marginal glosses, reluctantly supplied to meet modern expectations, and introductory short essays on important topics like 'The Dreamer', 'Lollardy and Lollers', 'Friars', and 'Peres the Plouhman'. The text is accurate. Its readings are revised in the light of the two fully collated editions that have appeared since 1978, Schmidt's parallel-text edition (1995), and especially Russell and Kane's Athlone edition of the C text (1997) with its full apparatus of variants. In one passus (C.20) Pearsall revises his 1978 text in some fifty readings that bring it into accord with the Athlone text, whereas he does not accept some 125 Athlone emendations of either the copy-text, San Marino, Huntington Library, MS Hm 143, or the archetype of the C-text manuscript tradition. Pearsall terms his text 'less "interventionist"' than the Athlone text, and in fact it is much closer to Schmidt's text. Lawrence Warner's proposals about the early development of the C text are mentioned but not absorbed into the presentation. Hoyt Duggan and Thomas Cable have made important findings about the prosody of the second half-lines of the big fourteenth alliterative poems, but no editor, including Pearsall, has yet exploited these findings as an instrument of textual criticism. The equally important question of L's alliterative practice also has never been resolved in full and convincing published studies. Though future exploration of these topics will fund still more authentic texts, all readers of the poem are indebted to Pearsall's pioneering work. (SAB)

3. Bond, Christopher, 'Medieval Harrowings of Hell and Spenser's House of Mammon', *English Literary Renaissance*, 37 (2007), 175–92.

This essay investigates the relations between *The Fairie Queene*, II.7, in which Guyon visits the House of Mammon, and the two most important imaginings of the Harrowing of Hell in medieval literature, L's and that of the mystery cycles. Most important is the concept of 'the guiler beguiled', in which 'resides a complex and serious theological issue: that Christ's trickery of Satan by disguising His divinity in a human body was a legitimate and fitting payback for Satan's trickery of Eve in the Garden of Eden. The associations of Guyon's journey through the House of Mammon with the Harrowing of Hell thus influence our understanding not only of Spenser's attitude toward his sources but also of the meaning of the episode itself' (p. 190). Spenser was the not only the first great Renaissance poet, but the last great medieval one: 'The House of Mammon's association with the Harrowing of Hell provides a further example of Spenser's inclusion, under the guise of an original story, of material that was, at least to Calvinists, highly dubious. And in a poem in which classical and Continental models receive the bulk of scholarly attention, this material was also, through the conduits of L and the mystery cycles, a peculiarly English ingredient' (p. 192).

4. Burrow, J. A., 'Conscience on Knights, Kings, and Conquerors: *Piers Plowman* **B.19.26–198',** *YLS,* **23 (2009), 85–95.**

Prompted in part by Sarah Wood's article in *YLS,* 21, and also by Stephen Barney's 2006 *Penn Commentary,* this essay reconsiders the argument in the account of the life of Christ given by Conscience (B.19.26–198). Conscience distinguishes three phases there: as a knight, known as *filius Mariae,* up to his first miracle, at Cana; as a king, *filius* David, in his public ministry and on the Cross; and as a conqueror, Christus, at and after the Harrowing of Hell. Wood describes the whole speech as a 'sermon on Christ's kingship'; but I argue that this is to elide distinctions that Conscience is careful to make. Thus, the gifts offered by the three kings represent, in this context, virtues that are to be understood as knightly, not kingly (as Wood and Barney suggest). In particular, undue emphasis on kingship obscures the fact that the chief point of the passage lies in its representation of Christ as conqueror. It is not as a king but as a conqueror that he has the power to cast down or raise up his subjects, and it is this conqueror's privilege that he deputes to Peter as that power of the keys with which the rest of the poem is to be much concerned. (JAB)

5. Cable, Thomas, 'Progress in Middle English Alliterative Metrics', *YLS,* **23 (2009), 243–64.**

The prevailing view of the metres of English poetry composed during the past eight centuries — both 'accentual' and 'accentual syllabic' — is that relative stress is the most important feature. By 'relative' is meant a comparison of adjacent syllables to determine only 'more' or 'less'. In simultaneous, transforming discoveries Ad Putter, Judith Jefferson and Myra Stokes, and Nicolay Yakovlev, complicate this neat, binary picture by showing that the poems grouped as the 'Alliterative Revival' incorporate an additional metrical feature. Whether designated as 'secondary stress' or as a 'non-schwa vowel', a phonological element is avoided in certain positions in the verse. The demonstration of this systematic avoidance leads to a new understanding of the metre of *PPl* and other alliterative poems. Along the way, both studies establish the regular presence of historical -*e*, but they come to different conclusions about 'extended', or three-beat, verses. In addition to pointing the way for future research on extended verses, the combined effect of the two studies is to lay out the question of the asymmetry, or 'hetero-morphicity', of the long line — the extent to which the patterns of the two halves of the line belong to mutually exclusive sets. With the inclusion of the features 'heavy final dip' and 'extra-long dip' (both disallowed in the b-verse), Putter, Jefferson, and Stokes find the asymmetry of a-verses and-b verses to be categorical, while Yakovlev concludes from the 'non-schwa' principle that the mutually exclusive sets are more pervasive than previously thought but are best described as 'rhythmical preferences'. (TC)

6. Catto, Jeremy, 'Written English: The Making of the Language, 1370– 1400', *Past and Present*, 179 (2003), 24–59.

This essay argues that later Middle English was the result not of natural developments, but of a conscious attempt by writers like L, Chaucer, and Gower to develop a more flexible and precise form of English. The flexibility and pre-cision of Latin had stunted the development of English, whose use was limited to less complex communication. Readers of the period apparently learned their letters in Latin, not English. The language of *The Book of the Duchess* was novel, heralding similarly novel writings such as *PPl*, whose English was much more subtle, precise, and expressive than was that of earlier writers. While it is not clear exactly how the change was made to English by L and his contemporaries, it is clear that crucial to the new development was the fact that the Ricardians were influenced by Latin styles and were able to accommodate Latin and French readily in their new form of the vernacular. It seems that L wrote for a progressive and educated audience familiar with Latin, which would have sympathized with his attempt to reach out to a popular audience through the use of the new form of English. While the motive for experiment must have been strong among the Ricardians, the change in English was not driven by nationalism, but by the desire firstly that impromptu translations of Latin religious texts might be avoided in religious instruction, and secondly that English might take its place alongside other illustrious vernaculars.

7. Davlin, Mary Clemente, 'William Langland', in *The Blackwell Companion to the Bible in English Literature*, ed. by Rebecca Lemon, Emma Mason, Jonathan Roberts, and Christopher Rowland (Oxford: Wiley-Blackwell, 2009), pp. 116–33.

A chapter in Blackwell's book on the Bible in English Literature, a reference book intended especially for undergraduates, 'William Langland' reviews recent knowledge of biblical quotations in *PPl*, ways in which various characters in the poem read the Bible, retelling of Bible stories and re-creations of biblical characters, personifications of the Bible, the effect upon the poem of biblical genres and styles, and the centrality of the Bible in the ideas and ideals of *PPl*. (MCD)

8. Duggan, Hoyt N., 'Notes on the Metre of *Piers Plowman*: Twenty Years On', in *Approaches to the Metres of Alliterative Verse*, ed. by Judith Jefferson and Ad Putter, Leeds Texts and Monographs, n.s., 17 (Leeds: Leeds Studies in English, 2009), pp. 159–86.

Duggan's retractions. Revisiting his essay in *YLS*, 1, which argued that L followed the same basic metrical rules that govern other alliterative poems, Duggan now says 'there is very little evidence that [L] felt constrained by (or perhaps was more than generally aware of) the metrical constraints that bound other poets' (p. 169). For instance, in *PPl* and only there, 'a word in the first or second dip of a b-verse from a closed class may carry alliteration without bearing linguistic or metrical stress' (p. 162). L is also prone to writing b-verses that are 'both semantically and syllabically heavier than is the norm with other poets' (p. 169). Similarly, a significant number of lines end with two or more unstressed syllables. 'Perhaps the most striking difference between L's metrical practice and that of the other alliterative poets is that he did not steadily make alliteration coincide with metrical stress' (p. 172). This immensely increases the number of lines acceptable under the definition of 'metrical'. Passages that editors have long taken to record draft material that L died before he could revise, such as C.Prol.114–24, would in fact have seemed to him unremarkable.

9. Echard, Siân, *Printing the Middle Ages* (Philadelphia: University of Pennsylvania Press, 2008).

The Introduction to this book, 'Plowmen and Pastiche: Representing the Medieval Book' (pp. 1–20), traces the fate of the frontispiece of Cambridge, Trinity College, MS R.3.14, the image of plowing, which serves as 'a rich instance of the general argument of this book, which is that from an early period, the texts of the Middle Ages have been understood at least in part in terms of their appearance' (p. 2). Echard discusses the adaptation of the image in various nineteenth-century works (e.g., Wright's edition), in which the image 'can be seen as a crystallization of the process by which many medieval texts have made their way into our hands' (p. 17).

10. Galloway, Andrew, 'The Economy of Need in Late Medieval English Literature', *Viator*, 40 (2009), 309–31.

Since the eighteenth century, economic thought has made identity legible in terms of production, consumption, and profit. This essay argues that, in contrast, in later medieval culture social thought was often framed in terms of an economy of need. The essay establishes that claim in the realms of canonists and theologians, but it also argues that, in a context where the blurring or transformation of the idea of need can be traced on many sides, late medieval vernacular English writers — preachers, prose writers, poets — as well as artists addressing vernacular culture, more fully emphasized this 'economy of need', pursuing its details and contradictions. The London writers (Gower, Chaucer, and L) especially elaborated the contradictions of this frame of thought. The concept and its contradictions help explain many of their poetry's preoccupations, even as their critical scrutiny shows how the idea of an 'economy of need' would ultimately collapse. (AG; from the journal's abstract)

11. Garrison, Jennifer, 'Failed Signification: *Corpus Christi* and *Corpus Mysticum* in *Piers Plowman*', *YLS*, 23 (2009), 97–123.

This essay explores L's Eucharistic theology and argues that *PPl*'s penultimate passus constitutes a poetic engagement in later medieval theological discussions of the Eucharist as an allegorical sign. L links the seemingly disparate elements of the passus — Will falling asleep during Mass, the discussion of names of Christ, Christ's vita, Pentecost, the founding of the church, Unity's invitation to and rejection of the Eucharist — through the concept of signification as it is elaborated in Eucharistic theology. For L, the power of the Eucharist lies in its unification of the two halves of the allegorical sign: the material appearance of bread unites with Christ's body, and the consecrated host which signifies the Christian community becomes one with that community through Eucharistic reception. Both Will and the Christians in Unity fail to receive the Eucharist in the penultimate passus because they refuse to recognize their role in the

Eucharist's signification and to transform their own divided social body into the perfect reflection of the unified body of Christ. L suggests that proper Eucharistic reception requires Christians to understand the Eucharist as a sign of both Christ's physical body (*corpus Christi*) and Christ's corporate body (*corpus mysticum*). L's interest in the corporate body is not a slight to belief in the Real Presence but rather stems from his sense of the inseparability of the two as sacramentally related concepts. (JG)

12. Green, Richard Firth, 'Langland and Audelay', in *My Wyl and My Wrytyng: Essays on John the Blind Audelay*, ed. by Susanna Fein (Kalamazoo: Medieval Institute Publications, 2009), pp. 153–69.

Green agrees with Simpson (against Pearsall; see below) that Audelay's references to Meed indicate his knowledge of *PPl*. Green pays special attention to similarities between passūs 2, 3, 5, and 6 of *PPl* B and *Marcolf and Solomon*, in which Audelay experiments with alliterative verse. Audelay shares a striking proportion of stock phrases with L, which does not seem coincidental. Audelay shares with L a homiletic alliterative vocabulary not used in most of the romances. In addition, Audelay and L share several broad aspects of style, such as direct addresses to the audience preceded by phrases like 'Look thou!' Both poets refrain from clearly signalling changes between 'speakers'; both depend heavily on Latin passages; and both run Latin and English phrases together. Moreover, both try to make theological mysteries more concrete — where L compares the Trinity to a hand and a torch, Audelay compares it to the sun. Yet Audelay was not significantly influenced by L's political and religious opinions, being more positive about friars and more orthodox than his predecessor. If Susanna Fein is correct in arguing that Audelay's poetry is a record of his own spiritual quest, then L's search for Saint Truth would stand as an obvious model for him.

13. Hanna, Ralph, 'William Langland', in *The Cambridge Companion to Medieval English Literature, 1100–1500*, ed. by Larry Scanlon (Cambridge: Cambridge University Press, 2009), pp. 125–38.

Hanna provides basic information about L and his sources; the A, B, and C texts; the episodic structure of the narrative; and the number and content of Will's dreams. Concentrating on the B text, he raises the problem of the poem's ambiguous and complex narrative and personnel. He proffers a number of examples to illustrate the poem's character: Will's meeting with the friars (passus 8); his conversation with Lady Holy Church (passus 1); the character of Piers;

and Piers's discussion of the question of sin (passus 5). While the meaning of the poem's allegory is spiritual and religious, the letter of the poem can often be interpreted as though L had merely written a romance: language at once offers instruction, and conceals it. The moral import of the poem is often lost on those who most need instruction. Hanna then discusses Piers's description of Truth's castle in relation to all three versions of the poem, observing that this episode reveals the greatness of *PPl*, and the compelling nature of the intellectual statement L makes in it.

14. Horobin, Simon, 'Adam Pinkhurst and the Copying of British Library, MS Additional 35287 of the B Version of *Piers Plowman*', *YLS*, 23 (2009), 61–83.

British Library, MS Additional MS 35287 [M] is an early fifteenth-century copy of the B text copied by a scribe using a provincial dialect and an inaccurate exemplar. The text was subsequently heavily corrected by a contemporary scribe who made numerous changes to its text and to its dialect and spelling. This essay argues on palaeographical, linguistic, and textual grounds that the hand responsible for these corrections was the professional London scrivener Adam Pinkhurst, also responsible for copying the Hengwrt and Ellesmere manuscripts of the *Canterbury Tales*, using an exemplar closely related to Cambridge, Trinity College, MS B.15.17 [W], a manuscript argued by Horobin and Mooney to have been copied by this same copyist. The remainder of the essay considers the implications of this identification for our understanding of Pinkhurst's role in the London book trade and the production and circulation of early copies of the B version of *PPl*. (SH)

15. Huber, Emily Rebekah, '"For Y am sorwe, and sorwe ys Y": Melancholy, Despair, and Pathology in Middle English Literature' (unpublished doctoral dissertation, University of Rochester, 2008), abstract in *DAI-A*, 69.8 (2009), 3145.

16. Johnston, Michael, 'Robert Thornton and *The Siege of Jerusalem*', *YLS*, 23 (2009), 125–62.

This essay examines the function of *The Siege of Jerusalem* within the so-called London Thornton Manuscript (London, British Library, MS Additional 31042). This romance has received much critical attention of late, most of which has suggested that it subtly challenges dominant ideas of anti-Judaism. By examining the interpretation of *The Siege* encouraged by this manuscript, the essay argues that Robert Thornton, the manuscript compiler, has gone to great lengths to place this text within a Christian imperialist historiography founded on the supersession of Jews and Muslims. It begins with a survey of the surviving manuscripts containing *The Siege*, in which Thornton's manuscript does the most explicit work to encourage an anti-Jewish response from its reader. It then turns to the opening two texts of Thornton's manuscript, *Cursor mundi* and the Northern *Passion*. In his copy of these two texts, Thornton has on occasion edited the text, and in other places he on occasion preserves unique readings. Both his editorial decisions and the unique readings he has preserved work to heighten the anti-Jewish sentiment of the opening two texts. The essay then turns to the two texts that Thornton has placed after *The Siege*: *The Sege of Melayne* and *Roland and Otuel*, both Charlemagne romances, arguing that the triumphalism of these texts serves as a capstone to Thornton's compilation, offering the destruction of the Saracens as the finale to this Christian historiography. The essay ends by returning to modern scholarship's tendency to read *The Siege* as offering a nuanced challenge to late medieval anti-Judaism. Many moments in the text can support such readings; however, if such nuance was invested in the text by its monastic author, it was seemingly lost on Thornton. (TS)

17. Karnes, Michelle, 'Will's Imagination in *Piers Plowman*', *JEGP: Journal of English and Germanic Philology*, 108 (2009), 27–58.

Argues that Imaginatif functions in *PPl* to reconcile 'clergie' and 'kynde knowynge', to harmonize the lessons that Will has learned from his instructors on the one hand and from his experience of the natural world on the other. Will seeks spiritual enlightenment from the natural world, in this quest following the lead of many a Christian before him, but he initially misunderstands the mechanism of natural theology. As his interactions with Thought and Wit show, he reaches flawed conclusions when he follows his rational faculties wherever they are disposed to go. He needs 'clergie' to steer his investigations and to derive spiritually profitable conclusions from them. Imaginatif is both Will's teacher in this matter and the very means by which Will is able to reconcile the two bodies of knowledge. Aristotelian philosophy in the Middle Ages typically assigned imagination the job of bridging sense and intellect, matter and spirit, and this much attested cognitive function of imagination casts light on what Imaginatif and imagination can do for Will. With their aid, Will is better able to reconcile the natural and the spiritual so that, by the end of the poem, he simply is living biblical narrative; his experience of the world has become spiritual. Imagination not only makes Will a better reader of the natural world but also of poetry, and the poem becomes more vivid as Will becomes adept in using his imagination as it was intended to be used. By calling attention to the cognitive work of imagination, then, this article shows what Imaginatif means and how Will puts Imaginatif's teachings to work in the poem. (MK)

18. Kennedy, Kathleen E., *Maintenance, Meed, and Marriage in Medieval English Literature* (New York: Palgrave, 2009).

Maintenance, Meed, and Marriage in Medieval English Literature explores how the relationship between husbands and wives were used as an analogy to relationships between men through an exploration of literary and documentary sources. The Meed passus in *PPl* provide the best example of the legal practice of coverture in Middle English literature, and are a focal point of the book. Meed's inability to act because she is a woman contrasts with her duty to act as a lord, and conversely suggests some ways in which men were constrained as well. Investigating these passūs in this fashion provides an opportunity to identify both female and male characters in Middle English texts who are experiencing similar tension. An earlier version of the material on *PPl* appeared as 'Retaining Men (and a Retaining Woman) in *PPl*', *YLS*, 20 (2006), 191–214. (KEK)

19. Little, Katherine, 'The "Other" Past of Pastoral: Langland's *Piers Plowman* and Spenser's *Shepheardes Calender*', *Exemplaria: A Journal of Theory in Medieval and Renaissance Studies*, 21 (2009), 160–78.

Argues that the emergence of pastoral in sixteenth-century England deliberately responded to a medieval poetry of rural labour. It takes as its focus Edmund Spenser's *Shepheardes Calender*, typically considered the first English pastoral, demonstrating that Spenser's attempt to write a new, Virgilian shepherd in the pastoral mode is haunted by the medieval rural labourer and the religious reformism with which he was associated: the Piers of *PPl* and the *PPl* tradition. Spenser's shepherd Piers in the May and October eclogues is less an homage to L's poem and its Reformation imitations than the sign of a 'splitting', to borrow a term from Pierre Macherey, that demonstrates 'the play of history'. That history is the shift in the symbolic imagination around labour that occurs in the wake of the Reformation. Spenser's Piers reveals the process by which labour is detached from its medieval, reformist content and appropriated for the pastoral. (KL; adapted from the abstract for the journal)

20. Morgan, Gerald, 'The Dignity of Langland's Meed', *Modern Language Review*, 104 (2009), 623–39.

This article examines the scholarly practice of referring to L's Meed as 'Lady' Meed in defiance of L's own practice. The representation of Meed as an allegorical personification takes its place as a precise if complex element in a systematic argument about the relation of material and spiritual goods (the subject of the first vision). In this respect Meed is to be contrasted and not identified with the ladies of medieval literary allegories, notably the Beatrice and Matilda of Dante's *Commedia* and the Lady Holy Church of *PPl* itself. (GM; adapted from the journal's abstract)

21. Newman, Barbara, 'Redeeming the Time: Langland, Julian, and the Art of Lifelong Revision', *YLS*, 23 (2009), 1–32.

This essay compares *PPl* with Julian's *Revelation of Love* as exemplars of an aesthetic of process, deeply marked by their authors' lifelong revisions. Beginning with the works' unwieldy, asymmetrical form, it argues that their refusal of formal closure marks an aesthetic stance linked to broader similarities. L and Julian both reject the normative separation of ordinary consciousness from the dreaming or visionary state, along with sharp distinctions between ordinary time and the privileged time of revelation. The texts thus develop complex temporalities atypical of their respective genres. Dream time and waking time in *PPl* are not synchronized, nor are the times of seeing, reflecting, and writing clearly delineated in *A Revelation of Love*. The essay goes on to link the internal temporality of each text (the time between visions) with its external temporality (the time between versions). It argues that Julian drafted a 'B text' between 1388 and 1393 before interpolating Chapters 44–63 at a later date, inserting the parable of the Lord and the Servant with its interpretation. This important new material alters the book's visionary focus in a kind of reverse typology, such that the literal vision of Christ crucified now anticipates the symbolic vision of the suffering servant — which may have been influenced by L's figure of Piers Plowman. Finally, the article sketches a relationship between two temporal frames in *PPl*, a cyclical frame shaped by the liturgical calendar and a linear one governed by the three ages of salvation history, with Piers serving as pivotal figure at the turn of the ages. But his role at these pivot points (the tearing of the pardon and the Tree of Charity) is eliminated in C, suggesting L's choice of intellectual clarity over affective compression in his last revisions — a choice markedly contrasting with Julian's. (BN)

22. Pates, Stella, '*Piers Plowman* Manuscript Trinity College: Dublin 212 — The Annals Revisited', *Notes & Queries*, 56 (2009), 336–40.

This note connects the individual Annals, recorded by the scribe who wrote the famous ascription of *PPl* to 'William de Longland', with the family histories of the Lords of Tewkesbury, their relations, and their associates. This web of connections points to Tewkesbury Abbey as site of its copying.

23. Paxson, James J., 'The Personificational Face in *Piers Plowman* Rethought through Levinas and Bronowski: Postmodern Philosophy, Scientific Humanism and Problems in Late Medieval Personification Allegory', in *Levinas and Medieval Literature: The 'Difficult Reading' of English and Rabbinic Texts*, ed. by Ann W. Astell and J. A. Jackson (Pittsburgh: Duquesne University Press, 2009), pp. 137–56.

This essay rethinks the cryptic depiction of the face of Anima in *PPl* B, passus 15, using a spectrum of postmodern theorists (including Paul de Man and Deleuze and Guattari) whom the author brackets between two unexpected thinkers: the rationalist and phenomenological philosopher Emmanuel Levinas and the mathematician, poet, historian of science, and great proponent of scientific humanism, Jacob Bronowski. The argument hinges as well on the two thinkers' shared position as Jews who had survived or escaped the violence of the Holocaust only to build careers in response to that violence which grew from the collapse of reason in Europe under the Nazis. In opening up understanding of L's striking personificational face, the essay implies that a prefiguration of the Levinasian 'face' could be construed in Bronowski's 1973 thought experiment, and technologically contingent demonstration, about the face of another death-camp survivor, one Stephan Borgrajewicz, as it gets 'viewed' according to the spectrum of electromagnetic radiations (radio, ultraviolet, X-ray, etc.). The now somewhat neglected thinking of Bronowski might help us to better understand the key concept of Levinas's face and, in turn, the centrality of the allegorical device prosopopeia — the 'making/unmaking of face' — in the poetics of L's *PPl*. (JJP)

24. Pearsall, Derek, 'The Idea of Universal Salvation in *Piers Plowman* B and C', *Journal of Medieval and Early Modern Studies*, 39 (2009), 257–81.

This essay takes up Nicholas Watson's important and influential article, 'Visions of Inclusion: Universal Salvation and Vernacular Theology in Pre-Reformation England', and argues that, for WL at least, the promise of universal salvation is at best ambiguous. The essay examines in detail Christ's speech after he has harrowed hell, the principal locus for the expression of L's views on the matter, but attempts to place this speech in the context of and as the climactic statement of L's salvation theology as it develops through the poem. Important variations between the B and C texts in their treatment of the subject are given special attention. The emphasis is always on the continuously evolving drama of *PPl* as a poem searching for the truth of belief rather than as a poem that expounds a system of already-existing belief. (DP; adapted from the journal)

25. ——, 'Audelay's *Marcolf and Solomon* and the Langlandian Tradition', in *My Wyl and My Wrytyng: Essays on John the Blind Audelay*, ed. by Susanna Fein (Kalamazoo: Medieval Institute Publications, 2009), pp. 138–52.

Although James Simpson is right to note that both *PPl* and Audelay's *Marcolf and Solomon* show a reluctance to express criticisms of the church too strongly, nevertheless Audelay differs from L in expressing undisguised admiration for the Friars' way of life. On the question of endowment the two poets are diametrically opposed, L being against and Audelay for it; Audelay does not engage in the anticlericalism of the Langlandian tradition. The two poems share many alliterative phrases, but they are part of the common stock of the alliterative tradition. Pearsall contends that the Langlandian feel of *Marcolf and Solomon* is known by intuition, not solid textual evidence — other than that provided by Audelay's reference to Meed. These similarities show not that L influenced Audelay, but that both poets drew upon a common tradition. The reference to Meed in *Marcolf and Solomon* may only be the result of Piers the Plowman and his story attaining a place in popular mythology. Pearsall's goal is not to deny that Audelay might have known *PPl*, but to provide a fresh explanation of the relations between *PPl* and *Marcolf and Solomon*.

26. Raskolnikov, Masha, *Body Against Soul: Gender and 'Sowlehele' in Middle English Allegory* (Columbus: Ohio State University Press, 2009).

In medieval allegory, body and soul were often pitted against one another in debate. In this book, Raskolnikov argues that such debates function as a mode of thinking about psychology, gender, and power in the Middle Ages. Neither theological nor medical in nature, works of *sowlehele* (soul-heal) described the self to itself in everyday language — moderns might call this kind of writing 'self-help'. Bringing together contemporary feminist and queer theory along with medieval psychological thought, *Body Against Soul* examines *PPl*, the 'Katherine Group', and the history of psychological allegory and debate. In so doing, it rewrites the history of the Body to include its recently neglected fellow, the Soul. The topic of this book is one that runs through all of Western history and remains of primary interest to modern theorists — how 'my' body relates to 'me'. In the allegorical tradition traced by this study, a male person could imagine himself as a being populated by female personifications, because Latin and Romance languages tended to gender abstract nouns as female. However, since Middle English had ceased to inflect abstract nouns as male or female, writers were free to gender abstractions like 'Will' or 'Reason' any way they liked. This permitted some psychological allegories to avoid the representational tension caused by placing a female soul inside a male body, instead creating surprisingly queer same-sex inner worlds. The didactic intent driving *sowlehele* is, it turns out, complicated by the erotics of the struggle to establish a hierarchy of the self's inner powers. An earlier version of the material on *PPl* appeared as 'Promising the Female, Delivering the Male: Transformations of Gender in *PPl* ', *YLS*, 19 (2005), 81–105. [adapted from the publisher's website]

27. Smith, D. Vance, 'Negative Langland', *YLS*, 23 (2009), 33–59.

Argues that 'our collective failure to come to terms with the poem — that is, terms that all readers of L can agree are essential to understanding such basic features as its form — is not a critical failure but a profound reading of the poem. [...] [W]hat appears to be an epiphenomenal feature, this failure to locate it firmly in one discursive universe, is in fact a consistent response to the poem's larger movement of negation' (pp. 34–35). The criticism of the poem that encourages us to make sense of it in conventional terms obscures its deep and extensive interest in negation as a philosophical, logical concept and as apophatic 'negative' theology. Like the important apophatic texts, *PPl* is centrally interested in the problem of names and naming because unknowability poses an almost insurmountable problem for traditional medieval linguistic theory. This problem is explored in the poem's meditation on the 'kynde name' and on the nature of love. (DVS)

28. Smith, Macklin, 'Langland's Alliterative Line(s)', *YLS*, 23 (2009), 163–216.

The 'alliterative' in 'alliterative long-line', although descriptively accurate, conveys something of its inordinate authority in the field of 'alliterative metrics'. Editors and other metrists have perforce depended on standards of authentic alliterative patterning in the line to distinguish authorial from scribal readings, and have treated the placement of alliterated stresses in relation to the caesura as the primary factor in their taxonomies of acceptable line types. Meanwhile the rhetorical and thematic functions of alliteration have been underestimated — at least in *PPl*. L evidently deployed alliteration with extraordinary versatility, both as a normative marker of metrically realized stress and as an optional prosodic feature. Within the line, he might alliterate two, three, or four metrical stresses, as well as extra stresses or non-stresses, and might insert a second alliterative grouping, arranging dual collocations an adjunctive, chiastic, or interlaced configurations. Beyond this, he might link adjacent lines in manifold ways, often coordinating their intralinear and interlinear collocations so as to mark expansive thematic associations. Much of this alliteration does not have a primarily metrical function. Taking Schmidt's taxonomy of alliterative line types as an initial framework but disputing some of its assumptions, this study addresses the poetic utilities of L's normative, enriched, 'extended', clustered, reduced, and mute-stave lines, as well as those with double alliteration. It argues for the inclusion of *xaa* a-verses within the prosodic field, identifying the chiastic *abb|ba* line as a particular variant. And it proposes a new taxonomy of interlinear alliteration: along with the well-recognized phenomena of running and translinear alliteration, eight other interlinear patterns enable discrete varieties of repetition, anticipation, and echo between and among lines. Alliteration in *PPl*, then, while certainly a line-based metrical marker, serves broader and more complex ends. (MS)

29. Stanley, E. G., 'An Allusion to *Piers Plowman* in Thomas Fuller's *Holy Warre*', *Notes & Queries*, 56 (2009), 201.

Thomas Fuller's *Historie of the Holy Warre* (1639) refers to *PPl* B.11.75–83.

30. Van Dijk, Conrad, 'Giving Each his Due: Langland, Gower, and the Question of Equity', *JEGP: Journal of English and Germanic Philology*, 108 (2008), 310–35.

This essay argues that L and Gower do not use equity strictly as a relaxation of the law or as an expression of mercy. Instead, the tendency for both poets is to link equity to the careful administration of the law. Equity is in fact associated with Ulpian's definition of Justice, which suggests that Justice means to 'give to each his due'. The aim of justice is to treat all equally before the law, with consistency and fairness. In developing this thesis, the essay looks at equity in the English courts and at the conflicting aphorisms about equity current in the fourteenth century. It examines various passages on equitable justice in the *Confessio Amantis* (particularly in Book VII) and in *PPl*, including the definition of the Spirit of

Justice in B passus 19 and the administration of justice in passus 4. The essay argues (against various traditional interpretations) that L does not create a radical contrast between the corruption of the common law and the equity of the king's chancery justice. Instead, both L and Gower appeal to the king to correct injustice, not necessarily by seeking new remedies, but by applying the existing law equally and consistently. The essay concludes with some thoughts about the implications all of this has for L's and Gower's views on the question of kingly sovereignty. (CVD)

31. Warner, Lawrence, 'Annual Bibliography, 2008', *YLS*, 23 (2009), 317–41.

Thirty-eight annotated items and a list of book reviews.

32. ——, 'The Gentleman's *Piers Plowman*: John Mitford and his Annotated Copy of the 1550 Edition of William Langland's Great Poem', *La Trobe Journal*, 84 (2009), 104–12, 130–31.

Identifies the Reverend John Mitford (1781–1859), editor of the *Gentleman's Magazine*, as the last of the 'gentleman scholars' of the pre-Skeat era who filled the flyleaves of their Crowleys and Rogerses with summaries of scholarship on the poem and lists of words and topics, and as the first to make what would become an important claim about *PPl*'s authorship. Mitford owned and annotated the Crowley held by the State Library of Victoria (Australia), and, this note points out, was anonymous reviewer of Thomas Wright's 1842 edition in that journal, an item that has not figured in histories of the poem's editorial and critical history because of its absence from DiMarco's *Reference Guide*. Mitford here suggests that 'persons of talent and leisure' — at least two, that is, in addition to the original author — were responsible for the variations to be found in the manuscripts. This, the first expression of such an idea, seems to have provided the foundation for George Marsh's very similar comments of 1862, which John Manly would later gratefully cite as support for his multiple authorship stance as 'an independent utterance from a scholar so distinguished for soundness of taste and sanity of judgment'. (LW)

33. ——, 'New Light on *Piers Plowman*'s Ownership ca. 1450–1600', *Journal of the Early Book Society*, 12 (2009), 185–94.

Three new or overlooked identifications of *PPl*'s owners. (1) One Thomas Danet († 1483), privy councillor and almoner to King Edward IV, owned London, British Library, MS Additional 35287 (M of B), undermining the belief that ownership of the poem was grounds for prosecution as a heretic. (2) One Joane Vane, 'some tyme priories of Dartforde in Kent', gifted a Crowley edition to William More, most likely the prominent landowner and administrator who sold to James Burbage the land that would become home to the King's Men theatre company. Vane is the second earliest identifiable woman owner of *PPl*. (3) Archbishop Parker's circle has connections with two MSS that, while known to students of Parker, have been overlooked by L scholars: Cambridge, Trinity College, MS R.3.14 (T of A and C), which includes additions in a sixteenth-century hand (including of the 'two monks' heads' passage Warner discusses in *YLS*, 21, to whose list of Tudor-era appearances this should be added), and Cambridge, Corpus Christi College, MS 293 (S of C). (LW)

34. Yakovlev, Nicolay, 'Prosodic Restrictions on the Short Dip in Late Middle English Alliterative Verse', *YLS*, 23 (2009), 217–42.

Recent reconstructions of late Middle English alliterative metre and of the authorial grammar of the relevant texts can be confirmed and developed further by an observation that monosyllabic dips in the second half-line may contain only syllables with either schwa or short final /i/. It follows that stem syllables of words with variable stress (e.g. *cómun/común*) and almost all suffixes cannot occur in monosyllabic dips. The restriction applies to verse-final dips and (possibly with a lesser regularity) to the monosyllabic dips between the two metrical stresses, but not to the monosyllabic dips in the verse-initial position. The relatively small number of counterexamples makes it difficult to determine whether the lesser regularity in the position between metrical stresses is due to scribal interference, but it is clear that such verses deserve close attention of a metrist or editor. The proposed rule is observed by most but not all longer alliterative poems, with *Mum and the Sothsegger* providing at least one straightforward exception. Corollaries of the rule include (a) metrical significance of more than two levels of linguistic stress and (b) rhythmical differentiation of the two half-lines, since non-schwa syllables are very frequent in monosyllabic dips in the first half-line. (NY)

Book Reviews

35. Barney, Stephen, *The Penn Commentary on 'Piers Plowman'*, V: *C Passūs 20–22; B Passūs 18–20* (Philadelphia: University of Pennsylvania Press, 2006). Rev. by George Shuffelton, *Studies in the Age of Chaucer*, 31 (2009), 301–04; shorter notice (no author listed), *Medium Ævum*, 78 (2009), 177–78.

36. Bowers, John M., *Chaucer and Langland: The Antagonistic Tradition* (Notre Dame: University of Notre Dame Press, 2007). Rev. by Matthew Giancarlo, *Speculum*, 84 (2009), 404–05; A. V. C. Schmidt, *Medium Ævum*, 78 (2009), 336–37; Pamela Luff Troyer, *Rocky Mountain Review*, 62 (2008), 96–98.

37. Cole, Andrew, *Literature and Heresy in the Age of Chaucer* (Cambridge: Cambridge University Press, 2008). Rev. by Linda R. Bates, *Marginalia*, 8 (2007–08) <http://www.marginalia.co.uk/journal/08cambridge/bates.php>; Ian Forrest, *Journal of Ecclesiastical History*, 60 (2009), 808–09; John M. Ganim, *Medieval Review*, 09.05.05 <http://hdl.handle.net/2027/spo.baj9928.0905.005>; Kantik Ghosh, *Studies in the Age of Chaucer*, 31 (2009), 301–04; J. Patrick Hornbeck II, *Church History*, 78 (2009), 678–80; Seth Lerer, *Times Literary Supplement* (30 January 2009), 23; Maura Nolan, *Studies in Philology*, 87.1–2 (2008), 185–91; Karen A. Winstead, *Review of English Studies*, 60 (2009), 479–80; Simon Yarrow, *History Today* (19 May 2009) <http://www.historytoday.com/MainArticle .aspx?m=33426&amid=30285010>.

38. Duggan, Hoyt N., and Ralph Hanna, eds, *The Piers Plowman Electronic Archive*, IV: *Oxford, Bodleian Library, Laud Misc. 581 (L)* (Cambridge: Published for the Medieval Academy of America and SEENET by Boydell & Brewer, 2004). Rev. by Karl Reichl, *Anglia*, 126 (2008), 551–57; Sarah Wood, *Notes & Queries*, 56 (2009), 450–51.

39. Eliason, Eric, Thorlac Turville-Petre, and Hoyt N. Duggan, eds, *The Piers Plowman Electronic Archive*, V: *London, British Library, MS Additional 35287 (M)* (Cambridge: Published for the Medieval Academy of America and SEENET by Boydell & Brewer, 2005). Rev. by Karl Reichl, *Anglia*, 126 (2008), 551–57; Sarah Wood, *Notes & Queries*, 56 (2009), 450–51.

40. Galloway, Andrew, *The Penn Commentary on 'Piers Plowman'*, I: *C Prologue–Passus 4, B Prologue–Passūs 4, A Prologue–Passūs 4* (Philadelphia: University of Pennsylvania Press, 2006). Rev. by George Shuffelton, *Studies in the Age of Chaucer*, 31 (2009), 301–04; shorter notice (no author listed), *Medium Ævum*, 78 (2009), 177–78.

41. Giancarlo, Matthew, *Parliament and Literature in Late Medieval England* (Cambridge: Cambridge University Press, 2007). Rev. by Andrew Breeze, *Modern Language Review*, 104 (2009), 544–45; Elizabeth Evershed, *Medium Ævum*, 78

(2009), 133–34; Sarah L. Peverley, *Medieval Review*, 09.04.11 <http://hdl .handle.net/2027/spo.baj9928.0904.011>; Claire Sponsler, *Journal of British Studies*, 48 (2009), 187–89; Lynn Staley, *Studies in the Age of Chaucer*, 31 (2009), 337–40; Marion Turner, *Review of English Studies*, 60 (2009), 299–301.

42. Heinrichs, Katherine, ed., *The Piers Plowman Electronic Archive*, III: *Oxford, Oriel College MS 79 (O)* (Cambridge: Published for the Medieval Academy of America and SEENET by Boydell & Brewer, 2004). Rev. by Karl Reichl, *Anglia*, 126 (2008), 551–57; Sarah Wood, *Notes & Queries*, 56 (2009), 450–51.

43. Kasten, Madeleine, *In Search of 'Kynde Knowynge': 'Piers Plowman' and the Origin of Allegory* (Amsterdam: Rodopi, 2007). Rev. by Denise Baker, *Speculum*, 84 (2009), 168–70.

44. Kelen, Sarah, *Langland's Early Modern Identities* (New York: Palgrave Macmillan, 2007). Rev. by John M. Bowers, *Medieval Review*, 09.01.06 <http://hdl .handle.net/2027/spo.baj9928.0901.006>; Philip Major, *Modern Language Review*, 104 (2009), 1108–09; Nandra Perry, *Renaissance Quarterly*, 62 (2009), 606–08; Paul Patterson, *YLS*, 23 (2009), 289–92.

45. Kerby-Fulton, Kathryn, *Books Under Suspicion: Censorship and Tolerance of Revelatory Writing in Late Medieval England* (Notre Dame: University of Notre Dame Press, 2006). Rev. by Mishtooni Bose, *Journal of the American Academy of Religion*, 77 (2009), 123–26; James Carley, *Times Literary Supplement* (8 June 2007), 25; Cindy Carlson, *Rocky Mountain Review*, 62 (2008), 98–100; Alexandra Gillespie, *English Historical Review*, 123 (2008), 715–17; Martha Dana Rust, *Journal of Educational and Behavioral Studies*, 10 (2007), 260–63; Nancy Bradley Warren, *Church History*, 77 (2008), 165–68.

46. Lightsey, Scott, *Manmade Marvels in Medieval Culture and Literature*. Rev. by Michael Calabrese, *YLS*, 23 (2009), 292–96; Sarah Stanbury, *Speculum*, 84 (2009), 1076–78.

47. Pearsall, Derek, *Piers Plowman: A New Annotated Edition of the C-Text* (Exeter: University of Exeter Press, 2008). Rev. by Stephen A. Barney, *YLS*, 23 (2009), 265–88 (see no. 2, above); Lawrence Warner, *Medieval Review*, 09.07.19 <http://hdl.handle.net/2022/3647>; Corinne J. Saunders, *Medium Ævum*, 78 (2009), 161–62.

48. Putter, Ad, Judith Jefferson, and Myra Stokes, *Studies in the Metre of Alliterative Verse* (Oxford: Society for the Study of Medieval Languages and Literature, 2007). Rev. by Thomas A. Bredehoft, *Review of English Studies*, 60 (2009), 802–04; Thomas Cable, *YLS*, 23 (2009), 243–64 (see no. 5, above).

49. Rayner, Samantha J., *Images of Kingship in Chaucer and his Ricardian Contemporaries* (Cambridge: Brewer, 2008). Rev. by Rebecca Davis, *YLS*, 23 (2009), 310–15; Siân Echard, *Review of English Studies*, 60 (2009), 483–84; Don Hoffman, *Arthuriana*, 19 (2009), 148–49; Robert J. Meyer-Lee, *Medieval Review*, 09.06.17 <http://hdl.handle.net/2027/spo.baj9928.0906.017>.

50. Scase, Wendy, *Literature and Complaint in England, 1272–1553* (Oxford: Oxford University Press, 2007). Rev. by Ethan Knapp, *Studies in the Age of Chaucer*, 31 (2009), 367–70; Thorlac Turville-Petre, *Medieval Review*, 09.05.12 <http://hdl.handle.net/2027/spo.baj9928.0905.012>.

51. Schoff, Rebecca L., *Reformations: Three Medieval Authors in Manuscript and Movable Type* (Turnhout: Brepols, 2007). Rev. by Robert Costomiris, *JEGP: Journal of English and Germanic Philology*, 108 (2009), 408–11; Bryan P. Davis, *Journal of the Early Book Society*, 12 (2009), 307–09; Thomas Prendergast, *Speculum*, 84 (2009), 1109–11.

52. Simpson, James, *'Piers Plowman': An Introduction*, 2nd, rev. edn (Exeter: University of Exeter Press, 2007). Rev. by J. Patrick Hornbeck II, *YLS*, 23 (2009), 296–302.

53. Wheeler, Bonnie, ed., *Mindful Spirit in Late Medieval Literature: Essays in Honor of Elizabeth D. Kirk* (New York: Palgrave Macmillan, 2006). Rev. by Kevin Gustafson, *JEGP: Journal of English and Germanic Philology*, 108 (2009), 255–56; Nancy Bradley Warren, *YLS*, 23 (2009), 308–10.

54. Zeeman, Nicolette, *'Piers Plowman' and the Medieval Discourse of Desire* (Cambridge: Cambridge University Press, 2006). Rev. by D. Vance Smith, *YLS*, 23 (2009), 302–07; Sarah Wood, *Notes & Queries*, 56 (2009), 449–50.

55. Zieman, Katherine, *Singing the New Song: Literacy and Liturgy in Late Medieval England* (Philadelphia: University of Pennsylvania Press, 2008). Rev. by Sam Barrett, *Studies in the Age of Chaucer*, 31 (2009), 392–94; Elisabeth Dutton,

Times Literary Supplement (31 July 2009), 27; John C. Hirsh, *Medium Ævum*, 78 (2009), 141–42; Michael Kuczynski, *Medieval Review*, 09.06.11 <http://hdl .handle.net/2027/spo.baj9928.0906.011]; Anne Sadedin, *Parergon*, 26. 2 (2009), 216–17.